PASSPORT
FRANCE

Passport to the World

Passport Argentina
Passport Brazil
Passport China
Passport Germany
Passport Hong Kong
Passport India
Passport Israel
Passport Italy
Passport Japan
Passport Korea
Passport Malaysia
Passport Mexico
Passport Philippines
Passport Russia
Passport Singapore
Passport South Africa
Passport Spain
Passport Taiwan
Passport Thailand
Passport United Kingdom
Passport USA
Passport Vietnam

PASSPORT
FRANCE

Your Pocket Guide
to
French Business,
Customs & Etiquette

Nadine Joseph

Passport Series Editor: Barbara Szerlip

WORLD TRADE PRESS®
Professional Books for International Trade

World Trade Press
1505 Fifth Avenue
San Rafael, California 94901 USA
Tel: (415) 454-9934
Fax: (415) 453-7980
USA Order Line: (800) 833-8586
E-mail: WorldPress@aol.com

"Passport to the World" concept: Edward Hinkelman
Cover and book design: Peter Jones
Illustrations: Tom Watson
Cover photography (lower, left image) by Jean-Daniel
Sudres, courtesy of The French Government of Tourism

Library of Congress Cataloging-in-Publication Data
Joseph, Nadine, 1952–
Passport France: your pocket guide to French business, customs & etiquette / Nadine Joseph
p. cm. -- (Passport to the world)
ISBN 1-885073-29-1 (pbk.)
1. Corporate culture--France. 2. Business etiquette--France.
3. Negotiation in business--France. 4. Intercultural communication.
I. Title. II. Series.
HD58.7.J65 1996
390'.00944-dc20
96-28184
CIP

Printed in the United States of America

Table of Contents
France

La Belle France

Overview

Business Environment

Customs & Etiquette

Additional Information

1 Doing Business Across Cultures

Although business operations around the world have become highly standardized, national traditions, attitudes and beliefs remain diverse. Public praise, for example, is much enjoyed by its recipient in the U.S. and Europe, but it's a source of embarrassment and discomfort for Asians. This is because Western cultures value individual thought and action, while Eastern cultures prize modesty and consensus.

While the primary focus of people in one culture might be to quickly get down to business, another culture concentrates on first developing personal relationships. Although their objectives may be the same, people from different cultures are likely to have different ways of achieving them.

You'll probably never know a particular culture as well as your own — not only is the language different, but the historical context within which its people operate is often misunderstood by outsiders.

Comparing Values Across Cultures	
One Culture:	**Another Culture:**
Values change	Values tradition
Favors specific communication	Favors ambiguous communication
Values analytical, linear problem solving	Values intuitive, lateral problem solving
Places emphasis on individual performance	Places emphasis on group performance
Considers verbal communication most important	Considers context & nonverbal communication most important
Focuses on task and product	Focuses on relationship and process
Places emphasis on promoting differing views	Places emphasis on harmony and consensus
Emphasizes competition	Emphasizes collaboration
Prefers informal tone	Prefers formal tone
Is flexible about schedules	Emphasizes rigid adherence to schedules

Passport France will offer some insights into the country and its inhabitants and help you understand how their traditions, values, business practices and communication styles differ from your own.

France
Quick Look

Official name	France
Land area	545,630 sq km (220,668 sqm)
Capital & largest city	Paris, 2.17 million
Elevations	Highest—Mont Blanc 4,810 m
	Lowest—sea level

People
Population (1994)	56.5 million
Density	104 persons per sq km
Distribution	75% urban, 25% rural
Annual growth (1995)	1.8%
Official language	French
Major religions	Roman Catholic 90%,
	Muslim 5%, Protestant 2%,
	Jewish 1%

Economy (1994)
GDP	US$1.285 trillion
	US$22,138 per capita
Foreign trade	Imports—US$17.6 billion
	Exports—US$14.7 billion
Principal trade partners	Germany 19%
	Italy 11%
	Spain 10%
	Netherlands, U.S.,
	United Kingdom 8% each
Currency	Franc (1FF=100 centimes)
Exchange rate (7/96)	5.03FF = US$1

Education and health
Literacy (1994)	99%
Universities (1994)	70 (public)
Life expectancy (1994)	Women—82.3 years
	Men—74.2 years
Infant mortality (1994)	6.6 per 1,000 live births

FRANCE

2 Country Facts

Geography and Demographics

France is the largest country in Western Europe. It is also the least crowded. Shaped like a hexagon, the landscape ranges from high mountains to plains, and from wine-growing valleys to pine forests bordering on miles and miles of duned beaches. France also boasts Europe's highest peak — Mont Blanc in the Alps rises to 4,810 meters (15,771 feet).

As a nation, its birth was rough. From the very start, France had its share of foreign invaders and foreign rule. In 51 B.C.E., the Romans conquered the Celtic people of France, called the Gaulois. Fiercely independent, the Gaulois belonged to 400 different tribes and spoke 72 different languages. (Today, they're lovingly satirized in the popular Astérix comics, in which the hero appears as a pun-spewing cross between Mickey Mouse and Batman — short and ugly but brave and wily, fighting foreigners single-handedly.) After Rome fell in the 9th century, Charlemagne and the Teutonic Franks took over. For the next few centuries, the Franks and the English battled for different pieces of the land.

As a result, the "French" are a blend of three different European stocks — Celtic, Roman and

Frank. The country is the creation of a monarchical dynasty that fashioned its territory by conquest, diplomatic ruses and opportunistic marriages. As a result, ancestry is considered less important than an attachment to the land, the language and *la culture française*. That's why the French are comfortable claiming Picasso (a Spaniard), Napoleon Bonaparte (a Corsican), Josephine Baker (an American) and Vincent van Gogh (a Dutchman) as their own.

Set up as a utopia of sorts after the French Revolution, France has always attracted its share of immigrants. One in four inhabitants is either an immigrant or has a parent or grandparent who was. Today, most foreigners living in France are from southern Europe (52 percent) or North Africa (26 percent), and their influence is finally being felt. If France was once viewed as only a high-brow intellectual mix of Rodin, Rousseau and Ravel, in the *banlieues* (suburbs) where the immigrants settled, that notion has been replaced — by a multiethic mix of Maghrebians (Arabs from France's former colonies in North Africa), Africans, Italians, Spaniards and gypsies. "French culture used to be a *baguette*, a béret and Camembert," a French-African actor told Newsweek. "Now it's us."

Climate

France is not a place of extremes — climatic or otherwise. It has three types of weather: oceanic (in the west), continental in the east, the interior and Paris, and mediterranean in the south and the Côte d'Azur (the Riviera). In the west, there's much rain and little difference in temperature between winter and summer. Most of France (eastern, central and Paris) has warm summers, cold winters and snow in the mountains. Parisian temperatures range from 3°C (37°F) in January to 23°C (73°F) in July. In the

south, the weather is hot and dry in the summer,
mild and wet in the winter. In the winter and
spring, *le mistral* (a cold, dry wind that travels at up
to 60 miles an hour) can blow continuously for several days.

The best months for travel are May, June, Sep-
tember and October. The advantage to spending a
humid July or August in Paris is that there are few
locals in town and less traffic than usual. The disadvantage is that the locals have been replaced by tourists from around the globe and that many of the best
restaurants (and some of the shops) are closed.

Business Hours

Most businesses are open from 9 A.M. to 6 P.M.
Monday through Friday. Some stores remain open
until 8 P.M. Some banks and shops are open on Satur-
days and closed on Mondays. Most airport currency
exchange offices are open from 6:30 A.M. to 11 P.M.

Almost everyone in France takes a two-hour
lunch break, usually between noon and 2 P.M. — the
only time that most restaurants serve lunch. Dinner
is served late, usually after 7 P.M., and in some areas,
after 8 P.M.

National Holidays

New Year's Day .... January 1
Easter Monday .... movable date
Assumption Day .... the Thursday 40
                                               days after Easter
Whit Monday .... movable date
(celebrate Christ's ascension into Heaven)
Labor Day........................... May 1
Le Huit Mai or Victory Day .. May 8
(celebrates the German defeat in Europe in 1945)

Bastille Day ....July 14
(France's independence day, commemorates the 1789 fall of the
Bastille prison, which held political prisoners)
All Saints Day ....November 1
(Christian feast that honors all the saints)
Armistice Day ....November 11
(commemorates end of WWI, during which one out of every
25 French citizens perished)
Christmas Day ....December 25

Holidays

A lot of creativity and planning are involved in
French celebrations. Many people take their "saint
day" (the saint they were named after) seriously —
they may throw a party, take the day off or accept
whimsical gifts. Each town and village has its own
particular *fête*, usually celebrated on *its* saint's day
or on the first day of the grape harvest.

New Year's is observed by kissing on the stroke
of midnight. On New Year's Day, candy, flowers or
books are often given to older members of the family. For children, there's Mardi Gras (Strove Tues-
day), with its parades and parties in February, and
Poisson d'avril (April Fool's Day), when people play
tricks on each other and pin red paper fish on
friends' and teachers' backs. On Easter Sunday and
Monday, children hunt for colored eggs and chocolate bells. Labor Day is mostly marked by parades,
while fireworks and street dancing are typical ways
to celebrate *Le Huit Mai* and Bastille Day. Beaujolais
Nouveau Day (the third Thursday in November) is
when the light, fruity wine (which is drunk fresh
rather than aged) is released at midnight.

(For more on holidays, see Chapter 17: Customs).

3   The French

A Love of Literature

The French are passionate about their language. It's more like a muse or a mistress than a mass of words. Almost half the nation reads at least ten books a year. Literature outranks politics in status, which is why authors are elected to high office (Lamartine, De Tocqueville and Chateaubriand were all foreign ministers) and politicians are expected to be literate — or better yet, literary.

The late President Charles de Gaulle's autobiography became a best-seller. President François Mitterand penned *several* best-sellers, and both his widow and his dog, Baltique, published memoirs of the great man (the latter is a 300-page parody). Prime minister Alain Juppé has written a book about his desire to retire to a house in Venice (where he can contemplate the meaning of life *sans* politics). Even current President Jacques Chirac (not a real writer) has described poetry as "a necessity for daily living." And he's right. It's not unusual for a French laborer to recite poetry or to quote directly from Montaigne or Montesquieu, even in the midst of a bar brawl.

Français, S'il Vous Plait

In the 12th century, Marco Polo wrote his famous travels in French. By the 1600s, French had been embraced as the language of diplomacy and culture in royal courts throughout Europe. During the 18th century, Catherine the Great of Russia carried on a lively, longterm correspondence with Voltaire in French. Yet before the 19th century, a quarter of the populace couldn't speak a word of it, and another quarter were incapable of having a decent conversation in it. The government began viewing *patois* (local dialects such as breton, occitan, alsatian and provençal) as a threat to French unity. In 1635, Richelieu instructed the French Academy to "labor with all care and diligence to give certain rules to our language, and to render it pure, eloquent, and capable of treating the arts and sciences." It became national policy that schoolchildren who spoke *patois* were punished. The offender was handed a bean, and as the day went on, the child would hand over the bean to the next child who spoke *patois*. At the end of the day, the last child holding the bean was beaten.

Today, even native French people concentrate all their efforts on mastering the language. And even professional authors can't ace *La Grande Dictée,* an annual, grammar trap-laden spelling bee that attracts 300,000 participants, is watched by another seven million on TV, and that receives detailed newspaper coverage.

But for all the language's difficulty, the French remain steadfastly attached to it. In 1990, when the government wanted to remove the "g" from *oignon* (onion) and the accent mark from words like *maître* and *huître*, people petitioned in protest, in what came to be known as the War of the Circumflex.

Discreet Charm of the Bourgeoisie

Class divisions are alive and well in France. The bourgeoisie (victorious against the ruling class in the French Revolution of 1789) run the show. It's hard, but not impossible, for the son of a plumber to become a doctor, lawyer, engineer or architect. He or she must do exceedingly well in school, compete to enter a prestigious university and join a well-established firm. But it's easier to succeed as *le fils à papa* (daddy's little boy).

Nowadays, the French aristocracy has little standing. It throws elegant balls and hosts fox hunts, but no one pays much attention. The French are more likely to follow the exploits of Princess Stephanie of Monaco than to care about their own counts, dukes or royal descendants.

The bourgeoisie is divided into three categories. The *haute bourgeoisie* are a kind of living gallery of France's illustrious past, the country's "who's who" (de Gaulle was among them). The *bonne bourgeoisie* (BCBG — *bon chic bon genre*) are the younger, up-and-coming leaders from the professions. As for the *petite bourgeoisie* (merchants and independent contractors), they're treated with disdain, partly because workers are able to infiltrate their ranks.

My Family, My Kingdom

The French feel protective about family. They pay attention to their children, pay homage to their parents and like to live within a few kilometers of each other. They consult with family members about everything from how to expand their business (they often go into business together) to where to go skiing in winter. Children tend to live at home until they marry.

The entire family — three or four generations

and often including all cousins — gathers for holidays, *fêtes* (celebrations) and ritualistic three-hour Sunday lunches. Not everywhere of course, but in some families, it's a scene straight out of a François Truffaut movie — with the children in smocked dresses and gloves or ironed cotton shirts and ties, sitting quietly during the entire meal like little angels. Family gatherings are a private affair. Only the most intimate of friends are ever invited to them.

A Mass of Contradictions — and Proud of It

Consistency isn't a French priority. On the contrary, it's dismissed as boring. The French are faddish — they'll wear the most outlandish outfits, if they've been designed by Pierre Cardin or Claude Montana. Yet they're also traditionalists. They love new American gadgets but won't serve California champagne. They adore bullet trains but won't rush their morning *toilette*. They love open space (*la campagne*) but often live in cramped apartments. Frenchmen would never dream of taking off their jackets at a cocktail party, but they'll parade naked (the women topless) on the beaches of St. Tropez. They wear perfume but abhor deodorant. They believe in codes and rights but break petty regulations about speed limits, pedestrian crossings, parking, smoking and standing in line.

French women are feminists but dress in sexy outfits. French men never comb their hair in public but will urinate anywhere. Dogs are welcome in certain chic restaurants (they sit on velvet cushions at the table) where children aren't tolerated.

Catholic — But Not Too Catholic

There's no official religion in France, though 90 percent of its 56 million citizens were born into Catholic families. Half of the country's 4 million foreigners are Arab or African, so there are many new mosques in urban areas. About 1 percent of the French are Jewish. Though most are fairly well assimilated, they've faced increasing anti-Semitism over the past decade or more — including desecrated cemeteries, bombed stores, and disparaging public remarks by right-wing politician Jean-Marie Le Pen. (Tolerance for religious differences was codified in the Edict of Nantes in 1598 and then revoked in 1685.)

French Catholicism varies by region. It's practiced less in Marseille than in Nantes, and less in Paris than in Brittany (where it's wedded to local customs). People all over France celebrate feast days and holidays, but only 16 percent attend church regularly. Most were baptized and over half went through religious weddings, but few go to confession. There's hostility to religion among teachers and leftists.

Church and state have been separated since the 19th century. Because the French don't take Catholicism too seriously, they tend to view other religions with suspicion. Just as they resent the Vatican's encroachment, they don't like the intrusion of non-European religions. There's controversy about Moslem girls wearing the *chador* (veil) to school. With the wails of the *muezzins* (Muslim criers) from the mosques, France's urban ghettos are beginning to sound and look more like Algiers than Paris.

Tolerance or Racism?

In the 18th century, the French began to colonize the world, extending the concept of *liberté, egalité, fraternité* (liberty, equality and fraternity). It was a shock to them when their ex-colonies chose independence over French citizenship.

But when it comes to foreigners settling in their own country, the French are ambivalent. They love the intellectuals, jazz musicians and exiled heads of state who flock to their borders. They've granted asylum to the Ayatollah Khomeini and the Shah of Iran, to Ho Chi Minh and the Khmer Rouge leaders, to Bébé Doc and Haitian poets. However, most racially different immigrants remain at the bottom of the socioeconomic ladder. All Muslims are labeled *arabes* and the children of former Algerians and Moroccans, although born in France, are often called *beurs* (which is akin to "kike").

Though the French don't like to think of themselves as being racist, racial polarization seems to be getting worse. Polls show that more than half the French complain of "too many Arabs," creating a cultural abscess. Immigrants feel that they're often branded as scapegoats for rising crime and joblessness.

Several parliamentary measures are currently being considered that would tighten existing immigration laws. Among them: One that would require visa applicants from "high migratory risk" countries to be fingerprinted, and one that would allow delinquent minors to be deported to their parents' country of origin, even if they were born in France.

Don't Worry — Be Happy

Changes are rocking France. The nation faces growing unemployment, the highest AIDS rates in Europe, strikes and terror bombings and the encroachment of insidious American trends — from munching *le Big Mac* on the Champs Elysees to popping Prozac, from joining 12-step programs (for everything from alcoholism to shopping) to plugging into the Internet. But even in adversity, the French cling to their optimism, their fighting spirit, their panache. They identify with heroes (both literary and real) who rose above poverty and defeat — from Cyrano de Bergerac and D'Artagnan to Napoleon and de Gaulle.

Unfortunately, their happiness isn't obvious — the French rarely smile at strangers or laugh in public. What a foreigner may detect, however, is a stubborn delight in daily pleasures: reading the newspaper alone at the café (though cafés are dying out), savoring a wedge of Camembert at the end of a two-hour lunch, or winning a heated argument.

Survival of the Smartest

The French like to be different — both from other nations and from one another. They define themselves in verbal duels, experimenting with new ideas, new theories, new conceits. They want to be considered *sérieux*: serious intellectuals who discuss everything from existentialism (a philosophy popularized by Jean-Paul Sartre that views the world as "absurd" and irrational) to Marxism, from ancient history to Impressionism.

If there's a shared idea among all of these budding philosophers, it's a strong belief in the survival of the smartest. The French respect those who express themselves with eloquence or who have proven themselves as authors or academics.

To arm themselves for intellectual combat, they turn to books and to their daily newspapers. Le Monde and Le Figaro contain more text than pictures, and they concentrate on analyzing significant world issues, rather than reporting on trivial events like the divorce of Prince Charles and Lady Di.

Super-Rational to Supernatural

Mathematican and philosopher René Descartes

(1596-1650) was the father of French thought. His most famous line, *"Je pense, donc je suis"* (I think, therefore I am), sums up his country's worldview in a nutshell.

The French thrive on Cartesian logic — abstract thinking and in-depth analyses. They love to break things down into fundamental parts and then put them all back together again, like a great puzzle. (Perhaps the most obvious manifestation of their love of the rational and the orderly can be seen in French formal gardens — nature transformed into complex, symmetrical geometries.)

And yet more French people than ever are consulting psychics. Last year, a total of 50,000 people (the highest number ever) declared income from their occupations as stargazers, mediums and psychic healers. By comparison, the nation only has 36,000 priests and 6,000 psychiatrists. There are also more exorcisms performed now in France than ever. A third of the population believes in the existence of the Devil.

The Only Truly Civilized People, Bien Entendu

The French believe that their contributions to world culture far outweigh everyone else's (and they couldn't care less if you disagree). France was, after all, the birthplace of Pierre-Auguste Renoir and Victor Hugo; of Marcel Duchamp and Maurice Ravel; of Simone de Beauvoir and Joan of Arc; of Francois Truffaut and Marcel Marceau. (And the Marquis de Sade, after whom the word "sadism" was coined.) Pierre and Marie Curie discovered radium here, the Cordon Bleu was founded here, and it was here that the Louvre was established as one of the finest art museums in existence. And is it elitist or merely objective to acknowledge that no other nation is really capable of *chic*? (Coco Chanel was, of course, French.) The Concorde, the airbus, the TGV (the fastest train in the world at 300 kph/ 186 mph), condoms, pasteurization (named after chemist Louis Pasteur) and leotards (after aerial gymnast Jules Léotard) are all French inventions.

Other Nations? The Butt of Jokes

- The Belgians, in particular, are targeted for disdain, ridiculed for their accents and their singsong way of speaking.

- The British are mocked for dressing badly, playing ridiculous games like cricket, and being cold, insensitive, perfidious (*perfide*), stingy and passionless.

- Americans are viewed as naive, conformist (they all wear jeans, sneakers and carry backpacks), boring (because they're always smiling), uninformed about the world, loud, money-hungry, and obsessed with physical fitness.

- Germans are considered untrustworthy, formal, reserved, organized, mechanical and dull.

- The Spanish are seen as proud and noisy.

- Italians are thought to be hot-tempered, garrulous and unethical.

- The Swiss are seen as obsessively clean — and boring. In Switzerland, lights are out at 8 P.M.

- The Chinese are respected for their hard work, intelligence and good manners, but they're also viewed as cold, distant and hypocritical.

- The Japanese are admired for their sushi, cinema and traditional arts but ridiculed for their ubiquitous cameras and for dressing alike.

 Cultural Stereotypes

While stereotypes about the French vary, some are common.

As Icy As Mont Blanc

The French are cold, negative and suspicious.

The French aren't crazy about strangers. Even French strangers. They like to maintain a mask of indifference in public and reserve their warmth and smiles for family and close friends.

This Gallic coolness is most prevalent in Paris (where most foreigners spend their time). In other regions, notably in the south and in the Pyrénées, people are actually warm, outgoing and friendly.

Better Rude Than Wrong

The French hate to take responsibility for their mistakes. They prefer to blame the victim than to apologize.

Someone dials the wrong number, then yells at you for not being the party they're trying to reach. A car hits a pedestrian and the driver starts cursing at the victim. *On n'a pas droit á l'erreur* (one doesn't have the right to make a mistake) is how the French put it. As children, they're taught to speak up only if they know the right answer, or else face ridicule. At work, bosses often cover up for their employees' mistakes and vice versa. It's the equivalent of "losing face" in Asian cultures. Admitting that you're wrong is viewed as a sign of weakness.

All Style And No Substance

The French are snobs, and they're formal to a fault. They care only about the Four F's — food, fashion, fragrance and frivolity.

True, the French pay attention to style. Yes, they do like to dress well, dine well and flirt, even at work. Sensuality makes life worthwhile; formality gives life structure.

But at the same time, they've managed to turn fragrance, fashion and food into major industries. They work hard, especially when they feel that they're tackling complex, important problems. They still have the fourth largest economy in the world. And they're not nicknamed "the Chinese of Europe" for nothing. Behind the suave exterior lies a sharp mind, which gears up for a challenge.

Better A Good Argument Than Boredom

The French are relentlessly confrontational. They've perfected the art of engueulade *(pointless, public, vulgar bickering).*

The French lose their composure at the slightest perceived insult. This trait dates back to Roman times: Tacitus wrote that the Gauls would have been victorious, had they not fought so much among themselves. They relish a good fight. A man steps on a woman's toe, then insults her. The French expect nothing less. Arguments are seen as games, as verbal jousts; they're a way to exercise one's lungs, to practice the art of debate, to expand one's vocabulary — to express that you exist.

The French also like to debate. They'll take opposite sides on an issue out of *esprit de contradiction* — the joy of engaging in a lively battle of wits. Unlike many Americans, they don't equate disagreement or lack of resolution with unfriendliness. But they *often* equate agreement with boredom. And, as the 19th century poet Alphonse de Lamartine once declared, the French "cannot bear to be boring."

Licentious

The French are sexual libertines.

Among the country's many proverbs are these:

- *Not every unfaithful wife feels remorse, but every faithful one feels regret.*
- *Make haste to give way to temptation before it's out of reach.*

France never went through a puritan, reformist or prohibitionist period. Wives and daughters parade topless on public beaches. Until recently, prostitution was totally legal. According to a recent survey, an estimated 2.2 million French couples "live in sin" (seven times as many as 20 years ago), and more than one in three babies are born "out of wedlock." Illegitimacy (except among staunch Catholics) no longer carries a stigma. President Chirac recently announced the birth of his first grandchild during a ceremony at the Elysée. Chirac's daughter, the child's mother, is unmarried.

Marital fidelity isn't expected. When the newspapers reported that Vincent Auriol (president of France after World War II) had lost his glass eye in a lover's bed, his popularity increased. Mitterand maintained two households — wife, sons and dogs in one, mistress, daughter and cats in the other. What the French found scandalous was that the press made such a *fuss* about it. (The two families met, for the first time, at his funeral in January, 1996.) The expression *cinq á sept* (five to seven) was coined to describe the two-hour period during which working people slip away from their offices to visit their lovers.

On the other hand, more than a third of the country (more than ever before) admits to being monogamous and to finding sex more satisfying with one partner over the years. And though the French may write a lot of erotic books, they don't necessarily buy them. The Story of O sold much better in the U.S. than in France.

5 Regional Differences

Vive la Difference

"How do you govern ... a people with 365 different cheeses," de Gaulle was once asked. His answer was typically French. "How can you live in a country without them?"

There are now 452 French cheeses. "A meal without cheese?" wrote the French humorist François Rabelais. "A fine lady lacking one eye!"

(Roquefort, a blue-mold cheese made of ewe's milk and aged in caves, comes from a village of the same name. Port Salut was named for the 19th century abbey where it was originally developed by Trappist monks. Montrachet, a log-shaped goat's-milk cheese made in Burgundy, is sometimes dusted with cinders. Camembert (cow's milk) takes it's name from a tiny hamlet in Normandy. Livarot, also from Normandy, is one of the oldest of French cheeses; it's usually bound in split reed ties to retain its cylindrical shape. Heart-shaped Guerbigny is made in a village in Picardy. Cervelle de canut (literally, "silk weaver's brains"), a fresh cheese seasoned with herbs, shallots, garlic and pepper, is popular in Lyon. And these are just a few....)

The Importance of Provincial Roots

Regionalism is alive and well. Each region boasts of its culinary specialties, its wines, its soccer and rugby teams, and its way of negotiating, entertaining and cutting deals. People often identify more strongly with their province than with their country and feel like foreigners when traveling beyond their localities. "I'm no Frenchman, really," confesses a 58-year-old builder in the southwest region. "I'm a Landais, and I have more in common with the Spaniards across the border than with Parisians in their fancy skyscrapers." Then again, a star soccer player from Marseille says he feels more at home in Rome "with its Mediterranean spirit" than in nearby Menton, where the people are "too *snob*."

The French attachment to provincial roots isn't surprising when you consider that only one in two Parisians was actually born in Paris. France has the highest proportion of families with second homes in the world — usually a country place that's been owned by their ancestors for generations.

As government becomes even more decentralized and as telecommunications grow, more French entrepreneurs are refusing to move their successful, international businesses to the capital. Jean Noel Bongrain sends cheeses all over the world from his headquarters in Iloud (in Haute-Marne), and Pierre Fabre refuses to leave Castres (outside of Toulouse), where he founded a billion-dollar pharmaceutical empire.

Dialects & Foreign Tongues

Because of France's linguistic chauvinism, other languages tend to be overlooked. Foreign tongues are, of course, spoken here — Arabic, Swahili, Turkish, Portuguese and English among others. And there are also regional *patois* — Breton (akin to Welsh) in Brittany, a German dialect in Alsace and Lorraine (only 85 percent of Alsatians speak French as their main language), Flemish in the northeast, Spanish, Catalan and Basque in the southwest, Provençal (in which troubadours sang their romances in the 12th century) and an Italian dialect in Corsica and the southeast. About 21 percent of all French claim to speak a regional language well and another 14 percent fairly well. And not everyone speaks the same *patois*. In Brittany, for example, every village has its own particular dialect, and the people think of themselves as being Bigoudens or Bidars, rather than Bretons.

Self-Determination

Of all the regional movements, the Basque and Corsicans have been the most vocal about demanding autonomy. Over the years, terrorists in both regions have been successful in planting bombs. In 1983, the French government outlawed a separatist group, the Corsican National Liberation Front, which had claimed responsibility for 370 out of 800 terrorist incidents the year before. About one in ten Corsicans are autonomists.

6 Government & Business

Traditionally, the role of the French government was to protect its industries and to promote its foods and wines overseas. At one point, the government even gave subsidies to owners of French cars, spouting a philosophy that one French comic summarized as "better inefficient and French than efficient and foreign." That protectionism is changing. Procedures have been streamlined and bureaucratic delays simplified. The European Union has made it harder for some other French habits to continue, as well: state subsidies and the overcharging of one state-owned company by another.

From Nationalization to Privatization

Three trends make this an auspicious period for foreign investment in France: decentralization, growing privatization of industries that were once nationalized and finally, France's participation in the European Union. The government is particularly eager to attract joint ventures in the high-tech industry.

Over the past several decades, France has decentralized its government, which means that many decisions about granting permits for new production plants are made at the local level, by the department, the city or the commune. Most other decisions (registering new corporations, for instance) are still made in Paris. Often, the local or regional chamber of commerce can act as an inter-mediary or broker, taking the place of a more costly *notaire* (a lawyer-notary public whose rates are set by the government) or lawyer.

A large portion of French industry is national-ized, and the government has been able to endorse several innovative ideas that turned into huge tech-nological (and sometimes even commercial) suc-cesses, including the TGV train, the airbus, the Concorde, and nuclear energy (France produces half of the E.U.'s nuclear energy).

But with growing privatization, France faces major changes. Many of the companies once owned by the state have inherited staffs that continue to enjoy the job security — and sometimes, the tradi-tional inefficiency — of public servants. In the past few years alone, the government has had to bail out five banks, an insurance company and Air France. Companies have also grown accustomed to the lux-ury of leaving infrastructure projects and planning to the state.

As 1999 (the date for European economic and monetary union) approaches, there will be even more changes. In 1998, for instance, when Euro-pean law opens all of Europe's telecommmunica-tions monopolies to competition, France's giant government-owned telecommunications company will be open to private capital.

The Art of Pantoufler

Business and government are so cozy that the word for migrating from the public to the private sector is *pantoufler* (literally, "slipper").

It's not unusual for both Socialists and Conservatives to move back and forth between the two in a "revolving door" scenario. In fact, it's taken for granted. Chambers of commerce play a quasi-governmental role, and they sometimes even operate airports. There are lots of ex-ministers in French industry. Of France's 200 biggest companies, over 40 are headed by ex-public servants.

Regulated Retail

The government has clamped down on hypermarkets, which are driving small shopkeepers (who can't compete with one-franc *baguettes*) out of business. New laws have placed a moratorium on the opening of big stores (over 3,230 square feet) and prevent others from selling goods at a loss. And stores that obtain discounts not noted on their invoices are forbidden to pass the savings onto customers.

According to one international study, deregulated retail can create up to five jobs for every thousand potential workers. In France, jobs are vanishing.

Fear of "Franglais"

No other country cares so much about preserving its language. An entire academy — l'Académie Française — works nonstop to preserve the purity of French, excising any words that may have slipped in from other tongues. And as far back as 1966, committees were established to invent French neologisms to supercede such Anglo-Americanisms as "fast food" restaurants (*restovites*) and "brainstorming" (*un remue-méninges*). Mitterand was once overheard complaining, "Must we give orders to our computers... in English?"

The French are so wary, in fact, of what they see

as the tyranny of English that, by law, all contracts with French companies must be written entirely in French — even if it increases the cost of the deal by 60 percent, as some have estimated. And in accordance with a 1994 law dubbed "the Toubon Law" (after ex-culture minister Jacques Toubon), all ads, product labels, instructions, advertisements and public signs have to appear in French, (or appear translated into French next to other languages). Only trademarks are exempt.

The government, along with five independent organizations (such as *Avenir de la Langue Française*, Future of the French Language) are on the lookout for violators. Recently, the British cosmetics firm The Body Shop was fined US$200 (out of a possible $5000) for selling products with English-only labels, including a "no-frizz" hair treatment cream and "pineapple" facial cleanser.

As of January 1, 1996, radio stations are fined if they don't play at least 40 percent French music (and half of it new), and French TV is required to broadcast 60 percent European-made films, 40 percent of which must be French. One leading private station was recently fined US$9 million for failing to comply.

Fewer Other Restraints

For companies used to navigating through myriad laws and regulations, doing business in France may seem somewhat less restrictive. Pollution laws, which are relatively recent, are rarely enforced. There are no laws against expense account abuse or nepotism, for example. In addition, the French are not litigious. This is partly because lawyers are so expensive and partly because the loser has to pay all the costs of a lawsuit (and the French are adverse to taking such a risk).

 The Work Environment

The most striking feature of a French office is its formality. The workplace is very hierarchical. Titles count. Executives rarely, if ever, go to lunch with their secretaries or their clerks, and in some companies, it's against the rules.

A Tightly Knit Elite

While intellectual accomplishments are highly respected (perhaps more so than in most corporate environments worldwide), what seems to count most in French business is one's blood. Seventy-five percent of the managers of the top 200 companies are the sons of wealthy, influential families — as compared with 25 percent in Germany and 10 percent in the United States. And they all know each other.

Many of the top businessmen and engineers have been in government at one point in their careers. They probably attended the "right" *lycée* (6th grade through the second year of college) and then graduated from one of the country's top two *grandes ecoles* — the Ecole Nationale d'Administration (known as ENA) or the even more elitist Ecole

Polytechnique (known as X) — where they were groomed for leadership posts.

ENA graduates are nicknamed *énarques*. Their ties are so strong that when they address each other, they drop the formal *vous* for the more intimate *tu*. The prestige of being part of a group that includes prime ministers and presidents is enormous.

Being an X entitles you to walk beneath your former classmates' crossed swords at your wedding and to write on the invitations, *ancien élève de l'Ecole Polytechnique.*

Security Above All Else

Historically, French industry has centered on employment rather than profitability. People are rarely fired, especially not after many years, or if their fathers and grandfathers once worked for the same company. "My secretary's husband left her for another woman," says a young businessman. "I would never fire her, even though she's a lousy secretary. She's been here too many years and is supporting too many children. It would be cruel and inhuman."

Until recently, students who graduated from France's universities were practically guaranteed good jobs. And many of those positions — as government lawyer, teacher or engineer — were for life. However, all that has changed. In 1995, unemployment suddenly jumped to twelve percent, and it's even higher among those under the age of 25. With job security being threatened, there's talk of "national preference" — hiring and maintaining native-born French people over immigrants.

Less Task Oriented

Because of the rigid hierarchy and lack of mobility in many French corporations, workers on the lower echelons — be they government bureaucrats or corporate secretaries — are less inclined to care about the tasks they're asked to perform. And they don't tend to be strong on teamwork. Executives often have secretaries who refuse to make coffee or to work overtime to make a deadline. They find they have to cajole employees into taking personal pride in a project.

Managers tend not to delegate and not to keep employees beneath their level informed about decisions. And they, too, are susceptible to a lack of motivation. In a survey by the Allensteig Institute cited in Polly Platt's <u>French or Foe</u>, managers in different European countries were asked how well they followed instructions from their bosses. The French scored lowest. However, when they understood the rationale for the project and were convinced that their input was valuable, they scored highest of all.

Not Defined by One's Job

A French person's work ethic is different from the one espoused by most Americans, Britons, Germans or Hong Kong Chinese, who tend to work nonstop and see money as an end in itself. An American may strive to be the first to produce a widget or to be the top salesman for his company in a given year. A Frenchman would find such ambitions crass.

A French worker is more than the sum of his successes on the job, and he would be insulted if you implied that work defines him. While the power and prestige of his position may be enjoyable, and while he may take pride in it, he remains modest about his personal accomplishments and silent about the wealth he accumulates. He picks his colleagues more for their shared philosophy of

life than for their business success. He works long
hours only when he has to. His weekends usually
remain sacred, reserved for his family.

Decision Making

Decisions are made at the top, not by consensus. You'd think that things would move at a light-
ning-fast pace as a result, but that's not the case.
The French fascination for details can make the
decision-making process a slow one.

While little brainstorming takes place during
meetings, there are, instead, time-consuming arguments about issues that may not be central to the
issue at hand — such as the rationale behind choosing system A over system B. The debate usually
focuses on a priori logical arguments, rather than
on spontaneous or creative solutions.

In addition, caution is a French management
staple. Managers in fairly large companies (as
opposed to young entrepreneurs) tend to be suspicious of risk and to distrust simple compromises or
solutions. If it takes twelve meetings to define an
issue, that's far more acceptable than rushing a
decision in order to make a deadline. Managers are
looking for full, sophisticated answers to their
questions and believe that these take time.

Door Code

Most foreigners who walk into a French office
are surprised by what they see: a hallway of doors,
all of them shut out of habit. But the closed door
has no real meaning in France. It implies neither
privacy, security nor secrecy. A French secretary
will simply knock on the door, open it and enter
without waiting for her boss to ask her to come in.

8 Women in Business

Only One Woman in the Panthéon

France has its heroines — Jeanne D'Arc (Joan of Arc) and Marianne, the symbol of the French Revolution — as well as several top female politicians (most recently, Simone Veil, Edith Cresson and Françoise Giroud). But societal equity has been slower in coming than most French feminists would like to admit.

In the 16th century, French women were considered chattel, classified along with children, lunatics and convicted criminals as having no legal rights. It's only since 1923 that women have even been allowed to open their own mail (as stipulated in an article of Napoleon's *code civil*). Suffrage didn't arrive until 1944; before that, even the three female ministers in socialist Leon's Blum's cabinet were forbidden to vote. And until 1965, no married woman was allowed to open her own bank account without her husband's written consent.

The prestigious Académie Française elected its first female member (novelist Marguerite Yourcenar) in 1974, and women still only hold two Académie seats out of forty. Only one metro station (out of 454) is named for a woman — Louise

Michel, an anarchist and teacher who took part in the Paris Commune and was subsequently deported to New Caledonia. And the only woman buried in the Panthéon, Sophie Berthelot, is there only because she happened to die at the same time as her husband Marcellin, who is buried there (he invented thermochemistry).

Hesitant Feminists

Most women in France work. Their average salary is about 75 percent that of their male co-workers, even though laws passed in 1972 require "professional equality" between the sexes. Women also hold the country's lowest-paying jobs, and two out of three earn minimum wage.

The good news is that women are increasingly moving into middle management. A handful are top executives. The higher their position, the harder it is to juggle family and career. A 38-year-old woman who graduated from ENA (the prestigious National School of Administration) remembers that when she took a senior post in a ministry, her male colleagues assured her, "You're one of us, one of the guys." But when she became a mother, they stuck ferociously to age-old traditions that she couldn't follow — long lunches and late-night meetings. "It was too much pressure and I felt like I was being sabotaged," she says.

For those who want to balance family with a job (as opposed to a high-pressure, high-visibility career), France is a haven. "Women don't define themselves by their career," says a wine executive. "It would be too narrow a definition." They marry later, on average, than in America — at age 25. And they stay in the work force. Part-time jobs are easy to find. Maternity benefits are generous, with over six months of paid leave. Women who've raised three or more children are entitled to a state-funded pension. The quality of publicly funded education for children is high. And abortion is not only legal, but it's paid for by the state.

Perhaps, as a result of the state's mother-friendliness, there's little feminist militancy. One opinion poll showed that only one fifth of French women had an "aggressive desire" for change, while another two-fifths wanted it but were unwilling to help bring it about. The rest were content with the way things are. Not surprising. Simone de Beauvoir's landmark feminist book, <u>The Second Sex</u>, sold more copies in the United States than it did in her native country.

Gallantry or Sexual Harassment?

French men still open doors for women (and are expected to), and they call older women *Madame* (because *Mademoiselle* would imply spinsterhood). They'll also stare at breasts, legs and *derrières*, whistle at anyone vaguely resembling Brigitte Bardot, and trade sexual banter in the office. Many will make a pass at any new woman in the office ("I wouldn't want to offend her by implying she's too ugly for me," explains a middle-aged journalist).

French women take it in their stride. "We can flirt and know it will go nowhere," says a young businesswoman. In American businesses, she argues, there may be little flirting, but there's often a sexual tension in the air.

Until recently, no one lifted an eyebrow. But a law passed in 1992 pinpoints sexual harassment as a crime. If convicted, a man can face a fine of up to 100,000 francs (US$20,000) and up to one year in prison. But the law only applies to "hierarchical superiors," so if a male colleague harasses a coworker, she has no grievance. "Nothing has really changed here," observes a 24-year-old public relations writer in Paris. "Nor should it. What's the big deal? A little flirtation. A little compliment. A little admiration."

Women Should Be Seen <u>and</u> Heard

In business, women who have clout dress elegantly, argue intelligently and play hardball at the negotiating table. They know the men in the room admire their brains as well as their bodies. "Remember to take the time to smile at each compliment," advises a female lawyer. "And then move on to your next point."

French businessmen like to poke fun at the "uniform" worn by most American female executives — namely, a dark, conservative, not-particularly-flattering suit, blouse and dark pumps, with no jewelry and little makeup. Frenchwomen see no need to abandon femininity and elegance in the business arena. They prefer soft colors, stylish clothes, silk scarfs, manicured nails, light makeup, and simple but elegant jewelry.

Walking to work in sneakers (with pumps in a handbag, even an elegant one) is a no-no in France. Sneakers or walking shoes are *never* worn in public, except when jogging, playing tennis or climbing mountains. Jogging suits are for jogging, not for strolling around the city on weekends.

Women should feel free to cajole and lobby for help or special consideration — but only in impeccable French. They should show their wit, intellect, ability to pun (the French love *jeux de mots* or word play) and understanding of politics, history and literature. Never be modest, passive or timid. These aren't perceived as admirable qualities in females of any stripe, businesswomen or otherwise.

9 Making Connections

Personal Relationships

The French trust each other if they've formed personal relationships, either through their families or through school. Family friendships often go back seven generations and include several intermarriages — so that, eventually, you have a scene out of the film "Cousin/Cousine," with everyone related to everyone else.

In school, exams are difficult, and competition weeds out the less intellectually nimble. Strong bonds develop among the brightest, those who make it into the elite schools and later into top posts in the government and industry. When applying for a job, it doesn't hurt if your father served in the same World War II Resistance unit as your potential boss or went to ENA with him.

Few French tycoons are *autodidactes* (self-taught). Many of the elite have also studied abroad, earning MBAs at Harvard, Stanford or Columbia, and they tend to be more open to foreigners. A personal introductory note from a friend is always helpful. A shared passion — whether for Bizet or Coltrane, Voltaire or Camus, Apple computers or even Lhasa apsos — will pique a French person's curiosity and most likely lead to a lunch invitation.

For many Westerners, developing a close relationship with a colleague is icing on the cake. But for the French, the long-term relationship *is* the cake. Keep in mind that the buzz phrase here is "relationship networking." If your host opens his photo album at the end of the last negotiating session to show you a picture of his yacht or his trip to the Himalayas, you've probably got yourself a deal.

Close Encounters ....

Although the french are *méfiants* (distrustful, wary) of foreigners, they let their guard down when on vacation — especially those who choose to travel outside of France. At Club Med in Morocco, for example, you might be invited to sit at a table with French executives and "bond." You may end up corresponding with each other and exchanging vacation photos. You may even discover that you've made new business connections in the process.

If you're a Freemason or a member of the Rotary Club in your own country, this can work to your advantage, in both the business and social realms. Find out the names of fellow members in the parts of France you'll be visiting and then contact them, either through the mail or by e-mail. Attend a meeting of the local French chapter or club. You may end up having special access (such as being invited to people's homes) that would not have been possible otherwise.

Le Système D

The French have built a bureaucracy of complicated and time-consuming procedures and regulations that govern almost everything. The *Défense d'Afficher* notices are a good case in point — an 1881 law allows the government and property owners to put up notices prohibiting others from putting up notices on the walls.

To counter this sea of red tape, there's another French invention, *le Système D*. The "D" stands for *débrouillard,* which means being able to get out of a tight fix. *Système D* is an alternative code of conduct. For instance, people discovered quickly that the 1881 law never mentioned drainpipes. So that's where they started posting ads and notices.

People try hard to abridge procedures, avoid taxes, and bulldoze through pet projects. This is usually done by finding the right bureaucrat or company employee to bend, manipulate or ignore a rule that no longer serves the purpose for which it was written. A plea for the exceptional exception — *le cas particulier* — is made and usually granted. "Without the *Systéme D*," observes a 32-year-old architect, "life in France would be hell."

The Power of Penmanship

Who would ever imagine that a nation raised on Cartesian logic would be so impressed by handwriting? Yet companies have been known to consult graphology experts before hiring or even interviewing a candidate. A young ad exec from Lyon found that agencies in Paris were lauding her as brilliant. "I soon discovered that my ads had not won them over," she laughs. "It was my handwriting — rounded, elegant and even. I phoned my mother that night to thank her for having me practice my *écriture* all those years."

10 Strategies for Success

From Walt Disney to Walt d'Isigny

The Euro Disney venture (1500 acres outside of Paris) is an excellent example of the importance of adapting one's business methodology to a particular culture. Opened to great fanfare in 1992, it took over three years to show a profit. This was due, in large part, to the shortsightedness of its American creators, who were convinced that what had worked for their theme parks in the U.S. and Tokyo would work just as well in Europe. Implicit was the belief that any cultural differences would be overcome by the Disney Company's superior management style.

But French employees hated the strict, 13-page dress code (a law suit was filed) and having to smile the "Disney smile" all day. European visitors wanted to sit down to leisurely lunches at about 12:30 P.M., not eat at arbitrary times or "graze" as they walked around *à l'américaine* (like in America). They wanted wine or beer (both forbidden), less souvenirs, and one-night-only stays (projected guest spending was off by 12 percent). And they resented the *à l'américaine* emphasis on glitz and size, rather than on having a unique experience.

Ten Golden Rules

1. Cultivate Relationships

"I was really impatient with all his talk about God and the universe," a German marketing exec says, recalling the first few meetings with his French counterpart. But by the second meeting, he had reread Teilhard de Chardin and could argue theology a little more intelligently. It wasn't until the fourth meeting that his French colleague even *mentioned* the joint project. You'll have to learn patience and to hone your debating skills. Don't be the one to bring up the deal first, but keep scheduling the next meeting.

2. Do an Exhaustive Analysis

Do your homework. Be prepared not only with the facts and figures of the deal but also with the history of your French colleague's company, its organizational charts, any precedents to your venture, and logical arguments, both pro and con. The French will expect as much, even when it comes to minor details.

3. Pick the Right Partner

The most important decision is to whom you should address your initial request. Make sure it's the person who makes the decisions, not his less powerful (but titled) brother. It should be your direct counterpart in the French corporation. Check out alternative business partners while you're in France.

4. Time on Your Side

Make sure you have large chunks of time to devote to your new business contact, if things work out. The French hate to be rushed. They want to feel that you'll make time for them.

5. Beware of Boredom

If your French counterpart suddenly stares into

space or stops gesturing, you've reached a nadir in your talks. You may want to bring up a controversial issue or give him a juicy piece of industry gossip to liven things up.

6. Keep It Formal

You'll probably use the formal *vous* (as opposed to the more familial *tu*) forever. Remember to call him *Monsieur X* until he offers to call you Bob and asks you call him Hervé — and even then, keep using *vous*. But don't count on achieving even that level of intimacy. Nor on taking off your jacket, loosening your tie or slumping in your chair.

Be aware that business hierarchies matter and that lower and higher levels don't mix. A foreign director of marketing for a high tech company made the *faux pas* of setting up a meeting with the junior product manager — the right person to help him out, but the wrong person in the company's hierarchy. Realizing his mistake, he then set up an *earlier* meeting with someone at his level in the French company and sent his subordinate to meet with the junior manager. "We talked about our wine cellars," he recalls. "And they ironed out the details of the deal."

7. Avoid Casting Personal Blame

One American executive might blurt out to another, "You were 10,000 tons short on your shipment, Charlie." But in addressing the same complaint to a French colleague, he should say, "I think something is wrong here." Failure is taboo, and so is blame. Either find a way to make an indirect reference to the problem or ignore it.

8. Be Diplomatic

Some of the shrewdest diplomats were French, and they perfected the art of finesse. You may well encounter businessmen as skilled as Talleyrand in their persuasive arguments and in their strategies.

(Charles Maurice de Talleyrand-Périgord, a 19th century statesman, served Napoleon, Czar Alexander I, Louis XVIII and King Louis Philippe. And true Frenchman that he was, he used the persuasive power of his country's famous cuisine to help restore the French monarchy. During the Congress of Vienna's peace settlement talks (1814), he began hosting embassy dinners four times a week that featured the culinary creations of Marie-Antoine Carême — *ris de veau Florentine*, eggs with crayfish tails, elaborate sculptural confections and extraordinary sorbets. Talleyrand was soon presiding over the Congress committees that had originally excluded him.

The collaboration between diplomat and chef lasted twelve years. Under the employ of the Russian czar Aleksandr I, Carême invented beef Stroganov and Charlotte Russe — while, at the same time, sending secret information from the Russian palace back to Talleyrand.)

9. Leave Money Until Last

Price is usually the most important consideration in making deals. But not so for the French, who find it vulgar to bring up money too early in the negotiations. Although they'll want the upper hand in a deal, you can build in other benefits. "We do want to feel that we've outplayed you," offers a French lawyer. "But if we've established a relationship, we also want to play with you again."

10. Relax Amidst the Storm

The French will get emotional in the heat of the debate. Be prepared for it and don't be afraid to argue, but try not to raise your voice. Your French colleagues will inevitably interrupt you. They may even turn bright red and gesture with their arms. "No better sign," says a German high tech manager. "It means they're deeply engaged and involved."

11 Time

Time Is Not Money

Time is a flexible concept in France. Things take longer than many foreigners expect. While Americans tend to think of time as something to be harnessed, compartmentalized or conquered, the French see it as more of a gift.

Meetings rarely begin on time, and they can be scheduled or cancelled without everyone ever being notified. So don't schedule only half an hour for closing your deal. Things move at a snail's (*escargot*'s) pace. And executives always wait for the chef or PDG (*président-directeur général*) to arrive before beginning any discussion. Some businessmen walk in late without making excuses or even appearing apologetic. Others take great pains to apologize and charm you with long stories about the traffic jam or the state crisis that they were forced to handle.

Most people are on time for lunch, but at least half an hour late for dinner. Trains and planes run on schedule, but gynecologists and general practitioners rarely do. Even the television broadcast schedule offers no guarantees.

In fact, the French habit of "polychronics" drives foreigners crazy. Executives almost seem to enjoy interruptions. They'll take a call from a wife or mistress in the middle of a presentation. They'll let a colleague walk in and join a one-on-one meeting. "It's not considered rude," explains a French vintner. "You don't want to offend a colleague or a friend."

On the other hand, the American tendency to time everything is the butt of French jokes. "He probably also times his lovemaking," a French lawyer says about an American colleague who times telephone consultations with clients.

The Meeting as Group Therapy

A meeting is more of a free-for-all than it is in the United States or elsewhere. It can take a half dozen of them to define an issue. The agenda is usually free-flowing, with several discussions going on at once and no time limit set for agenda items. People interrupt each other. It is an opportunity to exchange ideas and poll opinions. Much of the discussion may strike a foreigner as irrelevant to the issue at hand. And even if a formal decision is reached, no one may be charged with implementing it.

"We like to give everyone an opportunity to give their input on a proposal," says a high tech marketing exec, "in order to be thorough and thoughtful. Americans always want to rush everything. We would rather take our time and create the perfect product."

Mercurial Deadlines

The French don't view deadlines as sacrosanct. If *you* do, be sure to write it into the contract — in French — and make sure that everyone signs. That, however, won't be enough. You must also keep checking on people. Make it clear that the deadline is a *date butoir* (critical deadline) and not a *date cible* (general target date).

Even if the contract is signed and the deadline specified, the French may not meet it. They will usually produce the goods, but not necessarily on schedule. One reason is that efficiency is not a highly prized employee characteristic (loyalty is preferable). The other reason is that there is no fear of retribution or of lawsuits. French business proceeds at a gentleman's pace, and taking one's time is equated with prudence. And since most deals are hatched among friends, no friendship is worth spoiling over a missed deadline. The French are forgiving and expect you to be the same.

12 Business Meetings

Phone Phobia versus Cell Mania

Your first contact with a French colleague may well be on the telephone. And that's unfortunate, because some French business people don't trust phones. They find them intrusive. They prefer meeting eyeball-to-eyeball, especially before committing to even a brief business meeting. Don't expect warmth. Most people sound awkward and rushed (they may also have been raised in an era when telephones were a luxury and calls were more expensive). "I guess we don't visualize the person we're talking to," says a middle-aged entrepreneur. "The telephone is just another tool — and often a nuisance, when it interrupts us when we're deep in thought." Many people use the telephone only to complain. It's less awkward than complaining in person.

Then, of course, as elsewhere, there are the cell phone maniacs. They talk in their cars, on the boulevards, even in the cafés. They prefer to make the calls, not to receive them. A young transportation executive uses his cell phone at dinner to check on employees working overtime. But his answering machine is also on, so that he can monitor incoming calls. "I just hate being disturbed," he admits.

To be on the safe side, your first contact should be a letter (or even a fax) of introduction by a mutual friend or colleague, or a formal, elegant letter (or fax) introducing yourself. The way you write your letter may carry more weight than its content. Your turn-of-phrase, and even your handwriting style, will be seen a reflection of your background and character. Your letter should be written in impeccable formal French. You can briefly outline your experience and background, but make an effort not to appear boastful. Never exaggerate the importance of your proposal. Try to address the letter or fax to the person most likely to carry out the deal -- the person you've identified as having *piston* (the ability to further your career through helpful connections or mentors).

ASAP? How Un-French

Write your first letter months before your arrival, if possible. The French don't like to be rushed, especially by strangers. Nor do they answer letters and faxes immediately, if at all. They consider an immediate reply, and any pressure for one, to be *vulgaire* ("common"). As one executive puts it, "Exchanging letters and faxes is like a good conversation. It should flow, but there should be many pauses as well." You may want to write a follow-up letter a few weeks later. If you haven't received a reply, you may want to write a third letter near the time of your departure, mentioning the dates you'll be in France and requesting *une rencontre* (a meeting) — which should be one-on-one. If others on your team have to get involved, that should be done later, after personal contact has been established and solidified.

But then, even if a meeting is set, it won't necessarily take place. Before your host feels some kind of a personal commitment to you, he'll feel free to cancel your appointment if other pressing business comes up.

The First Meeting

When your first meeting *is* held, your French host will not necessarily go to great pains to make you feel comfortable. He may appear rushed and busy. He wants to feel superior, in a position of power. You're the supplicant — even if you feel that he should be salivating for your revolutionary product.

He's feeling you out — not on the business deal and not even on your character, honesty or efficiency. He wants to know if you're someone he wants to do business with over time, someone with whom he wishes to develop a social relationship. Do the two of you share a philosophy of life? Do you have similar backgrounds and education? Are you well connected in your country?

You can prepare for this meeting by researching your French colleague's company's history (as opposed to its net profits). You may flatter your French colleague by talking about his vision and the durability of his enterprise. The more you learn about his industry and his struggle to build a humane (though profitable) workplace, the closer you are to understanding him.

If you're fluent enough in French to conduct the meeting in it, you're at a big advantage. If you need an interpreter, it will make it harder to develop any kind of bond. "It's a barrier," notes a French commercial advisor. "The initial contact is not as good when a third party is involved." The French need to feel a sense of contact and a physical closeness, which an interpreter can destroy.

If you do need an interpreter, make your introductory comments in French. Look at your French counterpart throughout the discussions. And don't take notes. This is an intimate chat, at best.

Diplomas and Name-Dropping

The French are impressed by doctorate degrees and important social contacts, so it doesn't hurt to mention your Harvard MBA or your speeches at a national convention in Washington. But it should be done subtly. For instance, "When I was on a panel with _____ (president of Apple)." Or, "As a member of the board of alumni of Harvard, I .... " If you're name dropping, remember to use given names or nicknames, to show that you really know the people.

Most of the conversation will center around politics, philosophy, history and literature — a kind of cultural quiz to identify where you stand intellectually and whether you are someone he would like to get to know better over lunch. Try to refrain from quoting de Tocqueville (a 19th century French statesman who wrote insightfully about America). One French executive says that every American he meets does so to impress him.

Don't ask personal questions, and never mention your wife or children. "If he wants to find out about your family, he'll probably find out through the grapevine," observes a French businesswoman. An American who has a fairly close business relationship with a French government official recalls that the first time the Frenchman mentioned his wife was during their seventh lunch date. "Oh, my wife says I eat too much," the Frenchman said and went into no further detail. The American knew better than to pry.

No Pressure

If the first meeting is long, you're fortunate. If it turns into an invitation to join your French colleague for lunch, you have struck gold. But don't count on it.

Either your colleague will be interrupted by a phone call from his secretary or he'll look at his watch to signal the end of the meeting. The best way for you to conclude is with a phrase such as, "When I have the honor to have your answer." Don't appear to be in a hurry for his reply. Do thank him for his kindness. Follow up with a formally written thank you letter. (Dozens of books exist on how to write in French to everyone from a niece to a corporate executive. In each case, the degree of politeness and formality varies.) Then follow up that letter with a request for a second *rencontre*.

13 Negotiating with the French

Negotiation in France is an art not unlike cuisine and couture. (See Talleyrand, page 46). Negotiation is treated like a verbal duel (something the French excel at), and they prefer that proposals build up slowly, so that each of its building blocks can be analyzed and digested. Be prepared for long, drawn-out debates. The French won't allow anyone to bully them, con them or use "hard sell" techniques. Often the negotiations are like a roller coaster ride of emotions. Often, they're embellished with historical or literary allusions. And the French would often rather argue the pros and cons of an issue face-to-face than read a prepared summary that states the same points. Indeed, foreigners may find it wearing, even never-ending.

But remember: Even if the discussions become heated, your manners and your body language should remain conservative. Never resort to outbursts.

Tipped Chairs and Other Persuasions

It's best to have your facts organized into positive and negative reasons for the deal. Rationalize the negative away in terms of the benefits that outweigh them. Don't try to downplay or sweep aside any problems. An accomplished rhetorical style, however, will win you points.

The French like to have the upper hand. "He doesn't really want you to feel comfortable," observes a French wine exec. You may be kept waiting — either because your proposal isn't being well received, or just as a means of getting a negotiating edge." Pre-arranging for a secretary to interrupt a meeting is more common in France than in the U.S. The French may also set up appointments and not honor them, or they may bring along other people and conduct other business during your time slot.

A Parisian editor has a special seat for the writer he's negotiating with. The front legs of the chair are shorter, so that the writer is always in an awkward position, slipping forward in his seat. "They feel too awkward to ask for a better deal," he says.

Tips For Foreign Negotiators

Various tactics will help you in dealing with the French.

- **Be Totally Prepared**
  Your French counterpart will be well prepared and ready to argue every point. (However, he may not have planned much in the way of fallback positions.) Your analysis should be thorough and your presentation clear and concise.
- **Mention You've Looked Elsewhere**
  Subtlety is important here. But feel free to politely mention that you've spoken with competitors about cost options. Or you can mention that there are people in the market who provide services beyond what your counterpart is offering.
- **Never Take Notes**
  If you're the vice president or director, you

shouldn't be the one taking notes. That task is best left to subordinates. If it's a one-on-one meeting, confirm the terms of agreement afterward and arrange to have your staff (or your lawyers) iron out the details. Problems often arise, and you'll probably have to meet again to resolve them.

- **Try Flattery**

    By your appreciative look, you can let him know that you appreciate his taste in clothes or the decor of his conference room. Compliment him on his efforts to create a humane work environment (sponsoring a company tennis court or gym, hiring the children of employees, etc.) Most business leaders want to be known as having companies in which employees' families stay for generations. Do your homework, so that you can be specific. (You can be sure that he's done his homework about *your* background.)

- **Be Tactful.**

    Though the French like to argue and debate, they dislike being rigorously questioned, and criticism of a proposal may be taken as a criticism of the person responsible for drafting it.

The French Approach to Contracts

Even though a handshake between two executives signals a deal, it's not the final word. Funny things happen on the way to the written contract.

In one case, after two directors shook hands on a deal, the Americans wanted a 4-page contract and the French an 86-page contract. They ended up with a 12-page document, but, the American bitterly points out, it took six months to work it out.

And while, in some cases, the French may abide by a contract only as long as it suits them, a foreigner may be held to it, word for word.

14 Business Outside the Law

Underground Economy

From the moment you step off the curb outside of Charles De Gaulle or Orly airports, you'll see the US$250 billion underground economy at work. There will be taxi drivers trying to persuade you to hire them — without turning on the meter. On the streets, you can buy everything from Seiko watches to windup birds. Many shopkeepers will cut deals if you pay them in American dollars. And gypsy children (often from Eastern Europe) are extremely adept at removing wallets without offering anything in return.

Across the border, in Italian towns like San Remo, you'll find French designer bags, wallets, ties and scarves -- "seconds" produced in Italy and for sale at a fraction of their retail price. The government has vowed to search cars crossing back into France in order to confiscate these bargains (Louis Vuitton, etc.), but the border patrols are fairly lax.

Drugs, Illegal and Otherwise

Marseille has been a drug port of entry (opium, heroin, cocaine) for centuries. The guns of Fort St.

Nicholas (built by Louis XIV) face inland, not out to sea. Today, drug use is on the rise, although no more so than in other Western countries.

But more surprising is the increase in the use of legal, prescription drugs. More than 400,000 French people take Prozac, and 2 million more take other psychotropic drugs. Tobacco consumption has trebled in the last 30 years. And as can best be estimated, almost half the teenagers in urban areas have smoked marijuana.

Graft and Corruption

France has had more than its share of political scandals — ranging from rake-offs from public contracts to fraud and influence-peddling. While corruption has always been a part of French politics, its breadth, and the amounts involved, have risen sharply over the past 10 years. According to The Economist, the reasons for this shift are the higher costs of election campaigns and government decentralization (which increases the power of regional decision makers and therefore the opportunities for payoffs). The good news is that this shift seems to be "a French thing" that doesn't affect foreigners.

In 1995, a French tycoon was tried for spending US$6 million to buy influence. The press said he conducted his business à l'américaine, where "money is easy, the law doesn't count and politicians can be marketed like bars of soaps or cans of peas."

Prime minister Juppé authorized subsidized housing (domaine privé) for his son, his daughter, his ex-wife, his half-brother and himself. (The latter apartment, on the lovely Rue Jacob, featured a garden and a terrace. He was subsequently forced to move.) Soccer matches were rigged by a businessman. Water concessions in Grenoble were granted only after the mayor received US$4 million in gifts and favors. The mayor of Nice was in prison for pocketing millions in the name of a bogus opera association. His method for running the city included cooperating with organized crime. "You can't run Nice without the gangsters," another former mayor once said, "but you never give them a lift in your car."

Although there is a crackdown on corruption underway, the public is not too concerned. There is a tradition of corruption and a tradition of tolerating it. As one French commentator puts it, "In France, fiddles, great and small make people smile. What in the United States would send a politician into long-term retirement, here remains lackluster, almost insignificant." Tax fraud and tax evasion are rampant, and many deals are hatched for that express purpose. As one French businessman puts it, "Sometimes an invoice is not necessary. You understand?"

Sex and Prostitution

Prostitution was legal in France until 1946 (not coincidental, two years after women won the right to vote). Today, it's rampant, and sometimes pricey. It ranges from erotic peep shows to intimate all-night *clubs de rencontre*s. Some of the weirdest sex can be found in the Bois de Boulogne, the woods on the western edge of Paris where low class *belles de nuits*, young boys, transvestites and even housewives trying to make some extra pocket money congregate.

Rue St. Denis is a popular red-light district, and sexual favors can always be purchased near train stations and next to Les Halles. In Paris alone, there are some 20,000 full-time and 60,000 part-time prostitutes. The rates range from US$20 a throw (plus hotel room) to US$500 and up for fancier call-girls.

15   Names & Greetings

The French trust their instincts about people. As a result, first impressions count. To make a good first impression, a foreigner should respect traditions and pay attention to cues. There should always be a brief visual exchange — but not a smile — in addition to the traditional handshake, when you first meet someone.

Tu versus Vous

Foreigners always worry about whether to use the formal *vous* or the familiar *tu* when addressing French friends and colleagues. The former is always polite and safe. A 42-year-old teacher says he still calls his aging father *vous*, even though he helps him with his personal care. "*Tu*," he laughs "is only for kids and dogs." But that's the old school. In the advertising, journalism, theater and cinema professions, people call each other *tu*, even when they don't know each other particularly well, and those who don't are seen as snobs. In banks and business, however, the atmosphere remains formal. To be polite, always address your secretary or your interpreter as *vous*.

One executive says that when his boss addresses him as *tu*, it's usually the prologue to a request to work overtime. "You can demand more of a person you call 'tu'," he points out.

Vous/tu is like a boundary or a border. Once you start calling someone *tu*, even by accident, you're stuck with it. Changing back to *vous* would be considered insulting.

Order, Initials & Gender

French business people usually write their first names in full, followed by their family name. Sometimes, however, they write their family name first, in capital letters, for example: DURAND, Claude. With a double first name (which is quite common), they sometimes use two initials. For instance the philosopher/writer Sartre's first name, Jean-Paul, might be J.P. Marie-Claude would be M.C.

Women and men sometimes share the same first names, with the letter "e" added at the end to indicate which are feminine — for instance, Pascal/Pascale, Paul/Paule or René/Renée. From time to time, it's been fashionable to give boys' names to girls — such as Georges, Dominique or Claude. And the name Marie (as in Jean-Marie) may be given to a boy.

It's safest to address women as *Madame*, although young, unmarried women prefer to be called *Mademoiselle*. Women should be addressed by their surnames, as in *Bonjour, Madame Dupont* or *Bonsoir, Mademoiselle Renaud*.

A Nation of Titles

The French like titles, and many exist in the corporate hierarchy. The chief executive of a corporation is *Président-Directeur Général* (PDG). An

Administrateur is a senior officer. Each department is headed by a *Directeur-General*. The department is then divided into "Directions" (headed by a *directeur*) and then subdivided into "divisions," then into "services" and finally into "sections" — headed by a *chef de division*, a *chef de service* and a *chef de section* respectively.

In family names, a *de* or *d'* indicates nobility (or a desire for it). Academic titles (Ph.D., for example) aren't usually used.

Whole Lot of Shakin' Going On

The French shake hands both on meeting someone and on leaving a room. They do so with everyone they meet during the course of the day. On arriving at work, each employee shakes hands with everyone there — this ritual alone often takes half an hour. In an office of 20 people, that's 400 handshakes every morning and another 400 each evening.

Handshaking shows respect and personal recognition. And it's always accompanied by a personal greeting (*Bonjour, Monsieur Leconte*). Children are taught to shake hands before they learn how to walk. The handshake is a light grip and a single quick shake. As a general rule, women who wish to shake hands extend their hand first.

Faire la Bise

Good friends and family members greet and depart with a double cheek kiss. One usually starts with the right cheek. A triple kiss — and in some provinces, a quadruple kiss — is an even greater show of affection.

Some foreigners have reduced the intimacy of the kissing ritual by "kissing air" instead of touching lips to cheek. Women who don't really like one another, but who feel obliged to engage in the ritual, also kiss air.

The Business Card Exchange

Handshakes are often followed by an exchange of business cards. They tend to be larger in format than American ones (probably because French paper currency, and therefore wallets, are bigger). Make sure that your cards have the proper telephone codes so that your French colleague or friend can reach you.

When accepting a card, take a few moments to read it before tucking it into your wallet. It shows interest and respect.

Bataille de la Porte

Social standing becomes apparent when everyone heads out of the room or into the elevator. It's called the *bataille de la porte* (battle of the doorway). The doorway is not a first-come, first-serve situation. Rather, it's a test of *savoir faire* and etiquette. In France, you must pay attention to the rank and gender of those heading out the door with you. Women may go first. Junior executives let their seniors pass ahead of them. If your rank is superior, by all means, go through the doorway first.

Crazy.

Enchanté.

What can I do?

16 Communication Styles

Conversation Starters

The French can be reserved and formal, especially when meeting new people. But they love to discuss art and literature, cinema and cuisine, music and history. Ask about the St. Germain team's soccer exploits. Let them extol their favorite restaurant or wine. They'll be curious about your impressions as a tourist (so think about something clever to say about the newest exhibit at the Louvre), as well as about your academic background and interests. Remember that repartee and nuance are much admired, and that being well-read is considered a sign of intelligence.

Certain topics may make your French host or potential business partner uncomfortable:

- **Personal questions.** American executives love to talk about their families and to ask about other people's. In France, that's considered an invasion of privacy. Wait for your host to bring it up. However, you *could* talk about your Golden Retriever.

- **Age & salary.** It's impolite to ask someone's age or how much they earn. It's also consid-

ered crass to talk about how much money you
or your company makes.

- **Boasting.** Avoid going on about your personal or
  professional accomplishments (or risk being seen
  as immature). If asked, try to sound modest.

- **Politics, religion, etc.** Remarks about how you
  voted, what faith you subscribe to, divorce or
  psychiatry may be considered too personal,
  and therefore offensive.

- **The pace.** Keep the conversation moving from
  topic to topic. It should be like a ping pong
  game. You make a remark, then the next person
  adds their *bons mots*. Expect your host to interrupt you. And don't be offended if someone
  debates you on an issue.

- **Humor.** Don't tell racial, scatological or sexual
  jokes, but try to be witty, when it's appropriate.
  Keep in mind that humor doesn't translate well
  between cultures or languages.

- **The war.** Avoid talking about World War II,
  and don't ask what the French did during the
  Occupation, unless your host or business asso-
  ciate brings it up. (Many people, including
  some who went on to hold powerful government positions, collaborated with the Nazis.
  No one wishes to admit it.)

Nonverbal Communication

In France, appearances count. How you look in
public affects your status. The French are aware of
their bodies at all times. Both men and women sit
with their legs crossed at the knees. They stand up
straight, with arms at their sides and feet together.

Public displays of affection are common. People seem to need less space between them than
some Westerners do. For instance, when you xerox

a document, co-workers will lean over and watch closely, almost touching you and often curiously staring at your work.

Guidelines

The best way to be considered *bien élevé* (well bred) is to observe French body language and mimic it.

- **Be physical**

Remember, your initial daily contact with your host or business colleagues will be to shake hands, and if there are women and children, *faire la bise* (kiss on both cheeks). Shake the hand of every new person you meet.

In business meetings, lean over when making a point. Look your colleague or host in the eye.

- **Stay Close**

Britons, Americans and Germans stand 18 to 24 inches apart in formal situations. The French stand closer -- at a distance of 12 inches or less. When standing in line at the post office or at a bar, the French practically bump each other. They look over each other's shoulders and no one seems offended.

- **Don't Smile, Unless They Do**

The French are not big on smiling. They find it childish and phony. They prefer to offer an empty stare. If you smile at a French man, he'll think you're either poking fun at him, that you're hypo-critical, or that you're stupid. If you smile at a French woman, you are flirting with her.

- **Speak Softly**

The French people have been taught to modu-late their voices in public. Raising one's voice is considered *mal élevé* (of poor breeding) for two rea-sons: because it might disturb others and because you might be overheard. In business meetings, speak clearly and loudly enough to be heard by all. But never resort to shouting, even in the heat of an argument.

- **Don't Point**

    Pointing is considered rude. To indicate some-one or something, use your entire hand, with the palm open.

- **Keep the Conversation Moving**

    In business as well as at dinner parties, the con-versation should sizzle. The debate should move along, with each person in the room participating. You should neither be passive nor deliver a mono-logue. Plan what you'll say, so that your remarks are concise and cogent. Be witty. (*It's not enough to have wit,* goes one old French proverb. *You must know how to use it wittily.*) And don't overstate your case.

- **Posture Counts**

    Never look too relaxed. Always look in control of your body and your emotions. It's been said that traditional French chairs were made to be uncom-fortable so that people would hold themselves up straight in them. Slouching or putting your feet up on a desk are considered impolite. During a meet-ing or dinner, never rest your elbows on the table.

- **Be Aware of Protocol**

    Watch for subtle signs of hierarchy among your colleagues. The person in charge of making deci-sions will listen to all opinions and talk about reaching some compromise. Avoid trying to appeal directly to the boss (unless you share his level of authority). Remember that you're the outsider.

Customs

Gift Giving

The French appreciate quality and originality in the gifts they give and receive. Gifts shouldn't be extravagant, but they should appeal to the intellect or to one's aesthetic sense — for instance, an Ansel Adams' photography book, a particularly artistic Katchina doll, a new Chick Corea CD, or a controversial biography of Michel Foucault. The American habit of a simple verbal "Thank you" is considered glib and *mal élevé*. You should thank someone in writing for any gift or dinner invitation. Avoid gifts with large company name or logo.

If you've worked with French colleagues before, you might want to surprise them with gourmet food items (a good bottle of Scotch or dried apricots), or a useful electronic gadget. You might also want to give them tickets to see a particularly fabulous orchestra, band or jazz ensemble on tour from your native country.

When visiting someone's house, bring high-quality sweets (chocolate truffles, for example) or flowers (in odd-numbered amounts, often seven but never 13) — but not chrysanthemums (reserved for funerals), carnations (bad luck), red roses (reserved for lovers and socialists), or yellow roses (the color is associated with cuckoldry). A present for the children (Swatch watches, for instance) is also a nice idea.

Café Sitting

Cafés are a refuge from the hectic pace of work — a place to sit, read Le Monde, smoke Gitanes, people-watch and discuss politics. They offer espresso, citron pressé (fresh lemon juice with water) and *sirops* (mixed with water, they taste like fruit drinks). At lunch, you can usually order a *steak/frites* (steak with French fries). During the rest of the day, they serve *croque monsieur* (ham and cheese sandwich dipped into beaten egg, then fried), *croque madame* (the same, but with sliced mushrooms or tomatoes and no ham), salads, desserts and ice cream.

Unfortunately for tradition, the number of cafés has dropped sharply in the last ten years, as they must compete with *brasseries, bistros, bars,* wine bars and *salons de thé.*

Le Pique Nique

Forget about sprawling on the ground on an isolated grass meadow surrounded by sandwiches, beer cans and plastic forks. When the French have a picnic, they bring along a table and chairs, a tablecloth, cloth napkins, silverware, ceramic plates and wine glasses. Often, these are arranged on the side of a road or highway, with cars careening by. The meal consists of carefully prepared dishes, such as cassoulet or a salmon quiche.

Christmas

On Christmas eve, families decorate their trees, go to midnight mass, and then return home for *le réveillon*, a lavish late supper that varies according to the region. Foie gras and oysters are traditional, as is goose in Alsace, turkey with chestnuts in Burgundy, buckwheat cakes with sour cream in Brittany, and salt cod cooked with tomato sauce, red wine and anchovies in Provence. Provence also has a tradition of serving 13 desserts, however simple (including dried figs, raisins, hazelnuts and almonds, as their colors symbolize Franciscans, Dominicans, Carmelites and Augustinians, respectively).

Before bedtime, children set out their shoes for *Pere Noel* (Father Christmas) to fill with gifts. Adults often wait until New Year's Day to exchange their presents.

Twelfth Night is often celebrated with a special cake that contains a bean, a silver coin or a whole almond (to eliminate the danger of a broken tooth). The recipient of the bean is declared king or queen for the day.

In Paris, a giant creche is set up in front of the Hôtel de ville (the town hall) and all the main churches, and *les grands magasins* feature magnificent window displays. In some cities, Nativity plays are acted out. In La Camargue, calves are rounded up and branded. In Les Baux, a little cart with a newborn lamb is drawn into church by a ram, accompanied by shepherds.

Intellectual Comics

Tintin is as famous in France as Mickey Mouse is in the U.S. Like Mickey, he's inspired an elaborate line of goods (ranging from T-shirts, slippers and shower curtains to wristwatches and ceramic teapots), along with exclusive Tintin stores to sell them in, though he has yet to have a theme park to call home, à la Disneyland (though he has a web site in the U.S.).

The earnest young hero and his faithful fox terrier, Milou (Snowy), have been having marvelous adventures since 1929 — in *bande dessinée* or BD (comic strip) books with names like <u>The Blue Lotus</u>, <u>Explorers on the Moon</u>, <u>Land of Black Gold</u>, <u>The Calculus Affair</u>, <u>Cigars of the Pharaoh</u>, <u>Tintin in Tibet</u> and <u>Castafiore's Emerald</u>. The foes they encounter run the gamut from communists and money-grubbing capitalists to gangsters and wild Indians.

Ostensibly written for children, these books (as well as those featuring Astérix, who was "born" in the 1960s — see page 9) are popular with adults. In fact, some French intellectuals have gone so far as to speak of them in the same breath with Marcel Proust and to declare them an art form almost as worthy of attention as French cinema. *Bédéphiles* have their headquarters in Angouleme's Centre National de la Bande Dessinée and attend festivals in both France and Belgium (Tintin's creator, Georges Rémi, a.k.a. Hergé — R.G., his initials reversed — was Belgian).

Viager: The French Gamble

Though a French person may seem formal and conservative on the surface, beneath the polished exterior is often a risk-taker — that daredevil at the wheel of a Renault who cuts you off as you circle the Arc de Triomphe. He or she may also be dying to place a bet on the *tiercé* (the equivalent of the trifecta at most race tracks) or to buy a *Loterie Nationale* (state-run lottery) ticket, which are sold at every newspaper vendor.

The biggest gamble in France is the practice of *viager* (literally, "for life"), a form of reverse mortgage that can apply to anything from a one-room apartment to a grand chateau. This is how it works. An aging home owner receives periodic payments from an interested buyer, who stands to take over the property when the owner dies. The buyer hopes to purchase a home for below-market value; the original owner hopes to live forever and thereby receive more money than the house is worth.

In one famous case, a 44-year-old man had his eye on a beautiful house in Arles. In 1965, he made a down payment to the 90-year-old owner, one Mme Calment, and agreed to pay her an additional US$3,500 a year until her death. However, he died first (thirty years later, in 1995), while Mme Calment (who had known Vincent Van Gogh in her youth) lived on to celebrate her 121st birthday. His children are now heirs to the house. Mme Calment still lives in it and is happy to continue to collect $3,500 a year.

The payments are usually based on actuarial tables and on the property's value, not on the owner's health. About 1,000 viager properties are sold in France every year, many to buyers who live in Japan, South America and the U.S. Even former President John F. Kennedy apparently played the *viager* market. Potential buyers either call *viager* specialists — they're listed in the French "yellow pages" — or look for ads in Le Figaro or the real estate weekly, Particulier.

18 Dress & Appearance

One of the first famous dressmakers was Mademoiselle Bertin, who designed for Marie Antoinette. In the 18th century, the fashion was to have a few types of dresses and 250 ways of decorating them. The French have a real appreciation of fine workmanship, sensual materials, originality, harmony and style. There's also a cult of accessories — scarves, belts and jewelry and perfumes. Some couturiers (like Nina Ricci) derive nine-tenths of their income from the sale of designer fragrances.

France's top designers probably dress only 2,000 of the world's richest women and actresses — less than a third of them French. (Guy Laroche served only 75 clients a year.) But most French women pay attention to fashion and buy clothes bearing designer labels — even if they buy only two or three dresses a year.

Besides Ricci and Laroche, other well-known *couturiers* include Yves St. Laurent (an Alsatian born in Algeria), Kenzo (Japanese Parisian), Pierre Cardin and Schiaparelli. Christian Dior was a political science student turned picture dealer who decided to try his hand at clothing design.

"I can always tell the Americans in Paris,"

observes a French dentist. "They look sloppy, unkempt, casual in the way they dress. It's not *soigné*." Soigné means to have put care and thought into your appearance. To be clean isn't good enough. You have to be elegant. *Haute bourgeoisie* Parisians, in particular, never go out in casual clothes, even to walk the dog or to fetch the morning newspaper (and they "dress" to garden if the garden is in the front yard, where others will see them).

While French businessmen tend to prefer dark suits, they'll also wear the latest cologne, a trendy, colorful tie and carry a designer leather briefcase. On the Riviera and in resorts, they wear bright, colorful shirts and often sport gold neck chains. Shorts on men are considered boorish, except for tennis.

Summers are hot and humid, so summer clothes should be made of lightweight material. In the spring and fall, it often rains, so raincoats and umbrellas are necessary. Except in the south, winter requires wool suits, coats, hats and lined boots.

A Note on Bérets

Until 1923, bérets were worn only in the Pyrénées area. Suddenly adopted as a French fashion, 23 million of them were manufactured — about one for every Frenchman. The fashion faded in the 1950s; today, less than a million are bought each year. Bérets remain, for the most part, the hat on the guy in the old Renoir movie or on the elderly gentleman clutching a *baguette* in travel agency posters.

19 Reading the French

Style as Substance

No one has ever counted just how often the French speak with their hands. But it's at least a few dozen times an hour. The French communicate a lot with body language freely and deliberately. A colleague will raise his shoulders before, or even instead of, telling you that your marketing plan is ridiculous. A smile might indicate that you've gone overboard in your presentation. Although the French are fairly direct and outspoken, reading their body language can help you to quickly evaluate the impact of your words or your work.

- Eye contact is a statement of equality, and it's considered too personal to use with strangers. Therefore, on the street or in a restaurant, direct eye contact may be viewed as a "pick up." Refusing to meet someone's eye, on the other hand, is viewed as unfriendly.

- As mentioned earlier, the French are *méfiant* (wary) of smiles and laughter, especially among strangers. The French smile and laugh only when there's "a reason" — for a friend, a child, a joke, a lover. A French human resources magazine went so far as to list 13 different types of smiles and their meaning, from ephemeral (weak, cowardly) to mocking (meant to discredit someone). The point is that the French are so analytical that even smiles are deconstructed for meaning.

- Counting on one's fingers starts with the thumb, rather than the index finger.

- The French cover their mouths when yawning, coughing or using a toothpick (this is rarely done in public). Handkerchiefs are used when sneezing; blowing one's nose in public is vulgar.

- Snapping fingers (even to summon a waiter) is considered rude, as is slapping an open palm over a closed fist. Winking and pointing are impolite.

- The classic "okay" sign in the United States — thumb and forefinger forming a circle with other fingers pointed up — means "zero" or "worthless." Okay is simply thumbs up.

- The Gaelic shoulder shrug alone means "This is ridiculous." When palms are extended, it means "I'm not worried." If the palms are raised to the chest, it means, "What do you expect *me* to do about it?"

- Playing an imaginary flute is a way of indicating that someone is talking too much and has become boring.

- A hand wiped across the forehead means, "I've had it up to here" (*J'en ai ras le bol*). A finger circling the temple means "He's crazy" (*dingue*). Kissing one's fingertips conveys, "How delicious." Pulling the right cheek down at the eye means, "You're kidding" (*mon oeil*). Flicking fingers across one's cheek means, "How dull."

Entertaining:
Le Grand Repas

Mr. Boulanger Invents the Restaurant

In 1765, a man by the name of Boulanger sold bouillons made of broth, minced meats and grain designed to fortify his fellow Parisians after strenuous physical exercise and to strengthen pregnant women. A quasi-Biblical sign, hung above his shop, read: *Come to me all those whose stomachs labor and I shall restore you.* He called his concoctions *restorants* or *restaurants*.

In an effort to expand his business, Monsieur Boulanger added a dish of sheep's trotters in a white sauce to his offerings. As he wasn't a guild member, the *traiteurs* (who provided the public with stews) sued. But Parliament ruled in his favor (the meat hadn't been cooked in the sauce, they said, and was therefore not a stew) and news of his victory spread. Boulanger's establishment on rue de Louvre quickly became the fashionable place to dine.

Food As Spiritual Experience

At a business seminar in Nice, two marketing

executives are deep in conversation, not about soccer or the upcoming local elections, but about where to pick the finest mushrooms (French varieties include cèpes, chanterelles, girolles, pleurottes and morilles) and which sauce to prepare them with. The ability to turn eating into art is the mark of a Frenchman.

"He who invents a new dish will have rendered humanity a greater service than the scientist who discovers a planet," wrote Anthelme Brillat-Savarin, 19th century author of the classic Physiology of Taste. Just think of Marcel Proust's *petites madeleines* (seashell-shaped cakes named after a French pastry cook) in Remembrance of Things Past. Their smell alone brought back buried childhood memories and inspired one of the great novels of the 20th century.

An appreciative palate is almost a national prerequisite. Of course, there are always exceptions to the rule. The highly lauded Napoleon prided himself on careening through a meal in 18 minutes or less and his favorite dishes were macaroni and chicken. (But then, he was Corsican by birth.) The first French cookbooks date back to the Middle Ages; the nation's cuisine began to set a world standard in the 18th century. Since then, great chefs (almost exclusively male) have been treated like cultural high priests.

At least one of them — Auguste Escoffier — was awarded the prestigious Legion d'Honneur. "To know how to eat," he said, "is to know how to live." During his 62-year career, Escoffier directed the kitchens of both the Savoy and Carlton Hotels in London. (To avoid offending the delicate sensibilities of his lady customers, he called frogs' legs "nymphs.") He simplified and standardized recipes (so that the same dish could be produced again and again), invented *pêche Melba* (in honor of the Australian singer Nellie Melba), and personally prepared meals for Napoleon III, three French presidents, Queen Victoria, Edward VII, George V and Kaiser Wilhelm.

Paul Bocuse, France's number one chef, compares his feasts to an opera — in which he orchestrates the music and directs the lights, the decor and the choir. Most of the country's food critics like to express disdain for other cuisines. <u>Le Guide Michelin</u> can find no restaurants in Italy worthy of three stars (the highest rating) and hardly any in the U.S. Only 20 restaurants in France currently have that honor. (In 1967, the chef at Relais de Porquerolles shot himself after losing his three-star Michelin rating.)

From Pig's Feet to Nouvelle Cuisine

The French eat just about everything (genitals, brains, cow ears, Monsieur Boulanger's sheep trotters), and they don't always mince or process them into a paté. So a *pied de porc* will look exactly look like the pig's foot that it is when it arrives on your *charcuterie* (cold cuts) plate. They also enjoy horse meat, rabbit, wild boar, venison and perhaps half a dozen different varieties of chicken.

Besides giving the world exquisite, cholesterol-laden dishes redolent with butter and cream, the French also invented Nouvelle Cuisine (circa 1973), an alternative lighter fare. Well-heeled execs often dine on elaborate "take-out" food, from *coq au vin* (chicken cooked in red wine) to *quenelles* (poached fish dumplings), from *quiche Lorraine* (custard pie with bacon and cheese) to *tarte Tatin* (an upside-down carmelized apple tart).

The French spend more than a quarter of their income on food. Even the most modest worker will take his family out to a restaurant for special occasions. In a small village in the Alps, a plumber took a party of 20 relatives and friends out for a five-course meal. The next day, he went bankrupt.

Wine Replaces the Sun

Thirty years ago, the typical working class Frenchman started his day with a shot of wine, followed by a small cup of espresso. That's no longer the typical French breakfast, but you can still order the combination in any bar. *In winter, while you sleep, wine replaces the sun*, goes an old proverb.

Few French would dream of having a meal without a glass or two. (Escoffier recommended that dinner include a pony of marsala, a good bordeaux and, finally, champagne.) One million French produce two billion gallons of wine a year — a quarter of the world's production. The legal drinking age is 14. Children are served wine at family celebrations, and some as young as three are given a slightly watered-down version.

Most people still prefer the wines from their own region. About two million people drink half a gallon daily. The rest consume, on average, 15.5 liters per person per year, second only to the citizenry of Luxembourg. Even at McDonald's, people drink wine with their Big Macs. (Alcoholism is the nation's third highest cause of death.)

The Phoenicians introduced winemaking to France when they moved into the Rhone valley in 620 B.C. They brought a variety of *vinifera* (wine) grapes with them — like the syrah and the muscat, originally from Persia. The Romans continued the tradition. The great French wines are usually made from a blend of grapes (cabernet sauvignon, chardonnay, sauvignon blanc, merlot, muscat, pinot noir, Johannisberg reisling and chenin blanc among them). Until recently, the wines were named for the region or village in which they were grown and produced (such as Bordeaux or Côtes du Rhone), not after the grape's name (as in the United States).

Whites, Rosés and Reds

White wines usually include Sancerre (fruity and spritzy, made from sauvignon blanc grapes), Muscadet (dry), Pouilly Fuisse (named for a small village in Burgundy and made from chardonnay grapes), and Chablis (named for a small region near Paris, also made from chardonnay grapes). Rosé wines are made from a blend of different red grapes, with the skins removed before the berries are crushed. Provençals are lighter and perfume-like, while Tavel (from the Côtes du Rhone region) is more robust.

There's an incredible variety among reds. Bordeaux wines are mostly cabernet sauvignon grapes blended with a little merlot, while Burgundy wines are all pinot noir. (Good years include 1978, 1982 and 1985. Try the Margaux wines of the Medoc region of Bordeaux or the Meursault from Burgundy.) Beaujolais wines (lighter) are also made in southern Burgundy, but from a different grape, the gamay Beaujolais. Côtes du Rhones (intense and rich, especially the popular Chateauneuf du Pape) are a blend of up to nine different grape varieties.

The Two-Hour Lunch

Inviting your French colleagues to lunch is a great way to establish a rapport. But consider allowing *them* to choose the restaurant or bistro. When a young American lawyer suggested lunch to fellows with whom he was collaborating on a deal, they hemmed and hawed. The next day, he tried again, this time making it clear that he expected them to choose the place. *"Bien sur,"* one of his colleagues said with a look of relief. "We were worried yesterday that you would take us to McDonald's." Let them choose the wine, too, even if you're an oenophile. Suggest a toast, if no one else at the table has.

(The term *bistro,* by the way, caught on in the early 19th century. Russian Cossacks on leave in Paris would bang on the tables in their favorite eating establishments shouting "Bistro!" — Russian for "quick.")

If you're the one who suggested going out, be sure to pick up the tab. The French don't believe in "going Dutch" (splitting the check). Instead, they take turns inviting one another out. Remember that the tip is already included in the bill (*service compris*), as is *le couvert* (a cover charge for the tableware). Leave a few extra francs only if the service was first class.

Formal lunches can last from two to three hours and can include up to 12 courses. The French may order an *apéritif* (usually Dubonnet or vermouth), a *Kir* (white wine and *cassis,* a black currant liqueur) or whisky. The minimum is five to seven courses — some kind of fish or starter, soup, the main dish, a green salad, cheese, dessert and fruit. Espresso (*café pressé* or *café bien serré*) usually follows.

The Dinner Party

Consider yourself extraordinarily lucky if you're invited to a French colleague's home for cocktails or dinner. The French home is considered very private and invitations are usually reserved for intimate friends. (Also, Parisian apartments tend to be small and their kitchens old-fashioned.)

Some basic guest protocol:

- Never arrive early or exactly on time (it suggests that you're overly anxious) and never leave first.
- Better to be overdressed than underdressed.
- Never arrive empty-handed (see Gift-Giving in Chapter 17) but never bring wine. Almost everyone has his own *cave* (wine cellar) and specific tastes. (If they live in a small apartment, they'll rent a storage space elsewhere.) If you're an American and are dining with friends or close acquaintances, you could bring a US$50-$100 bottle of California wine and ask your host to taste and compare it with French wine.
- Stay in the living room; don't wander around the house or ask for a tour. The host or hostess will tell you to join him or her in the kitchen if either of them wants you there (which is rare). You're the guest and your place is in the *salon*.
- Never pour yourself a drink or a refill. Wait to be served.
- Rise when your host gives you your pre-dinner drink. Rise, if you're a man, every time a woman comes into the house for the first time.
- People rarely use someone else's bathroom, so don't ask to use the W.C. unless it's an emergency.

At some parties, only friends actually talk to each other before dinner is served. So don't feel offended. Remember not to ask personal questions, such as the first one that most Americans would, namely "How do you know Monsieur X, our host?"

If you're the honored guest, you'll be seated at the right of the host or hostess. Remember to eat all the food you're served (but you can refuse the cheese course without offending your host). Feel free to comment favorably on the food, but don't ask for the recipe — that's almost as personal as asking for your host's bra size.

The Importance of Table Manners

Poor French language skills are easily forgiven, but *faux pas* (mistakes) at the table are not.

The word "etiquette" derives from *estique*, an Old French word meaning "to stick." As daily rules were tacked up on walls in army posts, by the 16th century, the word had come to mean a label or ticket. So, etiquette can be seen as the "permit" that gets one into polite society.

The current edition of *Bottin Mondain* (a listing of the nation's social elite, about 0.5 percent of the populace) reminds its readers that the host and hostess should face each other across the center of the family (not at either end); that napkins should be draped lengthwise across the knees (but not opened fully); that knives should never be used to cut bread, foie gras or salad (fold the lettuce into small pieces with your fork); that only puddings made with cream are eaten with a spoon; that hands not engaged in eating should rest on the table (there are various amusing reasons given for this one); and that a lady's hand should never be kissed out of doors.

Here are a few other guidelines:

- The French eat in the continental style, with the fork in the left hand and the knife in the right. You should start with the utensils on the outside and work your way in. The silverware above your plate are for dessert. Often, another set of utensils will be brought for cheese and dessert. Knife and fork are placed parallel, across the plate, when you've finished eating.

- It's impolite to speak with your mouth full or to point with your knife.

- Salad is served *after* the main dish.

- Only bread and asparagus are eaten with the fingers. Chicken legs, all fruit (the French peel and cut theirs with their knife and eat it with a fork), pizzas and even sandwiches are cut and eaten with a fork.

- Don't cut the point off the cheeses (served after the salad and before the dessert). The technique is to cut cheese so that it retains its shape. And it's impolite to help oneself to cheese twice.

- Inebriation is *mal élevé*. Learn to sip your wine slowly and to take breaks to talk.

- Eat everything that's on your plate. "Americans are so wasteful," a 33-year-old engineer laments. "They never finish their food."

- In a restaurant or in someone's home, refrain from lightening up a cigarette until after the espresso or *digestif* (after-dinner drink) has been served. Don't smoke between courses, unless others do. (However, in cafés and bars, the French smoke non-stop.)

- If a Parisian mentions that he or she lives in *le Huitieme* (the 8th) or *le Seizieme* (the 16th), they're referring to prestigious *arrondissements* (areas of the city) and telling you, by association, that they're *quelqu'un* (someone worthwhile).

21 Socializing

The French work hard, but they have no appreciation of workaholics. Weekends are reserved for family, culture and relaxation. Leisure time is not scheduled. People "hang out" with each other *(traîner)*. "I might go shopping with my sisters and buy nothing," says a 39-year-old businesswoman and mother of two. "It is an excuse to be together and exchange ideas. We have no sense of 'wasting' time." They might garden, putter around at home, visit friends, or go to the beach. Weekend meals are long and leisurely — an opportunity to debate politics and literature.

Cinema Reigns

The French see a film a week, on average. The art of filmmaking, like the art of cuisine, is taken very seriously. The French film industry creates about 250 films annually, ranging from slapstick comedies to serious literary epics (where the emphasis is on mood, cinematography and philosophical discussion, rather than on plot surprises and clever repartee). Nearly a third of the industry's funds (800 million francs) come from govern-

ment subsidies. The state-run TV network also
commissions films. The prestigious Cannes Film
Festival, where many international films debut,
takes place every May, and there's an animation
festival in Annecy each June.

Not the Mall, but the Marché

Either with your new French friends, or on
your own, you may want to visit a *marché* (open air
market), where vegetables and fruit are hawked,
sometimes in loud sing-song monologues. The
merchants make puns and the ambience is festive.
Bring along a canvas, straw or string bag, as gro-
cery bags aren't provided. Ask for a kilo or 500
grammes of blood oranges, thick-stalked white
asparagus (fabulous) or garden-fresh leeks (the
French bake them into tarts). In many areas, the
produce will be picked out for you. (It pays to pay
attention. More than one amateur shopper has
taken home a purchase, only to discover old or
overly ripe produce in the bottom of the sack.)

Other *marchés* (where you can bargain) include
marchés de brocante (second hand) and Paris's *marché
aux puces* (flea market).

Le Grand Spectacle

Most French people avoid going to watch can-
can dancers in spectacular outfits, but for some reason, they believe that foreign tourists really enjoy *le
grand spectacle*. It's worth experiencing at least once,
just as you might sing in a karaoke club in Tokyo or
see the Rockettes at Radio City Music Hall in New
York. The two most likely spots you'll be taken to
are the Moulin Rouge and the Lido.

What the French do appreciate is jazz. In July,
there are festivals in Juan les Pins, Antibes and Nice.

The world-class line-up often includes Frenchmen
Stéphane Grapelli (jazz violin) and the grandson of
the legendary Django Reinhart (jazz guitar).

La Vie Sportive

Other activities foreigners may be invited to
include *pétanque* (a bowling game played in the
south), yachting, fishing, hunting or wine tasting.
Indoor windsurfing is a recent sports fad. Golf is
for the wealthy, as there are only private clubs.
(Avoid casual dress and wear an elegant hat.)

Many French people prefer to watch, rather
than participate. Ten million of them line the streets
each year to watch the *Tour de France* (millions more
watch on TV), as the world's greatest cyclists hurtle
up and down mountains, covering a few hundred
kilometers a day for over a month. Begun in 1903
(the women's version in 1984), the *tour* supposedly
follows the contour of the country. The last Sunday
in July, the day when the cyclists finally cross the
finish line on the Champs Elysées, is celebrated as a
holiday. The winner automatically becomes a
national hero — even if he's not French (the last
French winner was Laurent Fignon in 1988).

Club Med: A Strange Cocktail

When the French take a vacation (they get five
weeks off each year), most of them (81 percent) stay
in France. But for those with wanderlust, there's
Club Med. Started in the 1950s by Gerard Blitz as "a
strange cocktail of *la vie de chateau* and *la vie de sau-
vage*" (chateau life and "going primitive"). It was
designed to offer exotic destinations where the
French would encounter ONLY other French people.
Today, Club Med caters to many nationalities and
has sites worldwide, particularly in tropical locales.

22 Basic French Phrases

English	French
Yes No	*Oui* *Non*
Good morning Hello (daytime) Hello (evening) Hello (telephone)	*Bonjour* *Bonjour* *Bonsoir* *Allo?*
Good-bye	*Au revoir*
Please	*S'il vous plait*
Thank you	*Merci*
Pleased to meet you	*Enchanté*
Excuse me; I'm sorry	*Pardon*
My name is _____	*Je m'appelle _____*
I don't understand	*Je ne comprends pas*
See you tomorrow	*A demain*

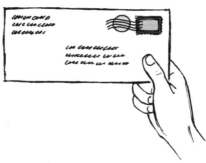

23   Correspondence

The order of information in a French mailing address is similar to that in most European countries. As in the U.S., postal codes are important. A sample address:

Monsieur DUPONT Alain
Editions Internationales S.A
Siege Social
Immeuble Louis XV
10, rue de la Victoire
37004 TOURS

Don't abbreviate Monsieur or Madame; the family name is usually capitalized and comes first. S.A. (*Societe Anonyme*) means it's a corporation. Note that *rue and avenue* (abbreviated as av.) aren't capitalized. The name of the city, town or commune is, however, capitalized. B.P (*boite postale*) is the equivalent of a Post Office Box. CEDEX (*Courrier d' Entreprise à Distribution Exceptionnelle*) is for special delivery of business mail.

For convenience, postage stamps are sold at local corner newsstands and *bureaux de tabac,* as well as in post offices.

 ## Useful Numbers

These are local Paris numbers. (In 1997, another digit will be added, for a total of nine.) If dialing from outside of France, dial your country's international access code and France's country code [33] first. From Paris to the provinces, dial 16 first. From the provinces to Paris, dial 16 plus 1 first.

- Medical Team and Ambulance 15
- Police 17
- Fire department 18
- Local telephone directory assistance 12
- International directory assistance ..... 19-33 plus country code
- Computer rentals 42-00-70-01
- Secretarial services 46-22-98-98
- Avis 48-62-34-34
- Europcar 49-75-47-47
- Air France 42-27-98-01
- British Airlines 47-78-14-14
- TWA 47-20-62-11
- French Chamber of Commerce 42-56-05-00
- SOS- Help (English) 47-23-80-80
- 24-hour dentist 43-37-51-00

Books & Internet Addresses

Travelers' Tales: France, edited by O'Reilly, O'Reilly & Habegger. Travelers' Tales, Inc., San Francisco, California, USA, 1995. Diverse first-person accounts offer a tantalizing look at French culture.

The Europeans by Luigi Barzini. Simon & Schuster, New York, USA, 1983. A witty journalist's views of how the national character of the different European nations was formed.

The French by Theodore Zeldin. First Vintage Books, New York, USA, 1984. A historian's thoughtful look at contemporary culture, based on interviews with people from all walks of life, including film star Brigitte Bardot and chef Paul Bocuse.

French or Foe? by Polly Platt. Culture Crossings, Ltd., England and Illinois, USA, 1995. A useful and amusing analysis of the similarities and differences between the French and American cultures by a cross-cultural trainer and journalist.

Village in the Vaucluse by Laurence Wylie. Harvard University Press, Cambridge, Mass., USA,

1974. A sociologist's study of a changing French village and how the Concorde has replaced the peasant as a symbol of national pride.

Web Sites

Usenet groups
  Clari-world.europe.france
  soc, culture.french
  fr.biz.produits

Webfoot's Guide to France
  http://www.wefoot.com/travel/guides/france/france.html

MINITEL in France
  http:/www.minitel.fr/English/Minitel/presentation.html

FranceNet (French)
  http://www.francenet.fr/franceweb/FW/CarnetRoute.html

Liste des Serveurs W3 en France
  http://web.urec.fr/docs/www_list-fr.html

Maison de France hotel rooms in Paris
  http://www.paris.org/

IMF: Radio France International
  http://town.hall.org/travel/france/rfi.html

Le Web Louvre
  http://mistral.enst.fr/^pioch/louvre/

Le Ministre de la Culture: Direction des Musées de France
  http://dmf.culture.fr/

Passport to

Your Pocket Guide to

PASSPORT CHINA

Your pocket guide to Chinese Business, Customs & Etiquette

Jenny Li

Other Passpo

Lecture Notes
Oncology

Mark Bower
Consultant Oncologist
Chelsea and Westminster Hospital
London

Jonathan Waxman
Professor of Oncology
Hammersmith Hospital
London

Blackwell
Publishing

Blackwell Publishing, Inc., 350 Main Street,Malden, Massachusetts 02148-5020, USA
Blackwell Publishing Ltd, 9600 Garsington Road, Oxford OX4 2DQ, UK
Blackwell Publishing Asia Pty Ltd, 550 Swanston Street, Carlton, Victoria 3053, Australia

First published 2006

2   2008

Library of Congress Cataloging-in-Publication Data

Bower, Mark.
  Lecture notes. Oncology / Mark Bower, Jonathan Waxman.
    p. ; cm.
  ISBN: 978-1-4051-2402-7 (alk. paper)
I. Cancer—Outlines, syllabi, etc.
  [DNLM: 1. Neoplasms. QZ 200 B786L 2006] I. Title: Oncology. II. Waxman, Jonathan. III. Title.

  RC254.5.B69 2006
  616.99'4—dc22

ISBN: 978-1-4051-2402-7

A catalogue record for this title is available from the British Library

Set in 8/12 Stone Serif by SNP Best-set Typesetter Ltd, Hong Kong
Printed and bound in India by Replika Press Pvt. Ltd

Commissioning Editor: Vicki Noyes
Development Editor: Karen Moore
Production Controller: Kate Charman

For further information on Blackwell Publishing, visit our website:
http://www.blackwellpublishing.com

The publisher's policy is to use permanent paper from mills that operate a sustainable forestry policy, and which
has been manufactured from pulp processed using acid-free and elementary chlorine-free practices. Furthermore,
the publisher ensures that the text paper and cover board used have met acceptable environmental accreditation
standards.

Contents

Colour plates fall between pages 154 and 155

v

Preface

Cancer affects one person in three and is currently the leading cause of mortality in the UK. Remarkably, oncology is given scant attention in the undergraduate curriculum, with many medical schools providing just two or three weeks training in what is the most important area of medicine. Cancer research leads 'medicine' by its nose to the frontiers of science where radical changes in our understanding of molecular biology have led to extraordinary advances in the treatment of our patients. We hope that *Lecture Notes: Oncology* will bring some of this excitement to our students, show them that there is hope, that we can get things better for our patients, and redress the deficits in the medical school curricula.

M.B. J.W.

Acknowledgements

Our thanks are to Sandie Coward for editorial assistance, to Professor Philip Gishen and Dr Chris Harvey for the provision of radiological images, to Professor Barbara Bain for haematology illustrations and for proof-reading, to Professor Hani Gabra, Dr David Vigushin, Dr Columba Quigley, and Dr Iain McNeish for their help in proof revision.

Part 1

Introduction to oncology

Chapter 1

What is cancer?

Cancer is not a single illness but a collection of many diseases that share common features. Cancer is widely viewed as a disease of genetic origin caused by mutations of DNA that make a cell multiply uncontrollably. The description and definitions of cancer, however, vary depending on the perspective as described below.

Epidemiological perspective

Cancer is a major cause of morbidity in the UK, with around 267 000 new cases diagnosed in 1999. There are more than 200 different types of cancer, but four of them—breast, lung, colorectal and prostate—account for over half of all new cases. Overall, it is estimated that one in three people will develop some form of cancer during their lifetime. In the 10-year period 1989–1998, the overall age standardized incidence rates for cancer increased by 1.6% in men and 6.3% in women. The fastest-growing cancers in men were malignant melanoma and prostate cancer, while in women, they were kidney cancer, non-Hodgkin's lymphoma and breast cancer.

Cancer incidence refers to the number of new cancer cases arising in a specified period of time. Prevalence refers to the number of people who have received a diagnosis of cancer who are alive at any given time, some of whom will be cured and others will not. Therefore, prevalence reflects both the incidence of cancer and its associated survival pattern. Overall, it is estimated that approximately 2% of the population of the UK (around 1.2 million people) are alive, having received a diagnosis of cancer. The single cancer that contributes most to this is breast cancer, with an estimated 172 000 women alive who have had a diagnosis of breast cancer.

Sociological perspective

Patients with cancer adopt a medically sanctioned form of deviant behaviour described in the 1950s by Talcott Parsons as 'the sick role'. In order to be excused their usual duties and to be considered not to be responsible for their condition, patients are expected to seek professional advice and to adhere to treatments in order to get well. Medical practitioners are empowered to sanction their temporary absence from the workforce and family duties, as well as to absolve them of blame. This behavioural model minimizes the impact of illness on society and reduces secondary gain that the patient benefits from as a consequence of their illness. As Ivan Illich pointed out, however, this sets up physicians as agents of social control by medicalizing health and contributing to iatrogenic illness—'a medical nemesis'. Of all the common medical diagnoses, cancer probably carries the greatest stigma and is associated with the most fear. The many different ways in which cancer affects people have been explored in the literature (see Table 1.1).

Table 1.1 Top 10 cancer books (in the authors' opinion).

	Title	Author
1	Cancer Ward	Alexander Solzhenitsyn
2	A Very Easy Death	Simone de Beauvoir
3	The Doctor	Anton Chekov
4	Age of Iron	JM Coetzee
5	The Cancer Journals	Audre Lorde
6	Patrimony, a True Story	Phillip Roth
7	Before I Say Goodbye	Ruth Picardie
8	Aids As Metaphor	Susan Sontag
9	The Black Swan	Thomas Mann
10	Dangerous Parking	Stuart Browne

Experimental perspective

In the laboratory, four characteristics define a cancer cell in culture:
1. clonal (all derived from a single parent cell)
2. grows on soft agar, in the absence of growth-factors
3. crosses artificial membranes in culture systems
4. forms tumours if injected into nude mice.[1]

Histopathological perspective

Cancer is usually defined by various histopathological features, most notably invasion and metastasis, that are observed by gross pathological and microscopic examinations. Staining for laminin may assist the histopathologist in identifying local invasion by tumours that breach the basement membrane. In addition, a number of microscopic features point to the diagnosis:
1. morphology different to normal cells
2. tumour architecture is less organized than that of the parent tissue
3. increased nuclear DNA and nuclear:cytoplasmic ratio
4. hyperchromatic nuclei with coarsening of chromatain and wrinkled nuclear edges
5. multinucleated or with macronucleoli
6. numerous and bizarre mitotic figures.

1 Nude mice are a mutant strain that lacks a thymus gland and T lymphocytes, and thus fail to reject a xenograft (transplant from another species). Nude mice are hairless owing to a mutation at a linked locus.

Cancers may be heterogenous with cells of varying sizes and orientation with respect to one another, despite their clonal origin.

Molecular perspective

The molecular features that identify cancer are described in 'Six steps to becoming a cancer' in Chapter 2:
1. grow without signal (self-sufficiency in growth stimuli)
2. do not stop growing (insensitivity to inhibitory stimuli)
3. do not die (evasion of apoptosis)
4. do not age (immortalization)
5. feed themselves (neoangiogenesis)
6. spread (invasion and metastasis).

How to read a histology report

The diagnosis of cancer is most commonly established following a histopathological report of a biopsy or tumour resection. A histopathological report should include both gross pathological features (tumour size, number and size of lymph nodes examined) and microscopic findings (tumour grade, architecture, mitotic rate, margin involvement and lymphovascular invasion). The grade and stage of a cancer are important prognostic factors that may influence therapy options (Box 1.1).

A histopathological definition of cancer

Malignancy is usually characterized by various behavioural features, most notably invasion and metastasis. The histopathologist, however, may have to identify a cancer without this information. Cancers are composed of clonal cells (all are the progeny of a single cell) and have lost control of their tissue organization and architecture. In addition to the natural history, a number of physical properties help to differentiate between benign and malignant tumours (Table 1.2). There is, however, no single histological feature that defines a cancer; nor indeed is there any single histological feature that separates benign from malignant tumours. In general, benign tumours are rarely

Box 1.1: Histopathology definitions

Quantitative changes

Too small

Atrophy
An acquired **diminution** of growth due to a decrease in the size or number of constituent parts of a tissue, such as decrease in size of the ovaries after the menopause.

Too big

Hypertrophy
Increase in the size of an organ or tissue due to an increase in the **size** of individual cells; for example, pregnant uterus.

Hyperplasia
Increase in the *size* of an organ due to an increase in the **number** of cells; for example, lactating breast.

Qualitative changes

Metaplasia
Replacement of one differentiated cell type by another. This implies changes in the differentiation programme and is usually a response to persistent injury. It is reversible so that removal of the source of injury results in reversion to the original cell type, such as metaplasia of laryngeal respiratory epithelium in a smoker. The chronic irritation leads to an exchange of one type of epithelium (normal respiratory columnar epithelium) for another (the more resilient squamous epithelium).

Dysplasia
Dysplastic changes do not necessarily revert to normal once the injury is removed. Dysplasia is usually considered to be part of the spectrum of changes leading to neoplasia, like cervical dysplasia initiated by human papillomavirus infection persists after eradication of the virus.

Invasion
The capacity to infiltrate the surrounding tissues and organs is a characteristic of cancer.

Metastasis
The ability to proliferate in distant parts of the body, after tumour cells have been transported by lymph or blood or along body spaces.

Table 1.2 Histological features of benign and malignant tumours.

Features of malignancy	Features of benign tumours
Macroscopic features	
Invade and metastasize	Do not invade or metastasize
Rapid growth	Slow growing
Not clearly demarcated	Clearly demarcated from surrounding tissue
Surface often ulcerated and necrotic	Surface smooth
Cut surface heterogenous	Cut surface homogenous
Microscopic features	
Often high mitotic rate	Low mitotic rate
Nuclei pleomorphic and hyperchromatic	Nuclear morphology often normal
Abnormal mitoses	Mitotic figures normal

life-threatening but may cause health problems on account of their location (by pressure or obstruction of adjacent organs) or by overproduction of hormones. In contrast, malignant tumours usually follow a progressive course and, unless successfully treated, are frequently fatal.

In situ or invasive?

Invasive cancers extend into the surrounding stroma. Tumours, on the other hand, which exhibit all the microscopic features of cancers but do not breach the original basement membrane, are termed *in situ* (non-invasive) cancers. Examples include *in situ* breast cancer confined to the ducts (ductal carcinoma *in situ* (DCIS)) or lobules (lobular carcinoma *in situ* (LCIS)). Similar preinvasive cancers have been found in many organs such as cervix, anus, prostate, and bronchus and are believed to represent a stage in the progression from dysplasia to cancer (Figs 1.1 and 1.2).

Histopathologist's nomenclature

The suffix *oma* usually denotes a benign tumour (although it simply means 'swelling' and some *omas* are not tumours, e.g. xanthoma). If a tumour

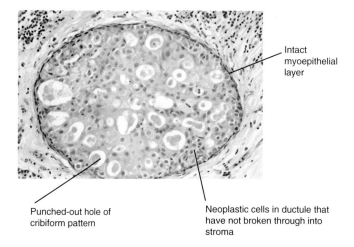

Intact
myoepithelial
layer

Punched-out hole of
cribiform pattern

Neoplastic cells in ductule that
have not broken through into
stroma

Figure 1.1 Histology of Intraductal carcinoma (Ductal carcinoma in situ— DCIS) of the breast, demonstrating neoplastic cells in breast ductule with intact myoepithelial layer. (See also colour plates between pages 154 and 155.)

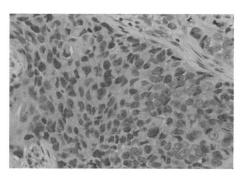

Figure 1.2 Histology of invasive ductal carcinoma of the breast with neoplastic cells invading breast stroma. (See also colour plates between pages 154 and 155.)

is malignant, the suffix -*carcinoma* (Greek for 'crab') is used for epithleial cancers or -*sarcoma* (Greek for 'flesh') for connective tissue cancers. The prefix is determined by the cells of origin of the tumour, e.g. *adeno-* for glandular epithelium, qualified by the tissue of origin, e.g. prostatic adenocarcinoma. There are numerous exceptions to this systematic nomenclature; for example, leukaemias and lymphomas are malignant tumours of bone marrow and lymphoid tissue, respectively. As a general rule, neoplasms are classified according to the type of normal tissue they most closely resemble. The four major categories are: epithelial, connective tissue, lymphoid and haemopoietic tissue, and germ cells (Tables

1.3–1.6). The latter arise in 'totipotential cells' and contain a variety of different mature and/or immature tissues from different germ layers, and these are given names with the root *terato-* (Greek for 'monster'). In addition, as with most fields of medicine where physicians try to leave their mark, there are a number of eponymous names. For example, Hodgkin's disease, used to describe seven cases in 1832 of the tumour that bears Hodgkin's name. Paradoxically re-examination of the specimens in 1926 revealed that the diagnosis was inaccurate in four of the seven cases.

Tumour grading

Tumours are graded according to the degree of tissue differentiation. Cancers that closely resemble their tissue of origin are graded as well-differentiated cancers, while cancers that retain little of their origin and have histological features of aggressive growth and high mitotic rates are graded as poorly differentiated cancers. The grade of the tumour is of prognostic significance.

In the case of breast cancer, the Scarff–Bloom–Richardson system is usually used to grade cancers based upon three features: the frequency of cell mitosis, tubule formation and nuclear pleomorphism. Each of these features is assigned a score ranging from 1 to 3 (1 indicating slower cell growth and 3 indicating faster cell growth). The scores of

Table 1.3 Nomenclature of epithelial tumours.

Epithelium	Benign tumour	Malignant tumour
Squamous	Squamous papilloma	Squamous carcinoma
Glandular	Adenoma	Adenocarcinoma
Transitional	Transitional papilloma	Transitional carcinoma
Liver	Hepatic adenoma	Hepatocellular carcinoma
Skin	Papilloma	Squamous cell carcinoma
		Basal cell carcinoma
Skin melanocyte	Naevus	Malignant melanoma

Table 1.4 Nomenclature of connective tissue tumours.

Tissue	Benign tumour	Malignant tumour
Bone	Osteoma	Osteosarcoma
Cartilage	Chondroma	Chondrosarcoma
Fat	Lipoma	Liposarcoma
Smooth muscle	Leiomyoma	Leiomyosarcoma
Striated muscle	Rhabdomyoma	Rhabdomyosarcoma
Blood vessel	Angioma	Angiosarcoma
Fibrous tissue	Fibroma	Fibrosarcoma

Table 1.5 Nomenclature of haematological tumours.

Tissue	Malignant tumour
Node lymphocyte	Lymphoma
Marrow lymphocyte	Lymphocytic leukaemia
Granulocyte	Myeloid leukaemia
Plasma cell	Myeloma

Table 1.6 Nomenclature of germ cell tumours.

Tissue	Benign tumour	Malignant tumour (male)	Malignant tumour (female)
Germ cell	Mature teratoma/dermoid cyst	Non-seminomatous germ cell tumour/malignant teratoma	Immature teratoma/embryonal carcinoma
	—	Seminoma	Dysgerminoma

each of the cells' features are then added together for a final sum that will range between 3 and 9. A tumour with a final sum of 3, 4 or 5 is considered a Grade 1 tumour (well differentiated). A sum of 6 or 7 is considered a Grade 2 tumour (moderately differentiated), and a sum of 8 or 9 is a Grade 3 tumour (poorly differentiated). The 5-year overall survival for grades 1, 2 and 3 is 95%, 75% and 50%, respectively.

Unknown primary identification (standard histological techniques)

Occasionally, patients may present with metastatic cancer without an obvious primary tumour site, and in addition to a careful clinical and radiological examination, the pathologist may provide a clue to the origins of the cancer. Most unknown primary cancers are adenocarcinoma (60%), and the remainder are poorly differentiated carcinomas (30%) and squamous cell carcinomas (5%). Light microscopy may provide pointers, such as the presence of melanin favours melanoma, while mucin production is common in gastrointestinal, breast and lung cancers but less common in ovarian cancers and rare in renal cell and thyroid cancers. Immunocytochemical staining of tissue samples can assist the pathologist in tissue identification.

Box 1.2: Cytokeratins

Cytokeratins (CKs) are intermediate filament proteins expressed in pairs comprising a type I (CK9–20) and a type II cytokeratin (CK1–8). Different tissues express different pairs, and immunocytochemical staining for cytokeratins can help identify the likely tissue origins of cancers cells. For example, in disseminated peritoneal metastases, CK7 expression favours an ovarian origin, whilst lack of CK7 is more common in colorectal cancer.

For example, the presence of oestrogen and progesterone receptors favours a diagnosis of breast cancer, while prostate-specific antigen and prostatic acid phosphatase staining points to prostatic adenocarcinoma; similarly, cytokeratin expression patterns may provide helpful hints (see Box 1.2). Cell-surface immunophenotyping is a sophistication of immunocytochemistry that is frequently applied to haematological malignancies. The pattern of immunoglobulin, T-cell receptor and cluster designation (CD) antigen expression on the surface of lymphomas is helpful in their diagnosis and classification. Immunophenotyping can be achieved by immunohistochemical staining, immunofluorescent staining or flow cytometry.

Unknown primary identification (special histological techniques)

The study of intracellular organelles by electron microscopy may identify the cellular origin of a tumour, such as the presence of melanosomes in melanomas and dense core neurosecretory granules in neuroendodermal tumours. Further laboratory techniques to aid diagnosis include molecular studies of DNA rearrangements that characterize malignancies. Monoclonal immunoglobulin gene rearrangements are present in B-cell malignancies, and rearrangements of T-cell receptors occur in T-cell tumours. In addition, a number of chromosomal translocations involving the immunoglobulin genes (heavy chain on chromosome 14q32, light chains on 2p12 and 22q11) and T-cell receptor genes (TCRα on 14q11, TCRβ on 7q35, TCRγ on 7p15, TCRδ on 14q11) occur in malignancies arising from these cell types. For instance, low-grade follicular lymphomas rearrange the Bcl-2 gene on 18q21, such as t(14;18)(q32;q21), most Burkitt lymphomas rearrange the Myc gene on 8q24, such as t(8;14)(q24;q32) and most mantle-cell lymphomas rearrange Bcl-1 on 11q13, such as t(11;14)(q13;q32). These rearrangements may be detected by karyotype analysis of mitotic chromosome preparations or by molecular techniques including Southern blotting and polymerase chain reaction (Box 1.3 and Table 1.7). Less commonly, these same methods may assist the diagnosis of solid tumours which are associated with specific chromosomal abnormalities, such as the i(12p) isochromosome found in germ-cell tumours and the t(11;22)(q24;q12) translocation seen in Ewing's sarcoma and peripheral neuroectodermal tumours. In addition to translocations, gene amplification may be detected and may have prognostic significance; for example, the amplification of the N-Myc oncogene in neuroblastoma is an adverse prognostic variable.

Tumour stage

In addition to the histological grade of a tumour, an important criterion in treatment decisions and the major determinant of outcome is the extent of spread or stage of a cancer. Staging a tumour is essentially an anatomical exercise that uses a combination of clinical examination and radiology. A uniform staging system is employed for most tumour sites, based upon the size of the primary Tumour, the presence of regional lymph Nodes and the presence of distant Metastases. The details of this TNM classification vary between different tumour sites. As always, there are exceptions including the staging system for lymphomas originally set out following a conference at Ann Arbour, in Michigan.

Radiology techniques

Staging depends to a large extent upon radiology, and this is the most commonly used tool to evaluate the response of cancers to therapies.

Box 1.3: The language of chromosomes—karyotype nomenclature

Each arm of a chromosome is divided into one to four major regions, depending on chromosomal length; each band, positively or negatively stained, is given a number, which rises as the distance from the centromere increases. The normal male is designated as 46,XY and the normal female as 46,XX (see Figure 1.3).

Polyploidy

Cell with more than one complete chromosome set or with multiples of the basic number of chromosomes characteristic of the species; in humans, this would be 69,92, etc.

Aneuploidy

Individual with one (or more) chromosome in addition to, or missing from, the complete chromosome set; for example, trisomy 21 (47XX +21).

Deletion

The loss of a chromosome segment from a normal chromosome.

Duplication

An extra piece of chromosome segment that may either be attached to the same or homologous chromosome, or be transposed to another chromosome in the genome.

Inversion

A change in linear sequence of the genes in a chromosome that results in the reverse order of genes in a chromosome segment. Inversions may be pericentric (two breaks on either side of the centromere) or paracentric (both breaks on the same arm).

Isochromosome

Breaks in one arm of a chromosome followed by duplication of the other arm of the chromosome to produce a chromosome with two arms that are both short (p) or both long arms (q).

Translocations

Translocations are the result of the reciprocal exchange of terminal segments of non-homologous chromosomes.

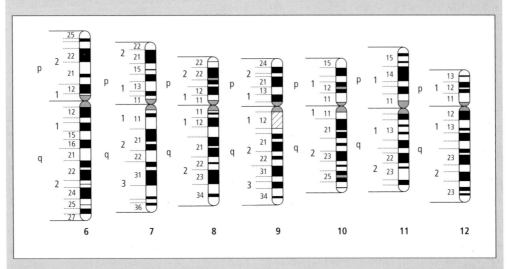

Figure 1.3 Karyotype nomenclature: For example, 11q23 designates the chromosome (11), the long arm (q), the second region distal to the centromere (2), and the third band (3) in that region.

Table 1.7 Examples of chromosomal abnormalities in cancers.

Chromosome defect	Karyotype	Tumour	Candidate gene
Monosomy	45, XY −22	Meningioma	NF2
Trisomy	47, XX +7	Papillary renal carcinoma	MET
Deletion	46, XY del (11) (p13)	Wilms tumour	WT1
Duplication	46, XX dup (2) (p23–24)	Neuroblastoma	N-myc
Inversion	46, XY inv (16) (p13q22)	AML (M4Eo)	MYH11/core binding factor b
Isochromosome	47, XX i (12p)	Testicular GCT	
Translocation	46, XX t (9;22) (q34;q11)	CML	bcr/abl

Table 1.8 Commonly used isotopes in nuclear imaging in oncology.

Isotope	Half life	Tracer	Oncological use
^{99}Tc	6 h	Methylene diphosphonate (MDP)	Bone scan
^{111}In	67 h	Octreotide	Neuroendocrine tumours
^{131}I	8 days	Sodium iodide	Thyroid cancer
^{131}I	8 days	Meta-iodobenzylguanidine (MIBG)	Phaeochromocytoma neuroblastoma
^{67}Ga	68 h	Gallium citrate	Lymphoma
^{18}F	110 min	Fluorodeoxyglucose (FDG)	Brain and soft tissue tumours

Anatomical imaging by plain films, computed tomography (CT), ultrasound and magnetic resonance imaging (MRI) are the standard methods. In addition, functional imaging using radiotracer isotopes to produce nuclear images is widely used in oncology (Table 1.8). The isotope-labelled tracers that are used diagnostically may also be used therapeutically (Fig. 1.4).

Performance status

In addition to the histological tumour grade and the stage or spread of a cancer, the patients' general status will determine how long they survive and may influence treatment decisions. Scales that measure the performance status or functional capacity of patients include the Eastern Cooperate Oncology Group (ECOG) grading system and Karnovsky scale (see Table 1.9). The performance status, however estimated, is an important prognostic indicator for almost all tumour types.

Prognosis—It's not cancer is it, doc?

Although a very significant stigma is attached to the diagnosis of cancer, for most of the general population the fear outweighs the reality, and comparison with other more 'palatable' illnesses yields results that are not always expected (Table 1.10).

Cancer epidemiology

Epidemiology in the UK

Cancer is now the commonest cause of death in the UK (if cardiovascular and cerebrovascular diseases are classed separately):
- one in three people in the UK will develop a cancer (250 000/year)
- one in four die of cancer (180 000/year)
- by 2008, it is estimated that one in three in the UK will die of cancer

The top 10 cancers diagnosed in the UK in 1998, excluding non-melanomatous skin cancers, are shown in Table 1.11.

Global epidemiology

The incidence of different cancers varies geographically with risk factors and the demographics of the local population (Fig. 1.5). There is, however, a general correlation between increasing wealth and

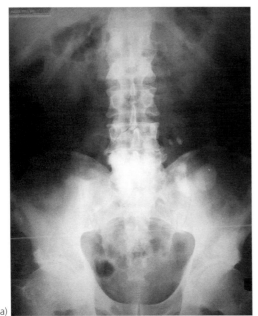

(a)

LT

(b)   POSTERIOR PELVIS

Figure 1.4 Plain pelvic radiograph (a) and corresponding area of Technetium pyrophosphate bone scan (b) of a patient with sclerotic bone metastases from prostate cancer.

Table 1.9 Functional capacity grading (ECOG) and Karnovsky performance scales.

ECOG functional capacity grading	
0	Asymptomatic
1	Symptomatic but fully ambulant
2	Symptomatic, ambulant >50% waking hours
3	Symptomatic, confined to bed >50% waking hours
4	Symptomatic, bedfast

Karnovsky performance status score (%)	
100	Normal; no complaints; no evidence of disease
90	Able to carry on normal activity; minor signs or symptoms
80	Normal activity with effort; some signs or symptoms
70	Care for self; unable to carry on normal activity or do active work
60	Requires occasional assistance, but able to care for most of needs
50	Requires considerable assistance and frequent medical care
40	Disabled; requires special care and assistance
30	Severely disabled; hospitalization indicated but death not imminent
20	Very sick; hospitalization necessary; active supportive treatment necessary
10	Moribund; fatal processes progressing rapidly

Table 1.10 Survival rates for various diseases.

	Myocardial infarction	Hodgkin's disease	Heart failure (NYHA* III/IV)	Metastatic breast cancer
1 yr survival rate	75%	90%	50%	60%
5 yr survival rate	45%	85%	15%	20%

*NYHA: New York Heart Association grading scale

Table 1.11 Commonest cancers diagnosed in UK.

Tumour	As percentage of all cancers diagnosed	Lifetime risk (men)	Lifetime risk (women)
Breast	15		1 in 9
Lung	15	1 in 13	1 in 23
Colorectal	13	1 in 18	1 in 20
Prostate	9	1 in 12	
Bladder	5	1 in 30	1 in 79
Stomach	4	1 in 44	1 in 86
Non-Hodgkin's lymphoma	3	1 in 69	1 in 83
Head and neck	3	1 in 70	1 in 85
Oesophageal	3	1 in 75	1 in 95
Ovarian	3		1 in 48
Other	27		

increasing cancer incidence, which is attributable to tobacco use, diet and increased longevity in wealthy populations. There are intriguing exceptions; for example, the Gulf states of Kuwait, Qatar, Bahrain, United Arab Emirates and Saudi Arabia have lower cancer incidences than would be predicted from their per capita gross national product.

Cancer charities

The UK has 600 cancer charities. Their efforts increase awareness of cancer, improve diagnosis and treatment capability and provide care for patients with the disease. The total income generated by the cancer charities in 2004 was £500 m; and the average charitable efficiency was 65%, providing £320 m for spending on patients' care and on research. The two largest UK cancer charities, the Imperial Cancer Research Fund (ICRF) and the Cancer Research Campaign (CRC), merged to from Cancer Research UK (CRUK) in 2002. CRUK is the largest volunteer-supported cancer research organization in the world, with 3000 scientists and an annual scientific spend of more than £250 m—raised almost entirely through public donations.

Cancer hospitals

Philanthropists and social reformers during the

19th century tried to provide free medical care for the poor. William Marsden, a young surgeon, opened a dispensary for advice and medicines in 1828. His grandly named London General Institution for the Gratuitous Cure of Malignant Diseases—a simple four-storey house in one of the poorest parts of the city—was conceived as a hospital to which the only passport should be poverty and disease, and where treatment was provided free of charge. The demand for Marsden's free services was overwhelming, and by 1844, his dispensary, now called the Royal Free Hospital, was treating 30000 patients a year. In 1846, when his wife died of cancer, Marsden opened a small house in Cannon Row, Westminster, for patients suffering from cancer. Within 10 years, the institution moved to Fulham Road and became known as The Cancer Hospital, of which Marsden was the senior surgeon. The Hospital was incorporated into the National Health Service in 1948 and renamed the Royal Marsden Hospital in 1954. Although other cancer hospitals have been established in Manchester (The Christie Hospital) and Glasgow (The Beatson Hospital), the Royal Marsden Hospital remains the most renown. With the recent emphasis on multidisciplinary approaches to cancer, single speciality hospitals are less *in vogue*, and the majority of cancer departments are in large teaching hospitals.

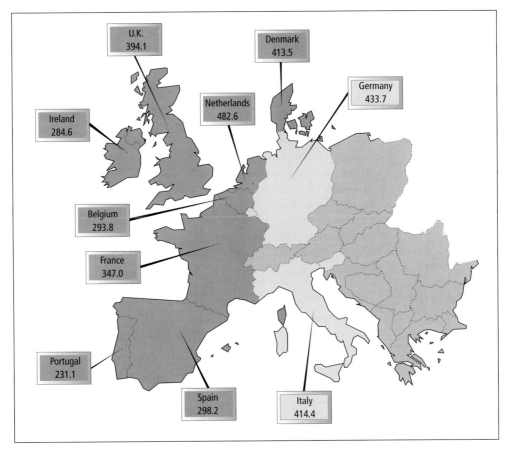

Figure 1.5 Map of cancer incidences in Europe (per 100 000 population).

Table 1.12 Rock star cancer deaths.

	Year of death	Age	Cause of death
George Harrison	2001	58	Non-small-cell lung cancer
Joey Ramone	2001	49	Non-Hodgkin's lymphoma
Ian Dury	2000	58	Colorectal cancer
Dusty Springfield	1999	60	Breast cancer
Carl Wilson (Beach Boys)	1998	52	Lung cancer
Linda McCartney	1998	57	Breast cancer
Frank Zappa	1993	53	Prostate cancer
Freddy Mercury	1991	45	Kaposi's sarcoma
Mel Appleby (Mel and Kim)	1990	24	Spinal tumour
Bob Marley	1981	36	Metastatic melanoma

Cancer celebrities

Celebrities influence public perceptions and behaviour inordinately, and this is true in oncology as elsewhere. Celebrities with cancer have contributed in three main ways; personal accounts bring patients' experiences into the limelight, reports of celebrity patients increase public awareness and may encourage health-seeking behaviour such as stopping smoking, and celebrity patients may support cancer charities and encourage donations. Prominent examples of patient's perspectives include John Diamond's account in *C: because cowards get cancer, too* and Ruth Picardie's *Before I say goodbye*, both moving accounts by accomplished journalists. Celebrity patients can influence the treatment choices that the public make. Following Nancy Reagan's mastectomy for localized breast cancer in 1987, there was a 25% fall in American women choosing breast-conserving surgery over mastectomy. Her husband's successful surgery for Dukes' B colon cancer while president in 1984 increased awareness and propelled the warning signs of colon cancer into the media. Successful cancer treatment is often most widely publicized, and no article describing Lance Armstrong's cycling victories seems complete without a mention of his treatment for metastatic non-seminomatous germ cell tumour, or of his two children conceived with stored sperm banked prior to chemotherapy. Other celebrity patients have used their wealth and fame to establish and support charitable projects to support cancer research and treatment, including Bob Champion, the steeple-chase jockey treated for testicular cancer in the 1970s, and Roy Castle, a lifelong non-smoker who was diagnosed with lung cancer in 1992. Of course, no one is immune to cancer, even rock stars whose deaths are traditionally associated with suicide and substance abuse (Table 1.12).

Chapter 2

The scientific basis of cancer

Six steps to becoming a cancer

At the molecular level, cancer cells are characterized by six acquired features:

1. self-sufficiency in growth stimuli ('keep on doubling')
2. insensitivity to inhibitory stimuli ('do not stop doubling')
3. evasion of apoptosis ('do not die')
4. immortalization ('do not age')
5. neoangiogenesis ('feed yourself')
6. invasion and metastasis ('spread').

It is not certain, but probable, that all six features are necessary to a greater or lesser extent. Some molecular changes in cancer cells may contribute to more than one of the six capabilities, for example, p53 may contribute to both avoidance of apoptosis and insensitivity to inhibitory stimuli. A number of mechanisms may contribute to the acquisition of these six properties, including genomic instability as a consequence of deficient DNA repair, or loss of cell-cycle arrest/death in response to DNA damage.

1. Autonomous growth signals

The instructions to cells to grow and start dividing are communicated by extracellular growth-factor ligands that bind cell surface receptors. This usually results in the reversible phosphorylation of tyrosine, threonine or serine residues of the recep-

tors. The transfer of these molecular switches from activated receptors to downstream signalling enzyme effectors, then to nonenzymatic second messengers in the cytoplasm and finally to nuclear transcription activators, is known as signal transduction (Figure 2.1). This cascade results in amplification of the initial stimulus. Cancers achieve self-sufficiency in growth-factors and are not dependent on these extracellular ligands for continued growth. The majority of dominant oncogenes act on this mechanism by:

• overproducing growth-factor receptors; for example glioblastomas produce platelet derived growth-factor (PDGF)
• overproducing growth-factors, such as epidermal growth-factor receptor (EGFR/erbB) overexpression in breast cancers
• mutations of the receptor or components of the signalling cascade that are constitutively active; for example mutations of Ras in lung and colonic cancers

2. Insensitivity to cell-cycle checkpoints

Many normal cells grow throughout their lifespan, and the co-ordination of their growth, differentiation, senescence and death is controlled, the normal cell cycle. Antiproliferative signals may be received by cells as soluble growth inhibitors or fixed inhibitors in the extracellular matrix. The inhibitors act on the cell-cycle clock (Box 2.1), most

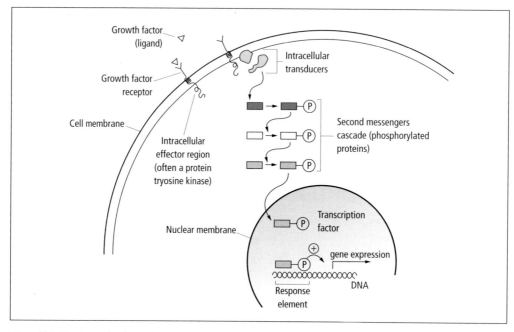

Figure 2.1 Signal transduction pathway.

Box 2.1: The cell cycle

Quiescent phase (G0)

Normal cells grown in culture will stop proliferating once they become confluent or are deprived of growth factors, and enter a quiescent state called G0. Most cells in normal tissue of adults are in a G0 state.

First gap phase (G1), duration: 10–14 hours

This occurs prior to DNA synthesis. Cells in G0 and G1 are receptive to growth signals, but once they have passed a restriction point (R), are committed to DNA synthesis (S phase).

Synthesis phase (S), duration: 3–6 hours

During this phase, DNA replication occurs, and the cell becomes diploid.

Second gap phase (G2), duration: 2–4 hours

This occurs after DNA synthesis and before mitosis (M) and completion of the cell cycle.

Mitosis (M), duration: 1 hour

This completes the cell cycle with splitting of the cell into two daughter cells.

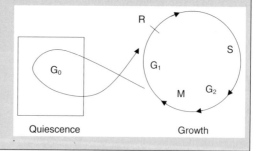

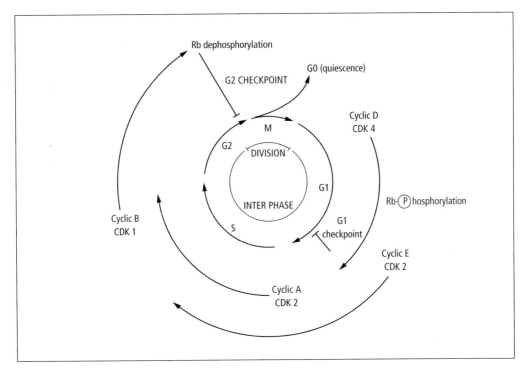

Figure 2.3 Rb phosphorylation and the cell cycle.

frequently arresting transit through G1 into the S phase. Cancer cells ignore these 'stop' signals.

The coordination of the cell-cycle, and its arrest at checkpoints in response to DNA damage, is achieved by sequential activation of kinase enzymes that ultimately phosphorylate and dephosphorylate the retinoblastoma protein (Rb). Periodic activation of these cyclin–cyclin-dependent kinase (Cdk) complexes drives the cell-cycle forward (Figure 2.3). Phosphorylation of Rb releases E2F, a transcription factor which promotes the expression of a number of target genes, resulting in cell proliferation. The brakes that balance this system are CDK inhibitors (CKIs). Interference in elements of the cell-cycle regulatory process is a common theme in malignancy (Table 2.2).

G1/S checkpoint

An important checkpoint, or restriction point, in

the cell-cycle occurs in G1, to ensure that, instead of being replicated, errors in DNA are either repaired, or the cell dies by apoptosis. This is initiated by damaged DNA and is coordinated by p53, the gene that is probably most commonly mutated in cancers. Additional checkpoints are present in the S and G2 phases, to allow cells to repair errors that occur during DNA duplication, and thus to prevent the propagation of these errors to daughter cells.

3. Evasion of apoptosis

Apoptosis is a pre-programmed sequence of cell suicide that occurs over a period of 30–120 minutes. Apoptosis commences with a condensation of the cellular organelles and a swelling of the endoplasmic reticulum. The plasma membrane remains intact, but the cell breaks up into several membrane-bound apoptotic bodies, which are phagocytosed. Confining the process within the

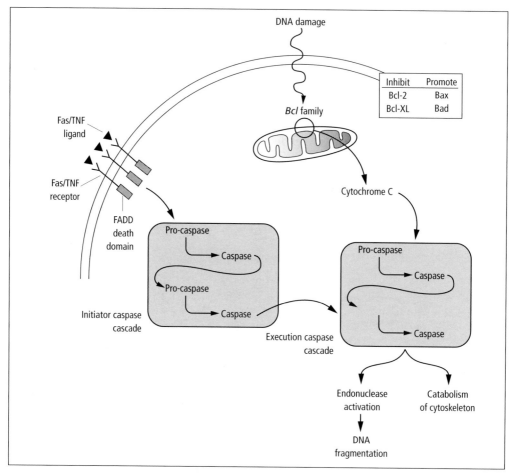

Figure 2.4 The apoptotic pathway.

cell membrane reduces activation of both inflammatory and immune responses. Amongst the molecules that control apoptosis are the Bcl-2 family that confusingly includes both pro-apoptosis members, e.g. Bax, and anti-apoptosis members, e.g. Bcl-2.

In mammalian cells, two pathways initiate apoptosis (Figure 2.4):

1. Intracellular triggers

DNA damage leads, via p53, to the activation of pro-apoptotic members of the Bcl-2 family. This

causes release of Cytochrome C from the mitochondria, which in turn activates the caspase cascade, a sequence of proteases.

2. Extracellular triggers

Binding of extracellular ligands to the cell surface death receptor superfamily, including CD95/Fas and tumour necrosis factor receptors, leads to a death-inducing cytoplasmic signalling complex that activates the caspase cascade and results in apoptosis. Evasion of this pathway is a prerequisite for malignant cell proliferation, and a number of

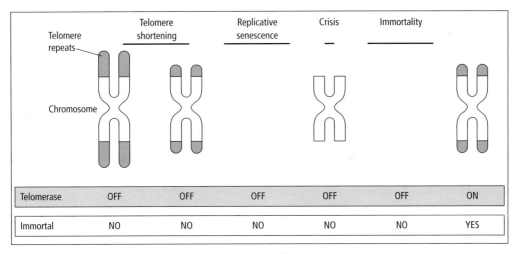

Figure 2.5 Telomerase, telomere length, senescence and immortalisation.

strategies to this end have been identified (Table 2.2).

4. Immortalization

In culture, cells can divide a limited number of times, up to the 'Hayflick limit' (60–70 doublings in the case of human cells in culture), before the cell population enters crisis and dies off. This senescence is attributed to progressive telomere loss, which acts as a mitotic clock (Figure 2.5). Telomeres are the end segments of chromosomes and are made up of thousands of copies of a short 6 base pair sequence. DNA replication always follows a 5'-to-3' direction, so that manufacturing the 3' ends of the chromosomes cannot be achieved by DNA polymerases, and in each generation, 50–100 base pairs are lost from the ends of the chromosomes. Eventually, the protective ends of chromosomes are eroded, and end-to-end chromosomal fusions occur, with karyotypic abnormalities and death of the affected cell.

Normal germ cells and cancer cells avoid this senescence, acquiring immortality in culture usually by upregulating the expression of human telomerase reverse transcriptase (hTERT) enzyme. This uses an RNA template and RNA dependent DNA polymerase to add the six base pair sequences back onto the ends of chromosomes, to compensate for the loss in DNA replication (Table 2.2). This process is abnormal in dyskeratosis congenita, an X-linked inherited condition, characterized by many abnormalities, including premature ageing, and an increased risk of skin and gut cancers which is due to mutations of a gene encoding dyskerin, which normally inhibits telomerase.

5. Angiogenesis

All tissues, including cancers, require a supply of oxygen and nutrients. For cancers to grow larger than about 0.4 mm in diameter, a new blood supply is needed. The growth of new blood vessels from pre-existing vasculature is termed angiogenesis. The 'angiogenic switch' denotes the ability of tumours to recruit new blood vessels and is necessary for tumour growth and metastasis. Angiogenesis is determined by the relative balance of angiogenesis promoters and inhibitors (Table 2.1).

Vascular endothelial growth-factors (VEGF-A to E) are a family of growth-factor homodimers that act via one of three plasma membrane receptors (VEGFR 1–3) on endothelial cells. Over-production of VEGF and/or FGF is a common theme in many tumours (Table 2.2). Angiogenesis may be measured by microscope as microvessel density in an area of tumour or by assays of angiogenic factors. These measures are of prognostic significance in several human tumours. Angiogenesis is becoming a major focus of anti-cancer drug development. It is an attractive target for several reasons. Angiogenesis is a normal process in growth and development but is quiescent in adult life except for wound healing and menstruation, so the side effects of drugs inhibiting this process are predicted to be minimal. As the target consists of normal endothelial cells without any genetic instability, there should be little capacity to acquire resistance. Each capillary supplies a large number of tumour cells, so the effects should be magnified in terms of tumour cell kill. Anti-angiogenic agents should furthermore have easy access to their target through the blood stream. In combination, these elements make anti-angiogenic therapies attractive and several phar-

maceutical companies have invested heavily in attempts to develop these agents.

6. Invasion and metastasis

The properties of tissue invasion and metastatic spread are histopathological hallmarks of malignant cancers that differentiate them from benign tumours (Figure 2.6). A number of sequential steps have been identified in the process of metastatic spread of cancers:

- motility and invasion
- embolism and circulation
- arrest in a distant capillary bed and adherence to endothelium
- extravasation into the target organ parenchyma (Box 2.2)

Central to many of these steps is the role of cell–cell adhesion that controls the interactions between cells, and cell–extracellular matrix interactions that influence the relationship between a cell and its environment. These interactions are regulated by cell adhesion molecules. Members of the cadherin and immunoglobulin superfamilies modulate cell–cell interactions, and integrins control cell–extracellular matrix interactions. Alterations of cadherin, adhesion molecule and integrin expression are common features of metastatic cancer cells (Table 2.2).

Tumours may migrate as single cells or as collections of cells. The former strategy is used by lymphoma and small-cell lung cancer cells

Table 2.1 Angiogenic factors and inhibitors.

Angiogenic factors	Angiogenic inhibitors
Vascular endothelial growth factors (VEGF-A to E)	Tissue metalloproteinase inhibitors (TIMP 1–4)
Fibroblast growth factors (FGF) (acidic FGF & basic FGF)	Plasminogen activator inhibitor (uPAI)
Transforming growth factors (TGF-α & TGF-β)	Thrombospondin
	Angiostatin
	Endostatin

Table 2.2 Examples of the six features and their molecular basis in different cancers.

Feature	Colorectal cancer	Glioma	Head and neck squamous cancer
1. Growth factor independence	K Ras mutation	EGFR amplification or mutation NF1 loss	EGFR mutation
2. Over-riding inhibitory signals	SMAD2/SMAD4 mutation	CDK4 / p16 mutation	Cyclin D amplification p16 & p21 mutation
3. Evasion of apoptosis	p53 mutation	p53 mutation / MDM2 overexpression	p53 mutation
4. Immortalisation	hTERT re-expression	hTERT re-expression	hTERT re-expression
5. Angiogenesis	VEGF expression	PDGF / PDGFR overexpression	Nitric Oxide pathway activation of VEGF
6. Invasion & Metastasis	APC, Inactivate E-cadherin	Cathepsin D, MMP-2 & -9 & UPA overexpression	Cathepsin D, MMP-1, -2 & -9 overexpression

Box 2.2: How cancers metastasize

Routes of metastasis

Breast-cancer cells that leave a primary tumour in blood vessels, will be carried in the blood first through the heart, and then to the capillary beds of the lungs. Some cancer cells might form metastases in the lung, while others pass through the lung to enter the systemic arterial system, where they are transported to remote organs, such as bone. By contrast, colon cancer cells will be taken by the hepato-portal circulatory system first to the liver. There is no direct flow from the lymphatic system to other organs, so cancer cells within it—for example, breast cancer cells—must enter the venous system to be transported to distant organs. Paths other than blood and lymphatic vessels are rarely used in metastasis. Transcoelomic spread across the abdominal cavity occurs for gastric tumours that metastasise to the ovaries (Krukenberg tumours). Spread within the cerebrospinal fluid is thought to be responsible for the metastasis of medulloblastoma up and down the spinal column.

Where cancers metastasize

Certain cancers tend to metastasize to particular organs, and this cannot be accounted for by blood flow alone. The basis for this tissue tropism has been found to relate to chemokine and chemokine receptor expression. Breast-cancer cells express high levels of the CXCR4 chemokine receptor. Lung tissue expresses high levels of a soluble ligand for the CXCR4 receptor. Therefore, breast-cancer cells that are taken to the lung, find a strong chemokine–receptor 'match', which may lead to chemokine-mediated signal activation. By contrast, in other organs where breast cancers less commonly metastasise, there are low levels of the ligand.

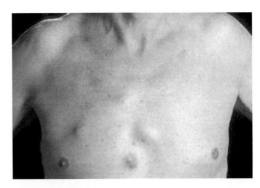

Figure 2.6 Patient with multiple cutaneous metastases from non-small cell lung cancer. (See also colour plates between pages 154 and 155.)

to prevent cells acquiring all six properties (see Table 2.2), including efficient mechanisms to correct errors in DNA and to eradicate cells with extensive DNA damage. In fact, DNA mutation is facilitated in cancer cells by error-prone DNA replication (mutator phenotype), including deficient DNA repair leading to genetic instability, and uncoupling of the DNA damage cell-cycle arrest/apoptosis response.

Genome instability

DNA damage or mutation will normally result in cell-cycle arrest followed by DNA repair or apoptosis. Interference in this process may occur either by deficient DNA damage recognition and repair, or by abnormal gatekeeping of the cell-cycle arrest/apoptosis response. This will result in the uncorrected accumulation of a large number of genetic abnormalities, which is referred to as 'genomic instability'. It is thought that this allows cells to acquire the six capabilities that characterize the cancer cell phenotype and physiology.

DNA repair

Environmental damage to DNA occurs commonly, and eukoryotes have developed several mechanisms for repairing their DNA.

Double-strand breaks in DNA
• homologous recombination, using the sister chromatid as a template

to metastasize. It requires changes in the cell–extracellular matrix interaction by integrins and matrix-degrading proteases. The latter strategy is common for most epithelial tumours. In addition, it requires changes in cell–cell adhesion through cadherins and other adhesion receptors, as well as cell–cell communication, via gap junctions (Box 2.2, Figure 2.7).

How to acquire the six capabilities

Cancer is a somatic genetic disease caused by DNA mutations. A number of mechanisms are in place

- non-homologous end joining (NHEJ) Single-strand breaks in DNA
- nucleotide excision repair (NER) for bulky lesions
- mismatch repair (MMR) for single mispaired bases and short deletions

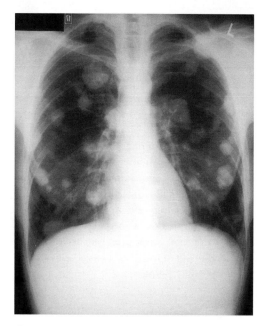

Figure 2.7 Plain chest radiograph, showing multiple rounded metastases of varying sizes in a man with metastatic testicular non-seminomatous germ cell tumour. Other tumours that commonly metastasise to the lungs include lung, breast, renal, thyroid cancers and sarcomas.

- base excision repair (BER) for alkylated bases

Hereditary mutations of the enzymes involved in DNA repair predispose to malignancy, as they confer genome instability (see Table 2.3).

DNA damage recognition

Another group of enzymes is required to recognize damaged DNA, leading to cell-cycle arrest to allow DNA repair to be completed before the damage is replicated and passed on to the progeny cells. A number of cancer-predisposing syndromes are associated with inherited mutations of these enzymes. Examples include p53, the inactivation of which is an early step in the development of many cancers. Patients with the Li–Fraumeni syndrome usually carry one mutant germ-line p53 allele and are at risk from the development of sarcomas, leukaemia and cancers of the breast, brain and adrenal glands.

Genetic causes of cancer

The causes of cancer may be usefully divided into genetic and environmental factors. The genetic factors are either germ-line mutations or somatic alterations. Germ-line mutations may be either inherited, in which case they follow a familial pattern, or may be new sporadic mutations. Some of the germ-line mutations have been outlined as mutator phenotypes (DNA-repair and damage

Table 2.3 Table of hereditary DNA repair syndromes.

DNA Repair Mechanism	Example of defect of DNA repair	Examples of cancers associated with defects
Homologous (sister chromatid) repair	Hereditatry breast and ovarian cancer (BRCA1)	Breast & ovarian cancers
Non-homologous end joining (NHEJ)	X-ray repair complementing defect gene (XRCC4; lethal)	None (lethal defect)
Nucleotide excision repair (NER)	Xeroderma pigmentosa (XP)	Skin cancers, leukaemia & melanoma
Mismatch repair (MMR)	Hereditary non-polyposis colon cancer (MSH & MLH)	Colon, endometrium, ovarian, pancreatic & gastric cancers
Base excision repair (BER)	Hereditary non-polyposis colon cancer (MYH)	Colon cancers

recognition genes). Other germ-line cancer predisposing mutations occur in tumour suppressor genes and oncogenes.

Oncogenes

The first clue to the identification of specific genes involved in the development of cancer came from the study of tumour viruses. Although cancer is generally not an infectious disease, some animal leukaemias, lymphomas and solid tumours, particularly sarcomas, can be caused by viruses. Oncogenes were identified following the discovery by Peyton Rous in 1911, that sarcomas could be induced in healthy chickens by injecting them with a cell-free extract of the tumour of a sick chicken. This was due to transmission of Rous sarcoma virus (RSV), an oncogenic retrovirus with just four genes;

- *gag*, which encodes the capsid protein
- *pol*, which encodes the reverse transcriptase
- *env*, which encodes the envelope protein
- *src*, which encodes a tyrosine kinase

It is the *src* gene which is necessary for cell transformation, and which is therefore an oncogene; literally a 'gene capable of causing cancer'. In the mid 1970s, it emerged that a homologous proto-oncogene (c-SRC) is present in the normal mammalian genome (the human *src* locus is on chromosome 20q12-q13), which has been hijacked by the retrovirus. The prefix *v-* denotes a viral sequence, and the prefix *c-* a cellular sequence. In 1965, 55 years after his discovery of RSV and at the age of 87, Peyton Rous was finally awarded a Nobel Prize. Around 50 oncogenes such as erbB, H-RAS and JUN have been identified by their presence in transforming retroviruses, and further oncogenes have been discovered both, by positional cloning of chromosomal translocations, such as Bcl-2 and BCR-ABL and by studies of transfections, like N-RAS and RET. Most oncogenes contribute to the autonomy of cancer in growth-factors, either as plasma membrane receptors as do RET and PTCH, signal transduction pathways components like PTEN, NF1&2 and VHL or transcription factors, for example, c-MYC and WT1; Table 2.4).

Tumour suppressor genes

In contrast to oncogenes, tumour suppressor genes act as cell-cycle brakes, slowing the proliferation of cells and mutations in these genes contributing to cancer. Germ-line mutations of tumour suppressor genes behave as autosomal dominant, familial cancer predispositions. Tumour suppressor genes require the loss of both functional alleles to support a cancer unlike oncogenes, where one mutant allele suffices. In 1971, Alfred Knudson proposed the two-hit model of tumour suppression, to account for the differences between familial and sporadic retinoblastoma in children. In familial cases, tumours arise at a younger age and are more frequently bilateral. Knudson hypothesized that these children inherit one defective retinoblastoma gene allele at birth, followed by the loss of function of the second allele after birth through a somatic mutation (Figure 2.8). Tumour suppressor genes, like oncogenes, are involved in a variety of functional categories including: cell-cycle regulation such as p53 and Rb; DNA repair and maintenance such as BRCA1 and 2, MLH1 and MSH2; signal transduction like NF1 and PTEN; and cell adhesion for example, APC; see Table 2.4 and Figure 2.9.

Environmental causes of cancer

The multitude of environmental factors that are associated with the development of malignancy may usefully be divided into three groups
- physical
- chemical
- biological

Physical causes of cancer

The major physical carcinogen is radiation. Radiation is ubiquitous and may either be ionizing like γ-rays from cosmic radiation and isotope decay, α-particles from radon and X-rays from medical imaging or non-ionizing like ultraviolet light from the sun, microwave and radiofrequency radiation from mobile phones, electromagnetic fields from electricity generators and pylons and

Table 2.4 Hereditary cancer predisposition syndromes.

Syndrome	Malignancies	Inheritance*	Gene	Function
Breast/ovarian	Breast, ovarian, colon, prostate	AD	BRCA1	Genome integrity
		AD	BRCA2	
Cowden syndrome	Breast, thyroid, GI, pancreas	AD	PTEN	Signal transduction (Tyrosine phosphatase)
Li Fraumeni	Sarcoma, breast, osteosarcoma, leukaemia, glioma, adrenocortical	AD	p53	Genome integrity
Familial polyposis coli	Colon, Upper GI	AD	APC	Cell adhesion
Hereditary non-polyposis colon cancer (Lynch type II)	Colon, endometrium, ovarian, pancreatic, gastric	AD	MSH2	DNA mismatch repair
		AD	MLH1	
		AD	PMS1	
		AD	PMS2	
MEN 1 (multiple endocrine neoplasia 1)	Pancreatic islet cell, pituitary adenoma	AD	MEN1	Transcription repressor
MEN 2 (multiple endocrine neoplasia 2)	Medullary thyroid, phaeochromocytoma	AD	RET	Signal transduction (receptor tyrosine kinase)
Neurofibromatos is 1	Neurofibrosarcoma, phaeochromocytoma, optic glioma	AD	NF1	Signal transduction (regulates GTPases)
Neurofibromatos is 2	Vestibular schwannoma	AD	NF2	Cell adhesion
von Hippel Lindau	Haemangioblastoma of retina & CNS, renal cell, phaeochromocytoma	AD	VHL	Ubiquination
Retinoblastoma	Retinoblastoma, osteosarcoma	AD	RB1	Cell cycle regulation
Xeroderma pigmentosa	Skin, leukaemia, melanoma	AR	XPA	DNA nucleotide excision repair
		AR	XPC	
		AR	XPD	
		AR	XPF	
Gorlin syndrome	Basal cell skin, brain	AD	PTCH	Signal transduction (Repressor of Hedgehog signalling)

*AD = autosomal dominant; AR = autosomal recessive

ultrasound radiation from imaging. Ionizing radiation requires 10–15 electronvolts (eV) and ejects electrons from atoms, yielding an ion pair. Ionizing radiation may be either electromagnetic (X-rays, γ-rays) or particulate (α-particles, neutrons). Non-ionizing radiation does not yield an ion pair but can still excite electrons resulting in chemical change.

Ultraviolet radiation

UV radiation in subdivided into three wavelength bands:
- UVA (313–400 nm)
- UVB (290–315 nm)
- UVC (220–290 nm)

UVC has the most potent effects on DNA, which absorbs most strongly at 254 nm. UVC, however, is quickly absorbed in air, which is why UVB is con-

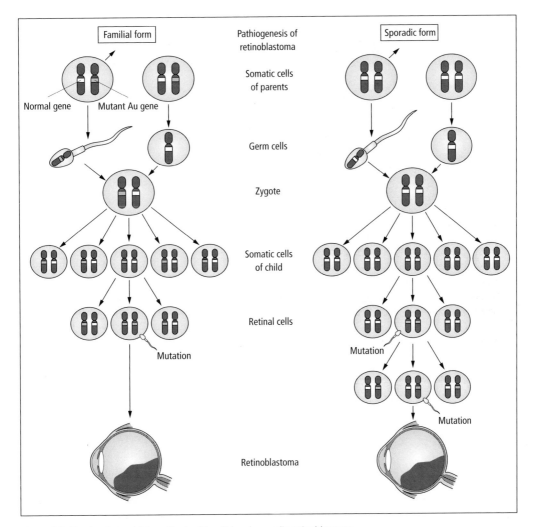

Figure 2.8 Knudson's two-hit hypothesis of familial and sporadic retinoblastoma.

sidered to be the greater environmental hazard. Most UV radiation is absorbed by atmospheric ozone in the stratosphere. This layer is being depleted in part due to chlorine in chlorofluorocarbons (CFCs), resulting in increasing UV exposure levels. One of the major lesions induced in DNA by UV radiation is the thymidine dimer, a covalent bonding of adjacent thymidine residues on the same DNA strand. This causes local distortion of the double helix, which is repaired by the nucleotide excision repair (NER) pathway. The seven identified Xeroderma Pigmentosa genes en-

code essential components that undertake NER, and hence Xeroderma Pigmentosa predisposes to UV induced skin malignancies. Melanin pigment in the skin normally absorbs UV radiation protecting the skin. While basal cell and squamous cell skin cancers increase with cumulative UV exposure, the relationship is less straightforward for melanoma. The evidence for an association with cancer for other forms of non-ionizing radiation (microwave, radiofrequency, ultrasound and electromagnetic radiation) is weak and inconsistent.

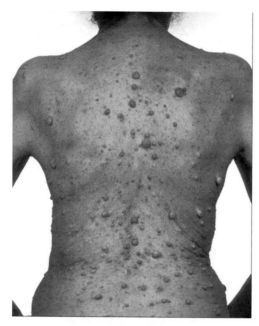

Table 2.5 How atomic bombs kill.

Timing	Effect
1–2 hours	Radiation sickness (acute nausea & vomiting)
2–10 days	Denuded intestinal epithelium (intractable diarrhoea, GI haemorrhage, septicaemia)
7–21 days	Pancytopenia (neutropenic sepsis, haemorrhage)
3–10 years	Acute myeloid leukaemia
10–50 years	Solid tumours (breast, bone, thyroid, lung, GI, ovary, skin)

Figure 2.9 Multiple dermal neurofibromata typical of peripheral neurofibromatosis, or type 1 NF, previously known eponymously as 'Von Recklinghausen's Disease'. This is due to a hereditary mutation of the NF1 neurofibromin gene on chromosome 2p22 that encodes a GTPase-activating protein that is involved in the signal transduction cascade. (See also colour plate between pages 154 and 155.)

Ionizing radiation

Natural sources

Exposure to natural sources of ionizing radiation varies in different populations. Higher altitude and further latitude from the equator are both associated with higher cosmic radiation exposure. In addition, various regions have higher natural background levels from radon. Radon is a colourless, odourless gas formed by decay as part of the uranium-238 series. The radon-222 isotope, along with a number of its progeny, is an α-particle emitter. Radon gas levels are normally quoted in becquerel [Bq] m^{-3} (1 Bq is one decay per second), and the average indoor levels in the UK are about 20 Bq m^{-3}. Some local geological factors such as granite with high levels of uranium produce high levels of radon in soil gas, but for this to escape to the surface the soil must be highly porous. In the UK, radon levels are particularly high in Devon and

Cornwall, Derbyshire and Northamptonshire. From the results of eight case-control studies, it is believed that radon exposure accounts for a small fraction of lung cancers, with a 14% increased risk for a person living for 30 years in a house with levels of 150 Bq m^{-3}.

Nuclear warfare

Most of the information on the induction of cancers by ionizing radiation comes from exposed populations, including Japanese people exposed to atomic bombs at Hiroshima ('Little Boy' was a U-235-enriched bomb) and Nagasaki ('Fat Man' was a plutonium-239 bomb). The estimated populations of the two cities at the time of bombing was 560 000, and approximately 200 000 people died within the first few months, of the acute effects of blast, burns and radiation exposure (see Table 2.5). The Radiation Effects Research Foundation has followed 86 000 survivors, and by 1990, 7827 of them had died of cancer. The excess risk of leukaemia was seen especially in those exposed as children, and was highest during the first 10 years after the bombing. The excess risk of solid tumours, however, occurred later and still persists (Table 2.6 and Box 2.3).

Medical radiation

The hazards of medical ionizing radiation may be difficult to determine, as ionizing radiation-induced tumours are not identifiable by a particular signature DNA mutation (unlike the thymidine

Table 2.6 Cancer deaths in survivors of Hiroshima and Nagasaki.

	Total number of deaths	Estimated number of deaths due to radiation	Percentage of deaths attributable to radiation
Leukaemia	176	89	51%
Solid tumours	4,687	339	7%
TOTAL	4,863	428	9%

Box 2.3: Chernobyl

On 26 April 1986, nuclear reactor number 4 at Chernobyl exploded in the world's worst nuclear accident. Over 10^{19} Bq of radioactive isotopes were released, including 5.2×10^{18} Bq of β-emitting isotopes of iodine that concentrate in the thyroid gland. An increase in thyroid cancer in children was first reported in 1990, but an excess of other tumours has not (yet?) been reported. Fallout from Chernobyl affected millions of people living within a few hundred kilometres of the reactor and caused a 30–100 fold increase in the incidence of thyroid cancer especially in children. The younger the child at exposure, the greater the risk is. The increase so far is almost entirely in papillary carcinoma of the thyroid, and the dominant subtype has solid papillary morphology. At a molecular level, these tumours show rearrangement of RET oncogene by inversion or translocation with partner genes to yield constitutively active c-RET tyrosine kinases.

Table 2.7 Diagnostic imaging radiation doses.

Imaging Procedure	Radiation dose	Equivalent to natural background radiation for
Chest X-ray	0.1 mSv	10 days
Chest CT scan	8 mSv	3 years
Abdominal CT scan	10 mSv	3 years
IVU	1.6 mSv	6 months
Brain CT scan	2 mSv	8 months
Mammogram	0.7 mSv	3 months

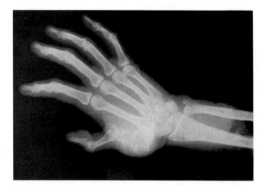

Figure 2.10 Osteosarcoma of first metacarpal, 15 years after radiotherapy for arthritis (no longer used). This radiograph shows cortical destruction, a soft tissue mass with internal calcification, and periosteal reaction.

dimers induced by UV radiation). Some tissues, such as breast, thyroid and bone marrow, are more susceptible to the carcinogenic effects of ionizing radiation, although tumours following radiation exposure have been described in every organ site. Well-described examples of iatrogenic tumours include acute leukaemias induced by radiation treatment for ankylosing spondylitis, prescribed in the late 1930s in the UK. 20000 Israelis received radiation for Tinea capitis (ringworm) in 1950s, and they suffered a significantly increased risk of developing meningioma by the 1980s. Similar increases in tumours have been observed in patients treated with radiotherapy, including men treated for prostate cancer, women treated for cervical cancers and Hodgkin's disease survivors. Diagnostic imaging radiation doses are shown in Table 2.7 and an example of an induced tumour in Figure 2.10.

Occupational radiation

The first clearly documented victims of occupational exposure to radiation were Marie Curie and her daughter, who both died of leukaemia. In the 1920s, watch dials were hand-painted with radium-based luminous paint. The women often licked their paint brushes to give them a sharp point and ingested the radium. Up to 3% of these women subsequently developed osteosarcomas after a latency of 5–10 years. Similarly, pitchblende (uranium oxide) and uranium miners in Czechoslovakia, Sweden, Newfoundland and Colorado who have been exposed to radon are at increased risk of lung cancers.

Chemical causes of cancer

Cancer is essentially a genetic disease arising from mutations of genes that affect the control of normal cell function (proto-oncogenes and tumour suppressor genes), or from polymorphic genes that govern enzyme systems that activate or detoxify environmental carcinogens (phase I and phase II enzyme reactions). Carcinogenic mutations can arise in several ways: through genotoxic environmental factors such as radiation and many chemical carcinogens, as spontaneous DNA aberrations occurring during normal cell replication, or as hereditary germ-line mutations. Chemical carcinogens may operate at any or all three stages. Chemical carcinogenesis has been defined as a multi-step process, following studies in the 1940s using polycyclic hydrocarbons and a murine skin cancer model system. This identified three steps: initiation, promotion and progression, as separate biological processes. The minority of chemical carcinogens act directly on DNA, such as alkylating agents, whilst the majority are pro-carcinogens that require metabolic activation to ultimate carcinogen forms. Many ultimate carcinogens are potent electrophiles, capable of accepting electrons such as epoxides derived from polycyclic hydrocarbons, vinyl chloride and aflatoxins; the N-hydroxylated metabolites of azo dyes; and the alkyldiazonium ions derived from nitrosamines.

Initiation

The key feature of initiation is the need for cell replication, without repair of the chemically induced DNA damage. Initiation is irreversible, usually involves simple DNA mutations that are 'fixed' by cell division, and results in no morphological changes to the cells. Single exposure to a carcinogen may be sufficient for initiation. For example, aflatoxin B1 is one of a family of mycotoxin contaminants of food crops such as grain and groundnuts. It is produced by *Aspergillus flavus*, which favours hot and humid conditions, and is therefore most likely to contaminate food in Africa and Asia. Aflatoxin B1 is oxidized by hepatic P450 microsomal enzymes into aflatoxin B1 2,3 epoxide, which binds to DNA bases, forming mutagenic adducts that preferentially induce GC to TA transversions. These transversions have been identified frequently in codon 249 of the p53 gene in hepatocellular carcinomas in patients from southern Africa and Qidong, China, who are exposed to high levels of aflatoxin B1.

Promotion

Promotion is a reversible process requiring multiple exposures to the carcinogen, usually with a dose–response threshold. Promotion does not usually involve DNA mutations, a process called non-genotoxic carcinogenesis, but provides a chemically mediated selective growth advantage. Thus, promotion results in clonal expansion of cells. In the 1940s it was noted that 5% of mice treated with benzopyrene developed tumours, but this figure rose to 80% when croton oil was added. Croton oil alone, however, produced no tumours. Subsequently it was found that tetradecanoylphorbol acetate (TPA), a natural component of croton oil from the seeds of *Croton tiglium*, a tree cultivated in India, which resemble castor seeds, interacts with the protein kinase C signal pathway, stimulating growth and thus acting as a promoter. TPA is the most widely used tumour promoter in cellular experimental models of oncogenesis. Similarly, oestrogens are believed to act as carcinogenic promoters. Indeed, transplacental diethylstilboestrol was shown to induce vaginal clear cell adenocarcinomas in young women whose mothers had been treated with DES during pregnancy.

Progression

Progression is an irreversible step that results in morphologically identifiable cellular changes and frequently involves multiple complex DNA changes, such as chromosomal alterations. Progression, and the accumulation of multiple genetic abnormalities that characterize cancer cells, may occur spontaneously or may be driven by chemical carcinogens. As these genetic changes may be acquired by individual cells, progression leads to heterogeneity of the cell population. Ultimately, some cells will acquire a mutator phenotype and the six genetic attributes that characterize a cancer cell.

Diet and cancer

A role for dietary constituents has been described for a number of cancers, and the evidence for some of these relationships is more robust than for others. Alcohol intake has been convincingly associated with an increased risk of oral, oesophageal and hepatic cancers. In contrast, dietary fat was believed to play an important role in breast cancer development based on animal studies, migrant studies and a few case-control trials. This led to great enthusiasm for reduced dietary fat intake to reduce the incidence of breast cancer. Results from large subsequent prospective studies, however, failed to confirm a strong relationship between dietary fat intake and breast cancer. Two paths may contribute to dietary carcinogenesis. Firstly, foodstuffs may include dietary genotoxins formed by contaminating moulds, products of storage or fermentation of food, products of cooking and food additives. Secondly, endogenous genotoxins, such as reactive oxygen species, may be formed and higher calorific intake may yield more genotoxins.

Biological causes of cancer

The association between infection and cancer is usually attributed to Peyton Rous, who described the acellular transmission of sarcoma between chickens in 1911. Six years earlier, however, Goebel had reported a link between bladder tumours and bilharzia. An estimated 15% of cancers globally are attributable to infections (11% by viruses, 4% by bacteria and 0.1% by helminths; Table 2.9).

Oncogenic human DNA viruses

Human papillomavirus (HPV)

The papillomaviruses are non-enveloped, icosahedral, double-stranded DNA viruses. Around 100 genotypes have been identified, and more than 30 of these infect the female genital tract. Some genotypes are associated with benign lesions, such as warts (HPV 6 and 11), whilst others, known as high-risk genotypes, are associated with invasive cancer (HPV 16, 18, 31, 33, 45, 51, 52, 58 and 59; Table 2.10). The prevalence of infection varies between populations but is 20–30% in women aged 20–25 years and declines to 5–10% in women over 40 years old. HPV is sexually transmitted, and the main determinant of infection is the number of sexual partners. Most infections are cleared spontaneously but a small proportion persists and is believed to be the origin of cervical dysplasia and invasive cancers. Latent infection is associated with cervical intraepithelial neoplasia (CIN), which is graded 1–3 according to the severity of cytological changes. The histological equivalent of these lesions is called 'squamous intraepithelial lesions', which may be low or high grade. Over 99% of invasive cervical cancers have detectable HPV DNA present, and HPV can transform cells in culture. The molecular basis of papillomavirus-induced neoplasia is attributed to two viral oncogenes, E6 and E7. HPV E6 inactivates p53, and E7 degrades Rb protein. High-risk HPV genotypes have also been associated with anal, penile, vaginal and vulval cancers. In addition, HPV is thought to play a role in the development of a number of other malignancies, including head and neck cancers, conjunctival squamous cancers, oesophageal cancers and possibly cutaneous squamous cell cancers. Studies have suggested that the detection of HPV in the cervix may be more sensitive for CIN than conventional cytological screening. Prophylactic HPV vaccines that induce neutralizing antibodies may prevent infection and the associated malignancies. Most of the vaccines have used virus-like particles constructed of major capsid proteins without viral DNA or enzymes present.

Box 2.4: A brief epidemiological history of smoking and cancer

Tobacco was one of the 'gifts' from the New World to the Old along with syphilis and potatoes. Nicotine is named after Jean Nicot, a 15th century French ambassador to Lisbon, who was a great advocate of smoking, and who, in 1559, sent tobacco to Catherine de Medici, the then Queen of France. Tobacco was subsequently introduced to England by Sir Walter Raleigh in 1586. Smoking was actively encouraged in soldiers in the Thirty Years War, Napoleonic campaigns, Crimean War and, most notably, the First World War. Smoking reduces fear and anxiety and suppresses appetite, and these effects were deemed beneficial to soldiers.

Early epidemiological links with non-lung cancers

In 1761, John Hill, a London doctor, wrote up several cases of nasal cancer amongst heavy tobacco snuff users and, in 1795, Thomas van Soemmering suggested a link between pipe smoking and lip cancer. The American Civil War Yankee general and later USA president, Ulysses S Grant, died in 1885 of throat cancer, and this was attributed to his cigars. In an early cohort study in the 1920s, Dr R Abbe observed that, of 90 patients with oral cancer, 89 were smokers.

Epidemiological links with lung cancer

In 1939, Dr Franz Müller of the University of Cologne performed what is generally recognised as the earliest case-control study of smoking, which showed that a very high proportion of lung-cancer patients were heavy smokers. The results, however, were dismissed as unreliable, because Hitler was a fanatical anti-smoker and had influ-enced the results. Shortly after the second world war, at a time when 90% of adult males in the UK smoked, Austin Bradford Hill, Edward Kennaway, Percy Stock and Richard Doll set out to investigate links between smoking and lung cancer, using a case-control dose-response strategy. Their case-control study was performed in 1948 in 20 London hospitals, interviewing one lung cancer patient for every two controls with gastric or colonic cancer. In all analyses, there was a dose-response relationship between the number of cigarettes smoked and the risk of lung cancer. This was published in 1950 in the British Medical Journal (BMJ).

In 1951, Doll and Hill set up a prospective cohort study of 60 000 doctors on the medical register, who were recruited via a letter in the BMJ. Forty-thousand replies were received and, in the following two and a half years, there were 789 deaths, including 36 from lung cancer. Doll and Hill found a significant increase in the risk of lung cancer with increased tobacco consumption (see Table 2.8). They noted, however, that the only two doctors, who definitely died of smoking, had died after setting fire to their beds whilst smoking in bed. This relationship was maintained in an update in 1993 of the original cohort, which now includes 20 000 deaths: 883 from lung cancer. The relative risk for smoking more than 25 g tobacco a day was 20-fold.

Similar findings were reported in the early 1950s in the USA by Ernst Wynder, a medical student, and Evarts Graham, a thoracic surgeon, who published the paper entitled 'Tobacco Smoking as a Possible Etiologic Factor in Bronchiogenic Carcinoma: A Study of 684 Proven Cases' in the Journal of the American Medical Association. Evarts, a chain smoker, did not take heed of his own findings and died himself of lung cancer.

Table 2.8

	N	Tobacco 1 g/d	Tobacco 15 g/d	Tobacco >25 g/d
Lung cancer deaths	36	0.4/10,000	0.6/10,000	1.1/10,000
All deaths	789	13/10,000	13/10,000	16/10,000

Hepatitis B virus

The hepatitis B virus is a double-stranded DNA virus that includes a single-stranded DNA region of variable length. The virus possesses a DNA-dependent DNA polymerase, as well as a reverse transcriptase, and replicates via an RNA intermediate. HBV has three main antigens; the 'Australian antigen' is as-sociated with the surface (HBsAg), the 'core antigen' (HBcAg) is internal, and the 'e antigen' (HBeAg) is part of the same capsid polypeptide as the HBcAg. All of these antigens elicit specific antibodies and are used diagnostically (Table 2.11).

Hepatitis B is one of the most common infections worldwide, with 2 billion people having been

Table 2.9 Cancers attributed to infection.

Infection	Cancer	Number of attributed cases worldwide per year
RNA viruses		
Human T-cell leukaemia virus	Leukaemia	3 000
HIV & Epstein Barr virus	Non-Hodgkin's lymphoma	9 000
HIV & Human herpesvirus 8	Kaposi's sarcoma	45 000
Hepatitis C virus	Hepatocellular cancer	110 000
DNA viruses		
Human papillomavirus	Cervical cancer	360 000
Hepatitis B virus	Hepatocellular cancer	230 000
Epstein Barr virus	Burkitt lymphoma, Hodgkin's disease, nasopharyngeal cancer	100 000
Bacteria		
Helicobacter pylori	Gastric cancer, Gastric lymphoma	350 000
Helminths		
Schistosoma haematobium	Bladder cancer	10 000
Liver flukes	Cholangiocarcinoma	1 000

Table 2.10 Human papillomavirus genotypes and associated conditions.

Human disease	HPV genotype
Skin warts	HPV-1, -2, -3, -7 & -10
Epidemodysplasia verruciformis	HPV-5, -8, -17 & -20
Anogenital warts-exophytic condylomas	HPV-6 & -11
Anogenital warts-flat condylomas	HPV-16, -18, -31, -33, -42, -43
Respiratory tract papillomas	HPV-6 & -11
Conjunctival papillomatosis	HPV-6 & -11
Focal epithelial hyperplasia	HPV-13 & -32

infected and 300–350 million chronic carriers. Hepatitis B is the ninth most common cause of death worldwide. Acute hepatitis B infection may be associated with extra-hepatic immune-mediated manifestations, and 1–4% patients develop a fulminant form. Following acute infection, up to 10% will develop chronic hepatitis: either chronic persistent hepatitis, which is asymptomatic with modest elevation of transaminases and little fibrosis, or chronic active hepatitis, which causes jaundice and cirrhosis and is associated with a 100-fold increased risk of hepatocellular cancer 15–60 years after infection. It is uncertain how hepatitis B leads to cancer. It is thought that either the X protein of hepatitis B interacts with p53, causing disruption of the cell-cycle control, or that the virus may act indirectly by causing an increased hepatic cell turnover associated with the cirrhosis. Treatment with alpha interferon and antiviral agents such as lamivudine or adefovir may lead to clearance of hepatitis B in chronic infection and recombinant sub-unit vaccines have been available since the early 1980s. The introduction of a mass immunization programme in Taiwan has been associated with a dramatic reduction in liver cancer in children there.

Epstein–Barr virus or human herpesvirus 4
The Epstein–Barr virus (EBV) is a ubiquitous double-stranded DNA gammaherpesvirus. It was first identified by Epstein and his colleagues by electron microscopy of a cell line derived from a patient with Burkitt lymphoma in 1964. Burkitt lymphoma had been described only a few years earlier in 1956 by Dennis Burkitt, a surgeon working in Uganda. The subsequent finding that EBV was the cause of infectious mononucleosis, arose

Table 2.11 Serological markers of Hepatitis B virus infection.

	HBs Ag	HBe Ag	Anti HBe	Anti HBs	Anti HBc	Anti HBc IgM
Acute infection	+	+/–	+/–	–	+	+++
Highly infectious carrier	+++	+	–	–	+	–
Low infectious carrier	+	–	+	–	+	–
Past infection	–	–	+	+	+	–
Past immunisation	–	–	–	+	–	–

Table 2.12 Diseases associated with Epstein–Barr virus infection.

Non-malignant
Infectious mononucleosis
X-linked lymphoproliferative syndrome (Duncan syndrome)
Oral hairy leukoplakia

Malignant
Burkitt lymphoma
Nasopharyngeal cancer
Post transplant lymphoproliferative disorder
Hodgkin's disease
Primary cerebral lymphoma
Primary effusion lymphoma (with HHV8)
Leiomyosarcoma in children with HIV
Nasal T/NK non-Hodgkin's lymphoma

serendipitously when a laboratory technician in Philadelphia developed mononucleosis and was found to have acquired antibodies to EBV. EBV infects over 90% of the world's population, is transmitted orally and, in normal adults, from 1 to 50 B lymphocytes per million are infected. A carcinogenic role for EBV has been confirmed for Burkitt lymphoma, Hodgkin's disease and immunosuppression-associated non-Hodgkin's lymphoma and nasopharyngeal cancer (Table 2.12). EBV is estimated to be responsible for 100 000 cancers per year worldwide.

Primary infection of epithelial cells by EBV is associated with the infection of some resting B lymphocytes. The majority of infected B cells have latent virus, with a small percentage undergoing spontaneous activation to lytic infection. During lytic infection, EBV replicates in the cell, and when the progeny virions are released, the host cell is destroyed. In contrast, during latent infection there is neither virus replication nor host cell destruction. Most infected B lymphocytes have latent virus, expressing at most 10 of the more than 80 genes of EBV. The roles of these latent genes include maintenance of the episomal virus DNA, growth and transformation of B cells and evasion of the host immune system. A number of these latent genes are thought to contribute to the oncogenicity of EBV. For example, latent membrane protein 1 (LMP-1) mimics a constitutively activated receptor for tumour necrosis factor (TNF), and BHRF1 and BALF1 are viral homologues of the anti-apoptotic protein bcl-2 that leads to evasion of programmed cell death. Thus, in contrast to retroviruses which generally possess a single oncogene, EBV uses a number of genes that contribute to the steps towards cancer.

Human herpesvirus-8 or Kaposi's sarcoma herpesvirus

Kaposi's sarcoma (KS) was originally described over a century ago and four forms have subsequently been recognized. The first is classic KS and is usually found on the lower legs of elderly men of Mediterranean or Jewish descent without any immunosuppression. A second form, endemic or African KS, is found in all age groups in sub-Saharan Africa, where, even before the HIV epidemic, it was as common as colorectal cancer is in Europe. A third form associated with iatrogenic immunosuppression was recognized in patients who had received an allogeneic organ transplant. The fourth and most common form of the disease is associated with AIDS. All forms of the disease are associated with human herpes virus-8 (HHV-8), which was identified in 1994. In addition, this virus is most prevalent in the populations at risk from KS. HHV-8 is also implicated in the pathogenesis of two rare lymphoproliferative diseases: primary effusion lymphoma and multicentric Castleman's disease. Like EBV, HHV-8 includes a number of cellular homologues that are thought to contribute to its oncogenic potential.

Oncogenic human RNA viruses

Hepatitis C virus

The hepatitis C virus (HCV) was identified in 1989 as the cause of transfusion-acquired non-A non-B hepatitis by Choo and colleagues. HCV is a single-stranded RNA virus belonging to the flavivirus genus whose member also lead to yellow fever and dengue fever. The prevalence of HCV varies geographically from 1–1.5% in Europe and USA to 3.5% in Africa. Transmission is chiefly parenteral, particularly by blood transfusion prior to the introduction of blood product screening. In contrast to HBV, 85% of patients develop persistent HCV and 65% progress to chronic liver disease including hepatocellular cancer, for which the relative risk is 20-fold (Table 2.13). The oncogenic mechanism for HCV remains unclear. Unlike retroviruses, there is no evidence of genome integration but cancer is preceded by cirrhosis, and it is hypothesized that the virus induces a cycle of inflammation, repair and regeneration and thus indirectly contributes to the formation of cancer. There are at least six genotypes of HCV and the diagnosis is usually made by enzyme immunoassay for anti-HCV antibodies and confirmed by polymerase chain reaction for HCV RNA. Treatment with pegylated

interferon and ribavarin leads to clearance of the virus in 40–60% of cases, depending in part upon the HCV genotype.

Human T cell leukaemia virus type 1

HTLV-1 is the main cause of adult T-cell leukaemia/lymphoma, a malignancy characterized by hypercalcaemia, lymphadenopathy, hepatosplenomegally and myelosuppression. It is associated with a particularly poor prognosis and occurs almost exclusively in areas where HTLV-1 is endemic, such as the Caribbean, Japan and West Africa, or in immigrants from these regions and their offspring. HTLV-1 is also associated with tropical spastic paraparesis and uveitis. HTLV-1 is an enveloped retrovirus that integrates into the host cellular genome. The virus is able to immortalize human T lymphocytes, and this property is attributable to a specific viral oncogene, *tax*. Tax is a trans-activating transcription factor that can also lead to repression of transcription. Adult T-cell leukaemia/lymphoma develops in 2–5% of HTLV-1-infected people and is commoner in those infected at a younger age.

Oncogenic bacteria

Helicobacter pylori

Helicobacter pylori is a spiral, flagellated Gram-negative bacteria that colonizes the human gastrointestinal tract. It causes gastritis leading to peptic ulceration, although many infections are asymptomatic. The discovery of *H. pylori*, and the recognition of its place in the pathogenesis of peptic ulcer disease, are chiefly due to Barry Marshall, who, in order to prove his point, swallowed a solution of the organism and developed acute gastritis

Table 2.13 Comparison of HIV and hepatitis B and C viruses.

	HCV	HBV	HIV
Global prevalence	3%	35%	0.5%
Global prevalence	170 million	1.2 billion	36.1 million
Chronic infection rate	2.3%	6%	0.5%
Chronic infection	129 million	350 million	36.1 million
Deaths per year	476,000	1.2 million	2.8 million
Annual death rate	0.40%	0.49%	7.80%

one week later. It is believed that half of the world's population is chronically infected with *H. pylori*. Prospective sero-epidemiological data suggest that *H. pylori* infection is associated with a 2- to 4-fold increase in the risk of gastric cancer as well as an increase in gastric low-grade mucosa-associated lymphoid tissue (MALT) lymphoma. As with the hepatitis viruses, the mechanism of oncogenesis is obscure, but is believed to be an indirect result of chronic inflammation and consequential epithelial cell proliferation. The combination of two antibiotics with either a bismuth preparation or a proton pump inhibitor for 14 days eradicates *H. pylori* in 80% of patients. Re-infection is common, however. *H. pylori* is very prevalent, and the time interval between *H. pylori* infection and gastric cancer is thought to be several decades. For these reasons, it may prove very difficult to assess the value of eradication interventions in reducing cancer risk.

Oncogenic helminths

Schistosomes

Schistosomes are parasitic blood flukes or flatworms belonging to the trematode class, whose intermediate hosts are snails. Three species infect humans; *Schistosoma haematobium*, *Schistosoma mansoni* and *Schistosoma japonica*. Humans are infected by contact with fresh water, where the parasite cercaria form penetrates the skin. It is estimated that 200 million people are infected with schistosomes (Table 2.14). Acute infection may produce swimmer's itch dermatitis and tropical pulmonary eosinophilia, although most people remain asymptomatic. The development of adult worms, days to weeks after infection, may cause Katayama fever, a systemic illness of fevers, rigors, myalgia, lymphadenopathy and hepatosplenomegally. Chronic infection leads to granuloma formation at sites of egg deposition; in the bladder for *S. haematobium* and in the bowel and liver for *S. mansoni* and *S. japonica*. The late sequelae include squamous cell carcinoma of the bladder in the case of *S. haematobium* and probably hepatocellular cancer with *S. japonica*. A single oral dose of praziquantel resolves the infection.

Liver flukes

Three species of food-borne liver flukes of the trematode class cause illness in humans. Infection is acquired by eating raw or undercooked fresh water fish, and the flukes migrate to the biliary tree and mature in the intrahepatic bile ducts. There are two intermediate hosts in the life cycle: snails and fish. As many as 17 million people are estimated to be infected (Table 2.15). Cholangiocarcinoma has been recognized as a complication of chronic infection, and case-control studies have found a five-fold increased risk with liver fluke infection. The oncogenic mechanism is again unclear, although chronic inflammation is believed to play a role. The antihelminth drug praziquantel is the treatment of choice.

Worldwide contributions to cancer

The current human world population is 6 billion and the global burden of cancer is estimated to be 10 million new cases and 6 million deaths

Table 2.14 Distribution of schistosomiasis.

Species	Geographical distribution	Number of humans infected
S. haematobium	North Africa, Middle East, sub-Saharan Africa	114 million
S. mansoni	Sub-Saharan Africa, Middle East, Brazil	83 million
S. japonica	China, The Philippines, Indonesia	1.5 million

Table 2.15 Distribution of liver fluke infection.

Species	Geographical distribution	Number of humans infected
Opisthorchis viverrini	Northern Thailand, Laos	9 million
Opisthorchis felineus	Kazakhastan, Ukraine	1.5 million
Clonorchis sinensis	China, Korea, Taiwan, Vietnam	7 million

Table 2.16 WHO cancer priority ladder.

WHO cancer priority ladder
1. Tobacco control
2. Infection control
3. Curable cancer programme
4. Early detection programme
5. Effective pain control
6. Sample cancer registry
7. Healthy eating programme
8. Referral guidelines
9. Clinical care guidelines
10. Nurse education
11. National cancer network
12. Clinical evaluation unit
13. Platform technology focus for region
14. Clinical research programme
15. Basic research programme
16. International aid programme

annually. Projections for 2020, when the global population is estimated to have risen to 8 billion, are 20 million new cases and 12 million deaths annually. Tobacco contributes to 3 million cases (chiefly lung, head and neck and bladder cancers), diet to an estimated 3 million cases (upper gas-trointestinal, colorectal) and infection to a further 1.5 million cases (cervical, stomach, liver, bladder and lymphomas) globally. Prevention by tobacco control, dietary advice and affordable food and infection control and immunization, could have a major impact in reducing the global burden of cancer. The differences in outcome for tumours between the so-called developed and developing world are most marked for the rare but curable cancers such as acute leukaemias, Hodgkin's disease and testicular cancers, where access to therapy dramatically improves survival. Small differences are recorded where screening programmes aimed at early detection are effective, such as for cervical and breast cancers, whilst there are small differences in outcome in the common tumours, like lung, stomach and liver cancers, where prevention has a major role. These observations have led to a WHO list of priorities to reduce global cancer that is headed not by scientific research or expensive chemotherapy but by tobacco and infection control (Table 2.16). In an optimistic scenario, the implementation of these priorities could reduce the estimated cancer incidence of 20 million in 2020 to 15 million and could reduce the expected mortality of 12 million to 6 million.

Chapter 3

The principles of cancer treatment

Appropriate care

The care of people with cancer requires careful deliberation and consultation with the patient. The appropriate care will depend upon the prognosis, the effectiveness and toxicity of any therapy and finally, most importantly, on the patient's wishes. To empower patients to participate in this decision-making process requires them to be fully informed, and the clear delivery of this information is essential. A number of resources are available to supplement the information divulged by clinicians to their patients. These include a number of web-based resources, as well as patient information leaflets published by charities including CancerBACUP and individual tumour-type patient groups. It is increasingly appreciated that the management of patients with cancer requires a multidisciplinary approach, involving a team of professionals including surgeons, clinical and medical oncologists, palliative care physicians, radiologists, histopathologists, specialist oncology and palliative care nurses, clinical psychologists, counsellors, dieticians, occupational therapists, physiotherapists, social workers and clinical geneticists.

The aims of therapy should be clearly identified before embarking on a course of treatment. Treatment may either be curative, aiming to save or extend life or palliative, aiming to improve the quality of life. When considering the management of individual tumour types, the maxim that prevention is better than cure should be recalled. Cancer prevention and screening are essential if the global burden of malignancy is to be minimized.

During the last quarter of the twentieth century, the role of chemotherapy, radiotherapy and endocrine therapy after primary surgery for localized breast cancer was recognized as additional treatments defined as *adjuvant therapies*. Thus, adjuvant therapy is treatment after the primary tumour has been removed surgically, and in the absence of detectable residual disease. While large clinical trials demonstrated the advantages of adjuvant therapy to a population of women with breast cancer, the benefits for an individual woman are not measurable. Partly for this reason, oncologists developed neoadjuvant treatments with a view to facilitating surgery. Neoadjuvant therapy, usually chemotherapy or endocrine therapy, is delivered prior to surgery or radiotherapy to downsize the tumour, thus demonstrating the sensitivity of the tumour and potentially reducing the extent of the surgical resection.

Surgical oncology

Surgery has three major roles in the management of people with cancer:
- to diagnose and stage the cancer
- to cure the cancer
- to palliate symptoms of the cancer

It is important to avoid unnecessary surgery in patients with extensive unresectable cancer, whilst ensuring that patients with potentially curative tumours are not denied surgery. Surgical oncology is the oldest discipline for the management of cancer. It attempted at curative resections from the beginning. Surgical oncology enjoyed a golden era at the end of the nineteenth century and early twentieth century prior to the First World War (Table 3.1). Subsequent developments in surgical oncology included the development of endocrine surgery for advanced disease. Surgical hormone ablation was pioneered by George Beatson for the management of breast cancer over 100 years ago (Table 3.2). More recent contributions from surgical oncology are the development of surgical prevention for individuals identified as at high risk of developing cancer (Table 3.3), and the use of more conservative function-preserving operations. Examples of the latter include wide local excision rather than mastectomy, and partial nephron-sparing nephrectomy rather than radical nephrectomy for small renal tumours.

In addition to curative operations for cancer, surgical oncology has made a major contribution to the palliation of patients with cancer. This ranges from the resection of metastases in a few rare circumstances where this is indicated, to the fixation of pathological fractures and the placement of vascular access devices. Finally, in combination with plastic surgery, the discipline of surgical oncology has developed reconstructive surgery to reduce some of the effects of tumour resections. Examples of this include breast reconstruction after mastectomy and reconstructive surgery of the face after excision of oral tumours, skin cancers, and head and neck tumours.

Radiotherapy

Radiotherapy involves the use of high-energy ionizing radiation, to cause DNA damage and ultimately cell death. The damage induced by ionizing radiation may be lethal or sub-lethal to the tumour cells. Ionizing radiation achieves this by ejection of an electron from an atom to yield an ion pair. This may lead to damage to DNA directly via molecular excitation or indirectly via the hydrolysis of water into free radicals (Figure 3.1). These free radicals are highly reactive and usually short-lived chemicals, characterized by the presence of an unpaired electron. The dose of radiotherapy is defined as the amount of energy deposited in tissues, and it is measured in Grays (Gy), after Hal Gray, a British pioneer of radiation biology and physics. One Gray

Table 3.1 Landmarks in radical surgical oncology.

Year	Surgeon	Operation
1881	Albert Billroth	Subtotal gastrectomy
1890	William Halsted	Radical mastectomy
1897	Carl Schlatter	Total gastrectomy
1898	Johann von Mikulicz	Oesophagogastrectomy
1900	Ernest Wertheim	Radical hysterectomy
1906	W. Ernest Miles	Abdominoperineal excision of rectum
1913	Franz Torek	Oesophagectomy
1913	Wilfred Trotter	Partial pharyngectomy
1933	Evarts Graham	Pneumonectomy
1935	AO Whipple	Pancreaticoduodenectomy

Table 3.2 Landmarks in endocrine surgery for advanced cancer.

Year	Surgeon	Operation
1896	George Beatson	Oophrectomy for breast cancer
1941	Charles Huggins & Clarence Hodges	Orchidectomy for prostate cancer
1951	Rolf Luft & Herbert Olivecrona	Hypophysectomy for breast cancer
1952	Charles Huggins & DM Bergenstal	Adrenalectomy for breast cancer

Table 3.3 Prophylactic surgery.

Indication	Prophylactic operation
Cryptorchidism	Orchidopexy
Polyposis coli / chronic ulcerative colitis	Colectomy
Familial medullary thyroid cancer (MEN 2 & 3)	Thyroidectomy
Familial breast cancer (BRCA 1 & 2)	Mastectomy
Familial ovarian cancer (BRCA 1 & 2)	Oophrectomy

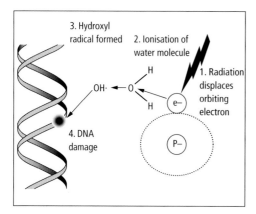

Figure 3.1 How radiation damages DNA.

is the dose absorbed when one joule is deposited in one kilogram of tissue. In each cell, one Gray damages approximately 10 000 DNA bases and 1000 deoxyribose sugars, causes 1000 single-strand and 40 double-strand breaks, and produces 150 DNA–protein crosslinks and 30 DNA–DNA crosslinks. Radiation can have an effect at any point in the cell-cycle, although it is only at the time of mitosis that cell death occurs. Therefore, there can be a lag-time of days, weeks or even months between the therapy and the full effects of the treatment becoming manifest.

Radiotherapy utilizes X-rays, electron beams and beta- or gamma-radiation produced by radioactive isotopes. X-rays are produced when a high-energy electron beam that is produced by heating an electrode in a vacuum, strikes matter. The energy of X-rays can be changed by altering the voltage input to the cathode of the X-ray tube that accelerates the electrons. Diagnostic radiology uses low-voltage equipment of, for example, 50 kV, producing X-rays of longer wavelength that are less penetrating. Therapeutic X-rays are produced by higher voltage machines of 30–50 MeV, producing shorter wavelength, more penetrating X-rays.

Radiotherapy is delivered in three ways; external beam radiotherapy, brachytherapy and radioisotope therapy. External beam radiotherapy involves the use of isotope sources or linear accelerators to deliver radiation from a distance. In the case of brachytherapy, the radioactive source is a solid radioactive nuclide emitting gamma-rays that is placed within the tumour or closely applied to the tumour. Finally, radioactive isotopes that are preferentially taken up in the target organ, may be administered orally or intravenously: for example, oral iodine-131 is given for the treatment of thyroid tumours, and strontium-89 is administered intravenously in palliative treatment of bone metastasis.

External beam radiotherapy

Superficial voltage machines operate at 50–150 kV, and their energy dose does not penetrate more than 1 cm below the surface of the skin. They are used chiefly to treat superficial skin cancers. Ortho-voltage machines that yield X-rays of 200–300 kV, penetrate to a depth of 3 cm. Metastases in bones close to the skin surface such as the ribs and sacrum are frequently treated on these machines. Mega-voltage radiotherapy machines usually use a cobalt-60 source that produces X-rays of 1.25 MeV on decaying to nickel-60. The cobalt-60 sources are contained within a protective lead shield, and an adjustable window in this shield allows regulation of the gamma ray beam. There is, however, considerable scatter of the beam, limiting the focus, and the relatively short half-life of the cobalt source means that it needs to be replaced every 3–4 years and that treatment times may become prolonged as the cobalt nears the replacement date. It is speculated that cobalt-60 sources could be used by terrorists to produce a 'dirty' bomb: a conventional

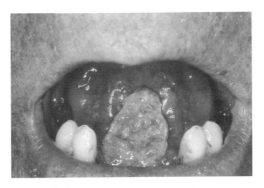

Figure 3.2 Squamous cell cancer of the oral cavity.

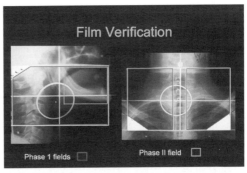

Figure 3.4 Radiological verification of radiotherapy fields.

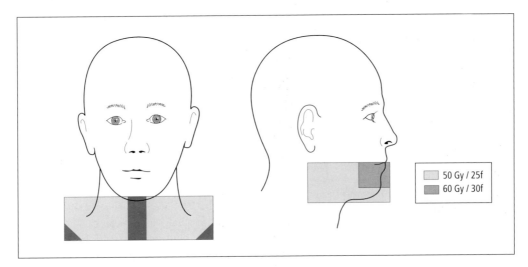

Figure 3.3 Diagram of planned radiotherapy fields.

explosive device to which radioactive material has been added.

Megavoltage machines have been replaced by linear accelerators, which produce a high-energy electron beam by accelerating electrons down a cylindrical waveguide before they bombard a fixed target, resulting in a high intensity 4–20 MeV electron beam with greater penetration and less scatter. The advantages of this electron beam over X-rays lie in the penetration and decay characteristics that allow an electron beam to deliver its high energy to deep seated tumours, whilst sparing normal tissues in its pathway. (Figure 3.2–3.5).

Brachytherapy

Brachytherapy employs sealed radionuclide sources that are implanted directly into a tumour or body cavity to deliver localized radiotherapy (Table 3.4). Examples of bachytherapy include radioactive iridium-192 needles or wires implanted into tumours of the breast, tongue and floor of the mouth. Sealed caesium-137 radioactive sources may also be placed into the vagina or rectum to treat cancers of the vagina, cervix, lower uterus, rectum or anus. Brachytherapy seeds are increasingly being used to treat localized prostate cancer. The major

Table 3.4 Radionuclides used for brachytherapy.

Source	Half-life	Mean XRay energy	Form
Cobalt-60	5.3 years	1.25 MeV	Pellets (beads, tubes, needles)
Caesium-137	30 years	0.66 MeV	Tubes, needles
Iridium-92	74 days	0.37 MeV	Wires, hairpins, cylinders
Iodine-125	60 days	0.03 MeV	Grains, seeds

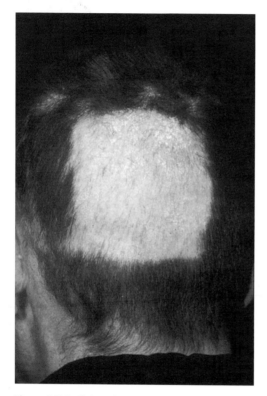

Figure 3.5 Radiation alopecia. Clearly demarcated scalp alopecia due to radiotherapy. (See also colour plates between pages 154 and 155.)

disadvantage of brachytherapy is the risk to staff handling the radioactive sources and caring for the patients. The exposure to radioactivity of all staff involved with brachytherapy must be monitored. Another method used to reduce exposure is to put in place inactive source holders while the patient is anaesthetized, and, once the source holders have been correctly located as determined by X-ray or ultrasound the patient is allowed to recover from the procedure. With the patient in a shielded room, the live radioactive source is then introduced, either manually or by remote control by a selectron. This routine is termed manual or remote 'afterloading' and is frequently used for tumours of the upper vagina, cervix and endometrium.

Radioisotope therapy

Radioactive isotopes can be given by mouth or injection and are taken up by a particular tissue where they remain. Radioisotope therapy can only be used where a tumour is inside a tissue that will preferentially accumulate a specific isotope, leaving other tissues unaffected. Examples are the thyroid, that will take up radioactive iodine, and bone, that naturally accumulates phosphorus, or will take up bone-seeking radiochemicals such as rhenium-186 hydroxyethylidine diphosphate (^{186}Re–HEDP; Table 3.5). A disadvantage of this approach is that the source cannot be recovered, limiting the degree of control over the total exposure to radiation.

Toxicity of radiotherapy

External beam radiotherapy is usually administered as repeated daily dose fractions rather than as a single large dose of radiotherapy, which would lead to severe damage to the normal tissues. Even with fractionation, normal tissues have a maximum tolerated dose as indicated in Table 3.6. The area to be irradiated is referred to as the 'radiation field'. This is marked out on the skin before treatment, and such markings often persist

Table 3.5 Systemically administered radionuclides used in oncology.

Radioisotope	Decay	Energy	Half-life	Uses in oncology
Iodine-131	β- and γ-emitter	Beta — 192 keV Gamma — 364 keV	8 days	Used in treating thyroid cancer and in imaging the thyroid gland.
Phosphorus-32	β-emitter	1.71 MeV	14 days	Used in the treatment of polycythemia vera.
Rhenium-188	β-emitter	2.12 MeV	17 hours	Used to irradiate coronary arteries via an angioplasty balloon and in relieving the pain of bone metastases.
Samarium-153	β- and γ-emitter	Beta — 825 keV Gamma — 103 keV	47 hours	Used in relieving the pain of bone metastases.
Strontium-89	β-emitter	1.481 MeV	50 days	Used in relieving the pain of bone metastases.

Table 3.6 Normal tissue tolerance of radiotherapy.

Tissue	Radiation effect	Dosage
Testis	Sterility	200 cGy
Eye	Cataract	1,000 cGy
Lung	Pneumonitis	2,000 cG
Kidney	Nephritis	2,500 cGy
Liver	Hepatitis	3,000 cGy
CNS	Necrosis	5,000 cGy
GI tract	Ulceration, haemorrhage	6,000 cGy

Table 3.7 Adverse early and late reactions to radiotherapy.

Timing	Tissue	Reaction
Early reactions	Skin	Dermatitis
	Oral mucosa	Stomatitis
	Bladder	Cystitis
	Oesophagus	Oesophagitis
	Bowel	Diarrhoea, ulceration
	Bone marrow	Myelosuppression
Late reactions	CNS	Necrosis
	Kidney	Nephritis
	Liver	Hepatitis
	Lung	Pneumonitis & fibrosis
	Vascular endothelium	Fibrosis

after treatment as tattooed dots. In general, radiation-related side-effects occur within the field of treatment, although a few systemic manifestations such as fatigue and nausea may occur. The toxicity of radiotherapy increases with both the volume of tissue irradiated and the dose given. The transient side-effects that develop during treatment tend to reflect the acute damage to normal healthy tissue. Careful planning of the beam size and shielding of surrounding tissue is therefore a prerequisite for successful therapy, because it helps to ensure that radiation fields give effective tumour eradication with an acceptable level of toxicity.

Radiotherapy-related toxicity can be usefully divided into early and late toxicities (Table 3.7). Early toxicity occurs in hours to weeks and includes systemic effects such as nausea, lethargy and myelosuppression which results when a large volume of bone marrow is within the treated area; for example, whole femur or pelvis radiation.

Localized skin toxicity is a common early side-effect, that may lead to local erythema, progressing to ulceration and desquamation in the more severe cases. Other early side-effects depend on the anatomy of the radiotherapy field; for example, alopecia (Figure 3.5) with cranial irradiation, oropharyngeal mucositis with head and neck radiotherapy, and diarrhoea, proctitis and cystitis with pelvic fields. These early reactions occur in tissues that are rapidly dividing and are usually present during, or shortly after, the course of radiotherapy. In most cases, they are reversible. Late side-effects may take months or years to manifest themselves and once again depend upon the site being irradiated. These late tissue reactions occur when slowly dividing cells attempt division, and these reactions are reversible less frequently. In some cases, the effects are believed to be mediated by fibrosis of the vascular endothelium. Examples of late reactions include necrosis in the central nervous system leading to transverse myelitis and paralysis with spinal cord radiation fields, radiation induced nephritis and osteomyelitis (Figure 3.5).

Radiosensitivity and radioresistance

Tumour resistance to radiotherapy appears to be an intrinsic property of the targeted cancer, rather than an acquired attribute selected for by the treatment, as is the case in chemotherapy. Indeed, the radiation sensitivities of many types of tumour are relatively predictable. The response of both malignant and normal tissues to fractionated radiation depends upon five 'r's:
- repair
- reassortment
- repopulation
- reoxygenation
- radiosensitivity

In this context, repair is recovery from sublethal damage and is dependent on DNA repair mechanisms. Reassortment refers to the cell-cycle phase of the tumour cells. Cells in the G2 and M phases are most susceptible to radiotherapy, and so after a first dose, cells in G1 and S will make up a greater proportion of the tumour cells still alive. Depending on the timing of the subsequent fraction of radiotherapy, these cells may have progressed or 'reassorted' to the G2 and M phases with increased sensitivity. Repopulation is the ability of tumour cells to grow and divide between doses of radiotherapy; this is a particular problem with prolonged fractionation and delayed fractions. Hypoxic cells are relatively radioresistant and after the first fractions of radiotherapy, the death of sensitive cells reduces the competition for oxygen in the tumour, so that cells that were hypoxic previously become reoxygenated and hence are more susceptible to radiation. Different cell lineages have different levels of radiosensitivity. These differences are in part intrinsic and independent of environmental factors. Amongst the factors that influence the radiosensitivity of tumours are the DNA repair genes, the production of free-radical-scavenging molecules, such as glutathione-S-transferases, superoxide dismutases, glutathione peroxidase, genes controlling apoptosis and cell-cycle regulatory genes.

Chemotherapy

Drug discovery

The origins of chemotherapy for cancer lie in the use of biological warfare during the First World War, most hauntingly described in Wilfred Owen's poem *Dulce et decorum est*. Following the extensive use of chlorine gas in trench warfare, the German army first released mustard gas at Ypres on the night of 12–13 July 1917. Mustard gas had been synthesized in 1854 by Victor Meyer and was noted to be a vesicant in 1887. As a weapon of mass destruction, mustard gas, or Yperite as it was then known, had the advantages over chlorine of requiring smaller doses, of being almost odourless, and of remaining active in the soil for weeks. The British gas casualties from 1914–1918 reveal the greater fatalities with mustard gas. Mustard gas exposure causes a severe blistering rash and conjunctivitis, followed by meyelosuppression after around 4 days. During the Second World War, the only use of mustard gas resulted in an 'own goal', when the Luftwaffe sank the USS John Harvey off Bari harbour in Southern Italy in 1943. The ship

was carrying 2000 M47A1 bombs containing a total of 100 tonnes of mustard gas, and the American sailors who survived the incident, developed conjunctivitis and skin blistering followed by a steep fall in their white-cell counts, as documented by the naval surgeon Colonel Stewart Alexander. Meanwhile, at Yale University, Alfred Gilman and Louis Goodman were using the closely related nitrogen mustard (mechlorethamine) initially in murine lymphoma models. In 1944, the first patient with lymphosarcoma (high-grade non-Hodgkin's lymphoma) was treated, and although Mr JD, a 48-year-old silversmith, achieved a temporary remission of his tumour, he later died of bone marrow failure.

The subsequent development of chemotherapy, following this fortuitous finding as a by-product of biological warfare, owes much to luck and trial and error, rather than to design. One serendipitous discovery was made by Barnett Rosenberg, a physicist at Michigan State University in 1965. He studied the effects of electric currents on *E.coli*, using platinum electrodes in a water bath. Rosenberg found that the bacteria stopped dividing but continued growing, leading to bacteria up to 300 times longer than normal. This was found to be due to cisplatin, a product from the platinum electrodes, which was interfering with DNA replication. By the end of the 1960s, a number of cytotoxic drugs from natural sources had been identified. In 1971, President Nixon, loosing the war in Vietnam, declared war on cancer, signing the Cancer Act and establishing a drug discovery programme at the National Cancer Institute. This project trawled though thousands of natural chemicals in search of potential cytotoxic agents. It was not until the 1990s, that rational drug design to target known tumour-related features emerged. Examples of this include trastuzumab, a monoclonal antibody raised against erbB2/neu/Her-2 in breast cancer, and imatinib, which inhibits the ATP-binding site of brc-abl fusion protein in chronic myeloid leukaemia.

Mechanisms of cytotoxic drugs

Amongst the many classifications of cytotoxic agents is a functional classification of cytotoxics (Table 3.8).

Alkylating agents

Alkylating agents transfer an alkyl group to the purine bases of DNA which are adenine and guanine. Bifunctional alkylating agents form covalent bonds between two different bases, resulting in interstrand or intrastrand cross-links, whilst monofunctional alkylating agents cannot form cross-links but cause adducts. Both forms of DNA alteration inhibit DNA synthesis, so alkyating agents act chiefly during the S phase of the cell-cycle. Bifunctional agents can act on more than one base and are more cytotoxic, whilst monofunctional agents are more mutagenic and carcinogenic. One of the mechanisms of tumour resistance to alkylating agents, is enzymatic removal of alkyl groups from purine bases and enhanced repair of cross-links.

Antimetabolites

Antimetabolites are structurally similar to natural compounds and in general interfere with cellular enzymes. These agents inhibit the metabolism of compounds necessary for DNA, RNA or protein synthesis. They include firstly, purine analogs; secondly, pyrimidine analogs; thirdly, folic acid analogs; and fourthly, 'others'—such as hydroxyurea. Most antimetabolites have their greatest activity during the S phase.

Intercalating agents

Intercalating agents disrupt the steric integrity of the DNA double helix. The exact mechanisms of this action remain uncertain, although it is known that anthracycline antibiotics intercalate into the DNA major groove between base pairs of the DNA double helix, and that this action is non-covalent and has no base sequence specificity. Platinum agents also intercalate and form intrastrand links similar to those formed by alkylating agents.

Table 3.8 A functional classification of cytotoxics.

Functional group	Chemical group	Examples
1. Alkylating agents		
	Nitrogen mustards	Chlorambucil, Cyclophosphamide, Melphalan
	Nitrosoureas	BCNU (carmustine), CCNU (lomustine)
	Tetrazine compounds	Dacarbazine, Temozolomide
	Aziridines	Mitomycin C, Thiotepa
	Methane sulphonic esters	Busulphan
2. Anti-metabolites		
	Purine analogues	6-Mercaptopurine, 6-Thioguanine
	Pyrimidine analogues	Cytarabine, Gemcytabine
	Dihydrofolate reductase inhibitors	Methotrexate, Ralitrexed
	Thymidylate synthetase inhibitors	5-Fluorouracil
	Ribonucleotide reductase inhibitors	Hydroxyurea
3. Intercalating agents		
	Platins	Cisplatin, Carboplatin, Oxaliplatin
	Anthracyclins	Doxorubicin, Daunorubicin
	Anthraquinones	Mitoxantrone
	Others	Bleomycin, Mitomycin C, Actinomycin D
4. Spindle cell poisons		
	Vinca alkaloids	Vincristine, Vinblastine, Vinorelbine
	Taxanes	Paclitaxel, Docetaxel
5. Topoisomerase inhibitors		
	Topoisomerase I inhibitors- Camptothecins	Topotecan, Irinotecan
	Topoisomerase II inhibitors- Epipodophylotoxins	Etoposide, Teniposide

Spindle poisons

Antimicrotubule drugs can be divided into two groups, those that stabilize microtubules by inhibiting depolymerization, e.g. taxanes, and those that are depolymerizing agents that inhibit polymerization of tubulin, e.g. vinca alkaloids. Spindle poisons inhibit the mitotic spindle function and therefore act in the M phase of the cell-cycle. Tubulin exists as α-tubulin and β-tubulin monomers in dynamic equilibrium with tubulin polymers that form microtubules. Resistance to spindle poisons may occur by mutations of β-tubulin, and these point-mutations do not confer cross-resistance between taxanes and vincas. Early spindle cell poisons included colchicine used for acute gout, familial Mediterranean fever and, rarely, psoriasis. Although colchicine, like vincas, causes depolymerization, it binds to a distinct site and is not used as a cytotoxic.

Topoisomerase inhibitors

Topoisomerase enzymes prevent DNA strands from becoming tangled, by cutting DNA and allowing it to wind or unwind. There are two mammalian classes of topoisomerases: topoisomerase I, which breaks single strands of DNA, and topoisomerase II, which breaks both strands of DNA. Topoisomerase I inhibitors act by inhibiting the re-ligation step of the nicking–closing reaction, trapping topoisomerase I in a covalent complex with DNA. Topoisomerase I inhibitors act in the S phase and belong to the camptothecin group. Camptothecin was discovered by the NCI screening of plant-derived

Table 3.9 Sensitivity and curability of selected cancers treated with chemotherapy.

Chemosensitivity	Tumour
Sensitive and curable	Leukaemias
	Lymphomas
	Germ cell tumours
	Childhood tumours
Sensitive and normally incurable (radical palliation)	Small cell lung cancer
	Myeloma
Moderately sensitive (palliation or adjuvant treatments)	Breast cancer
	Colorectal cancer
	Ovarian cancer
	Bladder cancer
Low sensitivity (chemotherapy of limited use)	Kidney cancer
	Melanoma
	Adult brain tumours
	Prostate cancer

compounds and was isolated from a Chinese small tree, *Camptotheca acuminata*. Topoisomerase II is inhibited by both, DNA intercalators, e.g. anthracyclines, and non-intercalators, e.g. epipodophyllotoxins.

Chemotherapy resistance

The major obstacle to successful cures with chemotherapy is the development of drug resistance by tumours. Indeed, the intrinsic resistance of some tumour-cell types accounts in part for the variable sensitivity of different cancers to chemotherapy (Table 3.9). In some circumstances, drug resistance is to a single drug only, whilst in other cases there is cross-resistance between different drugs. The latter mechanism is due to the expression of molecular efflux pumps in tumour-cell membranes. The most commonly found pump in multi-resistant tumour cells is P-glycoprotein (Pgp), or the multidrug resistance protein (MDR). This transmembrane protein pumps natural toxins out of cells, including most chemotherapy agents, and is normally present in selected cells of the body, such as renal proximal tubule cells, the apical mucosal cells of the colon and the canilicular surface of hepatocytes. Over-expression of Pgp/MDR by cancer cells confers a survival advantage in the

presence of chemotherapy by inducing tumour resistance.

Resistance to chemotherapy can be achieved by a number of mechanisms, including efficient repair of DNA, reduced drug uptake, increased drug efflux, decreased intracellular activation of the drug, increased intracellular inactivation of the drug, activation of biochemical pathways that bypass the pathway being blocked by the cytotoxic drug, and finally compensation for blocked enzyme pathways by increased enzyme production. An example of the last form of drug-specific resistance occurs with methotrexate, an antifolate antimetabolite that inhibits dihydrofolate reductase (DHFR). The first ever cancer cures with chemotherapy alone were reported with methotrexate for choriocarcinoma in 1963. In resistant tumour cells there is amplification of the DHFR gene, with many thousands of copies of the gene leading to higher levels of DHFR to overcome the inhibitory actions of methotrexate.

How chemotherapy is used

Cytotoxic drugs are rarely used as single agents but are usually administered in combinations in an attempt to improve treatment efficacy by reducing the development of drug resistance. A number of considerations are applied to the design of chemotherapy combinations. Only drugs that have proven activity as single agents should be included, and preference should be given to drugs with non-overlapping toxicities and different modes of action. Cycles or pulses of chemotherapy given intermittently are designed to allow for recovery of normal tissues between doses, without enabling the tumour cells to repopulate. Although this goal is frequently desirable, in recent years a number of continuous infusion chemotherapy regimens have been developed. The importance of choosing a suitable acronym for a chemotherapy regimen should not be underestimated. No single regimen has remained the gold standard of care for as long as the aptly named CHOP regimen for non-Hodgkin's lymphoma has, easily seeing off competition from the likes of ProMACE-CytaBOM. With greater experience of the benefits and disadvantages of chemotherapy, its safety has improved, and the indications for its use have expanded. As with radiotherapy and endocrine treatments, chemotherapy is increasingly used in an adjuvant context (Table 3.10).

In some circumstances, chemotherapy resistance may be overcome by escalating the cytotoxic dose. In many circumstances, the dose-limiting toxicity of chemotherapy is myelosuppression,and if this can be avoided, doses may be doubled or more before reaching the next dose-limiting toxicity, which is often mucosal damage. Autologous (from the patient him- or herself) and allogeneic (from a donor) bone marrow transplantation was developed to this end. Prior to high-dose chemotherapy, progenitor stem cells are harvested either from multiple bone marrow aspirations (BMT) or,

now more frequently, from the peripheral blood following growth-factor stimulation (PBSCT). These stem cells are immature haematopoietic cells which are capable of repopulating the bone marrow. The patient receives the conditioning high dose chemotherapy and/or radiotherapy, and subsequently the stem cells are re-infused as a transfusion. This approach has an appreciable mortality of 20–50% in the case of allogeneic BMT and of 5% with autologous PBSCT. Stem cell transplantation, however, has a clearly defined role in the management of a number of malignancies (Table 3.11).

Side-effects of chemotherapy

The main actions of chemotherapy are focussed on killing rapidly dividing cancer cells, and many of their toxicities arise because of the effects on normal cells with high rates of turnover. Indeed, the side-effects of chemotherapy may be divided into the predictable toxicities that are common, often dose-related, and usually related to the mechanism of action of the drug. In contrast, idiosyncratic side-effects are usually rarer, unrelated to dose or mechanism of action, but they tend to be drug-specific. The predictable effects of chemotherapy on fast-dividing normal cells (bone marrow, gastro-intestinal tract epithelium, hair follicles, spermatogonia) are a consequence of

Table 3.10 Cancers effectively treated by neoadjuvant and adjuvant chemotherapy.

Therapy	Tumour
Cancers effectively treated by neoadjuvant chemotherapy	Soft tissue sarcoma Osteosarcoma Locally advanced breast cancer
Cancers effectively treated by adjuvant chemotherapy	Wilm's tumour Osteosarcoma Breast cancer Colorectal cancer

Table 3.11 Cancers effectively treated by high dose chemotherapy and stem cell transplantation.

Disease	Stage	Transplant	Approximately 5 years of disease-free survival
CML	Stable phase	Allogeneic	30%
ALL	Second remission	Allogeneic/autologous	40%
AML	First remission	Allogeneic/autologous	50%
High grade non- Hodgkin's lymphoma	Responsive relapse	Autologous	45%
Hodgkin's disease	Responsive relapse	Autologous	45%
Neuroblastoma	High risk first line	Allogeneic/autologous	50%
Neuroblastoma	Relapsed	Allogeneic/autologous	25%
Non-seminomatous germ cell tumour	Responsive relapse	Autologous	50%
Myeloma	First line	Allogeneic/autologous	30%

inhibition of cell division and are especially found with cell-cycle-phase-specific cytotoxics. In contrast, the side-effects on slow-growing cell types will occur most frequently with drugs that are not cell-cycle specific, such as the alkylating agents that introduce DNA mutations into these cells, resulting in secondary leukaemias and other tumours.

The side-effects of chemotherapy may be divided into three time groups; immediate effects that occur within hours, delayed effects that occur within days, weeks or months but are generally manifested whilst the full course of chemotherapy treatment is on-going, and late effects that occur months, years or decades after the chemotherapy has ceased. The top five side-effects ranked by patients according to severity are nausea, fatigue, hair loss, concern about the effects on friends and family and, finally, vomiting. The immediate toxicities include nausea and vomiting, anaphylaxis, extravasation and tumour lysis. The delayed side-effects are the most abundant and include alopecia, myelosuppression, stomatitis and the majority of the unpredictable toxicities. The late effects of chemotherapy include infertility and secondary malignancies.

Early side-effects

Nausea and vomiting

Vomiting is a central reflex initiated in the vomiting centre of the medulla that coordinates the contraction of the diaphragm and abdominal muscles with relaxation of the cardiac sphincter, and the muscles of the throat. There are four inputs into the vomiting centre; the labyrinths (responsible for motion sickness, for example), the higher cortical centres (responsible, for example, for fear and anticipation), the vagus nerve sensory input from the gastrointestinal tract (particularly the small bowel), and the chemoreceptor trigger zone (CTZ). The CTZ is located in the area postrema adjacent to the fourth ventricle, where the blood–brain barrier is relatively deficient and chemicals in the blood and CSF are sensed, stimulating the vomiting centre. The different inputs to the vomiting centre rely

on different neurotransmitters, and this can be exploited pharmacologically in the control of symptoms (Figure 3.6). Chemotherapy chiefly acts on the gastrointestinal tract, causing serotonin (5-hydroxy tryptamine) release. It acts via the afferent vagus nerve. It also stimulates the chemoreceptor trigger zone, which employs the dopaminergic and muscarinic pathways. Occasionally, anticipatory vomiting is problematic, and this acts through the higher cortical centres, using gamma-aminobutyric acid (GABA) neurotransmission. In contrast, the labyrinthine pathways utilize histamine-1 receptors, and motion sickness is often successfully controlled with anti-histamines.

The likelihood of being sick with chemotherapy depends upon the emetogenicity of the cytotoxics used, as well as on host-related factors. Cisplatin and mustine are amongst the most emetogenic, whilst vinca alkaloids rarely cause nausea. Younger patients, women, patients who have been sick previously with chemotherapy, and patients who drink little or no alcohol, are all more likely to suffer with chemotherapy-induced vomiting. Acute vomiting within six hours of chemotherapy is best controlled by a combination of steroids and 5HT-3 receptor antagonists. Delayed vomiting occurring up to five days after the chemotherapy is best treated with steroids and dopamine antagonists. Anticipatory vomiting that occurs prior to receiving chemotherapy is treated with benzodiazepines.

Anaphylaxis

As with all medicines, anaphylaxis may occur with chemotherapy, and the most common culprits are taxanes and asparaginase. The incidence of hypersensitivity with paclitaxel is so high, that routine prophylaxis with steroids and antihistamines (H1 and H2) is administered to all patients receiving paclitaxel.

Extravasation

Extravasation is the inadvertent administration of chemotherapy into subcutaneous tissue. This leads to pain, erythema, inflammation and discomfort, which, if unrecognized and untreated, can lead to

47

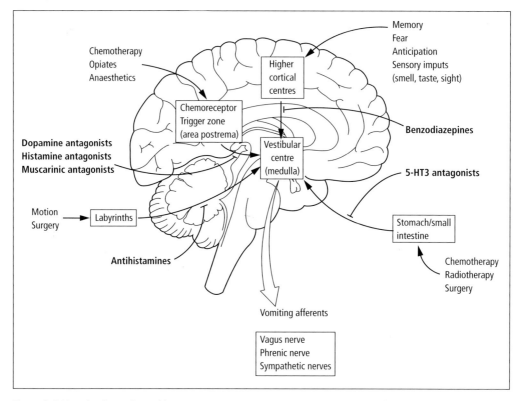

Figure 3.6 Neural pathways in vomiting.

tissue necrosis with the possibility of serious sequelae. Position, size and age of the cannulation site
are the factors with the greatest bearing on the likelihood that problems occur, and the experience of
the specialist administering the chemotherapy is
crucial in this aspect. The likelihood of damage occurring is determined by the cytotoxic drug, with
anthracyclines being especially likely to cause severe injury and one of the reasons why long-stay
catheters are used (Figure 3.7).

Tumour lysis

The rapid cytolysis of a large volume of cancer cells
at the start of chemotherapy occasionally results
in the 'tumour lysis syndrome' which is a form of
metabolic chaos. The destruction of tumour DNA
leads to hyperuricaemia from the breakdown of
nucleotide bases. The cytolysis causes hyperkalaemia by releasing intracellular potassium, and

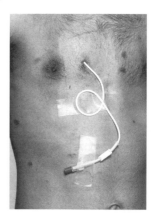

Figure 3.7 Patient with a Hickman line, a skin-tunnelled
long-term silicon catheter with a dacron cuff about 2 cm
above the exit site that acts as a barrier to microorganisms
and prevents catheter dislodgment. Hickman lines are used
for continuous infusional chemotherapy or for patients
with poor venous access. Hickman lines are placed in the
radiology department, using ultrasound guidance or in
theatres under general anaesthetic.

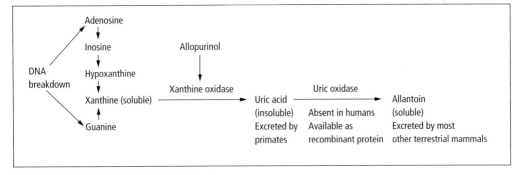

Figure 3.8 Purine catabolism pathway and the therapy of tumour lysis.

the breakdown of proteins and DNA causes hyper-phosphataemia and secondary hypocalcaemia. Acute renal failure may be a consequence of the high levels of urate and phosphate, while the high levels of potassium may lead to cardiac arrthymias. Tumour lysis only really occurs with acute leukaemias and high grade lymphomas, including Burkitt's lymphoma. Bulky tumours, poor renal function and high levels of urate before chemotherapy increase the risk of tumour lysis.

Uric acid is soluble at physiological pH levels but precipitates in the acidic environment of the renal tubules, leading to crystallization in the collecting ducts and ureters, and in turn to obstructive uropathy. Similarly, calcium phosphate is precipitated in the renal tubules and microvasculature, producing nephrocalcinosis. The most important issue in the management of tumour lysis is its prevention by a combination of hyperhydration, allopurinol and, rarely, by urinary alkalinization to pH levels of seven or higher, with sodium bicarbonate to reduce urate precipitation in the renal tubules. Allopurinol is an inhibitor of xanthine oxidase, the enzyme that catalyses the conversion of soluble xanthine, a product of purine catabolism, to uric acid. The treatment of established tumour lysis is an oncological emergency. The majority of patients who develop tumour lysis have chemosensitive tumours and are receiving potentially curative treatment. These patients should be considered candidates for urgent haemodialysis. A relatively new addition to the treatment is recombinant urate oxidase (rasburicase), which converts insoluble urate to soluble allantoin (see Figure 3.8).

Delayed predictable side-effects

The main predictable delayed side-effects of chemotherapy are alopecia, bone marrow suppression and gastrointestinal mucositis.

Alopecia and onychodystrophy

Hair loss with chemotherapy is both drug- and dose-dependent and is related to the frequency of cycle repetition. Long-term therapy may result in loss of pubic, axillary, and facial hair, in addition to scalp hair. The loss of scalp hair often occurs in an acute episode while washing, usually two to six weeks after starting chemotherapy. It should be emphasized to patients that alopecia from chemotherapy is reversible, with hair re-growth beginning between one and two months after completing chemotherapy. The hair may re-grow a lighter or darker colour and is often curlier initially. Doxorubicin and cyclophosphamide are the commonest culprits. Patients should be offered wigs, available on the NHS. Scalp cooling, below 22°C, may reduce alopecia by causing vasoconstriction and reducing circulation to hair follicles. The pharmacokinetic profiles of cytotoxics dictate that scalp cooling is only effective for taxanes and anthracyclines. Concerns have been raised over the potential risk of developing scalp and cerebral metastases with scalp cooling, due to reduced drug circulation to these sites. Along with alopecia, a frequent complication of chemotherapy is onychodytrophy or changes in the nails other than colour changes, which usually render the nails brittle and prone to

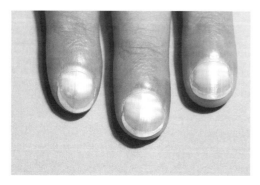

Figure 3.9 Beau lines. This image shows a man with Beau lines, transverse ridges that form as a result of temporary interference with nail growth, here shown following several cycles of chemotherapy. (See also colour plates between pages 154 and 155.)

shedding (onycholysis) and to fungal infection (onychomycosis). A common physical sign in patients who have received cyclical chemotherapy are Beau lines: horizontal grooves or lines on the nail plate that indicate cycles of arrested nail growth with chemotherapy cycles (Figure 3.9).

Myelotoxicity of chemotherapy

The myelosuppressive effects of chemotherapy may affect the circulating red cells, white cells and platelets (Figure 3.10). The manifestations in these three series are partly related to their circulatory life spans. In circulation, the half life of an erythrocyte is 120 days, of a leucocyte six to eight hours, and of a platelet seven days.

There will be a significant risk of severe myelosuppression, if chemotherapy is initiated when the total white cell count is below 3.0×10^9/L (or neutrophil count is below 1.5×10^9/L) and/or the platelet count is below 150×10^9/L. These values are the usual cut-offs for administering a cycle of chemotherapy, it may, however, be given at lower values to patients with haematological malignancies, or if supportive therapy is anticipated and when non-myelosuppressive regimens are employed. Myelosuppression is the dose-limiting toxicity for many cytotoxic agents; the main exceptions are vincristine, bleomycin, streptozotocin, and asparaginase which do not cause myelosuppression.

Anaemia is rarely a dose-limiting toxicity but is generally cumulative over successive cycles of chemotherapy. Anaemia is most troublesome with cisplatin, since the nephrotoxicity of this agent may decrease erythropoietin production from the kidneys in response to anaemia. The symptoms of anaemia include fatigue, lethargy and exertional dyspnoea, with haemoglobin levels in the range 8–10 g/dL. As the haemoglobin falls below 8 g/dL, reduced exercise capacity progresses to dyspnoea and tachycardia at rest, and to complications including cerebrovascular and cardiovascular ischaemia, such as transient ischaemic attacks and angina, respectively. The management of chemotherapy-induced anaemia is with transfusion and, at least with cisplatin-induced anaemia, recombinant erythropoietin may be beneficial (Box 3.1).

Neutropenia, defined as a neutrophil count below 1.0×10^9/L, is the commonest dose-limiting toxicity of chemotherapy and is a frequent cause of treatment delays and dose reductions. Neutropenia most often manifests itself as infection, and neutropenic sepsis is a medical emergency which, if left untreated, is potentially fatal. It is frequently overlooked by untrained medical staff, and delays in starting intravenous antibiotics can be fatal. Neutropenic sepsis is defined as a fever of 38.0°C or higher for at least two hours when the neutrophil count is below 1.0×10^9/L.

The treatment of neutropenic sepsis includes a thorough clinical history and physical examination to identify possible sources of infection (Figure 3.11). Initial management must include resuscitation measures for shock, if present. An infection screen should be performed, including blood cultures from peripheral veins as well as from any central access catheters, a urine sample for microscopy and culture, a chest X-ray and a throat swab for culture. Treatment should not be delayed awaiting the results of cultures. The most common organisms associated with neutropenic sepsis are common bacterial pathogens. Empirical antibiotic treatment should be instituted with broad-spectrum bactericidal antibiotics, and antibiotic regimens will be dictated by local antibiotic resistance patterns. The most common initial

Box 3.1: Haemopoietic growth factors

The proliferation and maturation of blood cell lineages in determined by haemopoietic growth factors or colony stimulating factors (CSFs). Bone marrow stromal cells produce many of these growth factors. Recombinant haemopoietic growth factors are administered to ameliorate chemotherapy-induced cytopenias. They are given parentrally to avoid proteolytic degradation in the gastrointestinal tract.

Erythropoietin

This growth factor is naturally produced by the kidney in response to hypoxia and stimulates red cell proliferation. It may be overproduced in renal-cell carcinoma, leading to paraneoplastic polycythemia. As well as its role in the treatment of anaemia of chronic renal failure, erythropoietin may be used to treat cytotoxic-induced anaemia, particularly where cisplatin is implicated.

Granulocyte colony stimulating factor (G-CSF)

G-CSF is a lineage-restricted growth-factor promoting granulocyte differentiation, while granulocyte-macrophage CSF (GM-CSF) is multifunctional, affecting granulocytes, monocytes, megakaryocytes and erythroid precursors but not basophils. Both CSFs are used in the treatment of chemotherapy and radiotherapy related neutropenia. Evidence-based guidelines are available that describe the rational use of G-CSF for four circumstances:

1. Primary prophylaxis (i.e. with first cycle of chemotherapy). Not routinely, occasionally for pre-existing neutropenia; for example, due to marrow infiltration.
2. Secondary prophylaxis. Only for curable tumours with proven importance of maintaining dose intensity (germ cell tumours, choriocarcinoma and lymphoma)
3. Febrile neutropenia. Data do not support routine G-CSF usage, but use in presence of pneumonia, hypotension, multi-organ failure and fungal infection.
4. Peripheral Blood Stem Cell mobilisation prior to harvesting for high-dose therapy and stem-cell rescue.

Thrombopoietin

Thrombopoietin (TPO) is constitutively produced by the liver and kidney and acts on many stages of megakaryocyte growth and differentiation. It has yet to become incorporated into routine clinical use. Interleukin-11, however, also raises platelet counts following chemotherapy and has been licensed for this indication in the US.

treatment regimens are a parentral combination of an aminoglycoside with either a cephalosporin or a broad-spectrum penicillin. Alternatively, mono-therapy with a cephalosporin may be used. If there is no response within 36–48 hours, the antibiotic regimen should be reviewed in the light of culture results, and consideration given to adding antifungal cover (such as amphotericin B). For patients with severe neutropenic sepsis as defined by hypotension, pneumonia or multi-organ failure, granulocyte-colony stimulating factor (G-CSF) should be administered. Following an episode of neutropenic sepsis, consideration should be given to reducing the chemotherapy dosage in subsequent cycles, or if dose intensity has been shown to influence the outcome (as for germ cell tumours and Hodgkin's disease), secondary prophylaxis with G-CSF to reduce the duration of neutropenia should be considered (Box 3.1).

Thrombocytopenia is a common side-effect of chemotherapy, particularly with carboplatin, that rarely causes clinical manifestations unless it is severe. Although petechiae and bruising may occur, major haemorrhage is very rare, unless the platelet count falls below 20×10^9/L. At platelet counts below 10×10^9/L there is an appreciable risk of gastrointestinal or cerebral haemorrhage, and prophylactic administration of pooled platelets is warranted. Growth-factor support for thrombocytopenia is currently investigational (Box 3.1), and chemotherapy dose-delays and -reductions may be necessary, following low platelet nadir counts.

Gastrointestinal tract mucositis

Mucositis is a frequent delayed side-effect of chemotherapy, occurring in 40–50% of patients and is even more common in patients receiving chemo-radiotherapy, or radiotherapy alone, for head and neck cancers. It is thought that chemotherapy and radiotherapy damage basal epithelial cells in the intestinal mucosa, leading to apoptosis, atrophy and ulceration. Once ulceration occurs, bacterial and fungal infection and activation of macrophages lead to further inflammation. Mucositis is associated with significant

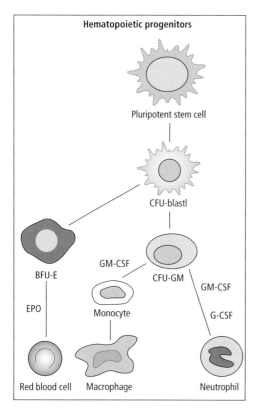

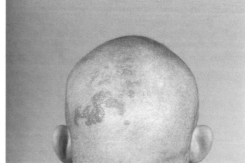

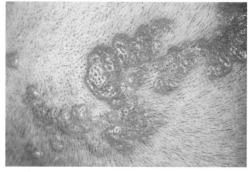

Figure 3.11 Herpes zoster of left C2 distribution erupts as an opportunistic infection during a course of chemotherapy for Hodgkin's disease.

Figure 3.10 Haematopoetic pathway. Abbreviations: CFU = Colony Forming Unit, BFU-E = Blast Forming Unit Erythroblast, CFU-GM = Colony Forming Unit Granulocyte Macrophage, GM-CSF = Granulocyte Macrophage Colony Stimulating Factor, G-CSF = Granulocyte Colony Stimulating Factor, EPO = Erythropoetin.

morbidity and mortality risk, and with chemotherapy dose reductions and delays. Sucking ice lollies during chemotherapy may reduce the incidence of mucositis with some cytotoxics, by a mechanism analogous to the cold cap treatment for the prevention of alopecia. Various 'magic mouthwashes' (usually a mild local anaesthetic in combination with an antiseptic) may provide symptomatic relief from mucositis. The time course of mucositis closely resembles that of neutropenia typically occurring 7–14 days after administration of chemotherapy. Recent developments in the management of mucositis include the investigational study of keratinocyte growth-factors as treatment for mucositis. In a few cases, specific antidotes reduce the incidence of mucositis, such as folinic acid rescue after methotrexate.

Delayed idiosyncratic side-effects

Many delayed side-effects of chemotherapy are drug-specific and are not immediately predictable from their mechanisms of action. The organs most frequently affected include the skin, nerves, heart, lungs and blood vessels.

Dermatological side-effects

Dermatological complications include the already-mentioned acute complications of extravasation and anaphylaxis, as well as idiosyncratic delayed toxicities. These include hyperpigmentation, which occurs commonly with 5-fluorouracil and bleomycin and may follow the lines of the veins into which the chemotherapy has been administered. A hand and foot syndrome of painful redness, scaling or shedding of the skin of the palms and soles may occur with continuous infusions of 5-fluorouracil chemotherapy and also with liposomal anthracycline chemotherapy. In the latter case, the cytotoxics are delivered in a liposome to dramatically prolong their half-life, mimicking the pharmacokinetics of a continuous infusion regimen. A third unusual dermatological side-effect of chemotherapy is radiation recall, an erythematous reaction of the skin in the area of a previous radiation field. Indeed, this may occur even when the radiation treatment took place decades earlier. It is most commonly seen with anthracycline and gemcitabine chemotherapy.

Cardiological side-effects

Acute arrythmias can occur during chemotherapy infusions or shortly thereafter, and this rare occurrence happens most frequently with taxanes. Similarly, 5-Fluorouracil rarely precipitates chest pain and acute myocardial infarction, pericarditis and cardiac shock. The most common cardiotoxicity of chemotherapy, however, is a dose-related dilated cardiomyopathy seen with anthracyclines. This usually presents with heart failure within eight months of the last anthracycline dose. Diuretics improve symptoms, and the early use of an angiotensin-converting enzyme inhibitor can increase the left ventricular ejection fraction, improving prognosis which nevertheless remains poor. This side-effect limits the total cumulative dosage of anthracyclines that can be administered. The maximum cumulative lifetime doses of the anthracyclines have been established, although cardiomyopathy may be seen at lower total doses particularly in children.

Neurological side-effects

Although only a few cytotoxics penetrate the cerebrospinal fluid, many cytotoxics cause neurotoxicity. Peripheral neuropathy, the most frequent neurotoxicity of chemotherapy, is commonly seen with vinca alkaloids, taxanes and platinum derivatives. The longest nerves are affected most, so the effect manifests as a symmetrical sensory loss over the feet and hands. This may progress to worsening paraesthesia, loss of tendon reflexes and eventually of muscle weakness. Features usually improve slowly over several months following cessation of chemotherapy, although residual deficits may persist indefinitely. The same cytotoxics may be responsible for an autonomic neuropathy leading to abdominal pain, constipation, paralytic ileus, urinary retention, bradycardia and postural hypotension. Acute encephalopathy is most commonly associated with ifosfamide, and symptoms include confusion, agitation, seizures, somnolence and coma. Cerebellar toxicity may follow cytarabine therapy and 5-Fluorouracil. Cisplatin-induced neurocytotoxicity is characterized by progressive loss of high-tone hearing and tinnitus.

The inadvertent intrathecal administration of vinca alkaloids is fatal, and this catastrophic clinical error has arisen because of confusion of the drug with a cytotoxic agent intended to be given intrathecally. Five such incidents have occurred in NHS hospitals in the past decade, representing an estimated rate of about three per 100000 intrathecal chemotherapy treatments. This recently resulted in the jailing of a junior doctor. A number of strict guidelines surrounding the administration of intrathecal chemotherapy are now in place to prevent this occurrence.

Pulmonary side-effects

Chronic pulmonary toxicity and fibrosis can occur with a number of cytotoxics, and the outcome is generally poor. Bleomycin is the most common culprit, and the risk increases with dose. The cardinal symptom of drug-induced pulmonary toxicity is dyspnea associated with a non-productive cough, fatigue, fever and malaise. Symptoms usually develop over several weeks to months. The chest X-ray classically shows reticulonodular infiltration at the bases and occasionally pleural effusions. Lung-function tests demonstrate a reduced diffusing capacity for carbon monoxide and restrictive ventilatory defects (Figures 3.12 and 3.13). The usual treatment is with corticosteroids, although there is little evidence to support this practice and the mortality is high.

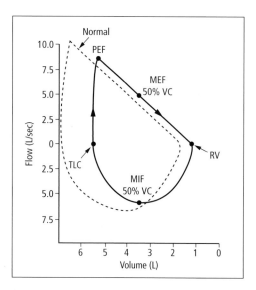

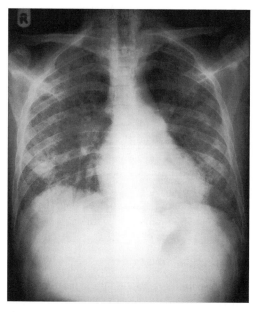

Figure 3.12 Lung flow loop showing restrictive deficit typical of belomycin fibrosis. Abbreviations: PEF = Peak Expiratory Flow, MEF = Mid Expiratory Flow, VC = Vital Capacity, TLC = Total Lung Capacity, MIF = Mid Inspiratory Flow, RV = Residual Volume.

Figure 3.13 Chest radiograph, demonstrating diffuse interstitial shadowing most prominent in the lower zones in a 35-year-old man treated with combination chemotherapy, including bleomycin for advanced germ-cell tumour of the testis.

Hepatic side-effects

Many cytotoxics cause elevated serum transaminases and bilirubin, and fatty infiltration and cholestasis may occur as the toxic effect progresses. Hepatic veno-occlusive disease (VOD) results from blockage of venous outflow in the small centrilobular hepatic vessels, following damage to cells in the area of the liver surrounding the central vein. This rare side-effect occurs with high-dose chemotherapy often as part of stem-cell transplantation. The clinical features are painful hepatomegaly, ascites, peripheral oedema, marked elevations in serum enzymes and bilirubin, as well as hepatic encephalopathy. The onset is often abrupt, occurring during the first post-transplant week, and the clinical course is fatal in up to 50% of cases.

Late side-effects

Gonadal side-effects

Chemotherapy causes a variety of toxic effects on male and female gonads, leading to infertility. Cytotoxic drugs given in the first trimester of pregnancy may have teratogenic effects, but not if given subsequently. If fertility is maintained or restored, there are concerns about the heritability of the cancer but no measured risk of mutagenic alterations to germ cells and subsequent increase in cancers in offspring of cancer patients.

Adult male gonadal toxicity

Male germ cells lie within the seminiferous epithelium and include stem spermatogonia, differentiating spermatogonia, spermatocytes, spermatids, and sperm. The differentiating spermatogonia actively proliferate and are therefore highly susceptible to cytotoxic agents. In contrast, the Leydig cells, which are found in the interstitium and produce androgens, and the Sertoli cells, which provide support and regulatory factors to the germ cells, do not proliferate in adults and so survive most cytotoxic therapies. Because later stage germ cells do not proliferate, they are not susceptible to chemotherapy.

Sperm counts do not fall immediately on starting chemotherapy, but may take 2–3 months to decline. Although minor falls in testosterone production may occur, only significant testicular radiation will produce testosterone deficiency. Men due to start chemotherapy should be offered sperm storage in order to enable them to father children in the future. Modern developments in *in vitro* fertilization are particularly relevant to the cancer patient. For those patients who were considered to be unsuitable for semen storage and remain azoospermic post treatment, the technique of intracytoplasmic sperm injection (ICSI) may be appropriate. It is useful to remember of course, that only one sperm is required to fertilize one ovum.

Adult female gonadal toxicity

In women, unlike men, the germ cells do not proliferate, whereas the somatic cells do, and this accounts for the different gonadal toxicity of chemotherapy in women and men. Female germ cells proliferate before birth as oogonia that arrest at the oocyte stage. At birth, a woman has one million oocytes, which are reduced to 300 000 at puberty. Oocytes are progressively lost by atresia, development and ovulation, until almost all are lost and menopause is reached. The interval from recruitment of primordial follicles to ovulation is 82 days, and when cytotoxics destroy maturing follicles, the result is temporary amenorrhea. If, however, the number of remaining primordial follicles falls below the minimum number necessary for menstrual cyclicity, irreversible ovarian failure occurs with permanent amenorrhea. This accounts for the increased risk of chemotherapy-induced menopause in older female patients. Permanent ovarian failure is often accompanied by vasomotor symptoms, whilst temporary amenorrhoea, which may last up to five years after chemotherapy, is usually asymptomatic. As in men, alkylating agents are the major culprits causing permanent gonadal failure in women. At present, ovum storage remains an unreliable method for routine usage and requires ovarian stimulation prior to egg harvesting, which introduces a delay prior to starting chemotherapy and is relatively contra-indicated in breast cancer. The storage of fertilized eggs is more successful.

Table 3.12 Table of carcinogenic medicines.

Carcinogenic drug	Associated tumour
Cytotoxics (especially alkylating agents & topoisomerase II inhibitors)	Acute myeloid leukaemia
Cyclophosphamide	Bladder cancer
Immunosuppression	Kaposi's sarcoma, post-transplantation lymphoproliferation
Oestrogens (unopposed)	Endometrial cancer
Oestrogens (transplacental)	Vaginal adenocarcinoma
Oral contraceptive pill	Hepatic adenoma
Androgenic anabolic steroids	Hepatocellular carcinoma
Phenacetin	Renal pelvis transitional cell cancer
Chloramphenicol	Acute leukaemia
Phenytoin	Lymphoma, neuroblastoma

Teratogenicity of chemotherapy

Many cytotoxics are teratogenic in murine models, although data in humans are thankfully limited. All alkylating agents are teratogenic, with limited information suggesting a significant risk of malformed infants if exposed in the first trimester: no increased risk is found for exposure during the second and third trimesters. Methotrexate is of course a potent abortifactant during early pregnancy. No clear evidence is available to support the timing of pregnancy following chemotherapy, although most clinicians advise a two to five years gap between chemotherapy and pregnancy.

Carcinogenicity of chemotherapy

Many cytotoxic agents are genotoxic, which accounts for their anti-tumour activity, but also carries the risk of inducing cancers; alkylating agents are the most potent carcinogens in this group (Table 3.12). The risk of induced malignancies depends not only on the cytotoxics administered, but also on the initial cancer diagnosis, with greatest risks in patients with Hodgkin's disease, where the second malignancy rate is 10–15% after 15 years. Two forms of secondary acute leukaemia following chemotherapy are widely recognized. Alkylating agents are carcinogenic, with acute leukaemias occurring in up to 5% of patients three to five years after exposure. They are associated with chromosome-5q or -7 deletions (Figure 3.14). Survival after secondary AML is poor: usually only a few months. There is also an increased incidence of solid tumours after administration of alkylating agents. Secondary acute leukaemia may also occur in patients treated with topoisomerase II inhibitors. These leukaemias occur two to three years after therapy and are associated with translocations of 11q23 (MLL gene) or 21q22 (AML1 gene) (Figure 3.14). Data on the development of secondary solid tumours are less clear, although cyclophosphamide is linked to a four-fold relative risk of bladder cancer and appears to be related to cumulative dose. Antimetabolites are generally not thought to be carcinogenic.

There is something particularly horrible about the development of second cancers after curative treatment of a first cancer, and for this reason, effort has been expended in developing alternative treatment programs that are not associated with increased cancer risk. The development of second cancers used to be a problem of particular poignancy in patients treated with alkylating-agent-based chemotherapy for Hodgkin's disease. This tumour commonly occurs in younger people, who are returned to a normal life expectancy before their devastating presentation with a second cancer. The alternative chemotherapy program, which is in current use for the treatment of Hodgkin's disease, is called ABVD. This was originally introduced by a group of Italian researchers, whose pronouncements about the effectiveness of ABVD chemotherapy were regarded with some scepticism by the medical community. However a randomized trial organized in North America showed that the Italian doctors were right.

Psychiatric dysfunction

It is generally thought that patients with cancer tend to be more depressed than the general population without malignancy. This, however, is far

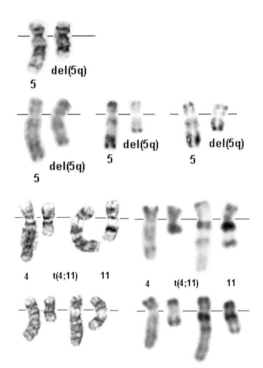

Figure 3.14 Chromosome translocation in secondary leukaemia. Partial karyotypes from two patients with secondary acute leukaemia follow chemotherapy. (a) deletions on the long arm of chromosome 5. These are characteristic of alkylating agent related secondary acute myeloid leukaemias that typically arise 3-5 years after chemotherapy and may be preceded by myelodysplasia. (b) the t(4:11) reciprocal chromosomal translocation commonly found in acute leukaemias that occur 2–3 years after chemotherapy with topoisomerase II inhibitors.

from the truth; so far from the truth, in fact, that it is a completely incorrect view. There is no difference in the incidence of mental illness between people affected with cancer and the general population. There is some controversy around the association between pre-morbid psychiatric conditions and the development of cancer. The only malignancy in which there has been shown to be an association is breast cancer, where early work described a link between pre-morbid depression and breast cancer. The link is weak. Patients with cancer go through a series of mental changes around the time of their diagnosis. Each of these stages may be protracted, even to the extent that the patient remains unable to grow beyond a particular phase. These symptoms are signs of a grief response, as seen in many other situations. Initially, patients deal with malignancy by denial. Their next move is to a grief response, progressing from there to acceptance of their situation.

Delayed side-effects in children

Growth disorders in children

Both growth disorders and mental changes are problems that are chiefly the result of the use of radiotherapy in childhood. Irradiation of the chest in the treatment of Hodgkin's disease is associated with destruction of the growing plates of the vertebrae and ribs, and with dysmorphic appearance in later life. For this reason, treatment with spinal radiotherapy is generally avoided in leukaemia and lymphoma occurring in childhood, with chemotherapy being the preferred option.

Mental change in children

Cerebral radiotherapy given as part of prophylaxis for CNS recurrence of leukaemia, may also cause significant problems. These problems are neither generally related to growth, nor to hormonal function, as the pituitary is relatively resistant to radiation. Personality defects, however, are described with increased incidence, as is global loss of cerebral function, manifested as a lower than expected IQ, personality change and occasionally fits. Although relatively resistant to radiation therapy, pituitary function can be damaged with loss of the gonadotrophs, leading to failure to achieve puberty. Loss of TSH production occurs with high-dosage radiotherapy, and even higher dosages of radiation therapy result in a loss of posterior pituitary function.

Gonadal toxicity in children

The germinal epithelium in the prepubertal testis does not appear to be any more resistant to cytotoxic therapy than in the adult, and the sterilizing effects of chemotherapy on prepubertal boys may be predicted from data in adults. In contrast, prepubertal girls are less susceptible to ovarian failure than adult women. Most chemotherapy regimens do not cause failure of pubertal development and menarche.

Hormonal therapy

Hormonal manipulation is an important part of managing cancers, the growth of which is dependent on hormones, namely breast and prostate cancers. The aims of endocrine therapy for cancer are to reduce the circulating levels of hormones, or to block their actions on the cancers. The origins of endocrine therapy for breast and prostate cancer are surgical oophrectomy and orchidectomy.

Breast cancer

Many breast cancers that produce oestrogen receptors rely for growth on supplies of oestrogen (see Figure 3.15). Luteinizing hormone releasing hormone (LHRH) agonists such as goserelin, cause down-regulation of pituitary LHRH receptors, and, via a decrease in LH/FSH (luteinizing hormone/ follicle stimulating hormone), leads to reduced plasma oestradiol. This is used in the neoadjuvant, adjuvant, and palliative setting in premenopausal women. Tamoxifen binds to oestrogen receptors and prevents oestradiol binding and is used in the neoadjuvant, adjuvant, and palliative setting in postmenopausal women. Aromatase inhibitors, such as anastrozole, bind and inhibit aromatase enzyme in peripheral tissues including adipose tissue, which converts androstenedione and other androgens into oestradiol and oestrone. This is the major source of oestradiol in postmenopausal women. Aromatase inhibitors are used in the palliative setting for women whose disease progresses on tamoxifen. All the above drugs can cause menopausal symptoms, namely hot flushes, sweats, and vaginal dryness. Specific and important adverse effects of tamoxifen are thromboembolic disease and uterine carcinoma.

Prostate cancer

The growth of prostatic carcinoma is under the control of androgens, hence the aim of hormonal therapy is to reduce testosterone levels or prevent

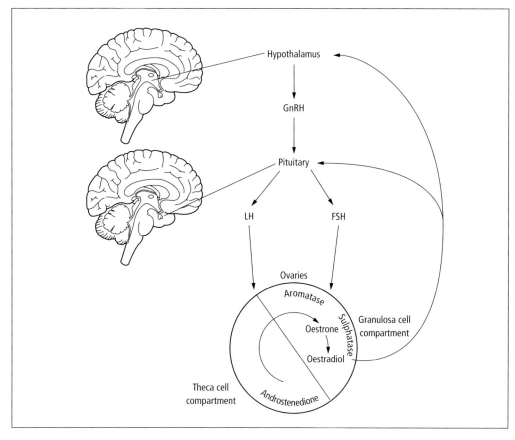

Figure 3.15 Hypothalamic-pituitary-gonadal axis in women.

it from binding to the androgen receptor. LHRH agonists cause down-regulation of pituitary LHRH receptors and via a decrease in LH lead to reduced serum testosterone and tissue dehydrotestosterone (Figure 3.16). They also have a direct effect on the tumour through tumour LHRH receptors. The adverse effects are impotence, loss of libido, gynaecomastia, hot flushes. Tumour flare, an increase in tumour size which can cause symptoms such as increase in bone pain and spinal cord compression, can occur with the initial use of these drugs, due to an initial increase in testosterone. Therefore, an anti-androgen such as bicalutamide, cyproterone and flutamide should be prescribed for one–two weeks before LHRH agonist therapy, to prevent this from happening. Anti-androgens act by blocking and preventing testosterone from attaching to the receptors in prostate cancer cells (see Figure 3.16).

The adverse effects of anti-androgens are hepatotoxicity, gynaecomastia, diarrhoea, and abdominal pain. 'Combined androgen blockade' or 'maximal androgen blockade' is a term used to describe the use of an LHRH agonist and androgen-receptor antagonist together. These agents are used alone or in combination for either locally advanced or metastatic prostate cancer.

Immunological therapy

As far back as the 1700s, it was recorded that certain infectious diseases could exert a beneficial therapeutic effect upon malignancy. Most prominent among the clinicians aiming to take advantage of these observations was a New York surgeon, William B. Coley. He used a bacterial vaccine to treat inoperable cancers and in 1893 reported high

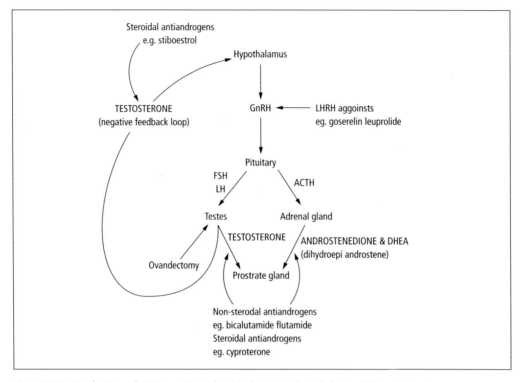

Figure 3.16 Site of actions of LHRH agonists and anti-androgens on hypothalamic, pituitary testis axis.

cure rates. Although a central role for the immune system in the surveillance and eradication of tumours has been postulated since then, immunotherapy has only a minor place in the treatment of cancers. Support for any role of immunity in the control of cancer comes from a number of observations. For some malignancies, a dense infiltration of lymphocytes in the tumour imparts a better prognosis. Cultivating and re-infusing these tumour-infiltrating lymphocytes occasionally results in some regression of the tumour. Conversely, people with immunodeficiencies have higher rates of cancers, but in general, these tumours are less common cancers and are caused by oncogenic viruses. Both passive and active specific immunotherapy and non-specific immunotherapy have a limited role in the management of cancer.

Passive specific immunotherapy

Passive immunotherapy with monoclonal anti-

bodies is an established treatment for breast cancer and non-Hodgkin's lymphoma. Monoclonal antibodies are produced by a single clone of B cells and may be humanized to reduce their immunogenicity. In 1975, Georges Kohler and Cesar Milstein developed a procedure to fuse myeloma cells with B-lymphocyte cells from the spleen of immunized mice. These fused hybridoma cell clones retained the ever-living characteristics of myeloma cells and the ability to secrete monoclonal antibodies against the antigen that the mouse was immunized with. Milstein and Kohler shared the 1984 Nobel Prize with Niels Jerne for this work. Cesar Milstein had left his native Argentina for Cambridge in 1963, following the military coup that deposed the moderate President Frondizi. He joins a long list of distinguished British Nobel laureates in physiology and medicine who arrived in Britain as political asylum seekers, including Max Perutz (discoverer of the structure of haemoglobin), Hans Krebs (who described the citric acid cycle) and Ernst Chain (who, together with Florey, developed the clinical application of Fleming's discovery of penicillin).

Two monoclonal antibodies are currently widely used in oncology; rituximab and trastuzumab. Rituximab is directed against CD20, a protein expressed on pre-B and mature B cells. This is non-specific, as it will ablate both normal and malignant B cells. The normal cells, however, are subsequently regenerated by the bone marrow from normal stem cells. This is effective in low-grade and follicular non-Hodgkin's lymphoma. Trastuzumab is directed against the human epidermal growth-factor receptor 2 (HER2), which is overexpressed in 30% of breast cancers and is associated with a poorer prognosis. It is used in metastatic breast cancer which is HER2 positive. Both these drugs can cause flu-like symptoms on infusion, such as chills and pyrexia. In addition, trastuzumab has been noted to be cardiotoxic especially when given with anthracyclines.

Active specific immunotherapy

Active cellular immunotherapy involves the harvesting and *ex vivo* activation of lymphokine-activated killer (LAK) cells (cytokine primed immune cells) and is an experimental treatment for renal cancers and melanoma. Other trial active immunotherapies include tumour vaccines. This technology is most often studied in these same tumour types, where occasional spontaneous regressions have been documented.

Non-specific immunotherapy

Global stimulation of the host cellular immune system in order to promote tumour rejection was probably the basis of Coley's adjuvant therapy. This has been replaced with the use of Bacillus Calmette-Guerin (BCG), which is administered intravesically (via a catheter into the bladder) to prevent recurrence of superficial bladder cancers, and with interferons and interleukins for renal cell cancer.

Interferon

There are three human interferons:

- interferon alpha, produced by leukocytes
- interferon beta, produced by fibroblasts
- interferon gamma, produced by T-lymphocytes.

Interferon alpha (IFN-α) is currently licensed for use and may act by enhancing the expression of HLA antigens on tumour cells, leading to increased recognition and lysis by cytotoxic T cells and natural killer cells. IFN-α is used on its own in the treatment of cancers like hairy cell leukaemia, chronic myeloid leukaemia, melanoma, renal cell cancer and Kaposi's sarcoma. The adverse effects of IFN-α are flu-like symptoms, fatigue, and myelosuppression.

Interleukin-2

Interleukin-2 (IL-2) is a cytokine, produced predominantly by activated CD4+ helper T-lymphocytes, which have been stimulated by antigen. It acts via a cell-surface receptor expressed also on activated T-cells, thus behaving as an autocrine growth-factor. In response to IL-2, CD4+ helper T cells are capable of differentiating from an initial common state (T_H0) into one of two apparently distinct types, called T_H1 and T_H2. The T_H1 pathway is essentially cell-mediated immunity, with the activation of macrophages, natural killer cells, cytotoxic T cells and a prolonged inflammatory response. The T_H2 pathway is essentially a humoral pathway, with the production of cytokines, which promote B cell growth and production of antibodies. IL-2 causes growth and proliferation of activated T-cells, thus expanding tumouricidal lymphokine activated killer (LAK) cells and may be used to treat melanoma and renal cell cancers. The adverse effects of IL-2 are fluid retention, multiorgan dysfunction, and bone marrow and hepatic toxicity.

Clinical trials

As new cytotoxic drugs are developed and other novel agents are found, it is essential to evaluate their potential in a structured fashion in clinical trials. A step-wise progression has been introduced that includes three phases of clinical trials. Phase I trials determine the toxicity, including the dose-limiting toxicities and the dose scheduling of a new agent. They enrol a small number of patients with resistant tumours. Phase II studies are designed to identify promising tumour types, using the dosing regimens established from the phase I trials. Phase III trials are larger, randomised comparisons that allocate patients either to the new treatment or the established standard therapy. In all phases of clinical trials, evaluations of response and toxicity are conducted, according to well established standards. The side-effects are measured, using the common toxicity criteria scale that rates the severity of side-effects on a four-point scale. The response to treatment is assessed using the RECIST criteria, which are largely radiological and

clinical measurements of the tumour size before and after treatment. A complete response is defined as the complete disappearance of all known disease, whilst a partial response roughly equates to a reduction of more than 50% in the size of measurable lesions, with no new lesions appearing. Although there is considerable debate as to whether these response criteria are appropriate for some of the novel therapies such as anti-angiogenic treatments, they are currently necessary for licensing approval of cancer drugs. The aims of clinical trials with a new agent include proving that it works, obtaining a license from the Food and Drug Administration (FDA) in the US and from the European Medicines Evaluation Agency

Box 3.2: How good a test is it?

The value of a diagnostic test in clinical medicine depends upon whether the result means what you think it does, and nowhere is this more relevant than in screening tests. The usefulness depends upon three factors; the sensitivity and specificity of the test, and the population prevalence of the condition.

Sensitivity

The sensitivity of a test is the ability of a test to pick up a condition:

Sensitivity = Number of true cases detected/All true cases.

A test that is 95% sensitive will detect 95% of all cases (or, put in another way, miss 5% of cases).

Specificity

The specificity of a test is the probability that a negative test is a true negative:

Specificity = Number of true negatives detected/All true negatives.

A specificity of 75% means that 75% of all negative tests are true negatives, or conversely that 25% of negative tests are actually positive for a condition.

The practical usefulness of a test in a given population can be summarized using:
- positive predictive value (the chance that a positive will be a true positive in that population) = true cases de-

tected/all positive test results (true positives and false positives)
- negative predictive value (the chance that a negative will be a true negative in that population)
= true negative results/all negative test results (true negatives and false negatives)

Prevalence and incidence

- Prevalence is the frequency of a condition in the community at a given point in time *(for example, the prevalence of cancer in children in USA is one in 330 children of less than 19 years of age).*
- Incidence is the frequency of a disease occurring over a period in time *(for example, the incidence of breast cancer in England in 1998 was 131 per 100 000 women).*

Running a trial

Ethics

The Declaration of Helsinki outlines an international basis of ethical clinical research. It describes the rights of patients, including the right to abstain from a study, access to adequate information about both potential benefits and hazards of involvement, the right to withdraw from the trial at any time and finally the desirability of giving written informed consent prior to enrolment. In the UK, research trials must be submitted to research ethics committees for review.

(continued on p. 62)

(continued)

Trial design

- Phase I trials determine the relationship between toxicity and dose schedules of the treatment
- Phase II trials identify tumour types for which the treatment appears promising
- Phase III trials assess the efficacy of the treatment compared to standard treatment, including toxicity

Randomization

Proper randomization should ensure unbiased comparisons. It achieves control for both known and unknown confounding factors.

Controlled

Controlled trials compare a 'new' test therapy with an existing treatment: either active or placebo.

Sample size

The number of patients (sample size) required in a trial will depend on the number of events (deaths or relapses) predicted with each treatment, and on the difference that you wish to be able to demonstrate between the two treatments of the trial. If you wish to detect a small difference between the two groups, more patients are needed.

Analysis

The 'intention to treat'-analysis compares the outcomes between all patients originally allocated one treatment, with all patients allocated to the other treatment.

Endpoints

Clinical-trial endpoints include overall survival duration, disease-free survival, time-to-disease progression, response rate, quality-of-life measures, adverse effects and treatment toxicity. The efficacy of treatment may be measured using the Response Evaluation Criteria In Solid Tumours (RECIST) criteria, which evaluate response in terms of radiological and clinical tumour shrinkage. The definitions broadly are:

- complete response: disappearance of all known disease
- partial response: >50% reduction in measurable lesions and no new lesions
- stable disease: lesions unchanged (<50% smaller or <25% larger)
- progressive disease: new lesions or measurable lesions >25% larger

Common Toxicity Criteria (CTC) scales

Grading scales exist to compare the side-effects of treatments in trials, including the CTC.

Interpreting the results

Evidence-based medicine

Over the last two decades there have been numerous advances in evidence processing, including the production of streamlined guides to aid critical appraisal of the literature, evidence-based abstraction services, online- and other forms of electronic literature searching, growing numbers of high-quality systematic reviews, and frequently updated textbooks in paper and electronic formats. All these initiatives have contributed to the emergence of evidence-based medicine as the optimal framework for clinical management.

Meta-analysis

Combining published data into a meta-analysis to provide an evidence base for clinical management is widely advocated. A meta-analysis may provide a more precise, less biased and more complete assessment of the available information than individual studies. The preferential publication, however, of striking results in small studies, and non-publication of larger negative studies ('publication bias'), may skew meta-analyses. Thus, the reliability of meta-analysis depends on the quality and quantity of the data that go into it.

Bias

Bias in a study is a design-flaw that results in an inevitable likelihood that the wrong result may be obtained. Bias cannot be controlled for at the analysis stage.

(continued on p. 63)

(continued)

There are three common potential biases in screening for cancer

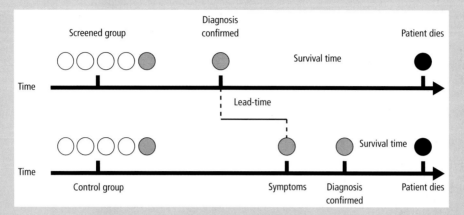

1. *Lead-time bias*: the diagnosis of disease is made earlier in the screened group, resulting in an apparent increase in survival time, although the time of death is the same in both groups.

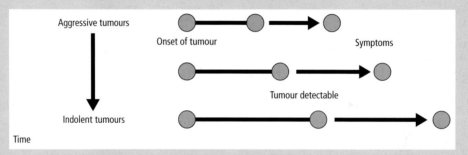

2. *Lag-time bias*: the probability of detecting disease is related to the growth rate of tumour. Aggressive, rapidly-growing tumours have a short potential screening period. More slowly-growing tumours have a longer potential screening period and are more likely to be detected when they are asymptomatic, causing an apparent improvement in survival.

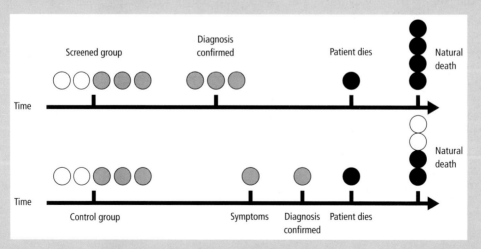

3. *Over-diagnosis bias*: the detection of very slow-growing tumours in the screened group produces an apparent increase in the number of cases. In contrast, these indolent tumours may remain silent in the control population, as they may never cause symptoms. In this diagram, two patients in the control group died with undiagnosed cancer that did not affect their natural life span.

(EMEA), as well as making money. In most cases, all the goals are complementary. There are examples from the biotechnology boom of the 1990s, however, where making money appeared to be the sole objective, and where venture capitalists earned a fortune without a drug ever achieving clinical use or benefiting any patients.

Randomized clinical trials are needed to establish evidence-based treatment protocols as well as to determine the value of new agents. Large clinical trials are a major focus of clinical activity in oncology, and patients are actively encouraged to participate in studies. The principles that underlie clinical trial management are outlined in Box 3.2.

Palliative care

Although it is widely thought that palliative care should only be offered when there is no chance of a cure, this attitude risks denying patients adequate analgesia and supportive care, irrespective of their prognosis. The concept that palliative care, to provide optimal symptom control and enhanced quality of life, should only be available to those patients with advanced disease, is absurd. The integration of palliative care into the early management of patients with cancer is recognized as benefiting patients and encouraging a more holistic attitude to their care. The discipline of palliative care throughout the globe owes much to the pioneering work of Dame Cecily Saunders. She started life as a nurse during the Second World War and became a social worker before training in medicine, which she viewed then as the only route to change the care of the dying. She advocated above all else that listening to patients is the best way to care for them. In 1967, she established the first ever hospice, St Christopher's Hospice in London, in order to meet the needs of the dying patient, which

are so often left unmet in a hospital. The hospice movement developed a comprehensive approach to dealing with the variety of symptoms experienced by patients with progressive debilitating illness, including promoting the safe use of opiate analgesia. This attitude has been developed to deliver whole-person care and to view the patient not in isolation but as part of a social unit that includes also family and friends.

Pain is the most feared and the most common symptom of advanced malignancy, and emotional, spiritual and psychological components may intensify physical pain. The relief of pain should therefore be viewed as part of a comprehensive pattern of care, encompassing all aspects of suffering. The physical component of pain cannot be treated in isolation, nor can a patient's anxieties be effectively addressed whilst they are suffering physically. It is obvious under these circumstances, that a multi-disciplinary approach is required. In addition to pain relief, expertise in the management of other common symptoms is essential, including constipation, diarrhoea, nausea, vomiting, dyspnoea and fatigue. In some circumstances, surgery or radiotherapy may provide valuable symptomatic palliation, for example for the relief of spinal cord compression. Moreover, in selected circumstances, palliative chemotherapy is indicated, even if the term seems to be a clinical oxymoron.

The delivery of palliative care has been hospice-based until recently. The hospice concept, however, has now extended to both the acute hospital and the community settings, where specialist teams work in partnership with primary care teams in the delivery of palliative care.

Community-based palliative care may enable patients to die at home or at least remain at home for as long as possible, which has long been known to be the favoured option of most patients.

Chapter 4

Cancer and people

Social and psychological aspects of cancer

Psychological carcinogenic risk factors

There is a great deal of speculation and anecdotal evidence connecting psychological factors and both the risk of developing cancer and its prognosis. Much of the research on the relationship between stressful life experiences and the onset of cancer has been poorly designed. The few existing well-conducted trials, however, have failed to establish any links. A large study of women with newly diagnosed breast cancer found that women who have a severely stressful life experience during the year before the diagnosis, or during the five years afterwards, do not seem to be at increased risk of developing a recurrence of the disease. Moreover, a meta-analysis addressing the influence of psychological coping strategies, including fighting spirit, helplessness/hopelessness, denial, and avoidance, on cancer survival and recurrence found that there was little consistent evidence that psychological coping styles play an important part in survival from, or recurrence of, cancer.

Psychological distress in cancer patients

Psychological distress is common in patients with cancer and is often overlooked or even deliberately neglected by clinicians. Over the last few decades, however, more oncologists have begun to appreciate that psychological distress and psychiatric disorders such as anxiety, depression and delirium are frequent co-morbid conditions. The outcome measures in clinical trials of new therapies increasingly include quality of life evaluation—rather than just assessing survival end-points. A number of factors have been found to be associated with an increased risk of psychological distress in patients with cancer (Table 4.1). Clinical features of anxiety include anorexia, fatigue, loss of libido, weight loss, anhedonia, insomnia and suicidal ideation. Many of these key symptoms are at times attributed to the cancer, and as few as one-third of cancer patients who might benefit from anti-depressants are prescribed them.

As well as pharmacological treatments, psychological interventions are employed frequently in the care of people with cancer. These interventions have a positive effect on both psychological morbidity and functional adjustment, and they may ameliorate disease and treatment-related symptoms. The most useful psychological intervention appears to be by a group of treatments termed 'cognitive behavioural psychotherapy'. These include behaviour therapy, behaviour modification, and cognitive therapy in various combinations. In behavioural therapy, a formal analysis of the patient's problem leads to an individualized programme of techniques aimed at changing their behaviour. Cognitive therapies explore how thoughts

Table 4.1 Factors associated with psychological morbidity in cancer patients.

Factors increasing risk of psychological morbidity
History of mood disorder
History of alcohol or drug misuse
Cancer or its treatment associated with visible deformity
Younger age
Poor social support
Low expectation of successful treatment outcome

Table 4.2 Ten top tips in communicating with patients.

1. Clarify patient's statements
2. Use open, not leading, questioning
3. Note verbal and non-verbal clues
4. Inquire about patient's psychosocial problems, e.g. depression
5. Keep patients to the point
6. Prevent needless repetition
7. Provide verbal and visual encouragement
8. Obtain precise information
9. Use brief questions
10. Avoid jargon

influence feelings and behaviour and aim to modify thought processes directly. These therapies consist of identifying maladaptive thought patterns, such as hopelessness in depression, and teaching patients to recognize and challenge these. Probably the most widely employed psychosocial intervention for cancer patients is supportive counselling which, along with information and patient education, empowers patients.

Psychosocial problems in cancer survivors

Even after successful curative treatment of cancer, patients continue to suffer psychological morbidity. The psychological sequelae in cancer survivors may relate to the illness and its treatment, as well as to family and personal issues. The majority of children who survive cancer cope well with long-term adjustment, but adults generally fare less well. Three well-recognized scenarios in this context are:
• the Lazarus Syndrome (difficulty with returning to normal life)
• the Damocles Syndrome (fear of recurrence and terror of minor symptoms)
• the Survivor Syndrome (guilt about surviving where others have died)
Cancer survivors also suffer social problems, including financial difficulties particularly with insurance and mortgages. They have also been found to have greater problems in obtaining employment and keeping jobs, and these may be compounded by frequent follow-up clinic visits.

Breaking bad news

Medical students have identified breaking bad news as their greatest fear in terms of communicating with patients, and in the first half of the twentieth century, it was routine practice to hide the diagnosis from patients with cancer. It is uncertain whether this was a paternalistic policy to protect the patient, or because physicians avoided a difficult task that many found unpleasant and that might lead them to question their practices. Although many students believe that good communication skills are innate, it is clear that, as with so many skills, the techniques can be taught and learnt (Table 4.2). The way in which the diagnosis is communicated to a patient is an important determinant of subsequent psychological stress, and even if the patients recall little of the conversation that followed, they state that the competence of the doctor at breaking bad news is critical to establishing trust.

Why do doctors fear breaking bad news? Obviously the information causes pain and distress to patients and their relatives, making us feel uncomfortable. We fear being blamed and provoking an emotional reaction. Breaking bad news reminds us of our own mortality and fears of our own death. Finally, we often worry about being unable to answer a patient's difficult questions, since we never know what the future holds for either our patients or ourselves. Breaking bad news to patients should not involve protecting them from the truth, but rather imparting the information in a sensitive manner at the patient's own pace.

Breaking bad news to patients requires preparation, and this aspect is very often overlooked. The setting for these discussions should be quiet, comfortable and confidential, so that the whole ward does not eavesdrop and that your bleep and mobile phone do not constantly intrude. An adequate period of time (at least 30 minutes) should be set aside and the patient should be asked if she or he would like someone else to be present. The conversation should open with a question to find out how much the patient already knows. An open question such as 'What have you already been told about your illness?' can reveal not only what has been said and how much has been understood, but also the emotional state of the patient 'I am so terrified it's cancer'. This opening gambit frequently takes care of much of the hard work for you. 'I think it's cancer but the doctors don't seem to want to say'. Under these circumstances, the diagnosis can be confirmed in an empathetic fashion. If this initial question does not open up a useful avenue, a 'warning shot' should be fired off: 'I have the results of your biopsy and I am afraid that the news is not good'. Following this warning shot, wait for the patient to respond and check if the patient wants to be told more. This cycle of warning shot, pause and checking should be repeated when elaborating on details of the diagnosis and treatment options. In this way the patient determines how much information is delivered. Certainly long monologues are overwhelming and confusing, and it is both useless and insensitive to use this opportunity to try to teach pathophysiology. Learning to identify and to acknowledge a patient's reaction is essential to breaking bad news. In general, prognostication in answer to: 'How long have I got, doc?', and the quoting of five-year mortality statistics, are rarely helpful. Few doctors can explain the implications of skewed distributions, medians and confidence intervals, let alone in a way that is accessible to patients. Many patients will ask for these predictions, hoping for reassurance. In these circumstances it is always easier to give the false reassurance, but this temptation must be resisted, as you will not be doing your patient a favour in the long run. After answering the patient's enquiries, it should be possible to synthesize their concerns and the medical issues into a concrete plan. Even in the bleakest of situations, setting short-term achievable plans leaves the patient with a goal for the future and with hope. The plan should include both an explicit arrangement for following up on the conversation, and a method for the patient to contact you if something arises before the next planned visit.

Coping strategies

Increased interaction and empathy with cancer patients has costs to health-care professionals that need to be appreciated and addressed. The improved communications brings health-care professionals closer to the patient and may increase feelings of inadequacy when faced with insoluble issues, and of failure when patients die. Health-care professionals dealing with dying patients and their families risk burnout, and although the medical profession is notoriously resistant to external help, a team spirit, adequate training through communication workshops and peer support are important elements in coping with these emotional stresses. Another technique that is frequently employed is distancing, which may protect the doctors from their feelings but often reduces their compassion and their capacity to care for patients. Although the burden of caring for people with cancer falls most heavily on doctors and nurses, other staff members may be affected. Indeed, when patients are dying, their distress and that of their care-givers trickles down to everyone in the clinic or ward.

Medical burnout

The depletion of physical and mental resources induced by excessive striving to reach an often unrealistic work-related goal, is termed 'burnout'. Burnout of staff working in cancer care is common, and victims often describe themselves as workaholics. The Maslach Burnout Inventory is a tool that measures burnout, and a quarter of consultant oncologists in the UK have scores that denote burnout. The consequences of medical burnout include emotional exhaustion, leading to psychological detachment from patients and the sensation that little is being achieved in terms of personal accomplishment. This may account for the high frequency of experienced oncologists changing roles in their 50s, taking on management positions or jobs with cancer charities, or immersing themselves increasingly in research rather than patient contact.

Unconventional treatments

The unmet emotional needs of patients have been held responsible for the increasing use of unconventional treatments for cancer. The void that patients may feel at a vulnerable stage in their lives may be filled with complementary treatments, alternative therapies or 'quackery'.

Complementary and alternative therapies

According to the Cochrane project, complementary and alternative medicine (CAM) is a broad domain of healing resources that encompasses all health systems, modalities and practices, as well as their accompanying theories and beliefs—other than those intrinsic to the politically dominant health system of a particular society or culture in a given historical period. Thus, while orthodox medicine is politically dominant, CAM practices outside this system, and is for the most part isolated from the universities and hospitals where health care is taught and delivered. As some CAM disciplines, such as acupuncture, become incorporated increasingly into conventional medicine, they loose their 'alternative' status. Indeed, it is this cooperation of health systems that led to the introduction of the term 'complimentary medicine' rather than the title 'alternative medicine'.

Every year around 20% of the population in the UK use CAM, and this is interpreted as a measure of disillusion with conventional medicine. In contrast, the prevalence of use in the USA is 40% and in Germany is over 60%. There is a prolonged history in Germany of CAM use, and, indeed, Samuel Hahnemann (1755–1843), who first described homoeopathy, was a German physician. The pan-

theon of complementary and alternative therapies includes alternative therapies with recognized professional bodies, such as acupuncture, chiropractic, herbal medicine, homoeopathy and osteopathy (Boxes 4.1–4.3) complementary therapies, such as Alexander Technique, aromatherapy, Bach and other flower extracts, body work therapies including massage, counselling stress therapy,

---

Box 4.1: Homeopathy—does it work?

The underlying principle of homeopathic medicine is the use of extremely low dose preparations, prescribed according to the belief that like should be cured with like. Treatments are chosen according to the symptoms that they elicit when administered to healthy people. Since raw onions cause crying, stinging eyes and a runny nose, *Allium cepa* (derived from onions) is used as a homeopathic remedy for hay-fever. The most notorious experimental trial, that attempted to explain the mechanism of action of homeopathy, was undertaken by Jacques Benveniste. He hypothesized that water had the ability to remember solutes that had been dissolved in it, after finding that very dilute solutions of allergens could elicit basophil responses. In a show-trial experiment, the then editor of *Nature*, Sir John Maddox, brought a team of independent referees to observe the experiments in Benveniste's laboratory. The observers included James Randi, a magician and investigator of the paranormal, and, under his scrutiny, Benveniste's team were unable to repeat the findings. Since that failure, Benveniste has continued to pursue the storage of memory in water, claiming to be able to store an electronic record in water that can be transferred back into an email format. These claims have been met with even greater scepticism and have earned him an unprecedented second IgNobel Prize, the tongue-in-cheek award given by the scientific community.

Despite these claims, the most widely believed theory of the mechanism of homeopathy remains a placebo effect, and more effort has been focused on establishing the efficacy of homeopathy. A meta-analysis published in the *Lancet*, examined over 100 randomized, placebo-controlled trials and found a significant odds ratio of 2.45 in favour of homoeopathy. Homoeopathic medicines can be purchased over the counter at chemists and health stores. In contrast to other forms of CAM, homeopathy is supported by the NHS; the National Homeopathic Hospital in London, and homeopathic remedies may be prescribed on the NHS by any doctor registered with the General Medical Council.

Box 4.2: Acupuncture

Acupuncture originated over 2000 years ago in China. It was used by William Osler, the most celebrated Canadian-born physician, who was both, Chief of Staff at Johns Hopkins University, and (subsequently) Regius Professor of Medicine at Oxford University, at the start of the twentieth century. The recent resurgence in popularity of acupuncture dates from President Nixon's visit to China in the 1970s. The stimulation of acupuncture points by fine needles is intended to control the 'Qi' energy circulating between organs along channels or meridians. The 12 main meridians correspond to 12 major functions or 'organs' of the body, and acupuncture points are located along these meridians. The analgesic actions of acupuncture may be explained by a conventional physiological gating model, and acupuncture is known to release endogenous opioids. There is convincing evidence supporting the value of acupuncture in the management of both nausea and acute pain. The evidence base for the use of acupuncture in chronic pain is less secure, and current evidence suggests that it is unlikely to be of benefit for obesity, smoking cessation and tinnitus. For most other conditions, the available evidence is insufficient to guide clinical decisions. Acupuncture appears to be a relatively safe treatment in the hands of suitably qualified practitioners, with serious adverse events being extremely rare. Despite this, it has been estimated that one million acupuncture treatments are given on the NHS in England each year, at an estimated cost of £26 million, equivalent to all other complementary therapies combined. A further two million acupuncture treatments are given in the private sector annually.

Box 4.3: Herbalism

The most widely used herbalism in the UK is Chinese and derives from the Daoist concepts of balancing the 'yin' and 'yang' elements of 'Qi' energy. The revenue from herbal products in the UK exceeds £40 million per year. Perhaps the most familiar example of herbal medicine is the use of St John's wort (*Hypericum perforatum*) for treating mild to moderate depression. Systematic reviews of randomized controlled trials confirm its efficacy over placebo and its equivalence to amitryptilline, with fewer side-effects. St John's wort is however not free of side-effects and has important drug interactions caused by inducing hepatic microsomal enzymes. Other more severe toxicities have been described with herbal medicines, including rapidly progressive interstitial renal fibrosis in several women, after taking Chinese herbs containing powdered extracts of *Stephania tetrandra* prescribed by a slimming clinic.

sis, may decline or stop conventional therapies, may waste money on ineffective therapies and may experience dangerous adverse effects from treatment. Moreover, the scientific academic training in medicine leads many doctors to question the value of these therapies, where a plausible mechanism of action is not available. At present, practitioners of complementary and alternative medicine in the UK are free to practice as they wish without clear regulation. Greater cooperation and respect between conventional doctors and complementary therapists would improve patient care.

'Quackery'

The word 'quack' is supposedly derived from 'quacksalver', a 17th-century variant spelling of 'quicksilver' or mercury, which was used in certain remedies that the public came to recognize as harmful. Pseudoscience uses the language and authority of science, without recognising its methods. It produces claims that cannot be proven or refuted and their practitioners may assume victim roles ('scientists are suppressing the truth'). A 'quack' may reasonably be defined as a pseudoscientist who is selling something, and a 'charlatan' as a cynical pseudoscientist who knows he or she is

hypnotherapy, meditation, reflexology, Shiatsu, healing, Maharishi Ayurvedic medicine, nutritional medicine and Yoga). There are alternative therapies that lack back up by professional organizations but are associated with traditional systems of healthcare like anthroposophical medicine, Chinese herbal medicine, Eastern medicine (Tibb), naturopathy and traditional Chinese medicine. Also to be considered there are other 'new age' alternative disciplines, e.g. crystal therapy, dowsing, iridology, kinesiology and radionics.

Many doctors remain concerned about the use of complementary and alternative medicines. These concerns may be based on a number of factors, including that patients may be seen by unqualified practitioners, may risk delayed or missed diagno-

deceiving the public. It is a sorry monument to human greed and stupidity that more money is spent on these health frauds every year than on medical research. 'Quacks' are convincing, because they tell people what they want to hear. Moreover, it is almost impossible for the cancer 'quack' to fail. When a patient deteriorates, the cancer 'quack' resorts to lines such as 'if only you had come to me sooner'. We should appreciate, however, that 'quacks' can teach us a great deal, while we retain an honest and informed practice of medicine. Their popularity is attributed to their patience and ability to listen carefully and to show both interest and affection. As well as this, 'quacks' encourage patients to take an active role in their health care thus empowering them. The internet appears to have made cancer 'quackery' even easier. While much health information on the web is evidence-based and of high quality, the open access has also been abused. Entrepreneurs have recognized the value of the web as a free-for-all market and have used it to promote fraudulent cancer treatments ranging from shark cartilage powder to 'The Zapper', a nine-volt electrical device for 'zapping away' cancers. (Boxes 4.4 and 4.5.)

Euthanasia

Euthanasia is the intentional killing by act or omission of a dependent human being for his or her alleged benefit. The term 'assisted suicide' is used when someone provides an individual with the information, guidance and means to take his or her own life, with the intention that they will be used for this purpose. Although active euthanasia remains illegal in the UK, it was legalized in Australia's Northern Territory in 1995, but this bill was overturned by the Australian parliament in 1997. In 1998, the Oregon state of the USA legalized assisted suicide following a ballot of the population. There were 129 deaths under Oregon's Physician Assisted Suicide Act between 1998 and 2002. Euthanasia was legalized in 2000 in Holland and in 2002 in Belgium. A survey published in 1994 showed that half of a mixture of hospital consultants and general practitioners questioned in

> **Box 4.4: The Luigi Di Bella Cure**
>
> This treatment is named after its proponent, Professor Luigi Di Bella (1912–2003), a retired physiologist, who lived in Modena, Italy. It is based on a combination of somatostatin, vitamins, retinoids, melatonin and bromocriptine. Adrenocorticotropic hormone (ACTH) and low doses of the oral chemotherapeutic agents cyclophosphamide and hydroxyurea are sometimes also included. It was claimed that the treatment stimulated the body's self-healing properties without damaging healthy cells. No scientific rationale or supportive experimental evidence was provided, and despite claims to have cured thousands of patients, no clinical results were published in peer-reviewed scientific journals. In December 1997, a judge in the southern Italian city of Maglie, ruled that the health authority should fund this treatment for a patient, and this pattern was followed elsewhere. Although the initial child patient died of cancer, unprecedented public interest in the unconventional therapy led to public demonstrations, with the right-wing media in Italy championing the cause. The socialist Italian government, under considerable pressure, decided to carry out phase II open-label studies in several cancer centres. Scrutiny of Di Bella's own clinical records of 3076 patients revealed that 50% of them lacked evidence that the patient had cancer in the first place, and a further 30% of them had no follow-up data. Adequate data were available for just 248 patients, of whom 244 had in addition received conventional treatments for their tumours. These findings rattled Di Bella's credibility, and in October 1998, the findings of the first clinical trial were published in the *British Medical Journal*. Of 386 patients, just three had shown a partial response. The findings however failed to shake Di Bella's confidence. He accused drug companies of conspiring against him, and suggested that the results were sabotaged by mainstream doctors. Even as late as 2003, some 3000 patients received Di Bella-based cancer treatments paid for by three Italian regional health services.

England had been asked by a patient to take active steps to hasten death, and that a third of those asked had complied with the patient's request. The reason for a patient choosing euthanasia is mostly out of fear of losing autonomy and/or bowel or bladder control, and an increasing proportion of the British public wishes to allow euthanasia for patients in certain incurable disease scenarios.

Box 4.5: Shark cartilage

In 1993, William Lane, a marine biologist and entrepreneur, published a book entitled *Sharks Don't Get Cancer*, following the discovery that some species of sharks have lower-than-predicted rates of cancer. The publication of the book preceded a prime-time television documentary focussing on a Cuban study of 29 cancer patients, who received shark-cartilage preparations. This resulted in patients clammering for shark cartilage, and a consequent devastation of North American shark populations. According to the National Marine Fisheries Service 'the Atlantic shark . . . is severely over-capitalized', and it is estimated that over 200 000 sharks are killed in American waters just for their cartilage every month. The powdered cartilage has modest anti-angiogenic activity *in vitro*: oral administration, however, results in the digestion of these proteins prior to absorption. An open-label phase II clinical trial, which was in part funded by shark cartilage manufacturers, found not a single responder amongst 58 patients, although both nausea and vomiting were reported. The company Cartilage Technologies subsequently announced that it would support no additional research on shark cartilage as a cancer remedy. It is, however, intriguing that squalamine, an aminosterol antibiotic isolated from shark livers, inhibits angiogenesis and suppresses the growth of tumour xenografts in animal models. Squalamine is easily synthesized without the need to fish sharks and is under clinical trial investigation in age-related macular degeneration as well as solid tumours.

Ethics

Four principles underpin medical ethics; respect for autonomy, nonmaleficence, beneficence and justice. In health-care decisions, respect for autonomy means that the patient is allowed to act intentionally, with understanding and without controlling influences. This is the basis of 'informed consent'. The principle of nonmaleficence requires that we do not intentionally cause harm or injury to a patient, through acts of either commission or omission. In common terms this is the same as 'avoiding negligence', and it is based on Hippocrates' (460–377 BC) original decree 'primum non nocere'. The principle of beneficence is the duty of health care professionals to provide

benefit to patients and prevent harm befalling them. These duties apply not only to the individual patient, but to society as a whole, and therein frequently lies the problem. In practice, double-effect reasoning, first attributed to Thomas Aquinas (1224-1274), may apply when an action has two outcomes: one good and one bad, and allows the lesser harm for a greater good.

Justice in health-care terms is defined as fairness in distribution of care, particularly when allocating scarce resources. A number of different political doctrines interpret this differently. Karl Marx (1818–1883) believed in egalitarianism 'from each according to his abilities, to each according to his needs'. Modern health care is rarely provided on this basis, however, but care is distributed according to a number of factors including need, effort, contribution, merit and free-market exchanges. Utilitarian philosophers, along somewhat similar lines, advocate a system that balances benefit between the collective public and the individual.

Perhaps the most interesting example of the rationing of health care is the Oregon health plan. The Oregon health plan was set up in 1987, with the focus on serving low-income people using federal funds, through a system that prioritizes heath care. An extensive list of more than 700 physical health, dental, drug dependency and mental health services was drawn up and their priority publicly debated in order to reflect a consensus of social values of Oregonians. A list of 587 approved procedures went into operation in 1994. The innovation that most sharply and controversially characterizes this systematic approach, is its commitment to provide a standard of health benefit based on ranking the effectiveness and value of all medical treatments. To determine which conditions are to be covered, Oregon's Health Services Commission ranks diagnoses from the most important (treatment with the greatest impact on health status) to the least important. This prioritization introduces a transparent approach to health-care rationing and was originally designed to use the savings achieved to extend coverage to more people. Moreover, it requires public involvement in health policies, and it incorporates public values into the rankings. The five top-ranking items were the diagnosis and treatment of head injury, insulin-dependent diabetes mellitus, peritonitis, acute glomerulonephritis, including dialysis, and pneumothorax. At the cut-off cusp, medical treatment of contact and atopic dermatitis and symptomatic urticaria are covered, as is repair of damaged knee ligaments, but the treatment of sexual dysfunction with psychotherapy or medical and surgical approaches does not make the cut, nor does the medical treatment of chronic anal fissure nor complex dental prostheses. Most interestingly, the Oregon Health Services Commission also excluded treatment for hepatocellular cancer and widely disseminated cancer.

The sociology of oncology

Inequality of health is not confined to the marked differences between wealthy and poor nations, but is recapitulated also within the UK. Only eight underground stations on the Jubilee 'tube' line separate Westminster from Canning Town in Newham, but the life expectancy of a child born in Westminster exceeds that of a child born in Newham by six years. Almost one year is lost for each stop travelled. How much of this disparity is attributable to differences in health care is uncertain, even in a state health monopoly that is free at the point of delivery. Certainly, Marxist health analysts, such as Howard Waitzkin, propose that doctor–patient encounters reproduce the dominant ideologies of the wider society, and that medicine

is a tool for social control. Modern medicine stands accused of serving the interests of capital, and of ensuring that people adhere to the accepted norms of behaviour. Many oncological health inequalities are behavioural, and medicine has branded these as self-inflicted, for example tobacco use and diet. Similar arguments have accused medicine of gender discrimination. Women are greater users of health care, because they live longer and because of the medicalization of reproductive health. It is also worth noting that the only national cancer screening programmes are for women and are mammography and cervical smears. Medicine has a long history of reinforcing a subordinate role for women in society, leading to both radical and reformist responses from the feminist movement. Equivalent responses relating to oncology would be the alternative medicine movement that wishes to 'overthrow' the current practice of oncology, and the complementary medicine that wishes to change cancer medicine from within, encouraging the adoption of a wider vision and more holistic approach.

The use of metaphors in cancer medicine has been attacked by both Susan Sontag and John Diamond, who use their personal experiences of cancer to describe the negative implications of these metaphors. Many of these metaphors are bellicose. The 'fight against cancer', for example, belittles the patient as a 'victim'. The use of these figures of speech may render cancer socially as well as physically devastating, and 'losing the battle against cancer' denigrates a patient's role in society.

Part 2

Types of cancer

Chapter 5

Breast cancer

Diseases of the breast, including tumours, have been attracting medical interest for more than 5000 years. The earliest written records of breast cancer are in the Edwin Smith papyrus, from ancient Egyptian civilizations of 3000 to 2500 BC. Hard and cold lumps were recognized as tumours, whilst abscesses were hot. The next major advances in the management of breast cancer occurred during the golden age of surgery at the end of the nineteenth century, following advances in antisepsis and anaesthesia. William Halsted in Baltimore described radical mastectomy in 1894. Moreover, in an early example of surgical audit, he reported a local recurrence rate in 50 women of only 6%. The next major advance in the management of breast cancer occurred in 1896 with the development of surgical oophrectomy as a treatment strategy for advanced breast cancer, which was pioneered by George Beatson in Glasgow. Although much of the focus during the following 75 years was on more and more aggressive surgery, the last few decades have been dominated by systemic therapy, genetics and prevention. These have all been encouraged by activists raising awareness of breast cancer. As a consequence, the survival rates of breast cancer have risen steadily over the last thirty years. A list of five-year survival of breast-cancer patients by stage of disease can be found in Table 5.1.

Epidemiology

Breast cancer is a common disease. According to the most recent figures, 37 500 women are affected annually and 11 750 die in England and Wales as a result of this condition. The likelihood of the development of breast cancer is affected by a positive family history of breast cancer, increasing age, diet, social class and nullparity. Breast cancer risk increases with age, plateauing during the menopausal years of 45–55. Women are at increased risk from breast cancer from non-vegetarian diets. It is not clear what the reason for this should be. Women who are more than two standard deviations above average height and weight are at a greater risk from breast cancer, as are women of social classes I and II. There is a protective effect of a full-term pregnancy, provided the pregnancy is achieved prior to the woman's 30th birthday. There is a minor protective effect of having more than five pregnancies, but probably no protective effect from breast feeding. A late menopause correlates with an increased risk of breast cancer, but there is little evidence that an early menarche predicates for increased risk. Oestrogen only hormone replacement therapy (HRT), as well as combined oestrogen and progestogen HRT, increase the risk of breast cancer in proportion to the duration of HRT administration. Both, the oral contraceptive pill, and alcohol and coffee consumption, have been linked to breast cancer, but the associations are controversial.

Table 5.1 Five-year survival of women with breast cancer by stage of disease.

Tumour stage	Stage definition	5-year survival
Stage I	Tumour <2 cm, no nodes	96%
Stage II	Tumour 2–5 cm and/or moveable axillary nodes	81%
Stage III	Chest wall or skin fixation and/or fixed axillary nodes	52%
Stage IV	Metastases	18%

A family history of breast cancer is a very important risk factor for breast cancer. If more than two first-degree relatives are affected, the risk to other female family members increases by a factor of two. There are clear links between breast cancer and other cancers, with associations between ovarian and endometrial cancer, and colonic tumours. Approximately 20% of breast cancer has an inherited genetic base involving the two genes BRCA1 and BRCA2. These will, if mutated, lead to a lifetime risk of breast cancer of up to 80% and up to 60% of ovarian cancer. BRCA1 has been located to chromosome 17q21 and is a tumour suppressor gene, the product of which is involved in cell cycle regulation.

The incidence of breast cancer is increasing in England and Wales, probably as a result of the introduction of the screening program. Death rates have fallen by nearly 30% over the last 15 years and survival chance increased from 65% to 75%. This is also likely to be due to the screening program, because of earlier detection of tumours at an earlier stage with a resulting better prognosis. There are also contributions to decreased mortality from the increased use of adjuvant chemotherapy and adjuvant hormonal therapy.

Presentation

Women with breast cancer generally present to their clinicians with a lump in their breast. On average, there is a delay of approximately 3 months between the woman first noting the mass in her breast and her seeing a hospital clinician. Alternative sources of referral are from breast-screening programmes, where mammographic detection leads to diagnosis of a previously unnoted breast lump. As a result of governmental concerns with the care of patients with breast cancer, the investigation and treatment of this disease has been prioritized. Patients in whom this condition is suspected ought to be seen in 'outpatients' within two weeks of receipt of the referral letter.

Outpatient diagnosis

The current standard is for women to be seen in a multidisciplinary setting which offers a 'one-stop shop' for diagnosis. Surgeons, with a special interest in breast cancer are located in a clinic with oncologists, with access to same-day cytology and imaging services. A careful history should be obtained from the patient prior to examination when seen in outpatients. The mass may be thought to be benign or malignant. Benign lumps are more likely in younger women and tend to be painful, enlarging before menstruation. Malignant lumps tend to be more common in older women and are generally painless: only 30% of malignant breast lumps are painful, and just 10% of lumps seen in new patients are malignant.

Diagnosis is by clinical, mammographic (Figure 5.1), ultrasonographic, cytological and histological means. After examination, mammography, that is, a soft tissue X-ray of the breast, aspiration cytology, which is removal of cells by means of a needle and syringe, and core biopsy should be performed to further assess the significance of the breast lump. In a younger woman, ultrasonography rather than mammography is the radiological investigation of choice. If there is confirmed malignancy, most women then proceed to surgery within two weeks of diagnosis (Figures 5.2 and 5.3).

Surgery

Surgery for breast cancer depends upon the clinical stage of the disease. If the mass is less than 5 cm in size and not fixed, the preferred treatment is removal of the lump, which is termed 'lumpectomy'. In most cases, lymph glands in the armpit are removed as well; this operation is termed axillary dissection. The reason for this is that if the nodes are affected by a cancer, there is an advantage in this group of women to additional chemotherapy. In the 'node-negative' woman there is a very much smaller advantage to additional chemotherapy. In an older woman there may be an argument against routine axillary dissection. The reason for this is that additional treatment with chemotherapy within this group of women is not dictated by lymph-node status, because the advantage is much smaller than in younger women and toxicity of the treatment outweighs these modest gains. It is clear,

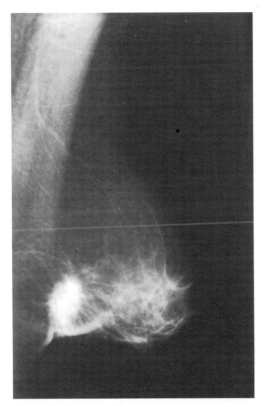

Figure 5.1 Lateral view of breast mammogram showing a large dense speculated mass highly suggestive of breast cancer.

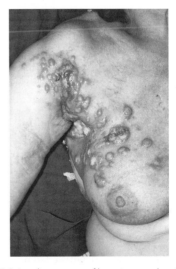

Figure 5.2 Local recurrence of breast cancer showing multiple ulcerating skin nodules. (See also colour plates between pages 154 and 155.)

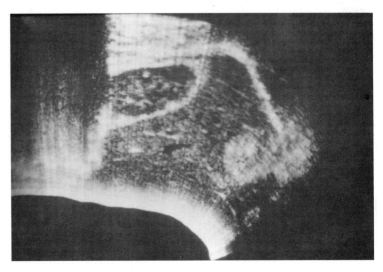

Figure 5.3 Breast ultrasound showing large echodense irregular primary breast cancer lesion.

however, that knowledge of the axillary nodal status does provide some prognostic information.

For a woman whose tumour measures 5–10 cm in size, the preferred surgical option is mastectomy, that is removal of the breast with axillary dissection. For more advanced breast cancer, the value of surgical treatment is much more contentious, and elderly women may be treated with hormonal therapy alone if the breast cancer expresses oestrogen receptors and/or progesterone receptors. In a younger woman, chemotherapy may be given in the first instance, to reduce the size of the tumour, and this may be then followed by surgery and radiotherapy. There is a major role for reconstructive surgery and this may be carried out at the time of primary surgery or at a later date upon completion of adjuvant radiotherapy or chemotherapy. The psychological gain is tremendous and needs to be considered in older as well as younger women.

Stage and grade

There are two main pathological variants of breast cancer; ductal and lobular, and these are both graded as given in Table 5.2.

This grading was first described by Bloom and Richardson, and bears their eponyms. As one might expect, poorly differentiated tumours have a

Table 5.2 Breast cancer grading and prognosis.

Grade		5-year survival
G1	Well-differentiated	95%
G2	Moderately differentiated	75%
G3	Poorly differentiated	50%

worse prognosis than moderately differentiated ones, which in turn have a worse prognosis than well-differentiated breast cancer. One may see pre-invasive changes, and these are described as either ductal (DCIS) or lobular carcinoma *in situ*. LCIS are additionally graded according to their microscopic features (Figures 1.1 and 1.2).

Stage is defined according to the classification of the Union Internationale Contre Le Cancer (UICC), which is updated every ten years or so (Table 5.3). The subscript 'P' denotes a pathological staging. There are many other staging systems.

Adjuvant radiotherapy

After lumpectomy, radiotherapy is given to the breast. This is done in order to reduce the risk of local recurrence of the tumour. Without radiation this risk is between 40% and 60%; whereas with radiation, the risk is reduced to approximately 4–6%, which is the same as that for more radical surgical procedures. Radiotherapy is generally given over a six-week period and requires daily attendance at hospital. The side-effects of radiation include tiredness and burning of the skin, which is generally mild. More serious consequences of radiation are seen only rarely and include damage to the brachial nerve plexus and, with more old-fashioned treatment machines and plans, damage to the coronary blood vessels.

Adjuvant hormonal therapy

Treatment with tamoxifen has been shown to have an advantage in terms of disease-free and over-

Table 5.3 TNM staging of breast cancer.

T stage—This defines the stage of the local breast tumour staging	N stage—This defines nodal involvement	M stage—This describes the involvement of distant organs
T0 No detectable primary tumour	N0 No nodes involved	M0 No metastases
T1 Tumour less than 2 cm	N1 Mobile axillary nodes	M1 Spread to distant organs
T2 Tumour measuring between 2 and 5 cm	N2 Fixed axillary nodes	
T3 Tumour measuring greater than 5 cm	N3 Involved supra or infraclavicular nodes	
T4 Tumour of any size extending into skin or chest wall		

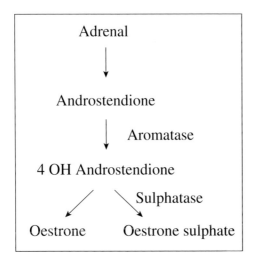

Figure 5.4 Peripheral oestrogen synthesis pathway.

all survival in both pre-menopausal and post-menopausal women and is now given routinely to this group of patients. It is usually recommended that treatment should extend for 5 years. There is no advantage to adjuvant tamoxifen in oestrogen receptor negative tumours. There have been changes in our understanding of the oestrogen receptor. Two different classes of oestrogen receptor, described as α and β, have been identified. Tamoxifen is a selective ERα-antagonist, which in turn has effects on the progesterone receptor. In postmenopausal women, recent studies suggest that a newer group of drugs, the aromatase inhibitors, may be even more effective than tamoxifen as adjuvant therapy. The current standard is to give sequential therapy with tamoxifen and then an aromatase inhibitor. Approximately 10% of circulating oestrogens derive from adrenal precursors, such as androstenedione, through the action of aromatase enzymes. The aromatase inhibitors block this action, limiting the synthesis of oestrone and oestrone sulphate produced by a second series of enzymes; the sulphatase system. See Figure 5.4.

There have been reports of cases of endometrial carcinoma associated with the use of tamoxifen. The estimated risk is one case per 20 000 women per year of use.

Adjuvant chemotherapy

Adjuvant chemotherapy has a significant place in the management of breast cancer. Although chemotherapy using the CMF (cyclophosphamide, methotrexate, 5FU) programme is probably the treatment of first choice, recently a large international study has shown that more intensive therapy using the FEC (5FU, epirubicin, cyclophosphamide) regimen is more effective. There has been recent interest in the use of docetaxel chemotherapy given in the adjuvant setting, with the possibility that survival may be improved. There is no evidence whatsoever that intensifying adjuvant therapy any further using, for example, high-dose treatments with bone marrow or peripheral blood stem cell-support improves the disease-free interval or the overall survival.

The treatment of metastatic breast cancer

The treatment of metastatic breast cancer depends very much upon the age of the patient and the sites of metastasis. It is only rarely curable, and so life quality issues are immediately important. When we described this point to one patient, she replied: 'my dear, it's death quality issues that bother me'. In older women whose metastases are in skin or in bone, the preferred treatment option is hormonal, provided that the tumour is oestrogen and/or progestogen receptor positive. The agent of first choice is tamoxifen because of its lack of toxicity and efficacy. Approximately 70% of women aged 70 respond to this therapy. In a premenopausal woman, hormonal therapy is generally less effective, and at the age of 30, just 10% of patients overall will respond to treatment at all. But oophorectomy (that is, removal of the ovaries by either radiotherapeutic, surgical or medical means) is generally the first therapeutic stratagem. An LHRH agonist is the least invasive of treatment options. It should be noted that the premenopausal ovary is relatively radioresistant and that radiation may not lead to menopause in all women treated. Treatment with other modalities of therapy will then proceed.

In both pre- and post-menopausal women,

radiation treatment is very effective in controlling bone pain. The addition of regular bisphosphonate therapy both relieves bone pain and reduces skeletal events such as fractures and spinal cord compression. If lungs or liver are affected, then chemotherapy is required. Overall, between 40% and 60% of patients respond to chemotherapy, and this response is for a median duration of one year. The median survival of women with metastatic breast cancer ranges between 18 and 24 months, with 5–10% alive after 5 years.

High-dose chemotherapy

Breast cancer responds to chemotherapy, but inevitably after responding, patients relapse and die. There have been attempts to maximize response rates by intensifying chemotherapy. High-dose treatments were popular in the early 1980s. Response rates were found to be higher than for conventional treatment; toxicity, however, was significantly worse, and death rates reached 20% as a result of the side-effects of treatment. Even more significantly, patients who responded and survived the toxicity, later relapsed, and the median duration of response was no better than that expected with conventional treatment.

In the 1990s, there was an increase in the numbers of patients receiving high-dose therapy for breast cancer. This was possible as a result of the improvement in supportive therapy, principally bone marrow rescue, either with stem cells or with marrow. Mortality has decreased and now is 5% in the best centres. Overall, there has been no significant improvement in the expectation for survival for patients with metastatic breast cancer, and only 20% of patients are alive two years after the transplantation. It has been recently argued that the relatively good results of intensive therapy reported in early studies are entirely the result of the selection of good prognosis patients for treatment with high-dose therapy, and that the same effects could be achieved with less intensive, conventional therapy. It may be the case that early, intensive therapy given to patients with poor-risk tumours as adjuvant treatment will lead to improved survival, but this has not been shown in any randomized study.

Carcinoma *in situ*

Carcinoma *in situ*, diagnosed by excision biopsy will progress to invasive cancer in 40% of patients over five years. Treatment with adjuvant radiotherapy will limit this progression rate to 1–4% per annum. An alternative to radiation therapy is mastectomy. Both radiotherapy and mastectomy are equally effective in local disease control. Lobular carcinoma *in situ* is associated with bilaterality, and mirror biopsy is recommended of the contralateral breast.

Paget's disease of the nipple

This is an eczematous condition of the nipple, associated in 80% of cases with an underlying ductal carcinoma, and in about 20% of cases with underlying ductal carcinoma *in situ*.

New therapies

One of the most interesting new approaches to breast cancer therapy is the use of antibody therapy directed against the c-erbB2 epidermal growth factor cell surface receptor, also known as HER2 (human epidermal growth factor receptor 2). A significant number (about 20%) of breast cancers overexpress c-erbB2. Trastuzumab which is a humanized murine monoclonal antibody, given in combination with chemotherapy, leads to a survival advantage compared with chemotherapy alone. It may be that this agent will have further efficacy in the adjuvant setting, and we await trials in this area with interest. Further hormonal therapies are also likely to become available with interest in the development of sulphatase inhibitors (Figure 5.4). Poor-prognosis breast cancer highly expresses EGFR. Therapy with gefitinib may be effective in these tumours. mTOR is a component of the P13K/Akt signalling pathway that mediates cell growth and proliferation. Inhibitors of this pathway, such as temsirolimus, have been shown to have activity in breast cancer. So, it is clear that there is hope that breast cancer will become a curable cancer within the next ten years.

Chapter 6

Central nervous system cancers

The first recognized resection of a primary brain tumour was performed in 1884 by Rickman Godlee in collaboration with the Westminster Hospital neurologist Alexander Bennett. It should be remembered that the removal of the cortical tumour was performed before any diagnostic imaging was available, but the surgeon knew to operate on the contralateral side to the signs! There are about 4400 people diagnosed with a brain tumour each year in the UK. That is the equivalent of about seven in every 100 000 people diagnosed each year. Brain tumours are slightly more common in men than in women. A further 300 children are diagnosed with brain tumours in the UK each year.

Epidemiology

Metastases to the brain are about ten times more common than primary brain tumours. The most common primary tumour sites amongst patients with brain metastases are lung, breast, melanoma and kidney. In addition, nasopharyngeal cancers may directly extend through the skull foramina. Meningeal metastases occur with leukaemia and lymphoma, breast and small-cell lung cancers, and from medulloblastoma and ependymal glioma as a route of spread. Primary tumours of the central nervous system (CNS) account for 2–5% of all cancers, and 2% of cancer deaths. Fewer than 20% of CNS cancers occur in the spinal cord. Each year, there are over 2500 new cases of brain cancer in

men, and over 1800 new cases in women, in the UK. There appears to be a modest increase in the incidence of primary brain tumours over the last two decades, particularly amongst the elderly. A more dramatic rise in the incidence of primary CNS lymphomas is attributable to the AIDS epidemic.

Aetiology

Although the cause of most adult brain tumours is not established, a number of inherited phakomatoses are associated with brain tumours. Phakomatoses are a group of familial conditions with unique cutaneous and neurological manifestations and dysplasias of a number of organ systems. They include neurofibromatosis (von Recklinghausen's Disease), tuberous sclerosis (Bourneville's Disease), von Hippel Lindau Disease (cerebroretinal angiomatosis), Sturge Weber Syndrome (ezcephalotrigeminal angiomatosis), Osler–Rendu–Weber Syndrome, and Fabry's Disease (angiokeratoma corporis diffusum). The first three of these are associated with brain tumours; von Reckinghausen's neurofibromatosis with cranial and root schwannomas, meningiomas, ependymomas, optic gliomas (Figure 2.9 in Part 1); tuberous sclerosis (Bourneville's Disease) with gliomas, ependymomas; von Hippel Lindau Disease with cerebellar and retinal haemagioblastoma (Table 6.1). In addition, an increased incidence of brain tumours is a feature of Gorlin's Basal Naevus

Table 6.1 Phakomatoses associated with brain tumours.

	Inheritance & genetics	Cutaneous manifestations	Eye	Nervous system	Brain tumours
Von Recklinghausen's neurofibromatosis NF-1	Autosomal dominant NF-1 gene (encodes neurofibromin that regulates GTPases in signal transduction)	Café au lait macules, axillary freckles	Lisch nodules (pigmented iris hamartomas)	Neurofibromata	Schwann cell tumours of spinal and cranial nerves, meningiomas, ependymomas, optic gliomas
Acoustic neurofibromatosis NF-2	Autosomal dominant NF-2 gene (encodes Merlin protein involved in cell adhesion)	Café au lait macules less common than in NF-1	Presenile cataracts	Bilateral acoustic neuromas Neurofibromata	Schwann cell-tumours of spinal and cranial nerves, meningiomas, astrocytomas, ependymomas, optic gliomas
Tuberous sclerosis	Autosomal dominant TSC 1 gene (encodes hamartin protein) TSC2 gene (encodes tuberin protein)	Adenoma sebaceum, Shagreen patches, Subungual fibromas, Café au lait spots		Seizures, mental retardation	Giant cell astrocytoma of foramen of Munro, gliomas, ependymomas
Von Hipple Lindau	Autosomal dominant VHL gene (encodes VHL protein involved in ubiquination)	Skin hamartomas	Retinal angiomas		Cerebellar haemagioblastomas, ependymomas, phaeochromocytoma

Syndrome (medulloblastoma), Turcot Syndrome (gliomas) and Li Fraumeni Syndrome (glioma). High-dose ionizing radiation to the head region administered in the past for benign conditions such as scalp tinea capitis fungal infection (ringworm), increases the risk of nerve sheath tumours, gliomas and meningiomas. There is much public concern that low frequency non-ionizing electromagnetic fields such as those emitted by 60 Hz power cables may increase the risk of brain tumours, but there is no consistent evidence to support this hypothesis. Similarly, despite scares, there is no evidence to support an association with wireless radiofrequency devices such as mobile phones.

Pathology

Primary nervous system tumours may be glial tumours, non-glial tumours or primary cerebral non-Hodgkin's lymphoma. Neuroectodermal tumours are classified on the basis of the predominant cell type and include all neoplasms with either central or peripheral nervous system-derived cell origins. After embryonic development ceases, neurons do not divide, but glial cells retain the ability to proliferate throughout life and thus most adult neurological tumours are derived from glial cells and termed gliomas. Seventy percent of primary brain tumours in adults are supratentorial, in contrast

Table 6.2 Brain tumours by age and site.

Adult	Child
Supratentorial	
Metastases	Craniopharyngioma
Glioma	Pinealoma
Meningioma	Optic glioma
Pituitary tumour	
Infratentorial	
Metastases	Medulloblastoma
Acoustic neuroma	Cerebellar astrocytoma
Cerebellar	Ependymoma of IVth ventricle
haemangioblastoma	

Table 6.3 Common presentation of brain tumours by site.

Tumour site	Common presentations
Frontal	Personality change
	Contralateral motor signs
	Dysphasia (dominant hemisphere)
Parietal	Contralateral sensory signs
	Visual field defects (optic radiation)
	Neglect
Occipital	Homonymous hemianopia
Temporal	Memory & behavioural disturbances
Posterior fossa	Raised intracranial pressure
	Ataxia & nystagmus
	Cranial nerve lesions

primary brain tumours in children are usually located below the tentorium (Table 6.2).

Gliomas account for 50% of brain tumours and are divided into grade I (noninfiltrating pilocytic astrocytoma), grade II (well to moderately differentiated astrocytoma), grade III (anaplastic astrocytoma) and grade IV (glioblastoma multiforme). The prognosis deteriorates with rising tumour grade. Other glial tumours include ependymomas, that arise from ependymal cells, usually lining the fourth ventricle, and oligodendrogliomas that arise from oligodendroglia. In the peripheral nervous system, neurofibromas and Schwannomas are the most frequent glial tumours. Medulloblastoma is a glial tumour of childhood usually arising in the cerebellum, which may be related to primitive neuroectodermal tumours elsewhere in the CNS. Non-glial brain tumours include pineal parenchymal tumours, extragonal germ cell tumours, craniopharyngiomas, meningiomas and choroid plexus tumours. Meningioma is the commonest nonglial tumour and constitutes 15% of brain tumours. The majority of spinal axis tumours in adults are extradural, metastatic carcinoma, lymphoma or sarcoma. Primary spinal cord tumours include extradural meningiomas (26%) and schwannomas (29%), intramedullary ependymomas (13%) and astrocytomas (13%).

Clinical presentation

Glial tumours

Glial tumours may produce both generalized and focal effects, and these will reflect the site of the tumour and the speed of its growth. General symptoms from the mass effect, increased intracranial pressure, oedema, midline shift and herniation syndromes are all seen, including progressive altered mental state and personality, headaches, seizures and papilloedema. Focal symptoms depend upon the location of the tumour (Table 6.3). Fewer than 10% of first fits are due to tumours and only 20% supratentorial tumours present with fits.

Meningioma

These tumours, which are more common in women, present as slowly growing masses producing headaches, seizures, motor and sensory symptoms and cranial neuropathies, depending on their site (Table 6.4). Meningiomas are one of the few tumours that produce characteristic changes on plain skull X-rays with bone erosion, calcification and hyperostosis.

Spinal axis tumours

For spinal axis tumours, the proportion of tumour sites is 50% thoracic, 30% lumbosacral and 20% cervical or foramen magnum. These tumours present with radicular symptoms, due to root infiltration, syringomyelic disturbance, due to central destruction by intramedullary tumours, or sensorimotor dysfunction, due to cord compression.

Table 6.4 Clinical features of meningiomas by site.

Site	Clinical features
Parasagital falx	Progressive spastic weakness
	Numbness of legs
Olfactory groove	Anosmia
	Visual loss
	Papilloedema (Foster Kennedy syndrome)
	Frontal lobe syndrome
Sella turcica	Visual field loss
Sphenoid wing	Cavernous sinus syndrome (medial)
	Exophthalmos & visual loss (middle)
	Temporal bone swelling & skull deformity (lateral)
Posterior fossa	Hydrocephalus (tentorium)
	Gait ataxia & cranial neuropathies V, VII, VIII, IX, X (cerebellopontine angle)
	Suboccipital pain, ipsilateral arm & leg weakness (foramen magnum)

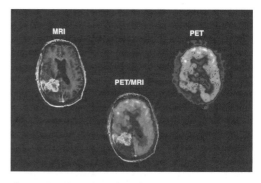

Figure 6.1 Co-registered and separate magnetic resonance (MR) and 18-fluorodeoxyglucose positron emission tomography (PET) scan images from a patient with a paraventricular high grade glioma demonstrating high glucose utilisation by the tumour. (See also colour plates between pages 154 and 155.)

Investigation/staging

Neuroradiology has developed into the most important investigation in patients with suspected brain tumours, following the introduction of computerized tomography (CT) in the mid 1970s by Geoffrey Hounsfield and magnetic resonance imaging in the 1980s. Newer techniques, such as positron emission tomography (PET), single photon emission computerized tomography (SPECT) and functional magnetic resonance imaging (MRI) have also found roles in the diagnosis and management of patients with brain tumours. MRI with gadolinium enhancement is the imaging technique of choice with advantages over CT particularly for posterior fossa tumours and non-enhancing low-grade gliomas. Positron emission tomography with [18]Fluorodeoxyglucose, which accumulates in metabolically active tissues, may help to differentiate tumour recurrence from radiation necrosis (Figure 6.1). Stereotactic biopsy is required to confirm the diagnosis, although occasionally tumours are diagnosed on clinical evidence, because biopsy might be hazardous, as in brain stem gliomas, for example.

Treatment

Some gliomas are curable by surgery alone and some by surgery and radiotherapy; the remainder require surgery, radiotherapy and chemotherapy, and these tumours are rarely curable. Surgical removal should be as complete as possible within the constraints of preserving neurological function. Radiation can increase the cure-rate or prolong disease-free survival in high-grade gliomas and may also be useful symptomatic therapy in patients with low-grade glioma, who relapse after initial therapy with surgery alone (Figure 6.2). Chemotherapy with nitrosurea or temozolomide may prolong disease-free survival in patients with oligodendrogliomas and high-grade gliomas, although its high toxicity may not always merit this approach.

Therapy of meningiomas is surgical resection, which may be repeated at relapse. Radiotherapy reduces relapse rates and should be considered for high-grade meningiomas or incompletely resected tumours. Relapse rates are 7% at five years if completely resected and 35–60% if incompletely resected.

Unlike with other brain tumours, surgical resection does not have a useful role in primary cerebral lymphomas. In immunocompetent patients, the combination of chemotherapy and radiotherapy produces median survivals of 40 months. In contrast, in the immunocompromized patients,

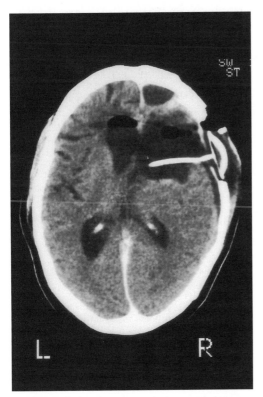

Figure 6.2 CT scan showing patient with an Omaya shunt (a closed CSF shunt joining the lateral ventricle with a reservoir below the scalp) in place that is leaking resulting in air seen in the right anterior brain and fluid accumulating around the shunt site. Omaya shunts may be placed to relieve non-communicating hydrocephalus caused by obstruction to CSF flow within the ventricular system, or to administer intrathecal chemotherapy.

especially those with HIV infection, the prognosis is far worse, with a median survival of under three months. Palliative radiotherapy or best supportive care are the appropriate treatment options here.

Complications of treatment

Early complications of cranial radiotherapy which occur in the first 3–4 months are due to reversible damage to myelin-producing oligodendrocytes. This recovers spontaneously after 3–6 months. It causes somnolence or exacerbation of existing

Table 6.5 Five-year survival rates of adult patients with brain tumours.

Tumour	5-year survival
Grade I glioma (cerebellar)	90–100%
Grade I glioma (other sites)	50–60%
Grade II (astrocytoma)	16–46%
Grade III (anaplastic astrocytoma)	10–30%
Grade IV (glioblastoma multiforme)	1–10%
Oligodendroglioma	50–80%
Meningioma	70–80%

symptoms in the brain and Lhermitte' sign (shooting numbness or paraesthesia precipitated by neck flexion) in the cord. Late complications include radiation necrosis, causing irreversible deficits due to vessel damage. This may mimic disease recurrence, is radiation dose related and occurs in up to 15% of patients, with the highest frequency in children also receiving chemotherapy. SPECT and PET scanning may differentiate radionecrosis and relapse.

Prognosis

The prognosis of glial tumours depends upon the histology, the grade and size of the tumour, on the age and performance status of patient and on the duration of the symptoms. The median survival for anaplastic astrocytoma is 18 months, for glioblastoma multiforme is 10–12 months. Meningiomas, if completely resected, are usually cured, and the median survival is over 10 years.

New therapies

The treatment of brain tumours may well improve in the next 5–10 years. The most important recent advance has been with the use of adjuvant chemotherapy. It is hoped that the application of temulozamide to radiotherapy for high-grade glioma will dramatically improve survival chances. Many high-grade gliomas express receptors for cErbB2/neu. Targetted antibody therapy delivered intravascularly may lead to further improvements in survival.

Chapter 7

Gastrointestinal cancers

Gastrointestinal malignancies have been attributed an important role in the history of Europe. Ferrante I of Arragon, the then King of Naples, was mummified and embalmed, following his death in 1494 and placed in a wooden sarcophagus at the Abbey of San Domenico Maggiore, Naples. In 1996, an autopsy was performed which revealed a large pelvic mass, and polymerase chain reaction (PCR) identified a mutation of the RAS oncogene, suggesting a colonic primary cancer. In 1821, Napoleon Bonaparte, the then Emperor of France, died in exile at Longwood House, St Helena. His health had been declining over a number of months with abdominal pain, weakness and vomiting, which he attributed to mistreatment by this English captors. An autopsy was performed following his death, which concluded that the cause of death was stomach cancer; and indeed, there was a strong history of stomach cancer in his family. Nineteen years later, Napoleon's grave was opened, and his body was returned to Paris to be finally interred in the magnificent tomb at the church of the Invalides, where it rests today. A popular alternative hypothesis proposed that his death was a consequence of chronic arsenic poisoning by his captors.

The gastrointestinal tract is one of the most frequent sites of cancer, and Table 7.1 shows the registration data for the most common tumours of the digestive system for South-East England in 2001 and the five-year survivals.

Gastrointestinal cancers include oesophageal cancer, gastric cancer, hepatobiliary cancer, pancreatic cancer and colorectal cancer, and these will be dealt with in more detail in the following five chapters.

Table 7.1 Gastrointestinal cancer registration data for South East England for 2001.

Tumour	Percentage of registrations		Rank of registration		Chance of cancer by age 75 years		Change in ASR 1987–1996		5-year survival
	Male	Female	Male	Female	Male	Female	Male	Female	
Oesophagus	3%	2%	6th	11th	1 in 103	1 in 278	+36%	+14%	8%
Gastric	4%	2%	5th	8th	1 in 79	1 in 263	−20%	−35%	13%
Pancreas	3%	3%	8th	6th	1 in 120	1 in 189	−2%	−8%	3%
Colorectal	12%	11%	3rd	2nd	1 in 30	1 in 44	+9%	−3%	41%

ASR = age standardized rate

Chapter 8

Oesophageal cancer

Epidemiology and pathogenesis

Cancer of the oesophagus is a relatively uncommon cancer in the UK, but the incidence is rising (Table 7.1). Worldwide, oesophageal cancer is the sixth most common cause of death from cancer. One-third are adenocarcinoma of the distal oesophagus and two third are squamous cell cancers, with 15% in the upper, 45% in the mid- and 40% in the lower portions of the oesophagus. Tobacco is a major risk factor for both histological types of oesophageal cancer, but the two types otherwise vary not only in their histology and anatomical distribution but also in their risk factors. Chronic irritation appears to be a major precipitant of squamous cell cancer and may be caused by alcohol, caustic injury, radiotherapy, or achalasia. The Plummer–Vinson Syndrome (or Patterson Kelly Brown Syndrome) of chronic iron-deficiency anaemia, dysphagia and oesophageal web is associated with squamous cell cancer of the oesophagus particularly in impoverished populations. Nonepidemolytic palmoplantar keratoderma, or tylosis, is an autosomal dominant abnormality, characterized by hyperkeratosis of the palms and soles. It carries a 95% risk of squamous cell cancer of the oesophagus by the age of 70. In contrast, the major precipitant of oesophageal adenocarcinoma appears to be gastro-oesophageal reflux. Related markers of reflux, such as hiatus hernia, obesity, frequent antacid and histamine H2 blockers, are also associated with an increased risk. Barrett's oesophagus develops in 5–8% of patients with reflux leading to metaplasia of the normal squamous epithelium of the lower oesophagus to columnar epithelium, which may be dysplastic. The annual rate of transformation to oesophageal adenocarcinoma is 0.5%. Over the last three decades, there has been a radical shift in the histology of oesophageal cancer in the USA, with a marked decline in squamous cell cancers and a rise in adenocarcinomas. This may reflect alterations in the number of smokers, and in obesity and nutrition of patients.

Prevention

Half of all incidences of oesophageal cancer could be prevented by giving up smoking, drinking less alcohol and improving diet, substituting fresh fruit and vegetables for poorly preserved, high salt foods contaminated with nitrosamine carcinogens or microbial toxins. Endoscopic surveillance is recommended every 2–5 years for patients with Barrett's oesophagus but the evidence that screening is effective is absent. Low-grade dysplasia requires aggressive antireflux management, whilst multi-focal or high-grade dysplasia should be treated by surgical resection.

Clinical presentation

Patients present with dysphagia or odynophagia,

Table 8.1 Five-year survival rates of patients with oesophageal cancer, according to stage at presentation.

Stage	Tumour	Node	Metastasis	5-year survival
0	Tis	N0	M0	>95%
I	T1	N0	M0	50–80%
IIA	T2–3	N0	M0	30–40%
IIB	T1–2	N1	M0	10–30%
III	T3–4	N0–1	M0	10–15%
IV	Any T	Any N	M1	<2%

Tis = carcinoma in situ, T1 = invasion of lamina propria, T2 = invasion of muscularis propria, T3 = invasion of adventitia, T4 = invasion of adjacent structures.

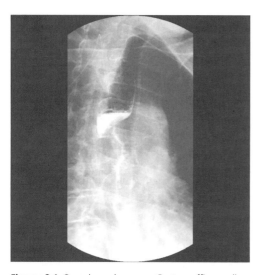

Figure 8.1 Oesophageal cancer. Gastrograffin swallow image showing a long tight stricture of the distal 1/3 of the oesophagus with shouldering that encroaches on the gastrooesophageal junction. This malignant stricture was due to adenocarcinoma of the oesophagus.

weight loss and, less frequently, with haematemesis. At the time of diagnosis, more than half of the patients will have locally advanced, unresectable disease or metastases present. Left supraclavicular lymphadenopathy (Virchow's node), hepatomegally and pleural effusion are common features of metastatic dissemination. The diagnosis is usually confirmed by upper GI endoscopy and barium studies (Figure 8.1).

Treatment

Only 40% of patients will have localized disease at presentation and are candidates for oesophagectomy with or without post-operative adjuvant chemoradiation. Surgery has a 5–20% mortality rate and may be complicated early by anastomotic leaks, and later by strictures, reflux and motility disorders. At diagnosis, 25% of patients will have local extension and are treated with palliative radiotherapy, which may cause oesophageal perforation and haemorrhage, pneumonitis and pulmonary fibrosis, as well as transverse myelitis. The remaining 35% of patients will have metastases at presentation and are usually treated symptomatically. Although cancer of the oesophagus is sensitive to chemotherapy, the duration of response is typically short and may be measured in weeks. Cisplatin-based combination regimens have higher response rates, but this may be offset by their greater toxicity. Adjuvant chemoradiotherapy, either prior to surgery (neoadjuvant), or following resection, has yet to be proven as being beneficial. Over the last 30 years, there has been a large number of trials that investigated the benefit of chemotherapy given in the adjuvant setting for carcinoma which had arisen at the junction of the oesophagus and stomach. Until a short time ago, no benefit had been shown, but recent trials have led to the consensus that chemotherapy is probably of benefit in the adjuvant setting, though this benefit is small.

Prognosis

The five-year survival of patients with oesophageal cancer according to stage at presentation is detailed in Table 8.1.

New therapies

As we write, sadly, there are no new therapies that these authors know of for oesophageal cancer.

Chapter 9

Gastric cancer

Epidemiology and pathogenesis

Gastric cancer is the sixth most common malignancy in the UK and constitutes approximately 5% of all cancers. The male to female ratio is 1.5 to 1. Currently nearly 6500 men and 3500 women are affected by the condition. There are 3500 male deaths and 2100 female deaths per year. The average of presentation is 65. Surprisingly, gastric cancer is the second most common cause of cancer-deaths worldwide. There are extreme geographical variations, with the incidence being five times higher in Japan than in the US.

The incidence of gastric cancer has fallen in the developed world over the last few decades. This is particularly the case for distal tumours of the stomach. It had been thought that one of the reasons for the decrease in the West is better food preservation. The reducing agents used to preserve food are thought to reduce the availability of free radicals within the stomach, a major cause of carcinogenesis, but this has not been proven in prospective studies. There is contradictory evidence for a protective benefit from fruit and vegetable intake, and also from the use of non-steroidal anti-inflammatory drugs.

Gastric cancer is more common in people with blood-group A, but the reason for this is not clear. Infection by *Helicobacter pylori* has been used to explain the aetiology of cancers developing in patients with atrophic gastritis. *Helicobacter*-infection is more common in patients with gastric cancer than in 'controls', in particularly in younger patients. Studies of the molecular biology of gastric cancer have not been very helpful in identifying putative tumour suppressor genes associated with this condition.

Presentation

Patients with gastric cancer generally present to their general practitioner with symptoms of abdominal pain. Classically, the pain is epigastric and worse with meals. The differential diagnosis includes benign peptic ulceration. The routine prescription of protein-pump inhibitors, without investigation by endoscopy, may lead to late diagnosis and the presence of advanced disease at diagnosis. Because the symptoms of gastric cancer are very similar to those of peptic ulceration, and because peptic ulceration is very common and not necessarily routinely investigated, early diagnosis of gastric cancer in the West presents a difficult problem. Walk-in endoscopy clinics, however, are becoming much more widely available in the UK, and it is hoped that they will impact upon survival figures for gastric cancer.

Outpatient diagnosis

After initial assessment, which should include a full blood count, liver function tests and chest X-ray, more specialized investigations should proceed. These should include endosocopy with biopsy, ultrasonography and CT-imaging of the abdomen and chest. There have been advances in endoscopic ultrasound that have allowed improvements in local staging of gastric tumours. These improvements are such, that mucosal invasion can be distinguished from submucosal invasion. Twenty years ago, the vast majority of patients with gastric cancer presented with inoperable disease. Currently, approximately 50% of tumours are operable at the time of presentation.

Surgery

The only significant chance for a cure rests with surgery. Laparoscopic staging is carried out prior to definitive laparotomy. There is considerable debate concerning the operative procedures of first choice. Older retrospective data suggested that survival was improved with total gastrectomy compared with subtotal gastrectomy. Randomized trials, however, have since shown equivalent survival, with lesser complications for subtotal gastrectomy for carcinoma of the antrum, compared with total gastrectomy. One recent randomized study showed equal five-year survival of patients with either subtotal or total gastrectomy with lymphadenectomy. Surgical developments have been led by the Japanese, who have to deal with the highest incidence of carcinoma of the stomach in the world. The current recommendation by the Japanese Society for Research in Gastric Cancer is for extensive lymphadenectomy, which involves the removal of the lymphatic chains along the coeliac axis, and hepatic and splenic arteries. This sort of dissection also has the advantage of allowing more accurate staging for gastric cancer and has been associated with improved survival. For early-stage disease, advances in endoscopic techniques have led to curative mucosal resection techniques equivalent to subtotal gastrectomy, with clear evidence of lesser morbidity. Tumours of the gastro-oesophageal junction are increasing in the West and are treated surgically by subtotal resection of the oesophagus, along with the cardia and gastric fundus.

Staging and pathology

The TNM staging system is widely used for staging gastric cancer, with the 'p'-prefix denoting pathological confirmation of the staging. Ninety-five percent of all gastric tumours are adenocarcinomas. The remainder are squamous cell cancers and lymphomas. Small cell cancers are reported only rarely.

Adjuvant treatment

In 30 years of adjuvant therapy investigation, no significant role for adjuvant radiation or chemotherapy had been found. Despite this, active trial work continued with the hope of improving prognosis and recent trials have shown a benefit to adjuvant treatment. These benefits continue to be debated.

Treatment of metastatic or locally inoperable gastric cancer

Patients with inoperable local disease or metastases may be treated with chemotherapy. Over the years, many treatment programmes have been introduced, and the majority have contained 5-Fluorouracil. There is considerable doubt as to whether or not combination therapy offers any improvement in response rates and the chance for survival, compared with single-agent 5-Fluorouracil treatment. In the 1970s, there was considerable enthusiasm for the introduction of combination therapy containing 5-Fluorouracil, Adriamycin (doxorubicin) and Mitomycin C. This treatment schedule, known as the 'FAM regime', was initially reported as leading to responses in 40% of patients, with a median duration of response of approximately nine months. Randomized trials have since shown that the same order of response can be obtained with single-agent 5-Fluorouracil, with the same expectations of survival. In recent times, there has been considerable support for combination chemotherapy using continuous infusion 5-Fluorouracil, Epirubicin and Cisplatin. Initially, a 70% response rate was reported, and the median survival of patients responding was seven months. The programme is well tolerated and offers patients reasonable quality of life.

Survival

In the West, more than 50% of patients present with advanced tumours. As a result, median survival rates for gastric cancer are around 30% at five years. The median survival of patients with advanced local disease or metastatic tumour is approximately six months.

Improving survival in gastric cancer

Patients with early gastric cancer have very good chances of survival, which can be in excess of 90%. For early-stage disease, surgery can be minimal, with advances in endoscopy, endoscopic ultrasonography and endoscopic surgery providing great improvements in limiting the morbidity of interventional therapies. Significant improvements have been seen in Japan as a result of the wide-scale implementation of screening endoscopy. In Japan, up to 40% of patients are found to have early-stage tumours, which contrasts with the situation in the West. One can only conclude that more widespread availability of endoscopic screening and of earlier referral by GPs remains the only significant chance for improved survival. The development of effective therapies based upon any understanding of the biological basis of this tumour group seems to be an unlikely possibility at this point.

Chapter 10

Hepatobiliary cancer

Epidemiology and pathogenesis

Hepatobiliary cancer is one of the most common malignant tumours in the world. The highest incidences are seen in South East Asia. In the United Kingdom hepatobiliary cancer is relatively uncommon. There are approximately 2500 men and women registered with the condition each year, and sadly 2200 deaths. Generally, there are more women than men affected by these tumours. Liver cancer is divided into four main groups of tumour: hepatocellular cancer, which accounts for 40% of this group; biliary tree cancers, also known as cholangiocarcinomas, which account for over 50%; and the rare hepatoblastomas and angiosarcomas which account for 1–2% of all liver cancers.

Hepatocellular cancer is associated with chronic hepatitis B-infection. This is prevalent in up to 15% of males in certain populations. The lifetime risk of developing a tumour is 40% in this group of men. There are significant concerns with regard to the increasing infection rates with hepatitis C in Europe. It is thought that the risk of developing hepatobiliary cancer in the presence of chronic hepatitis C infection is even greater than that associated with hepatitis B infection. Hepatocellular cancers are also associated with alcoholism, other hepatitides causing cirrhosis, and with exposure to *Aspergillus fumigatus*.

There is great interest in the role of the hepatitis-causing viruses in the aetiology of hepatocellular cancer, and this is for two reasons. Firstly, a vaccination program, if introduced widely, might lead to spectacular decreases in the incidence of the malignancy. Secondly, an understanding of the molecular mechanisms for the cause of this cancer may add significantly to our understanding of viral carcinogenesis. The hepatitis B-genome is incorporated at random into the human genome, and the effects of this integration are not clearly known. It is observed that a double mutation of the genome is a constant feature in 75% of all tumours, involving the 1762(T)/1764(A) of the hepatitis B viral genome. This is also detectable in plasma.

The aetiology of hepatoblastoma is not known. Hepatic angiosarcoma are known to be associated with exposure to polyvinyl choride monomer. The mechanism for this is not clear, and the development of this tumour does not always occur in those men and women, who have the heaviest exposure to PVC, as for example in those workers involved in autoclave cleaning in chemical works. When workers exposed to PVC are examined for their lifetime risk of developing angiosarcoma, this is clearly four times higher than in the general population. Where there is a coincident hepatitis B-positive serology, the risk increases 25-fold compared with the general population. PVC-exposure is also associated with the development of brain and lung tumours.

Tumours of the biliary tree, which are divided into intra- and extra-hepatic and gall-bladder

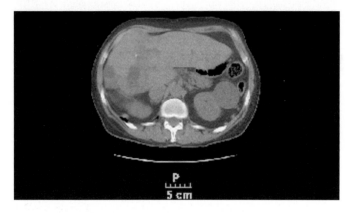

Figure 10.1 CT scan demonstrating intrahepatic dilated bile ducts that were due to cholangiocarcinoma. There is also a low attenuation metastasis in segment 7 of the liver and an incidental (benign) renal cyst.

cancers, are seen at increased frequency in patients with ulcerative colitis and primary sclerosing cholangitis. (Figure 10.1) In South-East Asia, where these tumours are common, they are seen in association with biliary infestion with liver flukes (*Clonorchis sinensis* and *Opisthorchis viverrini*).

Presentation

Patients with hepatobiliary cancer generally present with advanced disease. Typical presentations are with jaundice, liver pain and weight loss. A patient with a suspected diagnosis of hepatobiliary cancer should be referred to the appropriate surgical unit for investigation. The management of these conditions is very complex and should only be in centres of excellence with highly specialized surgical units, who achieve significantly better results.

Standard investigations for patients with hepatocellular cancer should include blood counts, liver-function tests, renal-function tests, chest X-rays, ultrasound assessment and CT imaging. Ultrasonography has developed considerably over the last decade, and these technical improvements have been matched by improved standards in endoscopic assessment of the patient. Hepatobiliary cancers are associated with raised serum levels of alpha fetoprotein, which is characteristically raised to many thousands of ng/mL. In patients with cirrhosis, who may have alpha fetoprotein levels raised to a few hundreds of ng/mL, increas-

ing levels are clues to the development of hepatobiliary cancer. CEA and CA199 are useful markers in the monitoring of hepatobiliary tumours.

Characteristically, patients with these tumours will commonly present with jaundice, and this presentation requires external stenting to stabilize the patient, enable investigations to take place and surgery to be considered. After staging, histological confirmation of the presence of a tumour should be obtained by percutaneous ERCP with needle aspiration or brush cytology or by liver biopsy.

Staging and grading

Hepatobiliary tumours are described as well, moderately or poorly differentiated. Staging for hepatic and billiary tract tumours is according to the TNM classification.

Treatment

Liver resection is the only treatment that offers a chance for cure for liver cancer. Surgery is limited by the degree of spread of the tumour and the presence or absence of background cirrhosis. The aim of surgery generally is to remove the lobe of the liver containing the tumour. It may be possible for patients with hepatobiliary cancer to be treated by liver transplantation and, if this is the case, the chance of survival increases dramatically. It is estimated that just 10% of patients with liver cancers have operable tumours. When curative surgery is

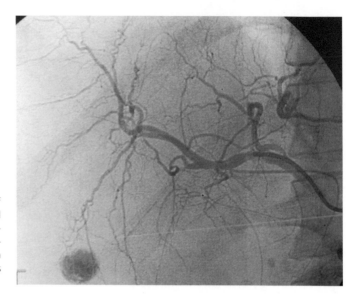

Figure 10.2 Selective angiography of right hepatic artery showing small area of hypervascularity due to hepatocellular carcinoma. As this was inoperable (there were 4 other lesions in different segments of the liver), it was treated by chemoembolisation.

not be possible, hepatic embolization, sclerotherapy and chemotherapy may be appropriate (Figure 10.2). Chemotherapy with boxorubicin or Mitoxantrone based regimens has, up to now, been the treatment of choice for this group of patients with inoperable disease. Tumours of the biliary tree are chemosensitive and very, very rarely operable. Similar treatment programmes are used in this condition.

Prognosis

Five-year survival for patients with operable liver cancer is in the order of 33% when management involves partial liver resection. The five-year survival of patients transplanted is 80%. The median survival of patients who are not treated with curative intent is 6–7 months. The median survival of patients in the Far East is much poorer, and the vast majority die within 2–3 months of diagnosis (Table 10.1).

New treatments for hepatobiliary cancer

We have great hope that mortality from liver tumours will decrease significantly in the next few

Table 10.1 Five-year survival rates of patients with hepatic and biliary tract cancers.

Tumour	5-year survival
Hepatocellular cancer	5%
Gall bladder cancer	5%
Cholangiocarcinoma	5%
Periampullary cholangiocarcinoma	50%

years. The reason for this is the development of effective campaigns for vaccination against hepatitis B. There is considerable concern in Europe that this will lead to increasing deaths from this condition. Unlike the hepatitis B-virus, however, the incorporation of the hepatitis C-virus genome into the host cell genome does not seem to be a random event. It has been localized to chromosome 17, where ubiquitination is inhibited, and it is hoped that an understanding of the mechanisms involving tumour development in hepatitis C infection will become elucidated. Chemotherapy has developed for tumours of both the liver and the biliary system, with new agents such as Gemcitabine producing significant responses in experimental trials.

Chapter 11

Pancreatic cancer

Epidemiology and pathogenesis

Carcinoma of the pancreas has increased in incidence over the last decade and is now the fifth most frequent cause of cancer deaths. There is an equal incidence between the sexes, and annually in the UK, there are about 6000 deaths. It is very sad to note, that registration figures, virtually equal mortality rates. There is an increased risk of developing pancreatic cancer with age, and it has been suggested that excess coffee consumption predisposes to the development of cancer of the pancreas. Smoking is also associated with an increased risk of this disease of between two- and five-fold. Pancreatic adenocarcinoma expresses a wide variety of hormone receptors, and these include receptors for somatostatin, gonadotrophin-releasing hormone, steroid hormones, insulin-like growth factors and vascular endothelial growth factors. It should be emphasized that these receptors are present in carcinomas, and that they are not present in the unusual secretory pancreatic tumours, such as gastrinomas, insulinomas or pancreatic carcinoids.

Presentation

Patients with carcinoma of the pancreas present with many different symptoms. These include abdominal and back pain, weight loss, anorexia and fatigue. In many patients the disease is asymp-

tomatic, until they present with obstructive jaundice. Other, less common presentations include superficial venous thrombosis and diabetes. Because of the position of the tumour, late presentation is very common. The patient with a suspected diagnosis of pancreatic cancer should be referred by his or her GP to a general surgeon or a gastroenterologist and be seen in outpatients within two weeks of receipt of the GP's letter of referral. The clinician should organize a number of tests, which include full blood count, renal and liver function tests, the measurement of serum levels of the tumour marker CA199, a chest X-ray and a CT scan of the abdomen. Abdominal ultrasonography is also helpful.

Investigation of the patient with pancreatic cancer is aimed at establishing the prognosis and defining operability. After the initial tests have been carried out, the patient should proceed to endoscopic retrograde cholangio-pancreatography (ERCP). At ERCP, cytology specimens may be obtained from brushings, suction of the pancreatic duct or biopsy. A failure to obtain a diagnosis by endoscopy should be followed by further investigation. Fine needle aspiration cytology under CT scan is usually successful at obtaining a tissue diagnosis.

Staging and grading

A commonly used staging system for pancreatic cancer is that of the Cancer Task Force and is as follows:

Stage I   No direct extension and no regional lymph node-involvement
Stage II   Direct extension into adjacent tissue. No lymph node-involvement
Stage III Regional lymph node-involvement with or without direct tumour extension
Stage IV Distant metastases
Ninety percent of pancreatic tumours are adeno-carcinomas of ductal origin, and approximately 10% are acinar. Tumours are graded as either well-, moderately, or poorly differentiated, or of endocrine origin.

Treatment

There is considerable nihilism attached, quite reasonably, to the treatment of a patient with pancreatic cancer. The initial management consists of relieving symptoms of pain and obstructive jaundice. For less than 20% of patients is there any hope for operability, as defined by imaging. With these, no attempt is made to proceed to surgery until the jaundice has completely resolved. Jaundice is dealt with by relief of biliary obstruction, either by endoscopic stenting or by percutaneous transhepatic stenting of the biliary system. Pain may be relieved by the use of opiates or may resolve with relief of biliary obstruction. At laparotomy, just 30% of those 20% of patients with radiologically operable disease turns out to have surgically operable tumours.

Pancreatic surgery requires a considerable degree of specialization and should not be carried out outside of the setting of a specialist treatment centre. The reason for this is simple: specialist centres achieve better survival rates and lower morbidity and mortality rates. The operation of choice is the Whipple's procedure, and this involves resection of the pancreas, distal stomach and upper duodenum. There are modifications of this procedure, such as the pylorus conserving pancreatico-duodenectomy, that are associated with less postoperative morbidity and equivalent efficacy.

Thirty years ago, surgery for pancreatic cancer was associated with a very high morbidity of approximately 25%. This has fallen in specialist centres to 5%, with the expectation that 20% of pa-

tients with operable disease will survive five years. Ampullary carcinomas of the pancreas generally present with early-stage disease because of their anatomical position. These tumours are associated with better prognoses than cancers of the rest of the pancreas. There is no role whatsoever for adjuvant chemotherapy or radiotherapy.

The treatment of inoperable disease

Patients with inoperable pancreatic cancer have a poor prognosis and the treatment of this condition is palliative. The median survival is 4–6 months. Active treatment with chemotherapy may be advised. The most successful chemotherapy programmes have response rates of up to 40%, but the median duration of survival of these responding patients is just one month more than might be expected without active treatment. Because pancreatic cancer is relatively common, a number of chemotherapy agents have been tried for this condition. The consensus view is that combination therapy using the more active agents, such as doxorubicin and Taxanes, given alone or in combination, is relatively ineffective. The more drugs are combined, the more toxicity, without an improvement in survival. The relatively recent application of Gemcitabine to this tumour has led to responses. The current consensus view is that single-agent Gemcitabine probably offers as good an opportunity for disease palliation as does any combination regimen, although in practice it is often combined with Cisplatin. Gemcitabine is easy to administer and has little toxicity. Quality of life issues are paramount in this condition because of the poor prognosis for inoperable disease.

An alternative approach to the management of pancreatic cancer is to treat symptoms. This is managed by stenting to relieve jaundice and by coeliac axis block. This procedure blocks the pain fibres originating from the pancreas and ensures good quality of life. The technique requires skill and is relatively well tolerated.

Prognosis

The outlook for patients with operable pancreatic

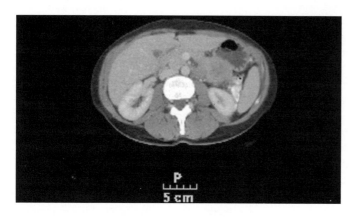

Figure 11.1 This CT scan shows a mass in the tail and body of the pancreas which has a low attenuation centre suggesting central necrosis of an adenocarcinoma of the pancreas.

Table 11.1 Clinical manifestations of secretory endocrine tumours.

Tumour	Major feature	Minor feature	Common sites	Malignant	MEN associated
Insulinoma	Neuroglycopenia (confusion, fits)	Permanent neurological deficits	Pancreas (β cells)	10%	10%
Gastrinoma (Zollinger–Elison syndrome)	Peptic ulceration	Diarrhoea, Weight loss, Malabsorption, Dumping	Pancreas Duodenum	40–60%	25%
VIPoma (Werner–Morrison syndrome)	Watery diarrhoea, Hypokalaemia Achlorhydria	Hypercalcaemia, Hyperglycaemia Hypomagnesaemia	Pancreas, Neuroblastoma SCLC, Phaeochromocytoma	40%	<5%
Glucagonoma	Migratory necrolyic erythema Mild diabetes mellitus Muscle wasting, anaemia	Diarrhoea, Thromboembolism Stomatitis, Hypoaminoacidaemia Encephalitis	Pancreas (α cells)	60%	<5%
Somatostatinoma	Diabetes mellitus, Cholelithiasis Steatorrhoea, Malabsorption	Anaemia, Diarrhoea Weight loss, Hypoglycaemia	Pancreas (β cells)	66%	Case reports only

SCLC = small cell lung cancer

cancer is unfortunately not particularly good, with a 20% chance of five-year survival. The outlook for those patients with locally advanced or metastastic disease is very poor, with a median survival of 3–4 months. Chemotherapy improves survival by a median of two weeks, and it is for this reason that there is such an emphasis upon quality of life in pancreatic cancer, rather than on the prospects for cure.

New treatments for pancreatic cancer

There has been considerable interest in the use of agents that block angiogenesis in malignancy. Pancreatic cancer has been studied in this context. In one laboratory experiment, replication-deficient retroviruses encoding truncated VEGF receptors

were used to block VEGF signalling in three pancreatic cell-lines that express VEGF mRNA. Interference with the ligand receptor system decreased growth. Transfer of suicide genes to tumour cells by retroviral vectors has also been applied in pancreatic cancer cell-lines. The vector that was used carried the herpes simplex virus thymidine kinase gene, and treatment with Ganciclovir inhibited gene-expression and cell-growth. The observation of the presence of peptide and steroid receptors in pancreatic cancer has led to treatment of these tumours with Octreotide, LHRH agonists, androgens and Tamoxifen. Although work in animal models has been promising, work in humans with cancer has unfortunately produced no significant benefit.

Pancreatic endocrine tumours

This is a very interesting group of tumours, interesting not only because of their biology, but also because patients with these tumours are expected to do well. Pancreatic endocrine tumours include carcinoids, insulinomas, glucagonomoas, gastrinomas and Vipomas. All except carcinoids, which may be non-secretory, synthesize hormones. The bizarre constellation of symptoms produced by carcinoids are well known even to medical students, as are the GI symptoms resulting from Vipomas, the hypo- and hyperglycaemia from insulinomas and glucagonoma. And I do hope that every medical student reading this book will be able to recount the ten skin conditions associated with carcinoid tumours, as well as describe the reasons for the effects of this tumour on the heart (Table 11.1).

What may not be well-known are the symptoms occasionally associated with gastrinoma, such as diarrhoea. These endocrine malignancies are associated with enormously long natural histories, which may date back over decades. The major treatment options include Octreotide to decrease hormonal secretion, and chemo-embolization to reduce the symptoms that result from tumour bulk. Octreotide has a median period of effect of one year in carcinoids. It leads to no clinical evidence of disease regression. Interferon may also lead to a reduction in secretory symptoms of carcinoid tumours. Embolization is a significant enterprise and is associated in even the best centres with mortality rates of 3–5%. It should therefore be considered with great care before it is undertaken.

Chapter 12

Colorectal cancer

Epidemiology and pathogenesis

Colorectal cancer is a major cause of morbidity in the West. Each year in England and Wales, there are approximately 29 000 people affected by the condition and approximately 23 000 deaths. In the 1960s and 1970s, there was increasing recognition of the possibility of a dietary basis to colorectal cancer. The disease was thought to be uncommon in the 'developing world', where a diet high in vegetable fibre was thought to be protective. High-fibre diet increases the transit time of the stool and decreases the colorectal epithelial exposure to carcinogens within the stool. This hypothesis has now largely been abandoned, and the idea that high-fibre diets are protective has been largely disproved.

Aspirin has been observed to have a protective effect against colorectal cancer, and epidemiological studies of Aspirin use have shown a consistent reduction of up to 50% in the risk of colorectal cancers. This decrease in risk is thought to be due to the inhibitory effect of Aspirin on cyclooxygenase-2, which is an enzyme found in high concentrations in colorectal tissue. In randomized studies, Aspirin has been shown to reduce the incidence of adenomatous polyps in patients screened after the excision of a primary colorectal tumour. There has, however, only been one single randomized trial of Aspirin prophylaxis, which has shown no evidence for a reduction in colorectal cancer incidence. Patients with ulcerative colitis are at risk from developing colonic tumours, and this risk rises to nearly 40% after 20-years follow-up.

There is a family history of colorectal cancer in up to 20% of patients with colorectal cancer. There are two significant familial causes for colorectal cancer: familial adenomatous polyposis (FAP) and hereditary non polyposis colorectal cancer (HNPCC). FAP and HNPCC constitute approximately 2% of all hereditary colorectal malignancy. FAP is an autosomal dominant condition, and the gene for FAP was mapped to chromosome 5q in 1987 and cloned in 1991. HNPPC is mainly sited in the right side of the colon and is associated with endometrial carcinoma, and also gastric, renal, ureteric and central nervous system malignancies. In this condition, the genetic abnormalities include microsatellite instability and mutated mismatch-repair genes. In the vast majority of non-inherited colorectal malignancy, the molecular changes consist of a cascade of events that include mutations in p53, deletion of the colorectal gene (DCC), together with mutations in K-ras and APC.

The numbers of patients with colonic cancers have increased by about 30% over the last 30 years, and the numbers of patients with rectal tumours rose by about 5% over the same period.

Presentation

Patients with colorectal tumours present to their general practitioners with a history of altered

bowel habit and rectal bleeding. This may also be accompanied by weight loss and abdominal pains. These symptoms are suggestive of malignancy, and accordingly an urgent referral should be made to a specialist bowel surgeon. The patient should ideally be seen within two weeks of receipt of the general practitioner's referral letter.

Outpatient diagnosis

In outpatients, the surgeon should take a full history from the patient and examine him or her. This should include a rectal examination, which may show the patient to have melaena. Proctoscopy and sigmoidoscopy should be performed in the outpatient setting. Blood tests should be organized, which should include a full blood count, renal function and liver function tests. A chest X-ray should be carried out and a barium enema or colonoscopy arranged as an outpatient procedure. The barium enema may show narrowing of the colon. In malignancy, this narrowing is typical and has the appearance of an apple core (Figure 12.1). Endoscopy may show a stenosing lesion or a polyp. Biopsies should be taken of the suspicious area.

Treatment

The suspicion of malignancy having been raised, the patient should be 'worked up' for surgery. As part of this work up, an assessment should be made of operability by CT scanning. The CT scan will show whether or not there are enlarged lymph-nodes within the abdomen and will define the possibility of further spread involving the liver. If there is no gross evidence of dissemination of cancer, the patient should be admitted to hospital for colectomy or an abdominoperitoneal resection. Removal of the primary is still considered in the presence of metastatic disease, to reduce the risk of perforation or obstruction.

The surgical plan depends upon the experience and practice of the clinician. There have been considerable developments in the area of laparoscopic surgery. If the patient is therefore considered to be an appropriate candidate, a laparoscopic colectomy might be performed. The results of rectal surgery are critically surgeon-dependent, and much better results are obtained in centres where the surgeon specializes in this procedure.

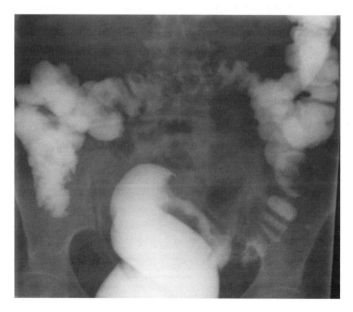

Figure 12.1 Barium enema investigation showing irregular stricture of the sigmoid colon with shouldering giving an apple core appearance typical of sigmoid colon cancer.

Surgery for colonic cancer

At operation, a midline incision should be performed and the abdominal contents inspected. The tumour should be mobilized and removed together with a good margin of normal tissue. The tumour should be inspected and frozen sections performed, to ensure that the resection edges of the apparently normal gut contain no tumour. An end to end-anastomosis is then made. If the patient is found to have 3–5 liver metastases at operation, these should be resected at an appropriate time, as successful resection is associated with a good prognosis and the possibility of cure. If there are more metastases, no operative action should be taken. Extensive resection of the lymph nodes should be performed, providing histopathological information which affects the patient's management.

Surgery for rectal cancers

The surgery that is performed depends upon the site of the carcinoma and a pre-operative assessment of operability. Tumours of the upper and middle third of the rectum are treated by anterior resection. In this procedure, the rectum is mobilized from the sacral hollow, and the tumour is removed together with an adequate margin of normal tissue. This normal margin ranges between 2 and 5 centimetres. The mesorectum and lateral pararectal tissue should be removed. Lesions of the lower third of the rectum are treated by abdominoperineal resection, which requires a permanent colostomy. The rectum is mobilized, and the peritoneum at the base of the bladder or posterior vagina is incized. The lateral ligaments are divided and the anus excised. The quality of surgery in rectal cancer is critically important. Extensive lymphadenectomy is associated with significantly improved chances for survival.

Tumour grading and staging

The tumour should be examined histologically. It is described as being either well-, moderately or poorly differentiated. A Dukes' Stage is given, and this reflects the degree of invasion of the tumour. Dukes' Stage A is specified when a tumour is confined to mucosa. Dukes' Stage B is a tumour that perforates the serosa, and Dukes' Stage C is given when lymph nodes are affected. Tumours of the colon are, furthermore, divided according to their anatomical sub-sites. These are the appendix, caecum, ascending colon, hepatic flexure, transverse colon, splenic flexure, descending colon and sigmoid colon. Finally, the tumour can be staged according to the TNM clinical classification system (see Table 12.1)

Complications of surgery

A neurogenic bladder is very common after pelvic surgery but will usually recover within ten days. Ureteric tears or transections may complicate surgery, but only rarely so. Sexual dysfunction in males is inevitable, and the most common problems are retrograde ejaculation and erectile impotence. Change in sexual function in women has

Table 12.1 TNM staging of colorectal cancer.

T refers to the tumour	N refers to the regional lymph nodes	M refers to metastatic state
T0—No evidence of primary tumour	N0—No nodes	M0—No distant metastases
T1—Tumour invades submucosa	N1—Metastasis in 1–3 pericolic nodes	M1—distant metastases
T2—Tumour invades muscularis	N2—Metastasis in 4 or more pericolic nodes	
T3—Tumour invades through muscularis	N3—Metastasis in any lymph node	
T4—Tumour perforates the peritoneum		

not been assessed. Surgery is complicated by a mortality rate of 1–2%.

Adjuvant treatment

Colonic cancer

Following recovery from surgery, no additional treatment is recommended for patients with Dukes' A or B disease. Patients with Dukes' C tumours, however, should receive adjuvant chemotherapy. The reason for this is that there is a survival advantage in this group of patients. Treatment should be with a 5-Fluorouracil-containing programme. There is considerable contention as to which is the optimal treatment schedule. In the late 1980s and early 1990s, the use of Levamisole was prevalent, but treatment with this agent is no longer recommended. There is hope that the use of newer agents, such as capecitabine and irinotecan, may convey additional benefit to adjuvant treatment, as may rescheduling 5FU-containing programmes with the addition of folinic acid.

Rectal cancer

Patients with rectal cancer may receive pre-operative radiotherapy. This has been shown to limit pelvic recurrence. It is disputed whether adjuvant radiotherapy improves survival. Alternatively, after the patient has recovered from surgery, he or she may receive pelvic radiotherapy. This has been shown in randomized studies to decrease the risk of pelvic recurrence by 5–10%. Patients with more advanced tumours (T_3 and T_4) may be treated with adjuvant 5FU-based chemotherapy prior to surgery, in addition to radiotherapy. There is increased post-operative morbidity with chemotherapy given in conjunction with radiotherapy.

Management of metastatic disease

In the situation where there are limited metastases from colorectal cancer, consideration is given to the possibility of curative surgical treatment. If the patient is fit, and there are 3–5 hepatic metastases or less than three pulmonary metastases, resection may be considered to be appropriate. If surgery is successful, then the prognosis is relatively good, with survival chances ranging up to 40% at five years.

Generally, however, metastatic colorectal carcinoma has a poor prognosis, and the current recommendation for appropriate treatment is with 5-fluorouracil regimens and radiotherapy. There is debate as to whether or not the addition of folinic acid is of an advantage to the patient. The current

Table 12.2 Screening scheme for colorectal cancer.

Low Risk 1 relative >45 years or 2 relatives >70 years	Action Reassure: no colonoscopy	Age
Low–moderate Risk 2 first degree relatives, average age 60–70 years	Single colonoscopy	Aged 55 years
Moderate Risk 2 first degree relatives, average age 50–60 years 1 first degree relative <45 years average age 50–60 years	5-yearly colonoscopy	Aged 35–65 years or starting 5 years before age when youngest relative's tumour was diagnosed
Moderate–High Risk 2 first degree relatives, average age <50 years 3 close relatives (not AC*)	3–5-yearly colonoscopy .	Begin age 30–35. Refer Genetics
High Risk 3 close relatives AC +ve (HNPCC) (FAP)	2-yearly colonoscopy Annual sigmoidoscopy from teens	Refer Genetics. Age 25–65 Refer Genetics

*Amsterdam Criteria

consensus is that there is a benefit at least in terms of remission rates, although no consensus has been reached regarding survival. The treatment regimen of first choice is called the 'De Gramont Regimen' and includes fortnightly 5-Flourouracil and folinic acid given for six months. New drugs have become available for the treatment of colorectal cancer, and there has been hope in the use of Irinotecan, a topoisomerase I-inhibitor. This agent, given in combination with 5-FU, is reasonably well-tolerated and increases response-rate, time to progression and survival. It is estimated that the development of new agents and their application has improved median survival from 9 to 18 months.

Screening

It is estimated that there may be a genetic predisposition to colorectal cancer in more than 20% of patients with these tumours. In the vast majority of colorectal cases there is, however, at present no direct evidence of there being a genetic risk. Patients with a risk of developing colorectal tumours can be stratified as having low, low–moderate, moderate, moderate–high or high risk of developing malignancy. The criteria for proceeding to screening for these patients are defined as in Table 12.2.

New therapies

This is one group of tumours where we are delighted to report that a host of golden apportunties for our patients have arisen. The development of drugs targetting angiogenesis such as bevacuvimab and the epidermal growth factor receptors such as cetuximab have led to real improvements is survival. Their prescription is a bankrupting issue for the NHS in the UK.

Chapter 13

Genitourinary cancers

The treatment of testicular cancer is one of the few solid cancers in adults that may be successfully cured even in the presence of metastases. This has only been achievable in the last 40 years, since the introduction of cisplatin chemotherapy. Cisplatin was discovered serendipitously by Barnett Rosenberg, a physicist at Michigan State University, in 1965. He studied the effects of electric currents on *E. coli* using platinum electrodes in a water bath and found that they stopped dividing but not growing, leading to bacteria up to 300 times longer than normal. This was found to be due to cisplatin, a product from the platinum electrodes, which was interfering with DNA replication. Following this, Professor Sir Alexander Haddow, the then head of the Chester Beatty Institute in London, showed that cisplatin was active against melanoma in mice, and clinical trials with human patients began in 1972.

The genitourinary tract is one of the most frequent sites of cancer in men and includes prostate cancer, which has emerged as the most common tumour in men (excluding non-melanomatous skin cancers). Table 13.1 shows the registration data for these tumours for South-East England in 2001 and the five-year survivals.

Cancer of the genitourinary tract includes cancers of the kidneys, bladder, prostate and testes, which are discussed in more detail in the next four chapters.

Table 13.1 Genitourinary cancer registration data for South East England from Thames for 2001.

Tumour	Percentage of registrations		Rank of registrations		Chance of cancer by age 75 years		Change in ASR 1987–1996	5-year survival
	Male	Female	Male	Female	Male	Female		
Prostate	22%	—	1st	—	1 in 24	—·	+48%	63%
Testis	2%	—	17th	—	1 in 286	—	+5%	96%
Kidney	2%	1%	11th	17th	1 in 139	1 in 303	+13%	37%
Bladder	5%	2%	4th	9th	1 in 68	1 in 238	−27%	53%

ASR = age standardized rate

Chapter 14

Kidney cancer

Epidemiology and pathogenesis

Renal carcinoma is not a particularly common cancer and causes approximately 2% of deaths from malignancy in the UK. There are about 4200 people who develop renal cancers in the UK per year and approximately 2300 deaths. Renal cancers may arise from the kidney nephrons or from the collecting systems. The histology is different for these two tumours and is described respectively as 'renal cell' for tumours arising from the nephrons and 'transitional cell' for tumours arising from the transitional cell epithelium of the collecting system. There is evidence for a genetic predisposition to this disease in a small percentage of patients. Renal cell cancer has an increased incidence in patients with Von Hippel-Lindau disease and tuberous sclerosis. Transitional cell tumours may be caused by tobacco.

There has been increasing interest in the molecular genetics of renal cell cancer. This is concentrated around the importance of the loss of heterozygosity at chromosome 3p and the inactivation of the Von Hippel-Lindau gene. Both are associated with the development of renal cell cancers. In one recent study there was loss of heterozygosity around chromosome 3p in 96% of conventional histology renal cell cancers, although in tumours with less common pathologies, such as the papillary and chromophobe variants, these changes are far less frequent. It is therefore likely that the loss of heterozygosity represents the loss of a specific tumour suppressor-gene for renal cell-cancer, and this fits in with conventional models for the development of malignancy. There are chromosomal changes in non-clear-cell tumours too. The PTEN/MMAC1 tumour suppressor-gene is lost in up to 90% of patients with chromophobe renal cell carcinoma, and so the molecular pathology of renal cell cancer defines a specific phenotype. Other changes have also been noted, involving chromosome 16q and 14q. A step-wise progression of molecular changes similar to those which are well-described in colorectal tumours seems to characterize renal cell cancer. These molecular changes are completely different from those seen in papillary tumours which are characterized by loss of the Y chromosome and multiple trisomy. In clear-cell renal cancer, Bp loss leads to inactivation of hypoxia-inducible factors. This in turn leads to activation of VEGFR and EGFR, with resultant new vessel formation and tumour development.

Presentation

Patients with renal cancers commonly present with pain in the loins, or blood in the urine. Other symptoms include joint pains, symptoms due to anaemia, a varicocele, generalized symptoms of malignancy, such as weight loss and cachexia, and symptoms due to a spread of the disease to metastatic sites such as brain, lung or bone. If a diagnosis of

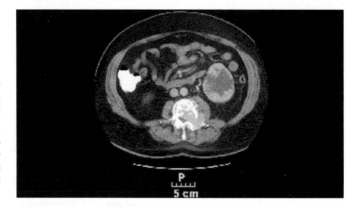

Figure 14.1 Renal cancer. This CT scan shows a left renal inferior pole mass. In addition there is erosion of the vertebral body and posterior elements of the 3rd lumbar vertebra. This is associated with extension into the spinal canal causing cauda equine compression and through the neural foramen into the psoas muscle.

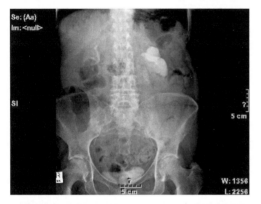

Figure 14.2 An intravenous urogram (IVU) image demonstrating obstruction of the left pelvi-calyceal system at the level of the pelvi-ureteric junction with a filling defect. These appearances were due to a transitional cell carcinoma of the renal pelvis. Transitional cell cancer of the renal pelvis arises in the collecting system and may be associated with TCC of the bladder and ureter. The biology, prognosis and treatment is similar to that of bladder cancer.

renal carcinoma is suspected, the patient should be referred to a urologist. Renal cell cancers are characteristically associated with paraneoplastic syndromes, which include polycythemia and pyrexia of unknown origin.

Outpatient diagnosis

The urologist will assess the patient in the outpatient clinic, taking a full medical history and examining the patient. Investigations to be

organized will include full blood count, liver and renal function tests and a chest X-ray. Further investigation will also include a CT scan of the abdomen (Figure 14.1) and the thorax to define operability. Angiography and an IVU (Figure 14.2) may also have to be performed.

Surgery

If the patient has no evidence of spread of the disease, then the urological surgeon will arrange for the patient to be admitted for nephrectomy. At operation, the kidney and vascular pedicle and associated lymph nodes are removed, together with the ureter and adrenal. Renal tumours have a propensity to invade along the renal vein. This invasion may extend into the IVC and right atrium. It does not represent a true invasion but a tumour thrombus. If this is suspected, then a combined approach involving an urologist and a vascular surgeon is advised in an attempt to fully resect the tumour.

Tumour grading and staging

The majority of renal tumours are adenocarcinomas of renal cell origin. Approximately 2% of renal cancers are of transitional cell histology, arising from the collecting system rather than from the renal parenchyma. Both adenocarcinomas and transitional cell tumours are described as well, poorly or moderately differentiated. Nuclear grading, into four Fuhrman categories, is strongly

correlated with prognosis. Only rarely is the kidney involved, either with a primary lymphoma or as the site of the spread of other cancers. The kidney can be the site of a rare non-metastasizing malignancy called an oncocytoma. The patient with renal cell carcinoma is staged according to the spread of the disease, using the TNM staging criteria.

Management of inoperable primary tumour

Locally advanced, inoperable kidney-cancer may cause significant symptoms, which may be poorly controlled by systemic palliative measures. These local symptoms can include haematuria, which may be so profound that regular blood transfusion is required; as well as loin pain, which may not respond to opiate analgesia. These symptoms can be treated by angioinfarction, where agents are introduced into the renal artery to occlude the tumour's blood supply. A number of different agents can be introduced into the renal artery. These include steel coils and chemotherapy pellets. By these means, successful symptom palliation is achieved in approximately 70–80% of all patients. The procedure does have significant morbidity, which includes a transient increase in pain, fever and, occasionally, shock due to the release of tumour products into the circulation. These symptoms peak a few hours after the procedure but may continue for up to ten days. There is a specific mortality associated with the procedure, ranging up to 5%. In hospitals where it is not possible to treat by angioinfarction, radiation to the kidney may be given.

Adjuvant treatment

Local radiotherapy to the tumour bed following nephrectomy leads to no survival advantage in patients with adenocarcinoma and has morbidity. This is therefore not recommended. Similarly, adjuvant chemotherapy has no survival advantage. The value of adjuvant immunotherapy continues to be investigated. Findings reported up to and including the year 2005, however, have shown no

benefit. This includes treatment with interleukin-2 (IL-2) for poor-prognosis tumours. The situation may possibly be different in transitional cell tumours. The outlook is very poor for these cancers, and so adjuvant chemotherapy is given in some centres.

Management of metastatic kidney cancer

Chemotherapy

Chemotherapy is generally ineffective in the treatment of adenocarcinoma of the kidney. The most active of the agents, which include the vinca alkaloids, produce responses in less than 10% of patients. Chemotherapy is given in the treatment of transitional cell-tumours. The response-rate of 60–70% is similar to that seen in patients with transitional cell-cancer of the bladder. Unfortunately, these responses are transient and last for a median time of 6–7 months.

Hormonal therapy

Initial reports of the efficacy of hormonal treatments in the management of renal cell cancer have proven to be incorrect. The use of hormonal therapies for renal cell cancer was based upon the observation over 30 years ago, of a response to orchiectomy in Syrian golden hamsters bearing renal cell tumours. The leap of logic from this observation to the use of medroxyprogesterone acetate is rather dizzy, but response rates of up to 30% were described to medroxyprogesterone acetate. This order of response has however not been confirmed, and the true response rate to hormonal agents is probably less than 2%. A wide variety of hormonal treatments has been used in this condition. They include tamoxifen and flutamide in addition to the progestagens. Transitional cell tumours do not respond to hormonal therapy.

Immunotherapy

The most important current therapy used for metastatic adenocarcinoma of the kidney is

immunotherapy. The first agents used were Bacillus Lalmette–Guerin (BCG) and *Corynebacterium parvum*, but these have now been replaced by the interferons and interleukin 2. The overall order of response to interferon therapy is 15%. Approximately 5% of patients have a complete response, and the median duration of a complete response is seven months. There is no incremental rise in response with dosages over three mega units weekly of interferon, merely increased toxicity. In 1985, the results of treatment with interleukin 2 were first published, and 60% of patients with kidney cancer were reported to respond to treatment. This high response-rate was not confirmed in subsequent studies, which were nevertheless encouraging in that, overall, approximately 20% of patients were seen to respond to treatment.

The most significant aspect to interleukin 2 treatment is that responses are durable. Those lucky patients who achieve a complete response are likely to be cured of their malignancy. In the original dosage regimen, treatment had significant toxicities. These toxicities are lower with subcutaneous low-dose scheduling of interleukin 2-treatments. Currently, interleukin 2 is given with interferon. Cytokine treatment may be improved by combination with chemotherapy, but this is controversial. Transitional cell tumours do not respond to immunotherapy.

Prognosis

The prognosis for localized adenocarcinoma of the kidney is variable. The survival rate for patients with good prognosis tumours is 60–80%, but if there is vascular or capsular invasion, only 40% survive one year. The median survival for patients with metastatic disease is 9 months. Overall, 10% of patients with metastatic renal cell cancer survive five years from diagnosis, and this group represents a curious feature of the malignancy. Even in the absence of metastases at presentation, the outlook for patients with transitional cell tumours is very poor, with 10% surviving for one year, and 5% for two years.

New therapies

It is now clear that there is a real chance for success in renal cell cancer. There have been new approaches to treatment which involve the use of dendritic cell therapies and non-myeloablative allogeneic peripheral blood stem-cell transplantation. In one study of this latter approach, 53% of patients with metastatic disease had regression of their tumours, and for those patients who had a complete response, remissions were maintained. There is, of course, some morbidity and mortality associated with either a graft-versus-host disease or with transplant-related problems. Much more important have been developments in the middle of this current decade, where an understanding of the molecular processes associated with renal cancer have led to new treatments, inhibiting angiogenesis which seems to offer real hope.

Chapter 15

Bladder cancer

Epidemiology and pathogenesis

Carcinoma of the bladder is common in the United Kingdom. Each year, approximately 11 500 men and women are registered with the disease and 5000 die. The average age at which patients with this condition present to their clinician is 65. The most important cause of bladder cancer is cigarette smoking. Workers in the dye, paint and rubber industries are also at increased risk of bladder cancer.

There have been many developments in our understanding of the molecular biology of bladder cancer, and, although these developments have not translated directly into treatment advances, they do provide significant prognostic information. Bladder tumours are thought to progress from a localized, superficial tumour to invasive and then metastatic disease. They are often multifocal. In an attempt to define the molecular events categorizing progression, it was originally noted that there was identical loss of heterozygosity in multifocal bladder tumours. This original description, however, of what was thought to be a primary genetic event in this cancer, has not been confirmed. Multiple loss of genetic material has been described, with the most common losses centred on chromosome 9q22, which is the site of a gene called patched (PTC). This is thought to be a tumour suppressor gene in basal cell carcinoma and medulloblastoma. There are other sites of chromosomal loss, particularly within chromosomes 3, 7 and 17. This loss of material can be used to follow up patients with

bladder cancer, using fluorescence *in situ* hybridization methodologies on urine cytology.

By far the most important of the recent findings in bladder cancer, however, has been the observation of overexpression of the human epidermal growth factor receptor (EGFR). This is reported in around 40% of the tumours of patients with bladder cancer. Overexpression correlates with a poor prognosis, and treatments directed against EGFR may well have some future role as therapies for this malignancy.

Presentation

The initial symptoms include haematuria, dysuria and frequency of micturition. These symptoms are, unfortunately, sometimes treated with antibiotics by GPs for a period of time, prior to referral to a specialist. New urinary tract infections in older women should always be investigated actively, and symptoms occurring in a man should always be considered to be pathological and a referral made. There is of course a differential diagnosis, but one should have a very high index of suspicion of malignancy. Referral should be promptly organized to a specialist urological surgeon. The patient will be seen in an outpatient clinic. A careful history should be taken and an examination made. The patient's symptoms should be investigated further by performing a blood count, renal function tests, liver function tests, bacteriological and cytological examination of urine, to examine for the presence

of infection and malignancy. An IVP may be ordered to examine the urothelial tract radiologically or an ultrasound investigation carried out.

Outpatient diagnosis

These investigations should be organized promptly and the patient reviewed with the result within two to three weeks. A flexible cystoscopy is then generally organized and this takes place in the Outpatient setting. If there is any suspicious appearance to the bladder, arrangements should then be made for a formal cystoscopy. The patient is anaesthetized for this procedure and the urethra and bladder carefully examined using a fibreoptic cystoscope. Any abnormal areas within the bladder should be biopsied together with areas of surrounding apparently normal looking bladder. The urologists at cystoscopy may describe a normal looking bladder or the presence of a papilloma or solid tumour. The suspicious areas are treated by diathermy and the pelvis carefully examined in order to describe the clinical staging of the tumour.

Tumour grading and staging

The tumour should then be examined pathologi-

cally and be given a grade according to differentiation. These grades are as follows:

G1 Well differentiated
G2 Moderately differentiated
G3 Poorly differentiated tumour

Lesions are further characterized pathologically by their microscopic appearance as either transitional cell carcinoma or squamous carcinoma. Approximately 90% of patients in the UK have transitional cell carcinomas. The rest are squamous carcinomas or adenocarcinomas. There may be squamous metaplasia present within a transitional cell carcinoma, and this is indicative of a poor prognosis.

The tumour should also be staged according to T (tumour) N (Node) M (metastatic categories) (Table 15.1).

Treatment of superficial bladder cancer

The majority of transitional cell carcinoma of the bladder present as superficial tumours. After resection by diathermy at cystoscopy, approximately 60% of these will recur. The recurrence rate is greater where there are multiple tumours, associated carcinoma *in situ* or poorly differentiated tumours. The outlook is best for solitary tumours, tumours with good histology and tumours without

Table 15.1 TNM staging of bladder cancer.

T Primary Tumour	N Nodal status	M Metastatic state
Tis Carcinoma *in situ*	N0 No lymph-node involvement	M0 No evidence of metastases
TA Papillary non-invasive tumour	N1 Single regional lymph-node involvement	M1 Distant metastases
T1 Superficial tumour, not invading beyond the lamina propria	N2 Bilateral regional lymph-node involvement	
T2 Tumour invading superficial muscle	N3 Fixed regional lymph-nodes	
T2A Tumour invading superficial muscle	N4 Juxta regional lymph-node involvement	
T2B Tumour penetrating through superficial muscle		
T3A Invasion of deep muscle		
T3B Invasion through bladder wall		
T4A Tumour invading prostate, uterus or vagina		
T4B Tumour fixed to the pelvic wall		

Note: A subscript 'P' is given to describe the pathological staging of the tumour

invasion of the lamina propria. There is controversy as to whether or not a solitary superficial but clearly non-invasive tumour should be followed up, because recurrence or further papilloma development is unusual. There is also debate as to whether or not these papillomata should be classified as malignant.

The recommendation for follow-up is slightly controversial, but in most practices, cystoscopy is performed three-monthly until the patient is tumour free and thereafter six-monthly for two years and yearly for three years. Practice varies throughout the UK.

If tumours are poorly controlled by cystoscopic diathermy but remain superficial, agents may be instilled into the bladder to try and control the disease. A number of different compounds are used, including BCG, interferon, thiotepa, adriamcyin, mitomycin C, mitrozantrone and epodyl. BCG is the treatment of choice for carcinoma *in situ*, and mitomycin C is the most popular treatment of multifocal superficial tumours. Maintenance BCG reduces recurrence rates.

Treatment of invasive bladder cancer

The treatment of muscle invasive carcinoma of the bladder is by radiation or with surgery. Both have similar efficacy in terms of the control of the disease. This varies according to clinical staging: 40–60% of T2 tumours, 25% of T3 tumours and 5% of T4 tumours are controlled by radiotherapy or surgery. In the UK, radiotherapy is the most widely practised treatment, because the patient keeps his or her bladder at the end of therapy. Radical cystectomy has a mortality of up to 3%, depending on which centre it is performed in. After cystectomy, patients must be nursed either in intensive care or in high-dependency beds. Continent bladders may be fashioned by the surgeon so that the patient does not require an ileostomy. Men are invariably rendered impotent by cystectomy. Little is known of the effects of cystectomy on female sexual function. There are well known electrolyte disorders associated with ileostomies.

Radical radiotherapy is generally given to a total dose of 6500 centiGrays over a six-week period. Treatment may be given to the whole pelvis, focusing down upon the bladder towards the end of treatment, or may be given to the bladder alone. There is a clear rationale for treating the bladder alone. Treatment of the whole pelvis is given with the aim of shrinking nodal disease, but this is unlikely in the dosage regimens used. If nodes in the pelvis are involved, there is a significant chance of distant nodal spread and so radiation of pelvic node is pointless. Whole pelvis radiotherapy has significantly greater toxicity than treatment to the bladder alone, and there is no logical reason for using whole pelvis radiotherapy.

During radiotherapy, the patient may get cystitis or proctitis. At the end of treatment, he or she may suffer from a small, shrunken bladder as a consequence of radiation fibrosis. Both cystitis and proctitis are common after radiotherapy to the bladder, occurring in up to 30% of patients.

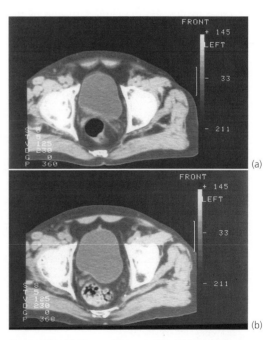

Figure 15.1 (a) CT scan demonstrating thickening of posterior bladder wall due to invasive bladder cancer and (b) same image after 4 cycles of platinum based combination chemotherapy showing reduction in bladder wall thickening.

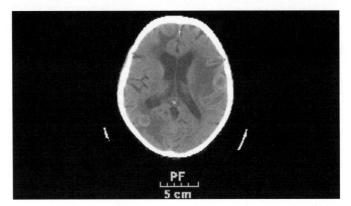

Figure 15.2 A man with a 3 year history of invasive baldder cancer treated with radical radiotherapy developed morning headaches and numbness of his right arm. His CT scan shown here shows two ring enhancing metastases in the left frontal and right parietal regions with marked surrounding oedema.

Chemotherapy has been given to patients with bladder cancer. Response rates seem to be similar to radiotherapy and surgery. The advantage to the patient is the avoidance of the long-term side-effects of radiotherapy and the retention of the bladder.

Treatment of metastatic bladder cancer

When bladder cancer has spread beyond the bladder it is conventionally treated with chemotherapy. Recent advances in the treatment of this disease mean that new hope is now offered to patients which metastatic cancer. A number of different programmes are used for treatment; including programmes which have the acronyms CMV, MVAC and MVMJ. New agents have become available for the treatment of bladder cancer. These include Gemcitabine. The standard treatment currently is combination therapy with Gemcitabine and Cisplatin, chosen for efficacy and comparative lack of toxicity (Figure 15.1).

Prognosis

The consensus view is that diathermy and intravesical chemotherapy prevent the progression of superficial to locally advanced or metastatic disease in 40% of cases. Overall, however, approximately 30% of patients with superficial tumours develop invasive disease. If there is associated carcinoma *in situ*, over 60% of patients will develop invasive cancer. Poorly differentiated superficial bladder cancers have a particularly poor prognosis and are treated aggressively. Despite treatment, just 20% of patients survive five years.

The results of treatment vary from centre to centre, but the overall expectation is for an initial response in approximately 50% of patients with metastatic disease, for a median duration of nine months. During the terminal phases of illness, patients require specialist care for symptom palliation. The disease may spread to bone, lung or liver, and opiate analgesia or local radiotherapy may be helpful in easing symptoms.

New prospects for treatment

The major prospects for the development of new treatments for bladder cancer are targeted at methods of inhibiting the activity of the epidermal growth factor-receptor. The first in development is Gefitib (Iressa), but this is just one of a family of at least six EGFR targeting therapies in development.

Chapter 16

Prostate cancer

Epidemiology and pathogenesis

Carcinoma of the prostate is the second most common cancer of men in the Western world. The latest incidence figures suggest that in England and Wales, 25 000 men were diagnosed as having prostate cancer and that there were approximately 10 000 deaths. Prostate cancer death rates have trebled in the last 30 years, and the incidence figures have increased so strikingly that the number of men affected by this cancer has overtaken lung cancer as the most common of all male cancers in the UK. This is also the case in the US, where prostate cancer has replaced lung cancer as the most common cancer of males.

How do we explain this increase in prostate cancer incidence? It is very unlikely that there is a genetic basis to this dramatic recent change in incidence. What is likely is that there is an environmental risk factor. This can be seen from studies on the incidence of cancer in the succeeding generations of migrating populations — as well as from dietary evidence, we believe. There were huge waves of migration from South-East Asia to North America and Hawaii at the turn of the 19th century. Prostate cancer has a very low incidence in Asia. The incidence of prostate cancer in the generations that followed these waves of migration increased, so that in two generations the incidence of prostate cancer was almost equivalent to that occurring in their Caucasian neighbours.

The second line of evidence comes from dietary studies, where it has been clearly shown that the incidence of prostate cancer in vegetarians is 50–75% that of the incidence in omnivores. There are striking correlates between prostate cancer and diets containing smoked foods and dairy produce, and protective benefits from diets that are rich in yellow beans.

The genetic basis to prostate cancer has not been clearly elucidated and the reason for this is that it is unlikely that there is one. There are links between familial breast cancer and prostate cancer, and overall the risk of developing prostate cancer is increased by just 1.3-fold if you have an affected father with the condition and by 2.5-fold if you have a brother affected.

No consistent genetic defect has been described in prostate cancer. Most have a multiplicity of observed changes. These include a loss of heterozygosity around a number of chromosomes, the most common of which is a loss of genetic material on chromosome 10p. The tumour suppressor-genes are infrequently mutated in prostate cancer — for example, retinoblastoma (RB) gene is mutated in just 5% of patients' tumours. No specific cell-surface molecular identity has been demonstrated to occur consistently in prostate cancer. EGFR positivity is described in up to 40% of tumours.

Prostate cancer is strikingly hormone-dependent. This is because the growth of prostatic tumours is regulated by the androgen receptor,

which is a member of the steroid super family of transcription factors, and the majority of treatments for prostate cancer have their effect through this receptor.

Presentation

Patients with prostate cancer commonly present with urinary frequency, a poor urine flow or difficulty with starting and stopping urination. Other associated symptoms on presentation include bone pain and general debility. Weight loss is rare. The patient with symptoms such as these should be referred by his GP to a urologist, who is a surgeon specializing in urinary problems.

Patients with a potential diagnosis of prostate cancer are diagnosed in general practice as a result of prostate-specific antigen (PSA) screening and referred directly to Oncology. In the UK between 2% and 6% of men are screened. PSA levels are not necessarily diagnostic of prostate cancer. Where levels are raised above the normal range of $4\,\mu g/L$ to between $4\,\mu g/L$ and $10\,\mu g/L$, the chance of the patient having prostate cancer is approximately 25%. At levels over $10\,\mu g/L$, the chance of diagnosing prostate cancer increases to 40%. Levels of this antigen may be elevated in benign prostatic hypertrophy. PSA is a serine protease and acts like drain cleaner for the prostate, dissolving the prostatic coagulum.

In outpatients, a careful history should be taken, a full examination made, routine blood-tests performed and levels of acid phosphatase and PSA assessed. In addition, plain X-rays of the chest and pelvis should be performed and a transrectal ultrasound and bone scan booked. See also Figures 16.1 and 16.2 and Figure 1.4.

Staging and grading

From the clinical findings an assessment can be made of the degree of prostate enlargement. If the prostate is malignant, it is staged as in Table 16.1.

The tumour grade can be described as well-, moderately or poorly differentiated. This is elaborated in the Gleason scoring system. The Gleason system scores prostatic tumours on a 1–10 scale, where ten is the most poorly differentiated. The combined Gleason grade describes the appearances of the two most common areas of prostatic malignancy.

If the X-rays show no evidence of metastases, a bone scan should be carried out. Transrectal ultrasound has low specificity for defining malignancy but a high specificity for describing the integrity of the prostatic capsule. In many centres, magnetic resonance is used as an adjunct to this procedure and has a reasonable specificity for describing prostatic staging. A CT scan should be used to define lymph node-spread. Transrectal ultrasonography should be combined with needle biopsy. As a standard, six cores are taken in general. Since diagnostic certainty is increased by carrying out more biopsies, eight, or even 12, needle cores are taken in many centres.

Treatment

Treatment of early stage prostate cancer

The treatment of prostate cancer depends upon clinical stage and is surrounded by controversy.

Table 16.1 TNM staging of prostate cancer.

T—Primary Tumour	N—Nodal status	M—Metastases
T0—No tumour palpable	N0—No nodes	M0—No metastases
T1—Tumour in one lobe of the prostate	N1—Homolateral nodes	M1—Metastases
T2—Tumour involving both prostate lobes	N2—Bilateral nodes	
T3—Tumour infiltrating out of the prostate to involve seminal vesicles	N3—Fixed regional nodes	
T4—Extensive tumour, fixed and infiltrating local structures	N4—Juxta-regional nodes	

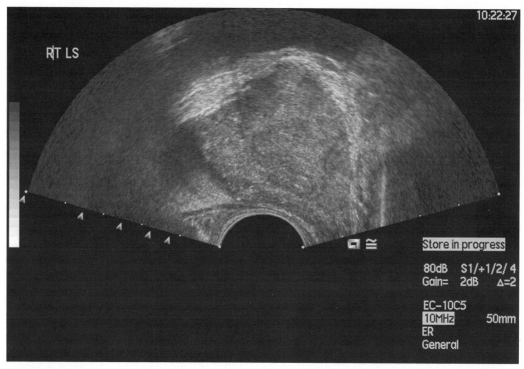

Figure 16.1 Transrectal ultrasound of the prostate gland showing extension of the primary tumour through the prostatic capsule (T3 disease).

Early-stage small-bulk prostate cancer, that is T1 and T2 disease, may be treated by observation, radiotherapy, or radical prostatectomy if there is no evidence of spread. The options for treatment depend upon the patient's overall state and preference. Observation involves regular follow-up without treatment. Radiotherapy involves approximately six weeks of attendance at hospital for prostatic irradiation, which is given in an attempt to sterilize the tumour. Radiotherapy has morbidity. Acutely, it may be associated with symptoms of cystitis and proctitis; post-treatment it may produce impotence in up to 70% of patients. Radical prostatectomy involves major pelvic surgery, with removal of the prostate and associated lymph glands. Modern anaesthetic techniques and surgical advances have meant that the morbidity is limited, but a degree of incontinence is reported in

up to 25% of patients, and a degree of impotence, which is under reported by surgeons, occurs in up to 90% of patients. It is agreed that morbidity has been reduced by the introduction of nerve-sparing techniques. There is an operative mortality of less than 1%.

The reason the patient can be offered the prospect of choice in determining what therapy he should have for the early-stage disease is that observation, radiotherapy and radical surgery have all been shown to offer the patient with good or moderate histology tumours the same overall chance of long-term survival. For younger patients, with poor histology surgery offers a better survival chance than radiotherapy. There has, however, been no randomized comparison of these three options involving significant patient numbers: hence this subject remains a matter for vocif-

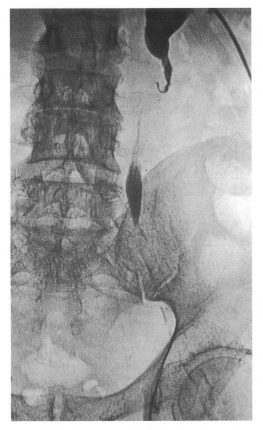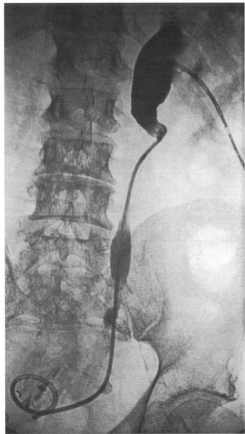

Figure 16.2 Antegrade nephrostogram showing irregular tapering and lack of contrast due to ureteric obstruction and hydronephrosis before and after passage of JJ stent to relive obstruction which was due to external compression by prostate cancer.

erous debate. A recent study of approximately 600 patients randomized to receive either watchful waiting or radiotherapy showed a better outlook for patients treated surgically.

In the early 1990s, investigations were initiated into the value of hormonal therapy given in addition to radiotherapy and surgery. No advantage to such 'neoadjuvant' hormonal therapy has been found in those patients proceeding to radical surgery. A number of randomized studies have shown an advantage to neoadjuvant hormonal therapy in patients receiving radiotherapy. The majority of studies have found a decreased risk of local relapse with hormonal therapy, and two major trials reported improved survival. There is controversy as to the suitable duration of treatment with adjuvant hormonal therapy.

Brachytherapy is a radiotherapy technique where local intensity of radiation is increased by the implantation of radioactive seeds or wires. This technique has been applied to localized prostate cancer. Excellent results have been claimed, but not proven, in any randomized trial. Recent publications have shown that the incidence of side-effects of brachytherapy is the same as for conventional radiation, and the efficacy of brachytherapy is no doubt similar to conventional radiation treatment.

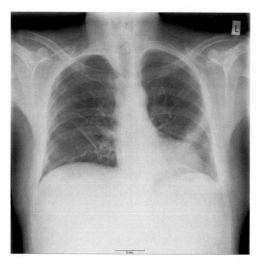

Figure 16.3 The chest X-Ray shows a sclerosis and expansion of the antero-lateral aspect of left 3rd rib. This appearance was due to metastasis from prostate cancer, although the differential radiological diagnosis would include lymphoma, osteopetrosis and Paget's disease.

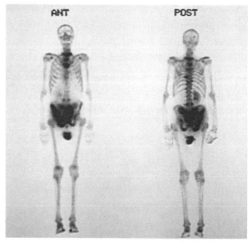

Figure 16.4 Bone scan showing multiple hot spots in the axial skeleton due to bone metastases and a non-functioning left kidney due to long-standing obstruction. The patient had locally advanced and metastatic prostate cancer.

Treatment of locally advanced or metastatic prostate cancer

When patients have locally advanced, that is T3 or T4, prostate cancer or metastatic disease, the treatment involves the use of hormonal therapy. Again, this area is one of considerable debate and controversy. Hormonal therapy for this condition was first described in the 1940s, when the disease was found to be dependent upon testosterone. For this reason, the first treatments offered in the 1940s were orchiectomy; that is, removal of the testes or oestrogen therapy.

The results of treatment were first analysed in the 1960s by the Veterans Administration Cooperative Urological Research Group (VACURG). In their studies, the VACURG randomized patients to treatment with oestrogens or placebo, or with orchiectomy or placebo, respectively. The overall survival of patients treated or untreated was the same, but there was an excess mortality rate from cardiovascular deaths in the oestrogen-treated group. The reason for this is that oestrogens cause an increased coaguability of blood and increased blood volumes.

Because orchiectomy is barbaric and oestrogen therapy is associated with morbidity and mortality, medical treatments for this condition have been sought which are not barbaric and have no side effects. The most effective of these new treatments which has the least morbidity associated with its use is a group of compounds called the gonadotrophin releasing hormone agonists. These include leuprorelin acetate, goserelin acetate and buserelin. These are currently given subcutaneously by monthly or three-monthly injection.

Effects of treatment delay

Later analyses of the VACURG study showed that all the patients who were initially given placebos were eventually treated with hormonal therapies by their primary care physicians. As survival of both groups of patients: 'treated' and 'untreated' was the same, the real conclusion of the study is that early, as compared with late, treatment offers the same prospect for survival. This important issue was investigated by the Medical Research Council (MRC) in a randomized prospective trial. The MRC trial was published, and initial analysis showed both, an increased risk of disease complications, and a more rapid rate of death in those patients who had delayed treatment. It would appear that this increased risk of complications and of death is confined to patients with metastatic cancer. In a review of the MRC trial in 2002, however, the principal author revised his conclusions and considered it to be uncertain whether or not there are a survival advantage and a reduced complication rate to early treatment.

Prognosis

Prognosis for small bulk localized disease

The outlook for small bulk localized disease depends upon grade. Observation, radiotherapy and surgery all lead to an equivalent survival of 80% at ten years for patients with well or moderately differentiated tumours. Patients with poorly differentiated, high Gleason grade tumours have a worse outlook with observation and radiotherapy than with surgery. Only 15% of patients survive ten years, compared with 60–80% of the latter treatment. It is argued that patient selection influences this result, as fitter patients, who will invariably do better than less well patients, are selected for surgery.

Prognosis for metastatic and large bulk localized disease

Prostate cancer is very responsive to treatment, and 80% of patients improve subjectively. After a period of approximately one year, however, most patients with metastatic cancer on presentation have PSA evidence of relapse. In relapse, treatment is palliative and hinges upon the use of radiotherapy and steroids. Blood transfusion is often necessary.

It has been shown in clinical trials that the addition of an anti-androgen to gonadotrophin-releasing hormone agonist therapy leads to an improvement in survival rate. The median survival for patients with metastatic tumours treated with combination anti-androgen therapy is three years, as opposed to two and a half years for patients treated with single-agent gonadotrophin-releasing hormone agonist or by orchiectomy. The prospects for survival for a patient with locally advanced disease without metastases are much better. The median survival of this group is four and a half years. It is not known whether there is an advantage to combination gonadotrophin-releasing hormone agonist and antiandrogen therapy in this patient group.

Screening

There is controversy also regarding the value of screening. Two recent reports, one from the Institute of Cancer Research, and the other from the University of York Health Economics Unit, have published findings similar to each-other. Both reports conclude that there is little value to screening because of the poor specificity of the diagnostic tools and the lack of a proven survival advantage to early treatment.

New treatments for prostate cancer

When biopsies from patients with recurrent tumour are examined and compared with biopsies on presentation, it is striking that up to 50% will show androgen receptor-mutations. This is in contradiction to the situation in breast cancer, where hormone receptor-amplification is the most commonly observed change. Over 700 mutations of the androgen receptor have been described, and these changes are a clue to the probable reason for the response to second-line hormonal therapy. The most commonly used second-line treatment is the withdrawal of antiandrogen therapy. Cessation of treatment with Flutamide, for example, given in combination with an LHRH agonist, will lead to a response in up to 40% of patients. This response is transient and is thought to occur because the mutation has led the tumour to depend upon the antiandrogen as a growth-factor. New treatments will thus have as their basis a molecular design which takes advantage of known androgen receptor-changes.

Chemotherapy has become more important in the treatment of recurrent disease, following to work in the early 1990s that showed good symptom palliation from the use of Mitoxantrone chemotherapy given with concurrent steroid. New treatments with drugs such as docetaxel have also shown promise. Responses have been seen to anti-angiogenesis agents such as thalidomide and to steroids such as calcitriol. Dendritic cell therapy, and vaccination approaches are also being trialled.

As time goes by, we have become more aware of the side-effects of hormonal therapy. The use of antiandrogen treatment is associated with osteoporosis, loss of muscle bulk, anaemia and neurological change, which includes both dementia and Parkinsonism. At present, the consensus view is that osteoporosis is best managed with bisphosphonates.

Until recently, men with prostate cancer represented a rather passive but extremely brave group of individuals who accepted their fate. The last two decades have seen significant changes in the way that men deal with their cancers, and prostate cancer has now become, quite rightly, politicized with the cause championed to good effect.

Chapter 17

Testis cancer

Epidemiology and pathogenesis

The treatment of testis cancer represents one of the major and wonderful triumphs of oncology. The application of modern treatments has led to a fall in death rates by 70% over the last 10–15 years, and currently fewer than 100 men a year die from this condition in UK of the over 2000 patients that present annually. The major pre-disposing factor to the development of testicular cancer is maldescent of the testes. There have been significant advances in the understanding of the molecular biology of adult male germ-cell tumours. It is over 15 years since the original identification of the characteristic cytogenetic marker of adult male germ-cell tumours: isochromosome 12p. An extra copy of chromosome 12p is present in 85% of all tumours, and in the remaining percentage there are tandem duplications embedded within other chromosomal material. The Cyclin D2-gene, which is concerned with the regulation of the cell-cycle, is mapped to this area. This suggests that the aberrant expression of Cyclin D2 leads to the disregulation of the normal cell-cycle and tumour development. This abnormality is present in both seminoma and teratoma. Testicular tumours also express c-KIT, stem cell factor receptor and PDGF alpha-receptor gene. These molecular findings suggest possible therapeutic options.

Presentation

Media campaigns have led to public awareness of testicular cancer as a curable condition and of the importance of early diagnosis. Generally, patients noticing testicular masses present to their GPs and are referred immediately to urology outpatients. There remain, however, a number of alarming instances, where GPs have treated patients with testicular tumours for epididymitis rather than referring them on. Patients with teratoma present during the second and third decade of their lives, generally with swelling of the testes and less frequently with pain. Men with seminoma may present in their third to fifth decades. Men with testicular cancer may have gynaecomastia. This is due to the production of steroid hormones by the malignancy, and clearly not to alpha fetoprotein (αFP) or human chorionic gonadotrophin (HCG) synthesis.

In urology outpatients, after examination, the patient should proceed to initial staging by routine haematology, biochemistry and measurement of αFP and HCG. A chest X-ray should be requested and an ultrasound examination of the testes ordered. The ultrasound will show features suggestive of testicular cancer, such as increased vascularity accompanying a mass. There may be additional features of microlithiasis, suggesting that the tumour has developed from carcinoma *in situ*. Carcinoma *in situ* is a bilateral condition with

121

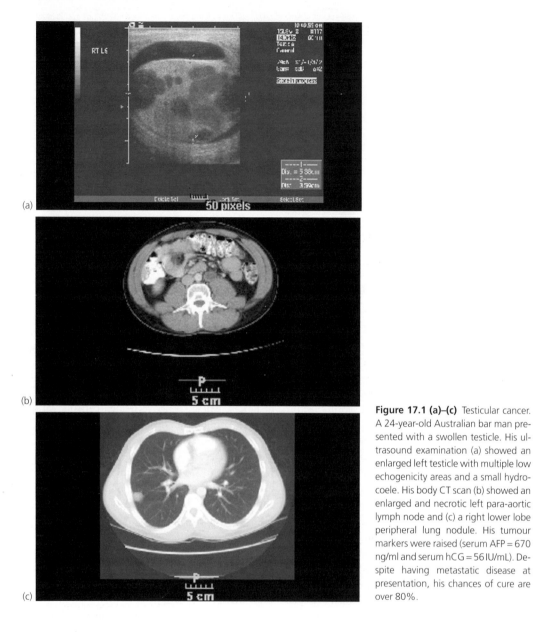

Figure 17.1 (a)–(c) Testicular cancer. A 24-year-old Australian bar man presented with a swollen testicle. His ultrasound examination (a) showed an enlarged left testicle with multiple low echogenicity areas and a small hydrocoele. His body CT scan (b) showed an enlarged and necrotic left para-aortic lymph node and (c) a right lower lobe peripheral lung nodule. His tumour markers were raised (serum AFP = 670 ng/ml and serum hCG = 56 IU/mL). Despite having metastatic disease at presentation, his chances of cure are over 80%.

a 3% subsequent chance of development of a second testicular tumour.

Following these investigations, arrangements should be made for the patient to proceed to orchiectomy. This is performed through a groin rather than a scrot alincision, which would lead to increased risk of scrotal spread of testicular cancer; particularly in cases where there are embryonal elements to the tumour. The testis is removed by the surgeon, cut in half, examined and sent for pathological examination (Figure 17.1).

Staging and grading

There are four main types of testicular tumour: seminoma, teratoma, lymphoma and small cell.

Teratoma constitutes approximately 75% of all testicular malignancies and appears cystic when examined by the naked eye. Pure seminoma constitutes 20% of tumours and is uniform in appearance. Approximately 5% of all testicular tumours are lymphoma, the appearance of which is generally uniform but with some areas of necrosis. Less than 1% of tumours are of small-cell origin. These tumours have no specific macroscopic features.

Microscopically, teratomas are constituted by a variety of different elements which may include, cartilage, muscle, bone and virtually any other tissue. Sub-types of teratoma are described, and they are called undifferentiated, differentiated or choriocarcinoma. Seminoma consists of uniform and large cells with darkly standing nuclei.

Having made a histological diagnosis, treatment is initiated and depends upon the stage at which the tumour has advanced. The following stages are described and determined by CT imaging of the chest, abdomen and pelvis:

Stage I Tumour confined to testes.

Stage II Tumour spread to abdominal lymph nodes.

Stage III Tumour spread to lymph nodes above the diaphragm.

Stage IV Tumour invading organs other than lymph nodes such as liver or lung.

The disease is further sub-staged according to the size of the metastatic deposits and the number of pulmonary metastases. In the US, retroperitoneal lymph node dissection is undertaken to stage testicular cancer, although this practice is disappearing. In our view, node dissection is not indicated as a routine staging procedure because of the major morbidity of the operation and also because of the side-effects, which include retrograde ejaculation. Node dissection for staging purposes is not part of medical practice in the UK, which relies on imaging.

Retrograde ejaculation is the ejaculation of sperm backwards into the bladder rather than forwards into the urethra. This phenomenon does not necessarily mean that the patient is functionally sterile, because sperm can be collected and artificial insemination techniques employed to successfully fertilize the patient's partner. In modern times, such IVF programs require aspiration of sperm from testes or testicular biopsy with sperm-retrieval, if collection of urine post-ejaculation with sperm-retrieval is unsuccessful.

Treatment

Treatment of stage I testicular cancer

The tumour stage of testicular cancer defines its treatment. If the tumour is localized to the testes, two actions are available to the clinician. The first activity for both seminoma and teratoma is observation without further therapy. If this policy is followed in the absence of poor prognosis pathology features, then the likelihood of any further treatment being required is 13% for testicular teratoma and 17% for seminoma. It should be noted that almost all patients who develop progressive disease during the period of observation without treatment are salvageable by chemotherapy.

In the UK, the majority of urologists refer patients with stage I seminoma for radiotherapy, following which the prognosis is excellent, with virtually no chance of relapse. The option of two courses of single-agent Carboplatin might also be offered. Evidence is emerging that this is as effective as radiation therapy and without the morbidity, two infusions being given at four-weekly intervals in contrast to three weeks of daily radiation therapy. Patients with stage I teratoma are generally referred for adjuvant chemotherapy using BEP chemotherapy: two to four courses are given. Treatment in certain circumstances might be modified, dropping Bleomycin from the treatment program to reduce the risk of lung damage.

Treatment of stage II testicular cancer

For Stage IIa seminoma, that is, with a nodal mass of less than 2 cm in diameter as defined by CT scanning, many clinicians in the UK advise treatment with radiotherapy. A consensus of opinion is now emerging, which follows the view that two courses of cytotoxic chemotherapy are equally as effective as radiation treatment in the control of this stage of disease. For stage IIb seminoma, that is, for patients with a disease mass of less than 5 cm, some clinicians, particularly radiotherapists, still treat with radiotherapy, but this is not generally advised in view of the side-effects of large field-radiotherapy. Chemotherapy should be given using either single-agent or combination therapy.

For all patients with greater than stage IIb disease, whether it is seminoma or teratoma, cytotoxic chemotherapy is given. Before the advent of cytotoxic chemotherapy for teratoma, the disease was invariably fatal. The development of effective chemotherapy programmes has bought about a revolution in the management of patients with malignancy, and now virtually all patients are cured by treatment.

Treatment of advanced testicular cancer

Treatment with cytotoxic agents was originally introduced into medical practice by Li in the early 1960s. As a result, approximately 8% of patients with advanced disease were cured, using a combination of agents that included actinomycin and chlorambucil. In the early 1970s, Samuels treated patients with vinblastine and bleomycin and produced remissions in approximately 50% of men treated. This treatment was of considerable toxicity because of the large dosages of vinblastine and bleomycin used and the relative lack of support programmes for patients with neutropenic sepsis and thrombocytopenia, which occur as a result of the use of these agents. In 1976, Einhorn introduced the BVP (bleomycin, vinblastine, and cis-platinum) program for the treatment of malignant testicular tumours. This regimen was enormously successful, and 70% of patients with advanced disease were cured. By substituting etoposide for vinblastine, less toxicity resulted with equivalent effect.

Over the last decade, there have been further refinements in the way that treatment has been given. Drug treatment which initially required six courses of five-day treatments, has now been reduced to four courses of three-day treatments. Substitution of drugs within this program to produce the modern three-day JEB (bleomycin, etoposide and carboplatin) program has meant that toxicity has been limited, and the expectation is that 95% of patients with good prognosis tumour are cured with this regimen, and 48% of patients with poor prognosis disease are cured with BEP chemotherapy. Extraordinarily, there has been further change in the collective view with regard to chemotherapy for testicular cancer, and many oncologists have reverted back to the original five-day BEP program. This is based upon analyses of huge numbers of patients and the realization of the superiority of this standard program.

Treatment of residual tumour masses

At the end of treatment, one problem may be that of a persistent mass. By this we mean a residual tumour at the site of the original metastatic disease. The approach to this problem is to proceed to surgery. Surgery may be very extensive and involve both thoracotomy and laparotomy. At surgery, the residual mass of tumour is excised as completely as possible, and this may require dacron grafting of major vessels or removal of a kidney in order to take away the tumour completely. This operative procedure is extremely intricate. Histological examination of the excised mass shows that in one-third of cases there is necrotic tumour, in one-third of cases there is differentiated teratoma and in one-third of cases there is undifferentiated cancer. If necrotic tumour is found, no further action is taken. If undifferentiated tumour is found, further chemotherapy is given and 30–40% of patients will be cured by a combination of chemotherapy and surgery. In those patients, who have residual differentiated tumour, it is important to remove the residual mass of the disease, because over a five-year period, approximately 50% of differentiated tumours undergo further malignant change, transforming to undifferentiated malignancy.

Unfortunately, a significant number of patients still have progressive or unresponsive tumours, and for these patients there is still a possibility of cure, which is in the range of 20–40%. Treatment programs such as VIP or high-dose therapy with stem-cell rescue are used to treat such patients.

Monitoring treatment

The effects of treatment are very closely monitored by measuring the serum levels of alpha feta protein and human chorionic gonadotrophin. These are hormones secreted by teratoma and seminoma. If the tumour is being treated effectively, then the levels of these hormones in the blood will decay over a known period, which is three to five days for alpha feta protein and approximately 12–36 hours for human chorionic gonadotrophin.

Side-effects of treatment

There are specific toxicities that relate to treatment. Cisplatin will cause renal damage, deafness and a peripheral neuropathy, which may manifest as numbness in the fingers or toes or complete loss of motor- and sensory function in the limbs. Bleomycin unfortunately causes pulmonary toxicity, that is, an irreversible and progressive loss of lung function, which is fatal in approximately 2% of patients treated (Figure 3.13). Testicular cancer and the drug regimen which is used generally causes sterility. By this we mean loss of functional spermatogenesis. In 80% of patients, however, there is recovery of spermatogenesis, which generally occurs at 18 months from the completion of treatment.

Prognosis

The treatment of teratoma and seminoma is highly complex and requires patient management in centres of excellence, where the delivery of chemotherapy and the maintenance of patients during neutropenic and thrombocytopenic episodes can be successfully achieved. In the best centres, 95% of patients with good prognosis tumours are cured, which is without doubt a significant advance in medical science, as young men with this malignant tumour can be returned to an active life within the community after treatment.

Prognostic indices have been described in detail by many authors. One of the more commonly used is described by the International Germ Cell Cancer Collaborative Group. Patients with non-seminoma are classified as having good prognosis disease with five-year survival of 92–95%, intermediate prognosis tumours with 72–80% five-year survival and poor prognosis tumours with 48% five-year survival. Patients with pure seminoma are described as having either good or intermediate prognosis disease. The classification into these categories is based on the presence or absence of non-nodal visceral metastases and serum levels of tumour markers. The influence of delay on prognosis is variably reported. Some authors link delay in excess of one year to a good prognosis, although this is described as being associated with a poor prognosis by other authors.

New treatments for testicular cancer

Testicular cancer remains an exclusively chemosensitive disease even at progression, and for this reason almost every new drug that has been developed for oncology has been applied to this condition. Amongst this new group of chemotherapy agents, the taxanes and gemcitabine have shown promise. Imatinib (Glivec), a c-KIT antagonist, has been applied to the treatment of testicular cancer, but information that is currently unpublished has indicated that unfortunately there have been no responses even in highly c-KIT-expressing tumours.

Chapter 18

Gynaecological cancers

In 1951, George and Margaret Gey and Mary Kubicek developed HeLa, the first human cancer continuous cell-line. It would proliferate in tissue culture and has been the basis of a great deal of research into cancer-biology and drug-development. The sample originated from the cervical cancer of a young black woman, Henrietta Lacks of Baltimore. Many thousands of tons of HeLa cells are now found in the incubators and freezers of laboratories around the world. Although the patient died less than a year after the cell-line was established, her family are said to be shocked by the development and proliferation of the cell line, which was obtained presumably without consent at the time.

Gynaecological tumours are not restricted to humans; female Asian elephants and rhinos are particularly susceptible to uterine fibromas.

Gynaecological cancers range from gestational trophoblastic tumours, which are associated with probably the highest survival of any malignant tumour, to ovarian cancers where fewer than a third of women will survive five years. The registration and prognosis data for the commoner tumours are shown in Table 18.1.

Gynaecological cancers include gestational trophoblastic disease, cervical cancer, endometrial cancer and ovarian cancer and will be discussed in more detail in the following four chapters.

Table 18.1 Gynaecological cancer registration data for South-East England from Thames in 1996.

	Percentage of female registrations	Rank of female registrations	Chance of cancer by age 75	Change in ASR 1987–1996	5-year survival
Cervix	2%	10th	1 in 159	−31%	63%
Endometrium	4%	5th	1 in 98	+5%	77%
Ovary	5%	4th	1 in 76	−7%	33%

ASR = age standardised rate

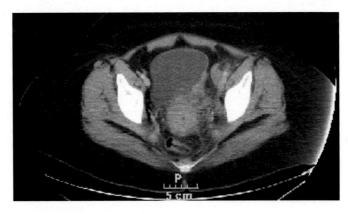

Figure 20.1 Cervical cancer, extensive locally infiltrating tumour. This CT scan of a 65 year old woman who had never had a cervical smear shows a bulky cervix with loss of the normal fat plane that separates it from the bladder. There is extension of the invasive cervical cancer into the postero-lateral bladder wall anteriorly and into the pelvic fat laterally. There is also an enlarged left external iliac lymph node. The staging was therefore T4N1M0 (IVA).

vaginal assessment. This may confirm the presence of a discharge and reveal a cervical mass (Figure 20.1).

Outpatient diagnosis

The GP should refer the patient to a gynaecologist who will repeat the examination, take smears from the cervix for cytological examination and then organize admission for examination under anaesthesia and cervical biopsy. Colposcopy should be performed as an outpatient procedure prior to admission. This technique allows direct visualization of the cervix with properly directed biopsies. After these assessments have been performed and a histological diagnosis has been obtained, staging investigations should be organized. These should include a full blood count, profile, chest X-ray and a CT or MR scan of the abdomen and pelvis.

Tumour grading and staging

Carcinoma of the cervix is staged as a result of these findings as follows:

Stage 0 Carcinoma in situ. Intraepithelial carcinoma Grades 1–3

Stage 1A Microscopic disease confined to the cervix.

Stage 1B Disease confined to the cervix and greater than Stage 1A

Stage 2A Carcinoma extending beyond the cervix without parametrial involvement

Stage 2B Parametrial involvement

Stage 3A Extension to the pelvic side wall

Stage 3B Extension to the pelvic wall with hydronephrosis or a non-functioning kidney

Stage 4A Extension beyond the true pelvis to adjacent organs

Stage 4B Spread to distant organs

Sixty-six percent of cervical cancers are squamous cell tumours. These are graded as G1, G2 or G3 tumours, according to their microscopic appearance. G1 tumours are well-differentiated, G2 tumours moderately and G3 tumours poorly differentiated. Fifteen percent are adenocarcinomas, and these are also graded G1–3. Other rarer tumours include small-cell cancers and lymphomas. Carcinomas *in situ* are graded I–III and abbreviated to CIN or CGIN, depending on whether squamous or adenocarcinoma cells are present.

Treatment

The treatment of cervical cancer depends upon the stage of disease. Stage 0 carcinoma of the cervix should be treated by cone biopsy or by surgical excision, Stage 1A disease can sometimes be managed by cone biopsy or local excision but usually by hysterectomy. Stage 1B and 2A cervical cancer is usually treated by either radical hysterectomy with pelvic lymphadenectomy or by pelvic irradiation. Both methods are equally effective in the long-term control of the disease. Stage 2B and 3 carcinoma of the cervix should be treated by pelvic radiotherapy and Stage 4 carinoma with chemotherapy.

Patients treated with pelvic radiotherapy with curative intent are frequently prescribed additional concurrent adjuvant chemotherapy. Typically, patients will be treated with weekly courses of single-agent Cisplatin. There is debate about the advantages of such additional chemotherapy. Progressive or metastatic cervical carcinoma is treated with combination chemotherapy usually using a PMB regimen which contains Cisplatin, Methotrexate and Bleomycin.

Carcinoma *in situ*

As a result of treatment, virtually 100% of patients with CIN disease are cured. Approximately 0.05–0.30% of treated women subsequently develop invasive carcinoma. If CIN is left untreated, then over a 30-year follow-up period, 10–40% of patients will develop invasive cancer. The evidence for this is based on data from a single study carried out in New Zealand of untreated patients with CIN. This study was carried out by a clinician who apparently was convinced that CIN did not progress.

Prognosis

Approximately 5% of patients treated for Stage 1A carcinoma of the cervix will progress to develop advanced disease. Sixty-five to 85% of all patients with Stage 1B and 2A carcinoma of the cervix survive five years after treatment by a radical hysterectomy or radiation. The chance for a cure is smaller in Stage 2B disease, and the expectation is that approximately 50–65% survive with radiotherapy alone. About 40–60% of patients with Stage IIIA, and 25–45% of patients with Stage 3B disease, survive five years and are treated with radiotherapy and frequently with chemotherapy.

These statistics are relevant to patients with squamous cancers or adenocarcinomas. Variant histologies, such as small-cell carcinomas, are associated with a poor prognosis, with the expectation that, even at an early stage, survival is less than 5% at five years.

Patients with Stage 4 cervical cancer do very poorly. In this situation, it is very unlikely that a cure will be achieved. Chemotherapy is the treatment of first choice. A number of agents have activity in the order of 15% and their combination is accompanied by some synergy of effect. The most commonly applied treatment programme involves the combination of Cisplatin, Methotrexate and Bleomycin. About 30–40% of patients will respond to treatment, but durable cures are rare. Chemotherapy is associated with toxicity, and this includes nausea and vomiting, hair loss, infections and kidney failure. Because of the toxicities of treatment, an alternative approach is to palliate symptoms with pain killers alone.

Terminal care

In the terminal phases of illness, patients with cervical cancer may have a number of problems which prove difficult to manage. These include fistulae from vagina to bladder and from rectum to vagina or bladder, as a result of local progression of the tumour. Obstruction of kidney function may occur as a result of blockage of the ureters, either by enlarged lymph nodes or by tumour from cervix growing within the pelvis, blocking the ureters. These situations can be treated surgically, in which case a colostomy or ileostomy may be formed, relieving bowel or ureteric obstruction or radiologically by passage of a stent to reverse obstructive damage to the kidneys.

New therapies

We hope that with the successful introduction of HPV vaccination and the institution of public health measures to eliminate smoking, there will be no need for treatment of cervical cancer in the future. In the developing would this utopian view may be a little optimistic.

Chapter 21

Endometrial cancer

Epidemiology and pathogenesis

The key to endometrial function lies in the effects of oestrogen and progesterone on the endometrium, enabling it to progress through the normal menstrual cycle and to prepare for embryo-implantation. Oestrogen stimulates proliferation in the glands and stroma. Progesterone inhibits mitotic activity and stimulates secretion in the glands and decidualization of the stroma, where the cells acquire more cytoplasm. It is therefore perhaps not surprising that unopposed oestrogens will promote continuous mitotic activity, leading to cancers. Endometrial cancer is associated with elevated endogenous levels of free oestrogens due to falls in sex hormone binding globlin or to increased aromatization and sulphation of androgens (androstenedione to oestrone). Thus, endometrial cancer is ten times more common in obese women, due to peripheral conversion of androstenedione to estrone by extraglandular aromatization in adipose tissue. Exogenous oestrogens also increase the risk of endometrial cancer. The use of unopposed oestrogens carries a four- to eight-fold relative risk especially in hormone replacement therapy, which is abrogated almost completely by combining progesterone with oestrogen. A great deal of attention has been paid to the induction of endometrial cancer by tamoxifen and has led to the development of new selective estrogen receptor modulators (SERMs), including raloxifene. Although the benefit of tamoxifen therapy for breast-cancer outweighs the potential increase in endometrial cancer, the relative risk is six-to seven-fold. Screening for endometrial cancer in women with breast-cancer taking tamoxifen has no proven benefit, but abnormal bleeding should prompt rapid investigation. Endometrial cancer is a feature of hereditary Lynch Type II non-polyposis colon cancer.

Epidemiology

Endometrial cancer is the fifth most common cancer in women in England and Wales (Table 18.1). It rarely develops before the menopause, and, since it causes abnormal vaginal bleeding, it can usually be diagnosed at an early stage.

Clinical presentation

These tumours present in post-menopausal women as uterine bleeding. Post-menopausal bleeding is always abnormal and requires prompt investigation. Hysteroscopy, which allows visual inspection of the uterine lining, is often used for diagnosis and can detect abnormalities in 95–100% of cases. The probability of endometrial cancer among women with post-menopausal bleeding who do not use HRT is 10%. If the trans-vaginal ultrasound scan is normal, this probability falls to 1%, so ultrasound allows the majority of women to be quickly reassured. Outpatient endometrial biopsy methods are now as accurate as dilatation and curettage (D&C), which requires a general anaesthetic.

Treatment and prognosis

The optimum treatment for endometrial cancer depends on the stage and grade of the disease and on the risk of tumour in lymph nodes. When the cancer is confined to the inner third of the myometrium, the lymph-nodes are likely to be clear, and total hysterectomy is usually sufficient as treatment. This applies to about 90% of women with endometrial cancer, and their five-year survival exceeds 70%. In women with tumour that extends beyond the inner half of the myometrium or with regional lymph node involvement, adjuvant pelvic radiotherapy is widely used. This has been shown to reduce the rate of local recurrence but may have long term sequelae, including lymphoedema. Neither chemotherapy, nor endocrine therapy, has been shown to reduce deaths in advanced endometrial cancer. Nevertheless, hormonal therapy is of use in the treatment of endometrial carcinoma, and excellent palliation is seen with treatments such as progestogens.

Chapter 22

Ovarian cancer

Epidemiology and pathogenesis

Carcinoma of the ovary is a common tumour affecting nearly 6000 women annually and leading to the death of 4500 women each year in the UK. Ovarian cancer is the fourth most frequent cause of cancer-death in women. The average age at which the disease occurs is approximately 60 years. By far the most common pathological subtype of ovarian cancer is epithelial, and this chapter concentrates virtually exclusively upon ovarian epithelial malignancy. There is a familial association between breast- and ovarian cancer. This relates to germline mutations in the BRCA1 and BRCA2 genes, which are associated with a risk approaching 60% of developing ovarian cancer. In an analysis of benign, borderline and malignant ovarian cancers, somatic loss of heterozygosity for BRCA1 was demonstrated in none of the benign, in 15% of the borderline and in 66% of the malignant cancers. There is controversy as to other associated risk factors of the development of ovarian cancer. For example, long-term oestrogen replacement therapy may be associated with the development of these tumours, and in one prospective study of over 31 000 post-menopausal women, the increased risk of the development of ovarian cancer was 1.7-fold. As in many other tumours HER-2 over expression is significantly associated with poorer survival prospects. HER-2 expression occurs in a minority of tumours; that is, in approximately 20% of patients.

Because ovarian cancer patients generally present with late-stage tumours, attempts have been made to reduce this risk by population screening. One of the largest published studies involved the prospective screening of nearly 4000 women by annual ultrasound examination and measurement of the serum tumour marker CA 125. This led to the identification of approximately 350 women with abnormalities, and 330 of these proceeded to laparotomy. In this group, there were 30 patients with ovarian tumours, the majority of which were at an advanced stage; so it seems that the value of screening using current technologies is low. Future screening programmes may benefit from a more refined approach. One technique involves the use of surface-enhanced laser absorption and ionization protein mass spectra. This rather complicated terminology describes the simple process of the separation of proteomic spectra from sera by electrophoresis. A number of protein patterns were identified in women with ovarian cancer, leading to a specificity of almost 90% in the identification of ovarian cancer. This would seem to be of interest in the development of more accurate screening technologies, particularly if the protein identities could be targeted, using a rapid diagnostic test. This approach of course assumes that ovarian cancer progresses by an orderly process according to early and late stage. This is by no means clear, however, and there is genetic evidence that early- and late-stage ovarian cancers may be different diseases that do not progress from one to the other.

Presentation

Patients with ovarian cancer usually present to their GPs with non-specific abdominal symptoms such as abdominal discomfort and swelling. There may be associated urinary frequency, alteration of bowel habit, tenesmus, colicky abdominal pain or post-menopausal bleeding. Patients with disseminated disease may have loss of appetite and weight. Early repletion is another common finding in the history. A patient with these symptoms should be examined by her GP, and if there is abdominal swelling or a pelvic mass, the patient should be referred on to a specialist gynaecologist for his or her views as to the patient's management. It is unfortunately the nature of ovarian cancer to present late, and almost 70% of patients have advanced disease at diagnosis. Patients with early-stage, localized tumours are often diagnosed as a result of investigation of another medical condition.

The specialist should see the patient in outpatients and take a full clinical history and examine the patient. The examination should include a pelvic assessment. If the patient is thought clinically to have ovarian cancer, the investigations organized should include a full blood count, routine biochemistry, chest X-ray, a pelvic ultrasound and an abdominal and pelvic CT scan, together with measurement of serum levels of CA-125. Ovarian cancer secretes CA-125, which is a glycoprotein. Approximately 80% of patients with advanced ovarian cancer have elevated CA-125 levels. Raised CA-125 levels may also occur in patients with almost any gynaecological, pancreatic, breast, colon, lung or hepatocellular tumour. CA-125 levels are elevated in a number of benign conditions including endometriosis, pancreatitis, pelvic inflammatory disease and peritonitis. Changing levels may be used to monitor treatment. If the tumour is operable, the patient should then be booked for a laparotomy. Surgery should be undertaken in specialist centres by a surgical gynaecological oncologist. At operation, the abdominal contents are examined and, where possible, tumour de-bulking should be undertaken. This should include removal of the omentum, ovaries, fallopian tubes and uterus, with excision of all visible peritoneal deposits. The aim of surgery is to remove as much tumour as possible, optimally reducing the maximum diameter of any tumour deposit to 1 cm or less (Figures 22.1–22.4).

Staging and grading

Ninety-five percent of ovarian cancers are epithelial tumours. The classification of tumours is as in Table 22.1.

An attempt should be made to stage the patient's tumour. The staging used is the FIGO classification which is as follows:

Stage 1 Growth limited to the ovaries
Stage 1A One ovary, no malignant ascites
Stage 1B Both ovaries, no malignant ascites

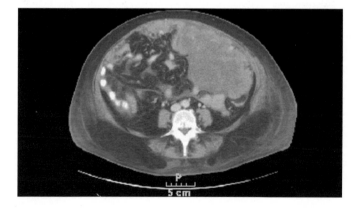

Figure 22.1 Ovarian cancer. CT scan shows an omental cake of metastatic ovarian cancer deposits anteriorly with a large lobulated mass that extends from the midline to the left flank.

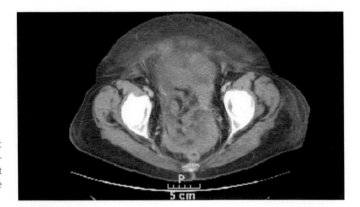

Figure 22.2 Ovarian cancer: pelvic mass. The CT scan shows a huge lobulated heterogenous pelvic mass that extends anteriorly. This mass was due to epithelial ovarian cancer.

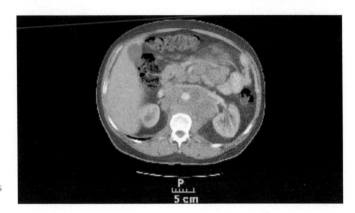

Figure 22.3 Lymph node metastases from ovarian cancer.

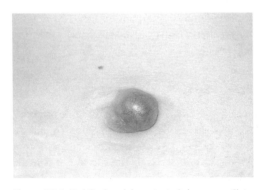

Figure 22.4 Umbilical nodule metastasis known as Sister Mary Joseph nodule which usually denotes transcoelomic spread from an ovarian or gastric primary. The eponym appears to have been given for Sister Mary Joseph Dempsey (1856–1929) who was a surgical assistant to Dr. William Mayo. This eponym is one of very few given for a nurse. (See also colour plates between pages 154 and 155.)

Stage 1C Tumour on ovarian surface or capsular rupture or ascites positive for malignant cell

Stage 2 Growth involving one or both ovaries with pelvic extension

Stage 3 Growth involving one or both ovaries with peritoneal implants or superficial liver metastases or abdominopelvic lymph node involvement

Stage 4 Tumour metastasing to liver parenchyma, pleura or other visceral metastatic sites

Treatment

Treatment is defined by the FIGO staging system. If the tumour is confined to one ovary, the gynaecological oncologist may choose to observe the patient after definitive surgery. For Stage 1 A and B ovarian cancer, patients derive no benefit from

137

Table 22.1 Pathological classification of ovarian tumours.

A. Epithelial	Serous
	Mucinous
	Endometrioid
	Clear cell
	Brenner
	Mixed
	Undifferentiated
	Unclassified
B. Sex cord/stromal	Granulosa
	Androblastoma
	Gynandroblastoma
	Unclassified
C. Lipid cell	
D. Gonadoblastoma	
E. Soft tissue	
F. Germ cell	Dysgerminoma
	Endodermal sinus
	Embryonal
	Polyembryonal
	Teratoma
	Mixed
G. Unclassifiable	
H. Metastatic	

adjuvant chemotherapy, and studies suggest that all patients with more advanced stages can be offered chemotherapy with benefit. Most specialists would agree that Stage 1A or 1B well-differentiated tumours can be observed, but adjuvant chemotherapy is increasingly offered to most patients with grade 2 and upwards disease irrespective of stage, and Stage 1C and upwards irrespective of grade. Patients with early stage ovarian cancer are usually offered single agent carboplatin as adjuvant chemotherapy. Ovarian cancer is chemosensitive, and there is a long history of the use of chemical agents in the treatment of this condition. The discovery of responsiveness to single-agent treatments led to the use of combination chemotherapy programmes. Intensive treatment using multiple drug regimens was advocated throughout the 1970s and early 1980s.

For patients with advanced ovarian cancer it was thought during the early 1990s, that single-agent therapy carboplatin was just as effective as combination treatments in terms of overall survival, although it was thought that there might be a minor advantage in terms of initial response rates and response duration to combination programmes. In the late 1990s, fashions changed again and treatment involved the use of combination therapy. There was evidence from randomized studies that combination therapy with cisplatin and paclitaxel had the highest response rates and in two high-profile studies showed superiority over another platinum-based regime in terms of disease-free result and overall survival. In this century, treatment recommendations have come full-cycle, and in the results of the ICON 3-study, a large trial conducted in the UK and Italy, single-agent carboplatin was not shown to be inferior to carboplatin and paclitaxel together. Ovarian cancer is, however, a highly heterogenous condition of many entities, and current advice from the National Institute for Clinical Excellence (NICE) is that the patient and oncologist should discuss whether better benefit might be obtained from single-agent carboplatin or carboplatin and paclitaxel on a case-by-case-basis.

Non-epithelial ovarian cancer is treated initially, where possible, by surgery. The procedures may range from oophorectomy to extensive tumour debulking. In relapse, or where a patient has presented with gross metastatic disease, treatment may involve similar chemotherapy programmes to that used for testicular cancer. Occasional responses are seen to hormonal therapy, using LHRH agonists for those patients with ovarian malignancies secreting sex steroids.

Prognosis

Localized ovarian cancer constitutes 24% of all presenting patients. Patients with Stage 1A and 1B ovarian cancer have an excellent outlook, with a 95% chance of survival. The survival of patients with Stage 1C disease with ovarian cyst rupture is variably reported and depends on tumour grade. In one series, just 63% of patients survived five years. Approximately 60–80% of patients with advanced ovarian cancer respond to chemotherapy for ovarian cancer. The median survival for this group of patients is 2.5 years, with under 30% of patients surviving for five years.

New treatments for ovarian cancer

The explosion of targeted biotherapies informed by the results of the Human Genome Project is beginning to find its way into ovarian cancer clinical trials. The main targets under consideration currently are the EGF receptor's tyrosine kinase intracellular domain and its extracellular ligand-binding component, and VEGF and its receptor, the IGF/PI3Kinase pathway. Treatments are being developed from an understanding of platinum resistance which may take its origin from BRCA1 mutant-states and MSH4 suppressed-states which may respectively mediate platinum sensitivity and resistance.

Other targets for the modern therapy of ovarian cancer include small molecular weight inhibitors ('nibs') and monoclonal antibodies ('mabs'), and treatment with these agents has in some senses undergone a renaissance. The early antibody studies, with radioisotope-labelled antibodies directed against the human milk fat globulin given intraperitoneally as an adjuvant to systemic chemotherapy, produced some exciting, but non-reproducible, survival data. The development of new antibodies that are relatively specific to ovarian cancer is now offering real promise.

Chapter 23

Head and neck cancers

Introduction

To the oncologist, the head and neck comprises six regions: the nasopharynx (the area behind the nose and pharynx), the oral cavity (including the lips, floor of the mouth, tongue, cheeks, gums and hard palate), the oropharynx (the base of the tongue, the tonsillar region, the soft palate and pharyngeal walls), the hypopharynx (the lower throat), the larynx (including the vocal cords and both supraglottis and subglottis) and the nasal cavity (the ethmoid and maxillary sinuses and the parotid, submandibular and minor salivary glands) (Figure 23.1). Although lymphomas, sarcomas, melanomas and other tumours may affect these regions, the term 'head and neck cancers' generally refer to squamous tumours, which make up 90% of cancers at these sites. Cancers of the nasopharynx include not only squamous cancers but also non-keratinizing transitional-cell cancers and undifferentiated lymphepitheliomas. The latter are the most common, and, unlike most other head and neck cancers, they frequently spread to distant sites. Tumours of the salivary glands are the most heterogeneous group of tumours of any tissue in the body, with almost 40 histological types of salivary gland tumours. Salivary gland tumours are more often benign than malignant. Sigmund Freud of course succumbed to cancer of the head and neck in 1939, attributed to smoking.

Epidemiology and pathogenesis

Head and neck cancers comprise 5% of all cancers in the UK and account for 2.5% of cancer-deaths. They are twice as common in men as women and generally occur in those over 50 years old. The sites in order of frequency are: larynx, oral cavity, pharynx and salivary glands. Over 90% are squamous carcinomas. Cancer of the head and neck is often preventable, and, if diagnosed early, is usually curable. Patients, however, often have advanced disease at the time of diagnosis. This is incurable or requires aggressive treatment, which leaves them functionally disabled. The optimum management of these tumours requires a multidisciplinary approach, including oncologists, otorhinlaryngologists, oromaxillofacial surgeons, and plastic surgeons, along with clinical nurse specialists, speech and language therapists, dieticians, and prosthetics technicians.

The incidence of head and neck cancers varies geographically, as does the most common anatomical site of these cancers. Smoking, high alcohol intake and poor oral hygiene are well established risk factors for the development of head and neck tumours. In addition, Epstein Barr virus is implicated in the aetiology of nasopharyngeal carcinoma in Southern China, betel nut-chewing in oral cancer in Asia and wood dust-inhalation by furniture makers, who may contract nasal cavity adenocarcinomas. In the UK, the incidence and

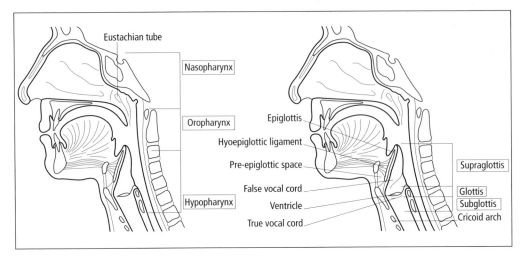

Figure 23.1 The head and neck.

mortality are greater in deprived populations, most notably for carcinoma of the tongue.

Primary prevention by smoking cessation and alcohol abstention are the most effective methods of reducing the risk of head and neck cancers. Increasing awareness of head and neck cancers may encourage earlier referral and diagnosis at a stage when the cancer is still curable. In this respect, dentists play an important role in examining the oral mucosa. Retinoids may reduce the risk of both recurrence and second primary tumours in patients following primary therapy. Moreover, they may reduce malignant transformation in precancerous conditions such as leukoplakia.

Clinical presentation

Most head and neck tumours present as malignant ulcers with raised indurated edges on a surface mucosa. Oral tumours present as non-healing ulcers with ipsilateral otalgia. Oropharyngeal tumours present with dysphagia, pain and otalgia. Hypopharyngeal tumours present with dysphagia, odynophagia, referred otalgia and neck nodes. Laryngeal cancers present with persistent hoarseness, pain, otalgia, dyspnoea and stridor. Nasopharyngeal cancers present with a bloody nasal discharge, nasal obstruction, conductive deafness,

atypical facial pain, diplopia, hoarseness and Horner's Syndrome. Nasal and sinus tumours present with a bloody discharge or obstruction. Salivary gland tumours present as painless swellings or facial nerve palsies. Cervical lymph node enlargement as the presenting feature is not uncommon, particularly when the primary tumour lies in certain hidden sites, such as the base of the tongue, the supraglottis and the nasopharynx. Systemic metastases are uncommon at presentation (10%). Synchronous or metachronous tumours of the upper aerodigestive tract occur in 10–15% of patients.

A number of criteria for urgent referral have been established (Table 23.1). Diagnostic surgical resection of cervical nodes, without first determining the site of the primary tumour, may compromise subsequent therapy, increases the morbidity and worsens the outcome.

Treatment

The approach to managing these tumours varies according to their site, but in general the primary site and potential for cervical lymph node metastases should be considered. Small early Stage 1 and 2 tumours, where there are no regional lymph node metastases, should be treated with surgery or

Table 23.1 Indications for urgent referral for suspected head and neck cancer.

Hoarseness persisting for >6 weeks
Ulceration of oral mucosa persisting for >3 weeks
Oral swellings persisting for >3 weeks
All red or red-and-white patches on the oral mucosa
Dysphagia persisting for >3 weeks
Unilateral nasal obstruction, particularly when associated with purulent discharge
Unexplained tooth mobility not associated with periodontal disease
Unresolved neck masses for >3 weeks
Cranial neuropathies
Orbital masses

radiotherapy with 60–69% cure rates. The decision between surgery and radiotherapy is often determined by the anatomical site and the long-term morbidity. Function is generally better after radiotherapy but requires daily attendance for 4–6 weeks, whilst surgical treatment is quicker, but patients need to be fit for anaesthesia.

More advanced tumours are usually managed surgically, providing that the tumour is respectable. This is followed by adjuvant radiotherapy if the margins are insufficient, or if there is extranodal spread, multiple lymph-node involvement or poorly differentiated histology. The resection of large tumours may leave sizeable defects, requiring myocutaneous flaps. Inoperable or recurrent disease may be treated with combinations of chemotherapy and radiotherapy, but outcomes generally remain poor, and in many cases of advanced disease, symptomatic palliation is a more valued approach.

If cervical lymph-node metastases are present, surgical resection is recommended, and, recently, more limited and selective neck dissection has been advocated. This preserves function, especially in relation to the accessory nerve, which, if sacrificed, usually gives rise to a stiff and painful shoulder. A scoring index can be used to predict the likelihood of metastasis to cervical lymph nodes. If the expected incidence of lymph node involvement exceeds 20%, neck dissection is usually recommended.

The addition of chemotherapy to radiotherapy, the use of altered radiotherapy fractionation, as well as intensity modulated radiotherapy have all improved the delivery of radiotherapy for patients with advanced head and neck tumours, resulting in modest improvements in survival and declines in morbidity. Recurrent or metastatic tumour may be palliated with further surgery or radiotherapy to aid local control, and systemic chemotherapy has a response rate of around 30%. Second malignancies are frequent in patients who have been successfully treated for head and neck tumours with an annual rate of 3%, and all patients should be encouraged to give up smoking and drinking to lower this risk. In addition, a number of studies have addressed the role of retinoids and β-carotene as secondary prophylaxis, but none have proved to have any significant effect.

Quality of life-issues are especially important in head and neck cancers, given the anatomical site of the disease and the consequences of treatment, which can affect facial appearance, speech, swallowing, and breathing. These cancers have enormous socio-psychological impact and may result in physical disability. These concerns must be addressed sympathetically with patients. Rehabilitation following treatment for head and neck cancers needs input from many professionals, particularly speech- and language-therapists, dieticians, and prosthetics technicians. Rehabilitation, furthermore, requires enormous patience and effort on behalf of the patient. For example, 40% of patients will achieve communication by oesophageal speech, following total laryngectomy.

Prognosis

Five-year survival rates for patients with head and neck tumours are listed in Table 23.2.

Salivary gland tumours

Salivary gland tumours represent around 5% of all head and neck cancers and affect both genders equally. They are most common in the sixth and seventh decade of life. Over half of the tumours are benign, and 80% originate in the parotid gland.

Table 23.2 Five-year survival rates for head and neck tumours.

Tumour	5-year survival
Larynx	68%
Larynx (Glottic)	85%
Larynx (Supraglottic)	55%
Oral cavity	54%
Oropharynx	45%
Nasopharynx	45%
Hypopharynx	25%
Salivary glands	60%

Approximately 25% of parotid tumours, 40% of submandibular tumours and over 90% of sublingual gland tumours are malignant. Histologically, the most common benign tumour is the pleomorphic adenoma, and the most common malignant tumour is the mucoepidermoid carcinoma. Most patients present with painless swelling of the parotid, submandibular or sublingual glands. Facial numbness or weakness due to cranial nerve involvement usually indicates malignancy and is an ominous sign. Pleomorphic adenomas, although not malignant, often recur if not completely excised, and a small proportion may become malignant if left untreated. Early-stage, low-grade malignant salivary gland tumours are usually curable by surgical resection alone. The prognosis is best for parotid tumours, then submandibular tumours; the least favorable sites are the sublingual and minor salivary glands. Larger or high-grade tumours require post-operative radiotherapy. Complications of surgical treatment for parotid neoplasms include facial nerve palsy and Frey's Syndrome which is gustatory flushing and sweating of ipsilateral forehead.

New treatments

Head and neck tumours highly express receptors for EGFR. Recently, encouraging responses have been found to treatment with antibodies directed against EGFR, which is highly expressed in head and neck cancer (Figures 3.2–3.4).

Chapter 24

Endocrine cancers

Endocrine cancers are a group of tumours whose clinical manifestations seem to delight old-fastioned physicians almost as much as they concern the patients with these cancers. In particular the products that they secrete give rise to many unusual syndromes. The majority of endocrine tumours are rare, with an incidence of 0.5 per million of population per annum. But others are more common, such as carcinoid tumours, which have a reported incidence of 1.5 per 10^5 of population per annum. These tumours are frequently listed as occurring in the context of multiple endocrine neoplasia (MEN). MENs are due to gene mutations. The MEN 1 gene is encoded at chromosome 11q13. The gene product is called, imaginatively, menin and encodes a nuclear protein that partners with JunD, NF-κB and many other proteins. The function of menin is, however, not known, and is lost in MEN 1. Mutations in MEN 2 lead to changes in the RET proto-oncogene. RET gene encodes a receptor tyrosine kinase and mutations at different sites within the RET gene are associated with MEN type 2A and type 2B, Hirschsprung Disease (congenital aganglionic megacolon), and medullary thyroid carcinoma. This one-gene source of multiple diseases is of course a blow to traditional paradigms of genetic disease but should perhaps be seen in the context of the shrinking genome. The number of genes

Table 24.1 Features of multiple endocrine neoplasia syndromes.

	MEN-1 (Werner's Syndrome)	MEN-2A (Sipple's Syndrome)	MEN-2B (also known as MEN-3)
Components	Parathyroid hyperplasia or adenoma (90%)	Medullary thyroid cancer (100%)	Mucosal neuromas (100%)
	Pancreatic islets adenoma, carcinoma or more rarely diffuse hyperplasia (80%)	Phaeochromocytoma (50%) Parathryoid hyperplasia or adenoma (40%)	Medullary thyroid cancer (90%) Marfanoid habitus (65%)
	Pituitary anterior adenomas (65%)		Phaeochromocytoma (45%)
	Adrenal cortex hyperplasia or adenoma (40%)		
Genetic locus	Chromosome 11q13 Menin gene	Chromosome 10q11 RET gene	Chromosome 10q11 RET gene

postulated for the human genome has steadily fallen from the early days of the Human Genome Project, when it was speculated that 50 000–75 000 genes were present in the human genome, to the present 'post-genomic' era, when estimates have decreased to 25 000 genes only.

The MEN syndromes are described in Table 24.1.

Thyroid cancer, adrenal cancers and carcinoid tumours are discussed in detail in the following three chapters.

Chapter 25

Thyroid cancer

Epidemiology and pathogenesis

Thyroid cancers are relatively uncommon malignancies. There were 1100 patients registered in the UK with this condition and 280 deaths reported in the last national statistics publication. There is a 2.5 : 1 ratio of women to men affected with thyroid malignancies. Radiation exposure is the most common predisposing factor to the development of thyroid cancer, and it was reported for many thousands of people across Europe following the Chernobyl disaster and in Japanese populations after the atomic bomb devastations.

Thyroid cancer includes a number of clinical entities, ranging from the classical papillary, follicular, and anaplastic tumours to the atypic Hurthle and medullary cell carcinomas, as well as thyroid lymphoma. Mutations in BRAF(V599E) are seen in 40% of papillary carcinomas. Cyclin D1 overexpression is observed in approximately 50% of papillary carcinomas, while the transcription factor E2F1, which is part of the Rb oncogene signaling pathway, is upregulated in 80% of papillary and anaplastic thyroid carcinomas. Medullary thyroid carcinoma is associated with multiple endocrine neoplasia types 2A and 2B (Table 24.1). The RET gene encodes a transmembrane tyrosine kinase receptor. This gene is mutated in almost 100% of all MEN 2A patients and in 85% of patients with familial medullary thyroid carcinoma families.

Presentation

The most common presentation of thyroid malignancy is with a thyroid nodule or with cervical lymphadenopathy. Much less frequently, patients will present with features suggestive of advanced disease, such as vocal cord paralysis or with symptoms due to metastases.

Investigations

The diagnosis of a thyroid malignancy is made following routine investigations, which should include thyroid function, thyroid isotope scanning and thyroid ultrasound. Under ultrasound control, fine needle aspiration biopsy is used to obtain a cytological diagnosis and thereby define treatment. Other staging investigations should include CT scanning of the neck and thorax. Serum calcitonin levels are measured in patients with medullary thyroid carcinomas, while serum thyroglobulin can be used to monitor relapse in well-differentiated carcinomas after thyroid ablation.

Treatment

After initial staging, patients with thyroid malignancies proceed to surgery. In the majority of patients with thyroid cancers, the surgical options are either subtotal thyroid resection, removing the lobe bearing the tumour together with the thyroid isthmus, or total thyroidectomy. Generally, partial thryoidectomy is only considered in those patients with low-risk tumours, for example those with a single focus of papillary carcinoma measuring less than 1 cm in diameter. There is no evidence that routine lymph-node dissection has any added survival advantage. Subsequent to surgery, patients are treated with thyroid replacement, aiming to suppress TSH completely, which may be a driver for the development of recurrence.

When patients with thyroid tumours develop recurrent disease, further options for management may include surgery or radiation therapy. Surgery is the treatment of choice for patients with recurrent medullary carcinoma of the thyroid, which is relatively resistant to radiation therapy and chemotherapy. Radiation treatment is given both by using external beam radiotherapy and by treating with radioiodine, which localizes to thyroid tissue. Thyroid lymphomas are treated with standard

Table 25.1 Five-year survival rates for thyroid cancers.

Tumour	5-year survival
Papillary thyroid cancer	80%
Follicular thyroid cancer	60%
Anaplastic thyroid cancer	10%
Medullary thyroid cancer	50%

lymphoma chemotherapy. Their prognosis is said to be poor, but this information is based upon limited clinical studies and may not be true. This data, however, does lead most clinicians to recommend that chemotherapy is followed by adjuvant radiotherapy to the thyroid.

Prognosis

Table 25.1 shows the five-year survival rates for thyroid tumours according to histological subtype.

Chapter 26

Adrenal cancers

Adrenal cortical cancers

Epidemiology

Adrenal cortical cancers are likely to occur with an incidence of approximately one per million of population per annum. Adrenal cortical cancers are derived from the adrenal cortex and may be secretory. The major adrenal hormone products of these tumours include androgens, aldosterone and cortisol. Serum levels of these hormones may be elevated, and 24-hour urinary cortisol secretion may be increased.

Presentation

Patients with adrenal cortical cancers generally present with non-specific symptoms, such as weight loss and general fatigue, or specific symptoms relating to their anatomical position, which include abdominal or loin pain. Adrenal cortical cancers may also produce symptoms related to the hormones that they secrete. Women may be virilized by the excessive production of androgenic hormones. Occasionally, adrenal cortical cancers are picked up as a result of an abdominal ultrasound or CT scan carried out for another reason.

Investigations

The patient with a suspected diagnosis of adrenal cortical cancer will generally be investigated in an endocrinological or surgical outpatient setting where routine blood testing together with specific endocrinological investigations will be arranged. These will include measurement of the adrenal androgens, diurnal cortisol production, ACTH levels, 24-hour urinary cortisol levels, plain X-rays and CT scans of the abdomen, pelvis and chest (Figure 26.1).

Initial treatment

Once staging investigations have been completed, the patient with a suspected diagnosis of an adrenal cortical cancer should be referred on to a specialist endocrine surgeon. The patient will proceed to laparotomy, and an attempt is made to resect the tumour. Surgery is complex, and there may be a major morbidity and mortality associated with the procedure. There is no clinical advantage to any adjuvant treatment.

Treatment of metastatic or locally advanced adrenal cortical cancer

The secretory symptoms of adrenal cortical tumours are unpleasant. Attempts are made to block the production of hormones by an adrenal cortical cancer, using blocking agents such as Metyrapone and Ketoconazole, which inhibit steroidogenesis. Treatment may be given using OPDD, which is also

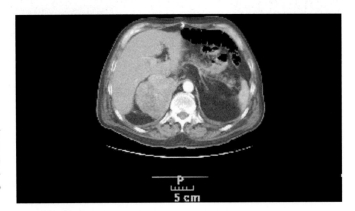

Figure 26.1 Adrenal tumour. This CT scan was performed on a 28-year old man with hypertension and shows a lobulated heterogeneous right adrenal mass which was due to phaeochromocytoma.

called 'Mitotane'. Mitotane is a selective adrenal poison that is structurally related to the chlorinated insecticide DDT. DDT is a cheap insecticide developed in the 1940s that has cumulative toxicity in mammals. It is estimated that DDT saved 500 million people globally from malaria. In 1962, however, Rachel Carson published *The Silent Spring*, in which she attributed the declining songbird population to widespread DDT use, and there since have been calls to ban DDT globally. The alternative insecticides are far more expensive, however, as they remain subject to patents owned by the pharmaceutical industry. Patients with adrenal cortical cancers are also prescribed chemotherapy. Approximately 40% of patients will respond and the most effective agents include doxorubicin and cisplatin.

Prognosis

The outlook for the majority of patients with adrenal cortical cancers is very poor, except in the patient with localized, small-bulk disease. For this group of patients, the expectation is for a 70% chance of complete cure following surgery. For patients with bulky tumours, the expectation is for a median survival of one year. Patients with metastatic tumours survive a median period of four months.

Adrenal medullary tumours

These uncommon tumours occurring in association with multiple endocrine neoplasia are a rare cause of hypertension. Phaeochromocytomas of the adrenal medulla produce their effects by secretion of catecholamines, resulting in intermittent, episodic or sustained hypertension, anxiety, tremor, palpitations, sweating, flushing, headaches, gastrointestinal disturbances and polyuria. Twenty-four-hour urinary collection for urinary free catecholamines (epinephrine, norepinephrine and dopamine) is now the most widely employed diagnostic test, although some centres also measure catecholamine metabolites such as metanephrines and vanilylmandelic acid (VMA). The treatment is surgical and the results of treatment generally excellent. Metastatic phaeochromocytoma may be treated with ^{131}I-MIBG (metiodobenzylguanidine), a catecholamine precursor, which may also be used to image the tumour.

Chapter 27

Carcinoid tumours

Carcinoid tumours (Figure 27.1) are neuroendocrine tumours that may arise in numerous anatomical sites particularly the gastrointestinal tract and lungs (Table 27.1). Much of their medical notoriety derives from their secretion of vasoactive compounds that give rise to the carcinoid syndrome. This usually follows the development of liver metastases, when first-pass metabolism of these products is bypassed.

Presentation

Patients with carcinoid tumours may be asymptomatic or may present with symptoms due to the secretory products of their tumour, if there is significant metastatic disease. These metabolic products cause diarrhoea, flushing and occasionally bronchospasm. These symptoms are so specific that there is little difficulty in making a diagnosis, which is often achieved in general practice.

Investigations

The presence of symptoms is likely to indicate that the patient with a carcinoid tumour has metastatic disease. The examinations of such a patient should be confined to establishing the extent of disease and obtaining a histological diagnosis. The investigations that are required include a blood count, liver function test, chest X-ray, and a CT scan of the chest and abdomen. Twenty-four-hour urinary

5HIAA (5 Hydroxy indole acetic acid) levels should be measured. This is because 5HIAA is the excretory product of the metabolites produced by carcinoids and results from the breakdown of 5HT (5-hydroxytryptophan or serotonin). There has been interest in the use of chromagranin A as a serum marker for carcinoid. This is a neurosecretory product, which is of value because we can monitor carcinoid using this as a blood test, rather than having to carry out 24-hour urinary collections to measure 5HIAA.

Treatment

Pharmacological control

These agents act to block the synthesis, release and peripheral blockade of circulating tumour products. The list of drugs used in the treatment of carcinoid symptoms include inhibitors of 5HT synthesis such as parachlorphenylalanine, peripheral 5HT antagonists such as cyproheptadine, antihistamines, and inhibitors of 5HT release such as somatostatin and its long acting analogues. The most frequently used somatostatin analogue is octreotide, and this leads to a relief of symptoms in 80% of patients for a median duration of ten months.

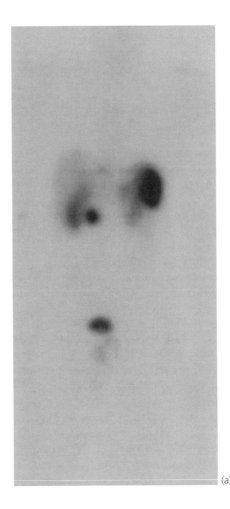

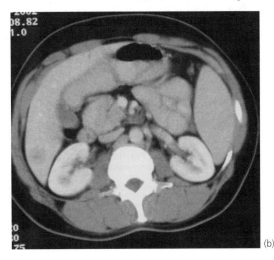

(b)

(a)

Figure 27.1 (a) [111]Indium-labelled somatostatin scan demonstrating a focus of carcinoid tumour in pancreas as well as normal tracer uptake in spleen and bladder. (b) Matched CT scan showing tumour in head of pancreas and liver metastases.

Table 27.1 Comparison of carcinoid tumours by site of origin.

	Foregut	Midgut	Hindgut
Site	Respiratory tract, pancreas, stomach, proximal duodenum	Jejunum, ileum, appendix, Meckle's diverticulum, ascending colon	Transverse & descending colon, rectum
Tumour products	Low 5HTP, Multihormones*	High 5HTP, Multihormones*	Rarely 5HTP, Multihormones*
Blood	5HTP, histamine, multihormones*, occasionally ACTH	5HT, multihormones*, rarely ACTH	Rarely 5HT or ACTH
Urine	5HTP, 5HT, 5HIAA, histamine	5HT, 5HIAA	Negative
Carcinoid syndrome	Occurs but is atypical	Occurs frequently with metastases	Rarely occurs
Metastasises to bone	Common	Rare	Common

*Multihormones include tachykinins (substance P, substance K, neuropeptide K), neurotensin, PYY, enkephalin, insulin, glucagon, glicentin, VIP, somatostatin, pancreatic polypeptide, ACTH, α-subunit of human chorionic gonadotrophin.
5HT = 5-hydroxytryptamine (serotonin), 5HTP = 5-hydroxytryptophan, 5HIAA = 5-hydroxyindole acetic acid.

Cytokines

Interferon has been used to treat patients with metastatic carcinoid tumours. Symptom relief will occur in between 50% and 60% of patients. Less than 5% of patients, however, achieve any significant tumour regression. Treatment with interferon is associated with significant side-effects, which may include flu-like symptoms; for this reason, it is not generally given.

Embolization

When metastatic disease in the liver is extensive, hepatic artery embolization may be considered. This involves selective cannulation of the artery with injection of embolic material. This will lead to sustained symptom relief in the majority of patients. There may be significant side effects from embolization, and so this procedure is not entered into without due consideration of the benefits. In some clinical series, mortality rates are 3–5%.

Prognosis

The prognosis for patients with metastatic carcinoid tumour is relatively good in comparison to that for most metastatic tumours. Patients with metastatic carcinoid commonly survive a considerable time and the expectation, even in the presence of liver disease, is that approximately 36% of patients will survive five years and 20% for ten years. In the absence of metastases and following resection of the primary, the outlook is excellent. Carcinoid tumours of different primary sites are thought to have different outlooks, but this is very much debated.

Chapter 28

Pituitary cancers

Pituitary tumours are common, and the most common are prolactinomas with an incidence of up to one in 3000 of the population per annum. Pituitary tumours arise from the anterior lobe and produce their effects by uncontrolled production of specific hormones, by destruction of normal pituitary tissues leading to hypopituitarism or by compressing adjacent structures such as the optic chiasm, hypothalamus and bony structures (Table 28.1). Secretory tumours produce syndromes which cause gross clinical signs and symptoms. The local symptoms include headaches and visual field-loss. The systemic symptoms produced depend upon the secreted product and range from acromegaly to pituitary Cushing's. Treatment options include blocking agents, such as Bromocriptine, neurosurgery and radiotherapy. The mainstay of therapy, however, is surgery, which is important in establishing the histological diagnosis, in decompressing the optic chiasm and in relieving obstructive hydrocephalus, as well as in completely excising the tumour. A trans-frontal approach is required for large tumours with extrasellar extension, while a trans-sphenoidal approach is safer and tolerated better for smaller tumours. Radiotherapy may be used as the primary treatment for intrasellar tumours and as an adjunct to surgery for larger tumours. The outlook is generally excellent.

Table 28.1 Comparison of clinical features of pituitary tumours.

Tumour	% of tumours	Morphology	Endocrine features	Neurological features
Prolactin-secreting adenoma	40%	Macroadenoma	Amenorrhoea, galactorrhoea, hypopituitarism in men	Headache, visual field defects
Non-secretory adenoma	20%	Macroadenoma	Hypopituitarism	Headache, visual field defects
Growth hormone-secreting adenoma	20%	Macroadenoma	Gigantism in children, acromegally in adults	Headache, visual field defects
Corticotropin-secreting adenoma	15%	Microadenoma	Cushing's Disease	Usually none
Gonadotropin-secreting adenoma	5%	Macroadenoma	Panhypopituirarism	Headache, visual field defects
Thyrotropin-secreting adenoma	<1%	Microadenoma	Hyperthyroidism	Usually none

Chapter 29

Parathyroid cancers

Parathyroid carcinomas are extremely rare, with an annual incidence ranging between 0.5 and one per million of the population. Parathyroid cancers secrete parathormone, and for this reason, the majority of patients present with hypercalcaemia. The hypercalcaemia is usually gross and, rather oddly, patients may be asymptomatic, with a calcium level that would normally be associated with death in the acute situation. The reason for this is that this condition generally has a long natural history and may have been present for many years prior to diagnosis. Calcium levels in excess of four are frequently reported and the patient's cellular processes will have adapted to this level of hypercalcaemia. The primary treatment for this condition is surgical. The outlook for patients with metastatic disease is awful.

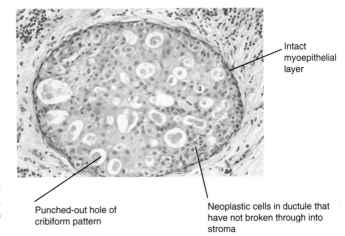

Figure 1.1 (p. 6) Histology of Intra-ductal carcinoma (ductal carcinoma in situ — DCIS) of the breast, demonstrating neoplastic cells in breast ductule with intact myoepithelial layer.

Intact myoepithelial layer

Punched-out hole of cribiform pattern

Neoplastic cells in ductule that have not broken through into stroma

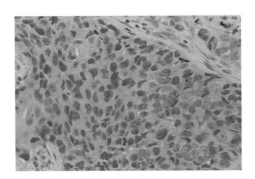

Figure 1.2 (p. 6) Histology of invasive ductal carcinoma of the breast with neoplastic cells invading breast stroma.

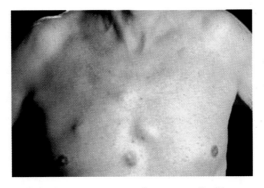

Figure 2.6 (p. 21) Patient with multiple cutaneous metastases from non-small cell lung cancer.

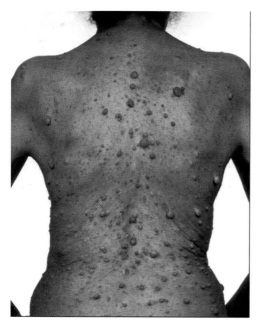

Figure 2.9 (p. 26) Multiple dermal neurofibromata typical of peripheral neurofibromatosis, or type 1 NF, previously known eponymously as 'Von Recklinghausen's Disease'.

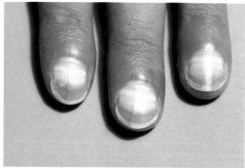

Figure 3.9 (p. 50) Beau lines, transverse ridges that form as a result of temporary interference with nail growth, here shown following several cycles of chemotherapy.

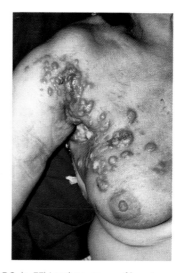

Figure 5.2 (p. 77) Local recurrence of breast cancer showing multiple ulcerating skin nodules.

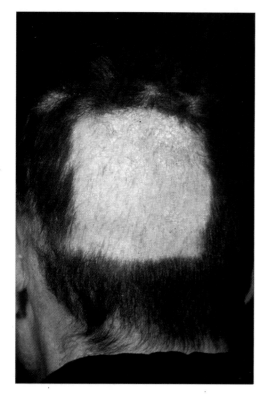

Figure 3.5 (p. 40) Radiation alopecia. Clearly demarcated scalp alopecia due to radiotherapy.

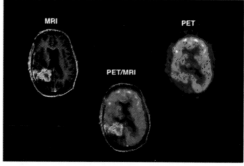

Figure 6.1 (p. 84) Co-registered and separate magnetic resonance (MR) and 18-fluorodeoxyglucose positron emission tomography (PET) scan images from a patient with a paraventricular high grade glioma demonstrating high glucose utilization by the tumour.

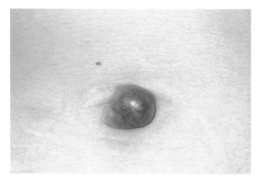

Figure 22.4 (p. 137) Umbilical nodule metastasis known as Sister Mary Joseph nodule which usually denotes transcoelomic spread from an ovarian or gastric primary.

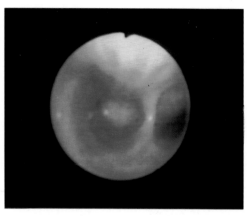

Figure 31.3 (p. 158) Appearance at bronchoscopy of a primary non-small cell lung tumour blocking the right main bronchus.

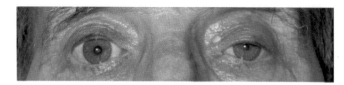

Figure 31.4 (p. 158) Unilateral ptosis and miosis (constricted pupil). The other features of Horner's syndrome are enophthalmos (sunken eye) and anhidrosis (no sweating) and is due to loss of sympathetic innervation due in the case to a Pancoast tumour of the left lung apex affecting the T1 nerve root (also associated with ipsilateral wasting of the small muscles of the hand).

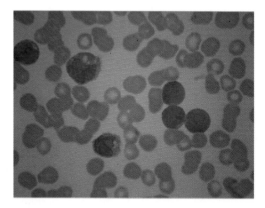

Figure 34.1 (p. 166) Peripheral blood film of acute myeloid leukaemia demonstrating myeloblasts. Occasionally Auer rods, needle like granules in the cytoplasm, are seen.

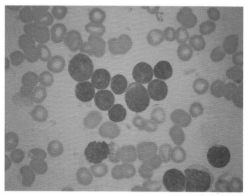

Figure 34.2 (p. 166) Peripheral blood film of acute lymphoid leukaemia demonstrating lymphoblasts with a very high nuclear to cytoplasmic ratio.

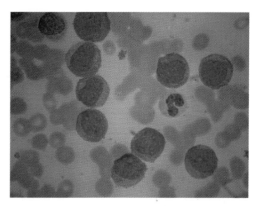

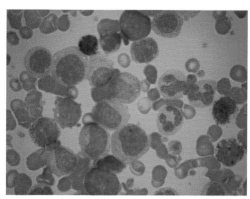

Figure 34.3 (p. 166) Bone marrow aspirate showing acute myeloid leukaemia with monocytic differentiation (AML-M5). This acute myelomonocytic subtype of AML is occasionally associated with gum infiltration and hypertrophy.

Figure 34.6 (p. 167) Peripheral blood film showing chronic myeloid leukaemia showing a spectrum of myeloid cells including eosinophils, basophils, and segmented neutrophils as well as immature myeloid cells.

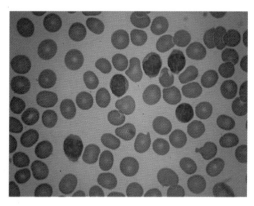

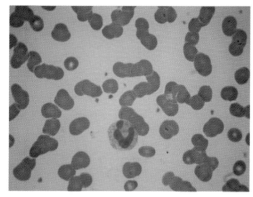

Figure 34.4 (p. 167) Peripheral blood film of chronic lymphocytic leukaemia showing multiple small B-cell lymphocytes with dense nuclei.

Figure 37.2 (p. 180) Peripheral blood film showing rouleaux formation with erythrocytes stacked up on each other, and a single neutrophil. Rouleaux are found with high levels in the blood of proteins such as fibrinogen or gammaglobulin.

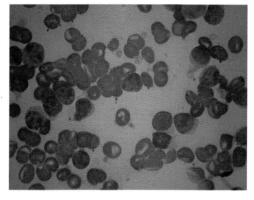

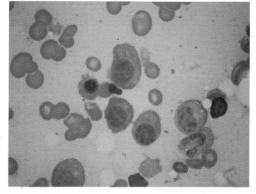

Figure 34.5 (p. 167) Bone marrow aspirate of an elderly asymptomatic man with a total white cell count of 28 × 10^9/L. There are many small lymphocytes present which were CD19 and CD5 positive B-cells.

Figure 37.3 (p. 181) Bone marrow aspirate of myeloma showing plasma cells with large eccentric nuclei and basophilic cytoplasm.

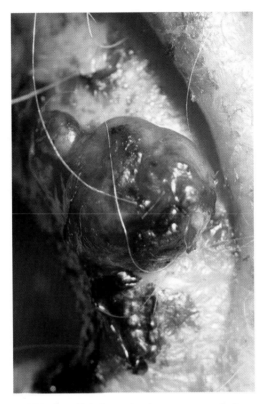

Figure 39.1 (p. 187) A large, raised, bleeding skin lesion on the pinna, a common site for squamous cell cancers of the skin. These tumours are related to UV exposure and may be preceded by actinic or solar keratoses.

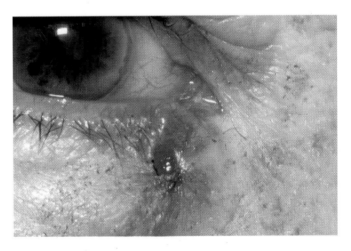

Figure 39.2 (p. 187) A pearly edged, ulcerated lesion characteristic of a basal cell cancer of the skin.

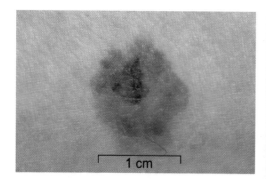

Figure 40.1 (p. 190) Atypical or dysplastic naevi are large naevi (moles) with irregular boarders and varied pigmentation. Atypical naevi are the precursors of melanomas.

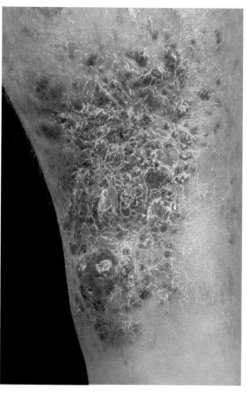

Figure 40.3 (p. 190) Irregular nodular pigmented lesion on the skin at the site of a previously excised malignant melanoma. This represents local recurrence of the melanoma.

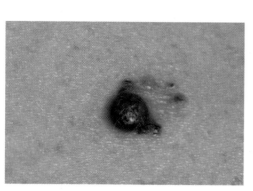

Figure 40.2 (p. 190) A pigmented nodular lesion with an irregular edge and adjacent satellite lesions. This was a nodular melanoma.

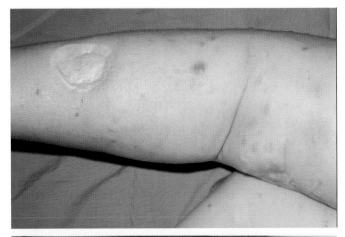

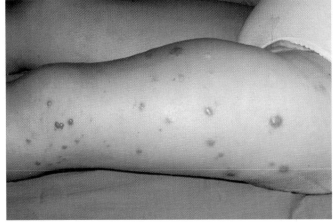

Figure 40.4 (p. 191) Multiple nodular skin metastases arising from a melanoma of the left calf that had been widely excised two years earlier, requiring a skin graft.

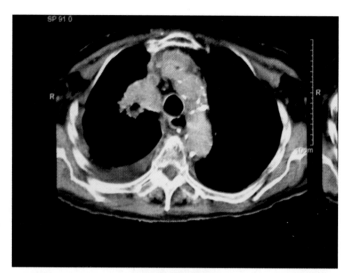

Figure 45.2 (p. 227) Finger-nail clubbing is characterised by increased longitudinal curving of the nail, loss of the angle between the nail and its bed and bogginess of the nail fold.

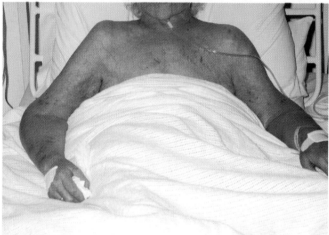

Figure 46.2 (p. 232) A 80-year-old woman presented with shortness of breath, headaches and swollen arms. The CT scan shows a large right hilar mass that was small cell lung cancer compressing the superior vena cava and collateral circulation. The clinical image also shows dilated veins on the anterior chest wall due to collateral circulation. The flow of blood in these veins will be from above as the blood is bypassing the obstructed superior vena cava to return via the patent inferior vena cava.

Chapter 30

Thoracic cancers

Table 30.1 Lung cancer registration data for South East England from Thames in 2001.

	Percentage of registrations		Rank of registrations		Chance of cancer by age 75 years		Change in ASR 1987–1996	5-year survival
	Male	Female	Male	Female	Male	Female		
Lung cancer	16%	10%	2nd	3rd	1 in 19	1 in 39	−25% (M) −3% (F)	7%

ASR = age standardized rate

In a celebrated television documentary 'Death in the West', produced in 1976 by Thames Television, the vice-president of Philip Morris attempted to dismiss established links between tobacco and cancer. During the interview he said: 'Too much of anything can kill you. Too much apple sauce can kill you.' And: 'If there were something harmful in tobacco smoke, we could remove it'. Despite numerous court cases since, the tobacco industry continues to target the young and encourage smoking. It took until 1999 for the Royal Family to withdraw its royal warrant from the tobacco multinational Gallaher, which entitled them to display 'By Appointment' on packs of Benson & Hedges cigarettes. This was despite the death of the last three kings from tobacco-related disease, including King George VI, who died of lung cancer.

Table 30.2 Five-year survival rates for lung cancer and mesothelioma.

Tumour	5-year survival
NSCLC	8%
SCLC	5%
Mesothelioma	5%

Thoracic cancers include primary lung cancers and mesotheliomas, although a number of other cancers may occur in the thorax: particularly haematological cancers. Primary lung cancer has recently been pushed into second place in the ranking order of cancer registration in men (Table 30.1) and has a very poor overall survival rate (Table 30.2)

Chapter 31

Lung cancer

Epidemiology and pathogenesis

Carcinoma of the bronchus is the second most common tumour of men and the second most common cancer of women. The overall prospects for survival are poor: only between five and eight percent of patients survive five years from diagnosis. Currently in the UK, there are approximately 31 000 men and women registered annually with carcinoma of the bronchus: 19 000 men and 12 000 women. The latest survival figures indicate that 17 500 of these men and nearly 11 000 of these women will die from their tumour.

The most important cause of carcinoma of the bronchus is smoking, and the incidence of lung cancer is directly related to the number of cigarettes smoked. Although the overall incidence of smoking is decreasing in the UK at a rate of a little under 1% per annum, there has been an increase in women smokers and in young smokers, and this bodes poorly for the future.

There are other risk factors for developing lung cancer. These include exposure to asbestos and heavy metals, such as nickel, and fibrotic disease of the lung. Air pollution is a significant factor in the development of lung cancers, and it is often said that living in London has the equivalent effect on lung-cancer incidence to smoking five cigarettes a day. Similarly, proximity to industrial pollution has a significant impact upon mortality rates.

As with so many other tumour groups, there is significant interest in the molecular biology of lung cancer. Amongst the first observations of the molecular changes in lung cancer were mutations in the Ras family of oncogenes which have GTPase activity and are important as second messengers linking events between the cell membrane and nucleus. The history of the molecular biology of lung cancer reads almost like a contemporaneous commentary on the development of our understanding of the molecular biology of cancer, and the next to be discovered were mutations in the tumour suppressor genes Rb and p53 present in at least 80% of all small-cell lung cancers. Loss of heterozygosity of a number of chromosomes has been observed in small-cell lung cancer. These include chromosomes 3, 9, 12, 13 and 17. The changes in chromosome 17 involve the c-erb-B2 oncogene and this has led to the development of new therapeutic approaches to the management of lung cancer.

More recently observations of abnormal DNA methylation of the cyclin D2 gene has been described in approximately 60% of small cell cancer lines. The cyclin D2 gene has a primary function in cell cycle regulation and has recently been brought to the general public's attention because of the awards of Nobel prizes to the scientists involved in this discovery.

Presentation

Patients with carcinoma of the bronchus generally present with a cough or haemoptysis. This may be associated with weight loss, and symptoms of metastatic cancer, such as bone pain or jaundice. Patients with chest symptoms suggestive of a diagnosis of carcinoma of the bronchus are generally referred promptly by general practitioners to a specialist chest physician. One of the concerns of oncologists in the 1990s was the lack of referral on from specialist chest physicians to oncologists, with patients regarded somewhat as property and their treatment proprietorial. One of the major changes that we have seen in this current decade has come about as a result of the central promotion of the philosophy of the multidisciplinary team. As a result, there is multi-specialty input into the management of lung-cancer patients and it is the view of these authors that the care of lung-cancer patients has generally improved throughout the country.

The signs of carcinoma of the bronchus are many and of particular interest is the observation of clubbing of the fingers occurring in non-small-cell carcinoma of the bronchus. The aetiology of finger clubbing, which is associated with hyper-trophic osteoarthropathy and polyarthralgias, has been postulated as including the secretion of PTH by tumours and also, more recently, the ectopic secretion of platelet-derived growth factor. Other clinical abnormalities may include Horner's syndrome or hoarseness, which are pointers to inoperability as a result of nerve entrapment by the tumour, and dysphagia which comes as a result of mediastinal nodal enlargement. Paraneoplastic syndromes are commonly associated with lung cancer, particularly small-cell carcinoma variant. These include cutaneous syndromes of dermatomyositis and acanthosis nigricans, the neurological complications of peripheral neuropathy and the Eaton–Lambert Syndrome. The endocrine features of ectopic PTH, ACTH and ADH secretion are all spectacular in their presentations.

Investigations should include a full blood count, liver-function tests, chest X-ray and sputum cytology. Bronchoscopy is organized and should proceed within a few days. Biopsies and washings are then obtained and examined microscopically. By these means, a histological diagnosis will be achieved. Diagnosis may not be achieved in the context of peripheral lesions and if this is the case, then needle biopsies under CT scanning or fluoroscopic imaging should be arranged. (Refer to

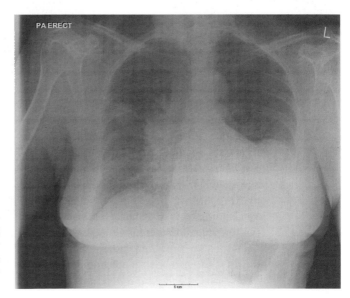

Figure 31.1 Chest X-ray of a 67-year old woman with T2N3M0 small cell lung cancer showing a right upper lobe primary lesion with extensive ipsilateral and contralateral hilar lymphadenopathy.

Figures 31.1–31.4 and to Figures 2.6, 45.1, 45.2, 45.6, 46.1 and 46.6 in Parts 1, 2 and 3.)

Pathology

There are a number of different variants of carcinoma of the bronchus, and these histological classifications are important in that they define the patient's further treatment. The main histological variants are squamous-cell carcinoma, small-cell carcinoma, adenocarcinoma and large-cell carcinoma. For treatment purposes, tumours are described as either being small- or non-small-cell

cancers. These constitute 95% of primary lung neoplasms. Squamous cell carcinoma accounts for approximately 40% of lung cancers, with adeno-carcinoma accounting for 30% and small-cell carcinoma 25% of all lung tumours. Approximately 10% of lung cancers are of mixed histology. Rarer variants include carcinoid tumours, lymphomas and hamartomas.

Staging

Lung-cancer staging is usually by the TNM classification. Staging should include a CT scan of the chest and abdomen, a radioisotope bone scan, a liver ultrasound and ideally a PET scan. Although not carried out routinely, examination of the bone marrow by aspiration and trephine in small-cell lung cancer shows the presence of metastases in 95% of patients. Pulmonary function tests to

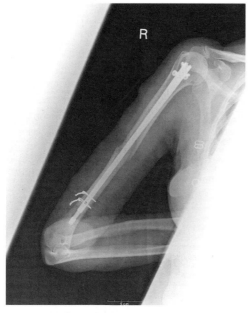

Figure 31.2 Pathological fracture of mid-humerus in a patient with metastatic non-small cell lung cancer. The fracture has been pinned with an intramedullary nail.

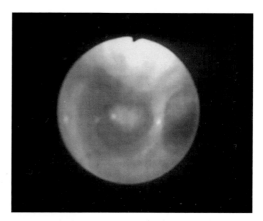

Figure 31.3 Appearance at bronchoscopy of a primary non-small cell lung tumour blocking the right main bronchus. (See also colour plates between pages 154 and 155.)

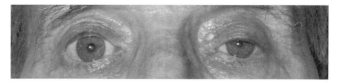

Figure 31.4 Unilateral ptosis and miosis (constricted pupil). The other features of Horner's syndrome are enophthalmos (sunken eye) and anhidrosis (no sweating) and is due to loss of sympathetic innervation due in the case to a Pancoast tumour of the left lung apex affecting the T1 nerve root (also associated with ipsilateral wasting of the small muscles of the hand). Horner (1831–1886) was a Swiss ophthalmologist, Pancoast (1875–1939) was an American radiologist. (See also colour plates between pages 154 and 155.)

assess vital capacity are essential, both to assess operability, and to ensure that the patient is not left with profound breathlessness following lung resection.

Treatment

Treatment of non-small-cell lung cancer

Non-small-cell lung cancer may be treated with either surgery or with radiation treatment. Surgery is only possible for patients with limited stage disease; that is, T1N0M0 and T2N0M0 disease, and a small number with T2N1M0 tumours. There is increasing surgical enthusiasm for operating on more extensive tumours, and it is not uncommon to find patients with T3 disease proceeding to surgery. The results of this approach are poor, however.

The UK falls below the European average in terms of the number of people proceeding to surgery because of issues of resource availability in terms of scans and surgeons. Surgery has a significant morbidity and mortality, and operability depends upon lung function prior to resection, together with cardiac status and the presence of other major illnesses. It is estimated that approximately 30% of patients with non-small-cell carcinoma of the lung have operable tumours. The five-year survival for this group of patients is variably quoted at between 5% and 40%. A review of 2675 patients gave a five-year survival of 30%. There is a sub-group variation in survival, depending upon pathological staging and histology. For example, if those operable patients with adenocarcinoma are considered, the expectation for survival ranges between 38% and 79% and averaging 65% at five years. If, on the other hand, operable patients under 40 years of age are considered, survival rises to 70%.

Radical radiotherapy, that is, radiotherapy given with curative intent, is considered for those patients who have inoperable disease by virtue of poor medical state rather than spread of the cancer. Five-year survival figures of 6% were reported in a review of 1487 patients. Conventionally, patients receive 6000 centiGrays over a six-week period.

More rapid treatment regimens are used particularly in the North of England, and similar survival figures are found.

For the majority of patients with more advanced cancer, palliative radiotherapy is the only treatment option. This is given to patients who have symptoms as a result of their disease which might include haemoptyses, breathlessness or chest pain. Radiotherapy is given according to various prescriptions; some radiotherapists advise a single dose of 1000–1500 centiGrays, others 3000 centiGrays in ten fractions over two weeks. Radiotherapy, too, has side-effects, and these include tiredness, oesophagitis and skin changes.

There is a limited place for chemotherapy in this condition. Response rates for the most active regimens are in the range of 15–25%. The median survival of responding patients is six to seven months, offering only minor survival advantage over palliative therapy. Combination therapy using regimens such as 'MIC' (mitomycin C, ifosfamide and cisplatin) is considered to be too toxic in view of the low response rates. Single-agent therapy using agents such as vinorelbine or platinum based doublets, have a role in the fitter patient, and may be used as primary therapy in rendering operable the surgically inoperable patient and as adjuvant therapy following surgery.

Treatment of small-cell lung cancer

Small-cell lung cancer is an entirely different disease from non-small-cell lung cancer. It is very rare for patients to have localized small-cell lung cancer, and approximately 95% of patients with small-cell lung cancer have metastatic disease at presentation.

The most important modality of treatment for small-cell lung cancer is chemotherapy. The current chemotherapy programme of first choice is etoposide and cisplatin. Approximately 80% of patients have an initial response to chemotherapy with this and similar programmes, and this generally includes a complete remission rate of up to 60% of patients. However the great majority of small cell lung cancers will recur after chemotherapy. Untreated, the median survival is three months. With treatment, 10–20% of patients will survive for two years and 5% for five years.

Treatment of paraneoplastic syndromes

Small-cell lung cancer is associated with many paraneoplastic syndromes, due to secretion by the tumour of specific growth factors and hormones. One of the commonest is hyponatraemia, due to inappropriate secretion of antidiuretic hormone. This is treated by water restriction or tetracyclines. Steroids are prescribed in high dose for the treatment of polymyositis, the Eaton–Lambert Syndrome and the peripheral neuropathies associated with small-cell lung cancer. Ectopic ACTH secretion may require high-dose therapy with adrenal enzyme blocking drugs such as Metyrapone and Ketoconazole. Unfortunately, these two agents do have toxicity in the dosages used and may make the patient feel awful. In this context, adrenalectomy may be rarely required.

New treatments for lung cancer

One of the most exciting developments of recent times has been that of specific therapies aimed at the molecular abnormalities expressed by cancer-cells. The observation of aberrant EGFR expression in non-small-cell lung cancer has led to the hope that agents directed against this receptor may provide a therapeutic advance. The most interest recently has been around the use of Gefitinib (Iressa) and Erlotinib (Tarceva), which are epidermal growth factor receptor tyrosine kinase inhibitors. There is some evidence of activity in non-small-cell lung cancer, with disease stability being the best outcome. Future investigations of these agents hinge around their combination with cytotoxic chemotherapy and radiotherapy. Side-effects are reported, the most common of which is an erythematous skin reaction.

Chapter 32

Mesothelioma

Epidemiology and pathogenesis

The incidence of mesothelioma has been steadily increasing, and it is estimated that the lifetime risk is around 0.5–1%. This tumour was originally described by occupational health doctors working in the asbestos factories in the East End of London around the time of the end of the First World War. It would appear, however, that this information was suppressed, and it wasn't until the 1960s that the association between mesothelioma and asbestos exposure was clearly publicised.

The development of mesothelioma is generally related to asbestos exposure, but this is not always the case. The development of mesothelioma is not related to the amount of exposure. It may not only occur in the asbestos worker but also in family members exposed to the fibres of asbestos brought home in their spouse's, father's or mother's clothes. There are no specific chromosomal changes associated with the development of mesothelioma, but there are a host of abnormalities that may occur, which are entirely non-specific. Different asbestos fibres have different properties and carcinogenicity. The most carcinogenic fibres tend to be the needle-shaped blue (crocidolite) and brown (amosite) asbestos rather than the commoner corkscrew-shaped white asbestos (chrysotile) (Table 32.1).

Presentation

Mesothelial tumours take their origins in the pleura or peritoneum. Patients with mesothelioma characteristically present with pleural effusions or ascites.

Investigations

The diagnosis of mesothelioma may be suspected from a chest X-ray (see Figure 32.1), where a patient may have pleural thickening and an effusion. CT scanning will show the extent of the pleural or peritoneal tumour. The next step in the investigatory process is to carry out a pleural or peritoneal biopsy. Multiple biopsies are usually required to make the diagnosis.

Possibly the most important aspect of the care of patients with mesothelioma is to ensure that the appropriate compensatory mechanisms are put in place. In the UK, industrial compensation is usually arranged for patients by their union officers and involves an examination of the tumour by a pathology panel. It is enormously important for the patient and his or her family that the clinician signposts this process.

Often a pleural biopsy may not be sufficient to obtain diagnostic material, in which case video-assisted thoracic screening may be required. Recurrent effusions are a dramatic problem for patients, and the intervention of a thoracic surgeon may be

Table 32.1 Types of asbestos and cancer risk.

Type	Colour	Morphology	Usage	Cancer risk	Mind
Crocidolite	blue	amphibole needles	10%	+++	S. Africa, Australia
Chrysotile	white	serpentine corkscrew	85%	+	Canada
Amosite	brown	amphibole needles	5%	++	S. Africa

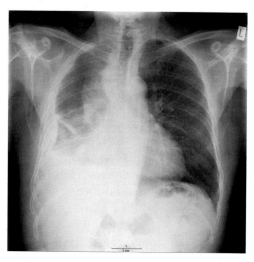

Figure 32.1 This chest X-Ray of a retired boiler maker shows diffuse circumferential pleural thickening of the right hemithorax and extending to the mediastinal pleura. In addition there is substantial volume loss of the right hemithorax. The appearances are due to mesothelioma.

required to strip the pleura and provide an effective pleurodesis.

Treatment

Unfortunately, the majority of patients with mesothelioma present with incurable disease. Treatment options are limited. Chemotherapy is ineffective, with response rates in the order of less than 10%. Radiation therapy may be helpful in controlling pain. Multiple pleurodeses are often required, with installation into the pleural cavities of materials such as talc, Tetracycline and Bleomycin. There have been times when cytokine treatment was thought to be effective, with Interferon being given into the thoracic cavity. This has, however, not proven to be a successful treatment option.

Prognosis

Unfortunately, the outlook for patients with mesothelioma is poor, with survival for patients with advanced disease ranging between 6 and 18 months.

New therapies

Recently responses have been reported for permetrexed, a dihydrofolate reductase inhibitor, and reductase. This is likely to become the standard.

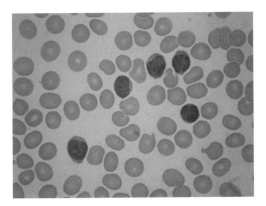

Figure 34.4 Peripheral blood film of chronic lymphocytic leukaemia showing multiple small B-cell lymphocytes with dense nuclei. (See also colour plates between pages 154 and 155.)

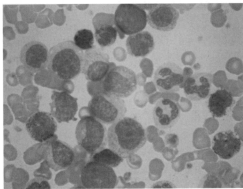

Figure 34.6 Peripheral blood film showing chronic myeloid leukaemia showing a spectrum of myeloid cells including eosinophils, basophils, and segmented neutrophils as well as immature myeloid cells. (See also colour plates between pages 154 and 155.)

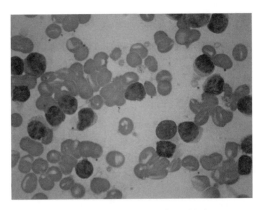

Figure 34.5 Bone marrow aspirate of an elderly asymptomatic man with a total white cell count of 28×10^9/L. There are many small lymphocytes present which were CD19 and CD5 positive B-cells. (See also colour plates between pages 154 and 155.)

Management

The management of acute leukaemia is complex. It requires psychological support of the individual and of the family, and active and urgent treatment, particularly for the acute leukaemias. Initial treatment involves attempts to stabilize the patient by transfusion of red cells and platelets, combined with treatment of infection by antibiotics to limit the complications that may occur with the initiation of chemotherapy. These mainly revolve around the tumour lysis syndrome. Rehydration is required, and the patient is started on allopurinol to prevent the metabolic abnormalities that are described in detail in Chapter 46 of this book.

The chemotherapy that is given to patients with leukaemia has evolved as a result of many clinical trials over very many years, involving the Medical Research Council (MRC) in the UK, and the Cancer and Leukaemia Group B in the USA. The mainstay of induction chemotherapy in adult has been the use of daunorubicin and cytosine arabinoside given in a daily schedule, the dosage and duration of which is varied and repeated upon recovery of haematological parameters.

During treatment, patients require supportive therapies with blood products such as platelets and red cells. Platelet support is given to keep platelet

leukaemia, five or six abnormalities are usually observed. Trisomy 12, for example, the most common cytogenetic abnormality, is found in just one-third of patients. Patients with CLL are classified using a number of different systems, most of which are helpful in describing survival related to lymphocytosis, lymph-node involvement and the presence or absence of anaemia or thrombocytopenia.

counts above 10×10^9/L, which limits the risk of spontaneous haemorrhage. There is a risk of immunization against platelets, which may require HLA-matched transfusions rather than random-donor platelet transfusion. Patients are of course at risk from neutropenic sepsis, which is treated with intravenous antibiotics. Prolonged neutropenia may be associated with fungal infection. In the context of persistent fever, particularly following transplantation, antifungal therapy is instituted. CT scanning may be appropriate in order to diagnose *Aspergillus* pneumonia. There is little evidence to suggest that any prophylactic antifungal treatment is of value, but randomized studies have shown that prophylaxis with antibiotics such as co-trimoxazole reduces the risk of *Pneumocystis* infection.

With recovery of the marrow, a further bone-marrow examination is carried out. The majority of patients will have entered complete remission just before course 2 chemotherapy. Generally, four to six cycles of treatment are given in all, and this may be followed by post-remission treatment using an allogenic autologous stem cell transplant. These approaches are used in younger patients who have entered their first remission. Approximately 50–55% of patients who receive a transplant will be cured, but there is no evidence of better survival after transplantation in the good prognosis patients.

The management of patients in transplant programmes is, of course, highly specialized, and medical training is focused on the recognition of the problems associated with profound and prolonged immunosuppression. The management of transplant patients has completely changed in recent years, because of the availability of recombinant growth factors. The use of GCSF in transplant programmes has reduced the period of profound neutropenia such that the average duration of stay on a transplant ward has decreased from 28 to 17 days.

The management of chronic phase CML has evolved over the years from the use of single-agent alkylating agents, such as busulfan and hydroxyurea, to the use of Interferon Alpha and then allogeneic stem-cell transplantation. Real hopes of cure came with the application of transplant programmes to CML. In the last few years, the introduction of Imatinib (Glevec), a novel compound which acts to inhibit the tyrosine kinase activity of the BCR–ABL oncoprotein, has been most encouraging. Between 80% and 90% of patients respond to Imatinib. In about half of these responding patients, a cytogenic response is also seen. There have been no serious adverse side-effects from treatment with this agent, which offers a dramatic improvement over conventional therapy. Unfortunately, late relapses do occur, although at present we do not know the median duration of response.

CLL may be an entirely indolent disease with an excellent prognosis, and for many patients treatment may not be necessary. Therapy, when it is required, is similar to treatment given for low-grade lymphoma, with single-agent chlorambucil, steroids and occasionally combination therapy, all being helpful.

Treatment of recurrent disease

Although 50% of patients with good-prognosis acute leukaemia survive, the majority of patients still die. Relapse generally occurs within the first two years. Patients are usually re-treated with chemotherapy, with a 50% chance of re-entering remission and a 10% chance of cure. It is usual in these situations to use a different induction drug regimen which is frequently more intensive, with a greater risk of treatment complications and death. Recurrence in chronic leukaemia may require stem-cell transplantation, but this is not the practice for CLL.

Leukaemia in young children

Acute lymphocytic leukaemia is the commonest childhood leukaemia. Overall, the prospects for cure are very good, with a chance in excess of 80% of a sustained remission. The treatment of acute childhood leukaemia owes a great debt to the MRC-organized trials, which have examined issues such as the duration of therapy both for induction and maintenance, the need for cranial irradiation to prevent central nervous system relapse and the value of the individual drugs within the treatment programmes. Because of the high likelihood of a cure, recent clinical trials have concentrated on trying to moderate the side-effects of treatment, and these are particularly important in limiting neurological toxicity, such as the effects upon intelligence, personality and pituitary function, and the effects on growth and fertility.

New therapies

In many ways, the future is 'here and now' for leukaemia. The treatment of chronic myeloid leukaemia has recently been transformed by the development of Imatinib. Imatinib binds to the BCR–ABL protein, inhibiting its kinase activity and effectively controlling disease driven by this kinase. Remissions in chronic myeloid leukaemia are seen with clearance of the Philadelphia chromosome, as shown by cytogenetic analysis.

In other leukaemias where there is a major genetic base, such as those arising in the context of Fanconi anaemia, haematopoietic stem-cells using target effectors may offer hope for cure. Haematological malignancies offer a solid chance for targeted delivery of molecular therapies, with the possibility that naked DNA strategies or interfering mRNA therapeutic approaches may reach their target and help us cure leukaemia.

Chapter 35

Hodgkin's disease

Epidemiology and pathogenesis

Hodgkin's disease is a relatively uncommon tumour, affecting approximately 1500 people each year in England and Wales. Currently, there are about 250 deaths annually. More men than women present with Hodgkin's disease, and there is a bimodal age distribution with peaks in the third and seventh decades. Little is known of the risk factors for the development of Hodgkin's disease, although there are minor associations with Down's syndrome and smoking. Geographical clustering has been noted, and there have been a few familial cases of Hodgkin's disease. Hodgkin's disease is also associated with sarcoidosis. The Epstein–Barr virus (EBV) genome is found incorporated within Reed Sternberg cells, but we do not know for certain whether this virus is a causal agent for Hodgkin's disease. The Reed Sternberg cell is thought to originate from lymphocytes affected by the Epstein–Barr virus. In HIV there is a six-fold increase in Hodgkin's disease.

There is significant interest in the origins of the Reed Sternberg cells which are the classical cells defining the presence of Hodgkin's lymphoma (Figure 35.1). Reed Sternberg cells have a specific immunophenotype, expressing CD15 and CD30, but not expressing CD20 or CD45. Immunoglobulin gene expression is mutated within Reed Sternberg cells, and there are functional rearrangements that lead to abnormal immune function. This leads to defective apoptosis, prolonged B-cell survival and, ultimately, to the development of Hodgkin's disease. EBV proteins remain present in up to 40% of Reed Sternberg cells and possibly provide a future target for immunotherapy.

Presentation

The presentation of Hodgkin's disease is usually with enlarged lymph nodes. This is generally painless and may be accompanied by constitutional symptoms which include profound sweating, sufficient to drench bedclothes, fevers greater than 38°C and weight loss exceeding 10% of body mass. These constitutional symptoms are prognostically important. There are other non-specific symptoms relating to the presentation of Hodgkin's disease, including alcohol-related pain and skin-itching.

Investigations

In clinic, a careful history should be obtained and an examination made. Investigations will be organized which include a full blood count and ESR, liver and renal function tests, a chest X-ray, CT scan of the chest and abdomen, bone marrow aspiration and trephine biopsy. The patient will be reviewed in outpatients with the results of these tests. Admission will then be organized for a biopsy of the lymph glands. The purpose of this investigations is to define the clinical stage of the

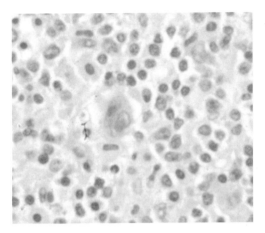

Figure 35.1 Histopathological sample demonstrating a Reed Sternberg cell (a large binucleated cell with prominent nucleoli surrounded by a clear space or lacunae) diagnostic of Hodgkin's disease.

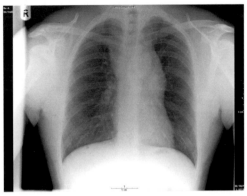

Figure 35.2 Hodgkin's disease, mediastinal mass. Chest X-Ray of a 20-year old male student showing infilling of the aorto-pulmonary window and a wide left paratracheal stripe due to mediastinal lymph node enlargement from Hodgkin's disease.

disease and the purpose of the biopsy to make a histological diagnosis. The examination of bone marrow examination is commonly undertaken in the investigation of patients with Hodgkin's disease. Less than 5% of men and women with Hodgkin's disease have bone marrow involvement, however, and this is generally only present in patients with advanced tumours of stages greater than IIB. There are strong arguments against carrying out this assessment except in advanced stage patients.

The investigation of Hodgkin's disease is a recapitulation of the history of imaging in the UK. Plain X-rays (Figure 35.2) remain helpful, but approaches such as lymphography have been replaced by CT and MR. There are significant errors in the accuracy of both CT and MR in defining hepatic and splenic involvement, with an error rate of up to 60% in the specificity for indicating involvement by lymphoma. Staging laparotomy has long been abandoned as an investigative tool, and the saga of the downside to staging diagnostic splenectomy continues to this day. It includes an ever-enlarging list of infection susceptibilities for which antibiotic therapy and immunization are recommended.

The pathology of Hodgkin's disease

Four different histological variants of Hodgkin's disease are described: nodular sclerosing, mixed cellularity, lymphocyte predominant and lymphocyte depleted Hodgkin's disease. Nodular sclerosing Hodgkin's disease is subclassified as grade I or II. Lymphocyte-predominant Hodgkin's disease is rare, constituting less than 5% of all histological phenotypes. The nodular sclerosing variant occurs in about 70% of all cases and is even more common in Hodgkin's disease affecting young women. The mixed cellularity variant is commonly associated with HIV-related malignancy and will often be diagnosed in the infradiaphragmatic presentations of Hodgkin's disease.

Staging

The results of the staging investigations will help the clinician to determine the clinical stage of the Hodgkin's disease, and this in turn defines treatment. In Stage I Hodgkin's disease, one lymph node or two contiguous lymph node groups are affected. In Stage II disease, two non-contiguous lymph node groups on the same side of the diaphragm are affected. In Stage III Hodgkin's disease, lymph node groups on both sides of the diaphragm are affected. In Stage IV Hodgkin's disease, there is extranodal spread to the liver, lung or bone but rarely to other sites.

The tumour is further classified as 'A 'or 'B'. 'A' defines a lack of constitutional symptoms and 'B' indicates the presence of the constitutional symptoms of Hodgkin's disease. Finally, the staging is defined by use of the subscript 'S', which indicates splenic involvement, or 'E' which, which defines extension to involve extranodal tissue in direct apposition to an enlarged lymph node group.

Treatment and side-effects

The purpose of staging is to define treatment groups. The current recommendations for treatment are as follows: Stage I and IIA Hodgkin's disease are generally treated with radiation. The exceptions are where there is bulky lymphadenopathy or constitutional symptoms. In these instances, chemotherapy may be the preferred option. Stage IIB–IV disease is generally treated with combination chemotherapy.

Radiation

Radiation treatment is generally given according to two well-defined treatment plans. Lymphadenopathy above the diaphragm is treated with mantle radiation which includes the lymph node groups in the neck, axillae and chest to a total dosage of 3500 centiGrays given over a period of four to six weeks. Infradiaphragmatic radiation is generally given in the inverted Y distribution which includes the para-aortic and iliac nodal groups. Treatment is given to a total dosage of 3500 centiGrays over a four- to six-week period.

Mantle radiotherapy may be complicated by radiation pneumonitis which is characterized by a period of breathlessness and fever and responds to steroids. It is invariably accompanied by loss of saliva production and oesophagitis. Infradiaphragmatic radiotherapy may be complicated by some minor bowel disturbance but generally is well tolerated. Radiation is usually avoided in children and adolescents as it may lead to gross growth disturbance. Infradiaphragmatic radiation may cause

sterility. In patients with good prognosis disease the radiation fields may be reduced to reduce toxicity. Thus extended field, or mini mantle treatments may be prescribed, in order to reduce radiotherapy toxicity.

Chemotherapy

Combination chemotherapy for Hodgkin's disease was introduced in the mid-1960s. The original treatment regimen, which has the acronym MOPP, combined mustine, vincristine (Oncovin), prednisone and procarbazine. These drugs are given intravenously and orally for two weeks and repeated every four weeks. Six cycles are administered. Treatment is associated with acute nausea and vomiting, sterility in 90% of males and 50% of females and the development of second tumours in approximately 5% of patients.

Chemotherapy treatments have been modified over the years in order to reduce side-effects. Six is a 'magic number' in oncology, and it is possible that four cycles of therapy are as effective as six cycles. The current recommendation is for a programme called ABVD which combines adriamycin, bleomycin, vinblastine and dacarbazine. These drugs cause neither sterility nor second malignancies and are of obvious advantage in a disease where there is a high expectation of cure. Randomized trials have shown an equivalence of ABVD to standard therapy with MOPP and to hybrid therapies.

Haemopoietic stem cell transplantation

High-dosage chemotherapy with either bone marrow transplantation or peripheral blood stem cell support is a relatively new and toxic treatment for drug-resistant Hodgkin's disease. The most commonly applied current programme in the UK uses 'mini-BEAM' or BEAM chemotherapy. Treatment is accompanied by either peripheral blood stem cell or bone marrow transplantation. Morbidity is high, and in certain groups, such as those pretreated with mediastinal radiotherapy, mortality reaches up to 30%. Long-term remissions occur in up to 40% of patients.

Prognosis

The results of treatment of Hodgkin's disease are considered to be one of the miracles of modern oncology, in that approximately 90% of patients with small-volume, early stage disease are curable with radiation and between 40% and 60% of patients with advanced disease are curable with chemotherapy. A poorer prognosis results from the presence of bulk disease, constitutional symptoms or poor prognosis histology. The patient who is 'cured' as a result of treatment is unfortunately at risk from late relapse; this may occur 15–30 years after diagnosis. This risk of a late relapse is small and largely confined to lymphocyte-predominant Hodgkin's disease.

Complications of chemotherapy

Hodgkin's disease is a tumour with significant cure rates, occurring in young people with an expectation of prolonged survival. This leads to a significant onus for providing a therapy that is without major long-term toxicity. Conventional chemotherapy and radiotherapy for Hodgkin's disease using alkylating agents is associated with the development of second tumours. The incidence of second tumours reaches approximately 5%, with staggering increases in the rates of acute leukaemias and lymphomas. The leukaemias present early, two to four years after the completion of chemotherapy. The solid tumours, such as breast, colorectal and lung cancer, occur late, sometimes 15–20 years after diagnosis. Sterility is also an important consequence of treatment with any alkylating agent-containing regimen, reaching up to 80% in males and 50% in females.

New therapies for Hodgkin's disease

The most important prospect for Hodgkin's disease remains the development of immunization programmes for EBV. EBV antigens are present in up to 40% of patients with Hodgkin's disease, and it is thought that this herpes virus might be a significant cause for the development of this 'B'-cell malignancy. Vaccination strategies have been developed, and it is hoped that these may lead to the elimination of a proportion of cases of Hodgkin's lymphoma. Other attempts have been made to develop cytotoxic lymphocyte-based immunotherapy for Hodgkin's disease. They have, however, not been successful, because of the facility of EBV to use multiple strategies to avoid detection. Attempts at immunotherapy have included down regulation of immunodominant antigens, together with cytokine secretion.

Combination chemotherapy regimens using hybrid treatment programmes have been investigated for the treatment of advanced Hodgkin's disease for the reason that, in this group of patients, a significant proportion of patients remain incurable. Although some studies have shown a small advantage to such hybrid regimens, the treatment carries the disadvantage of increased long-term toxicity from the alkylating-agent-containing regimens. A recent trial of 850 patients which compared ABVD with MOPP/ABVD has shown an identical complete remission and failure-free survival rate.

Where there is predominant CD20 expression, there are prospects for treatment with immunotherapy directed to this surface antigen, such as rituximab, which in a recent study has shown a response rate of 86% in a small group of patients.

Chapter 36

Non-Hodgkin's lymphoma

Epidemiology and pathogenesis

Non-Hodgkin's lymphoma is relatively common. In England and Wales there are just over 4000 deaths each year and 7500 patients presenting with this condition. There have been many descriptions of the pathological classification of this disease. Rather than achieving charity, however, most have tended to confuse the situation further because of their com-plexity. In terms of clinical practice, the most signi-ficant divisions are into high- and low-grade lymphoma.

High-grade lymphoma is much more common than low-grade lymphoma. About 1000 people with low-grade lymphoma present each year. Slightly more men are affected than women. Lymphomas arise from lymphoid organs or lymphatic tissue associated with other systems which contain lymphatic tissue. The latter, the so-called 'extra-nodal lymphomas' constitute up to 30% of all non-Hodgkin's lymphoma.

There have been extraordinary advances in our understanding of the molecular biology of lymphoma, and from this we have begun to understand some of the aetiological features involved in this condition. It is thought that Epstein–Barr virus infection is linked to the development of African Burkitt's lymphoma, certain other B-cell lymphomas, HIV-associated lymphomas and almost all lymphomas associated with the immunosup-

pression consequent to transplantation of heart, kidneys and lung.

The human T-cell leukaemia lymphoma virus type I (HTLVI) causes T-cell lymphoma and leukaemia endemic in the Caribbean and Japan. Other viruses associated with the development of lymphoma include hepatitis C and HHV8. *Helicobacter* infection in the stomach leads to a proliferation of gastric lymphoid tissue and the de-velopment of low-grade mucosa-associated tumours. Such tumours may respond to *Helicobacter pylori* eradication treatment, but unfortunately they may evolve into classical lymphoma despite eradication.

Presentation

Patients present with nodal enlargement which may be accompanied by constitutional symptoms including weight loss, sweating and fever. These symptoms, where weight loss is in excess of 10% of pre-morbid weight, sweating sufficient to drench night clothes, and fever exceeds 38°C, are described as 'B' symptoms. 'B' symptoms are less common in high-grade lymphoma than low grade malignancies. Patients with such symptoms should be referred to specialist centres where the chance for survival and the quality of survival are significantly better than in peripheral non-specialist centres. The care of patients with lymphoma should be by oncologists or haematolo-

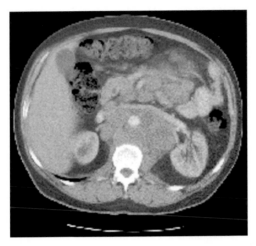

Figure 36.1 CT showing a large retroperitoneal mass encasing the aorta and causing anterior displacement of the left renal vein. The cause was high-grade B-cell non-Hodgkin's lymphoma.

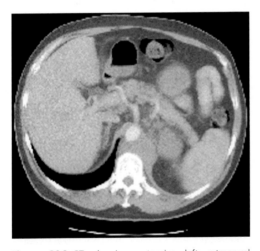

Figure 36.2 CT showing extensive left retrocrural adenopathy and a left adrenal mass due to high-grade B-cell non-Hodgkin's lymphoma.

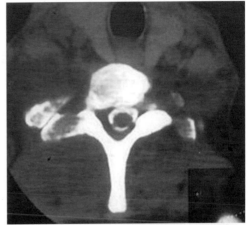

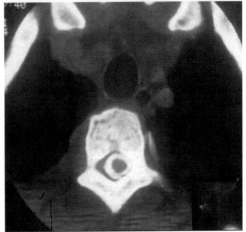

Figure 36.3 Compression of spinal cord at T1 (upper) and T2 (lower) by extradural mass of high grade non-Hodgkin's lymphoma.

gists, depending upon the specialist interests of the clinicians (Figures 36.1–36.3).

Stage and grade

In outpatients, a careful history is obtained from the patient who is then examined. The investiga-tions organized should include a blood count, renal and hepatic function tests, chest X-ray, bone marrow aspiration and trephine, and CT scan of the abdomen and chest. These investigations are done in order to define the extent of the disease. From these investigations the clinical staging is obtained. This is defined as follows:

Stage I Disease confined to one lymph node or two contiguous lymph node groups.

Stage II Disease on one side of the diaphragm in lymph node groups that are separate.

Stage III Disease on both sides of the diaphragm.

Stage IV Extra-nodal spread of lymphoma.

Table 36.1 World Health Organization (WHO) classification of lymphomas. (More common lymphomas are shown in bold.)

B-cell neoplasms	T-cell and NK-cell neoplasms
Precursor B-cell neoplasm	Precursor T-cell neoplasm
B-lymphoblastic leukaemia/lymphoma	**T-lymphoblastic leukaemia/lymphoma**
Mature B-cell neoplasms	Mature T-cell and NK-cell neoplasms
B-cell chronic lymphocytic leukaemia/small lymphocytic	**T-cell prolymphocytic leukaemia/lymphoma**
B-cell prolymphocytic leukaemia	T-cell large granular cell lymphocytic leukaemia
Lymphoplasmacytic lymphoma	NK cell leukaemia
Splenic marginal zone B-cell lymphoma	Adult T-cell leukaemia/lymphoma (± villous lymphocytes)
Hairy cell leukaemia	Extranodal NK-/T-cell lymphoma, nasal type
Plasma cell myeloma/plasmacytoma	Enteropathic-type intestinal T-cell lymphoma
Extranodal marginal zone lymphoma	Hepatosplenic γ/δ T-cell lymphoma
(of MALT type)	Subcutaneous panniculitis-like T-cell lymphoma
Nodal marginal zone lymphoma	**Mycosis fungoides**/Sézary syndrome
Follicular lymphoma	Primary cutaneous anaplastic large cell lymphoma
Mantle cell lymphoma	**Peripheral T-cell lymphoma, not otherwise**
Diffuse large B-cell lymphoma	**characterized**
Subtypes: **mediastinal (thymic)**	Angioimmunoblastic T-cell lymphoma
intravascular, primary effusion lymphoma	**Systemic anaplastic large cell lymphoma**
Burkitt's lymphoma/Burkitt cell leukaemi	

Preliminary investigations having been organized, the patient should then proceed to a lymph node biopsy. Lymph node biopsies used to be required to describe the architectural arrangement of the tumour. In modern times, they are no longer always considered to be necessary. Sufficient material can often be obtained from core needle biopsies to define the pathological diagnosis. There are many classification systems for non-Hodgkin's lymphoma, which include the WHO classification (Table 36.1), the Kiel classification, the Working Formulation and the Revised European and American Lymphoma Classification (REAL).

For the purposes of defining treatment, the most practical classification, however, is to describe the tumour as being low or high grade. A low-grade tumour tends to have a follicular nature and to contain relatively inactive cells. A high-grade tumour contains cells that have a high index of mitotic activity, and there is no follicular structure to the lymph node. An intermediate-grade tumour, which generally behaves clinically like a high-grade tumour, has some of the features of both high- and low-grade tumours. There are variant lymphomas, such as the Mantle Cell and Burkitt lymphomas, which are clinical entities with poor prognosis.

Many modern techniques have been applied to the pathological diagnosis of lymphoma. Immunophenotyping using monoclonal antibodies is the most helpful firstly, in initially distinguishing between a lymphoma or a carcinoma by using antibodies to the leukocyte common antigen (CD45), and secondly, in defining the lymphoma by using antibodies that are specific for B or T lymphocytes, such as CD20 or CD4, CD2 and CD3. T-cell receptor and immunoglubulin gene rearrangements are also carried out, and are helpful in describing tumour clonality. Fluorescent *in situ* hybridization is also useful. This is because of the observed cytogenetic abnormalities that are relatively specific for non-Hodgkin's lymphoma. Some of these are outlined in Table 36.2.

Table 36.2 Recurrent chromosomal translocations in NHL subtypes, resulting in oncogene dysregulation.

Histology	Translocation	Alteration of gene function	Mechanism/Features of translocation	Frequency (%)
Follicular lymphoma	t(14;18)(q32;21)	Upregulation of *BCL2* (inhibitor of apoptosis)	*BCL2* relocates to IgH locus. Error in physiological IgH rearrangement. Seen rarely in normal B cells	80
Burkitt's lymphoma	t(8;14)(q24;q32); t(2;8)(p12;q24); t(8;22)(q24;q11)	Upregulation of c-*MYC*; (transcription factor for cell cycle progression/proliferation)	c-*myc* relocates to IgH locus or to one of the light chain gene loci	100
Mantle cell lymphoma	t(11;14)(q13;q32)	Upregulation of *cyclin D1* (G1 cyclin)	*Cyclin D1* relocates to IgH	>90
Diffuse large B cell lymphoma[a]	t(3;14)(q27;32) & several others Involving 3q27	Deregulation of *BCL6* (zinc finger transcription factor)	*BCL6* relocates to IgH, IgL, IgK or one of many other non-Ig loci	30–40
Extranodal marginal zone lymphoma (MALT)	t(11;18)(q21;q21)	Gene fusion of *AP12* and *MLT/MALT1* genes (AP12 is inhibitor of apoptosis)	Gene fusion	20–35
Extranodal marginal zone lymphoma (MALT)	t(1;14)(q22;q32)	Deregulation of *BCL10* (apoptosis regulatory protein)	*BCL10* relocates to IgH locus	<5
Lymphoplasmacytic lymphoma	t(9;14)(q13;q32)	Deregulation of *PAX5* (paired homeobox transcription factor)	*PAX5* relocates to IgH locus	50
Anaplastic large cell lymphoma	t(2;5)(p23;q35) & others involving 2p23	Gene fusion of *ALK* (anaplastic lymphoma kinase, a receptor tyrosine kinase) and *NPM* (located at 5q35) or other gene malignant transforming capacity *in vitro* & *in vivo*	Gene fusion	50 *ALK-NPM*; 15 others

[a] BCL2 (30%) and c-*myc* (10%) rearrangements are also frequently seen in diffuse large B-cell NHL

Treatment

Low-grade non-Hodgkin's lymphoma

Low-grade tumours are generally disseminated at diagnosis. If they are localized, that is Stage I, small-bulk, peripheral, and without B symptoms, the treatment should be radiotherapy. For Stage II–IV disease, treatment is with chemotherapy with oral alkylating agents such as chlorambucil or with an intravenous chemotherapy programme known as CVP which uses cyclophosphamide, vincristine and prednisone. Chlorambucil has very little early toxicity but at high total dosages causes sterility and secondary MDS/AML. CVP leads to hair loss, but apart from this it is without significant morbidity. Both regimens may be associated with marrow toxicity which results in admissions with neutropenic sepsis or with thrombocytopenic bleeding.

Patients with Stage I non-Hodgkin's lymphoma have a 70–95% chance of cure with radiotherapy. The patient with disseminated low-grade lymphoma is not cured by treatment. Although 85% of patients achieve a complete response to therapy, this response is transient. After a median period of 18 months, the patient relapses and requires re-treatment. The average patient has four such episodes of response and relapse. Finally after a median period of seven and half years, there is transformation to high-grade lymphoma.

High-grade and intermediate-grade non-Hodgkin's lymphoma

Paradoxically, high-grade and intermediate-grade lymphomas are more likely to be confined to one lymph node group than low-grade tumours and are curable. Stage I disease may be treated with radiotherapy. Some clinicians will then proceed to treat with adjuvant chemotherapy. Patients with small bulk Stage I non-Hodgkin's lymphoma have a 95% chance of cure with radiation, and this chance is only minimally improved with chemotherapy. If the Stage I disease is bulky, chemotherapy alone may be given. Treatment is with the CHOP regimen, and there is little evidence that more complex regimens add to the chance of cure. Of all patients, 70–80% enter

remission, which is sustained in about 40–60% of cases.

High-dose therapy

Patients with poor prognosis lymphomas at presentation or with recurrent high-grade lymphoma may be considered for high-dose chemotherapy with auto or allogeneic bone marrow or other stem-cell support. These programs may be linked with attempts to purge marrow or peripheral blood stem cells of specific cell populations. Immunosuppression is required for patients receiving allografts. Prognosis depends on a number of risk factors. There is an associated mortality rate to these procedures which may exceed 10%.

New therapies

New agents have become available for the treatment of lymphoma. Amongst the most interesting are antibody treatments directed against B-cell antigens, such as rituximab. Rituximab is directed against CD20 and usually has very little toxicity apart from the possibility of a hypersensitivity response. It has been used mainly in the treatment of recurrent lymphoma. In more recent trials, however, rituximab has been prescribed as first-line therapy for patients with B-cell lymphomas. There are other anti-CD20, CD40 and CD8 antibody treatments, which show some promise if combined with radioisotopes such as I-131. Vaccine trials using patient-specific immunization with immunoglobulin idiotype are also underway. There is new hope for lymphoma patients!

Chapter 37

Myeloma

Epidemiology and pathogenesis

Myeloma is a relatively common haematological malignancy affecting 3000 people each year in England and Wales, and leading to 2000 deaths per year. There is an equal sex distribution and an increasing incidence with age. The rate of myeloma is higher amongst black populations, and the disease is associated with industrial and radiation exposure.

Multiple myeloma is a B-cell neoplasm characterized by the proliferation of plasma cells which synthesize and secrete monoclonal immunoglobulins or fragments thereof. The molecular basis of the transformation which characterizes this tumour is not clearly known. Karyotypic abnormalities have been identified in up to 50% of myeloma patients, but there is no clear, unifying change that underlies this transformation. Several molecular events have been described. These involve 14q32 translocations, chromosome 13 deletion and fibroblast growth factor receptor 3 (FGFR3) activation. These abnormalities are seen in no more than 20% of all myeloma patients. The translocations that have been described mostly involve the switch rearrangements of the heavy chain locus with partner genes such as FGFR3. Mutations have been observed in tumour suppressor genes and abnormalities of expression in apoptosis-related genes such as BCL-2. T cells secrete IL-6, which appears to be an essential growth factor for myeloma cells in culture.

Excessive secretion of IL-6 occurs in myeloma and this may be a primary cause for the condition.

The destructive bone lesions that are seen in myeloma are thought to be due to dysregulation of the osteoprotegerin rankl system. Rankl is the ligand for osteoprotegerin and an imbalance in this system leads to osteolysis.

Presentation

Patients with myeloma often present in a dramatic fashion with significant bone pain due to the lytic lesions that characterize this disease (Figure 37.1). Vertebral collapse is often a feature of presentation, and this may lead to symptoms of cord compression. Patients with myeloma may present with symptoms of hypercalcaemia, which every medical student reading this chapter is able to describe. Hypercalcaemia can be one of the precipitating factors for renal failure commonly observed in myeloma. The other causes include amyloidosis, precipitation of Bence–Jones protein, direct infiltration and infection. An excess of immunoglobulin may cause the hyperviscosity syndrome, which is more common with an IgG myeloma than an IgM myeloma. This is explained by the fact that a far greater proportion of patients have IgG than have IgM myelomas, which represents just 0.5% of all myeloma cases.

The raised paraprotein levels may cause other problems, including peripheral neuropathy.

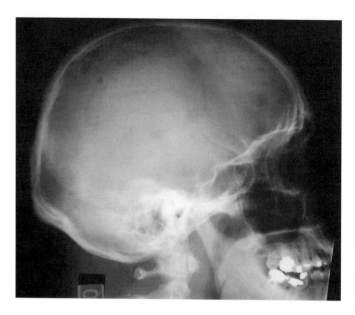

Figure 37.1 Skull radiograph of a 52-year old man with multiple myeloma showing multiple well defined lucencies that are fairly uniform in size, unlike bone metastases which usually vary in size.

Marrow infiltration with an excess of plasma cells leads to a decrease in numbers of other marrow constituents, causing anaemia, thrombocytopenia and neutropenia. This in turn has consequences for both the presentation and the clinical features of the disease as it evolves.

Investigations

The investigation of myeloma is relatively simple. It requires the examination of the peripheral blood, of paraprotein levels, blood count, $\beta 2$ microglobulin levels, renal function, calcium levels; assessment of the bone-marrow, examination of the urine for Bence–Jones protein urea and a skeletal survey. Bone-scanning is of low diagnostic value in myeloma. Myeloma is staged, and the staging has prognostic value. Two systems are used; those of Durie and Salmon, and that of the MRC (Tables 37.1–37.3 and Figures 37.2 and 37.3).

Treatment

The initial treatment of myeloma requires stabilization of the patient and correction of renal function abnormalities and hypercalcaemia. The patient will be started on allopurinol and may

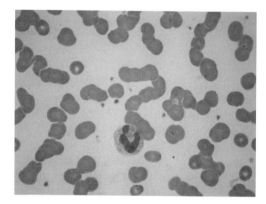

Figure 37.2 Peripheral blood film showing rouleaux formation with erythrocytes stacked up on each other, and a single neutrophil. Rouleaux are found at high levels in the blood of proteins such as fibrinogen or gammaglobulin. They are particularly prominent in diseases that cause a very high erythrocyte sedimentation rate (ESR), such as multiple myeloma, cancers, chronic infections (e.g. TB) and connective tissue diseases. (See also colour plates between pages 154 and 155.)

require hydration or transfusion. Hypercalcaemia will be treated with bisphosphonates, steroids and rehydration. Where there is significant bone pain, which is poorly responsive to opiates, radiotherapy may be required. A single fraction treatment will alleviate bone pain in approximately 80% of

Table 37.1 Diagnostic criteria for myeloma.

Major criteria	
I	Plasmacytoma or tissue biopsy
II	Bone marrow plasmacytosis >30%
III	Monoclonal (M) spike on electrophoresis >35 g/L (IgG peaks) or >20 g/L (IgA peaks) or kappa or lambda light-chain excretion >1.0 g/24 h
Minor criteria	Distant metastases
a	Bone-marrow plasmacytosis 10–30%
b	M spike present but less than above
c	Lytic bone lesions
d	The normal immunoglobulin levels decreased: IgM below 0.05 g/L or IgA below 0.01 g/L or IgG below 0.60 g/L
	Diagnosis of myeloma requires a minimum of one major plus one minor criteria *or* three minor criteria
Diagnostic criteria for MGUS	
I	Monoclonal gammopathy
II	Bone marrow plasma cells <10%
III	Monoclonal (M) component level IgG < 35 g/L IgA < 20 g/L kappa or lambda light chains <1.0 g/24 h
IV	No overt bone lesions
V	No symptoms to suggest myeloma

patients. Anaemia may require transfusion and significant hyperviscosity needs plasmaphoresis.

Chemotherapy for myeloma has a 50-year history, beginning with the use of alkylating agents such as melphalan and cyclophosphamide. These agents are still in use, given with or without prednisone, although the value of giving prednisone is not particularly clear. With this approach, the median survival for patients is 2.5 years. Clinical trials have investigated the benefits of more intensive therapy using combination chemotherapy programmes, and these appear to have no benefit compared with single-agent therapy. The exception to this view is that for younger patients, there may be a benefit to combination treatment, but this is by no means proven.

Infusional chemotherapy using vincristine, doxorubicin and dexamethasone was developed in the

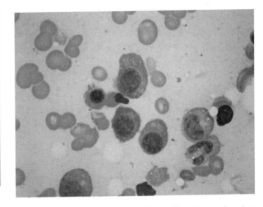

Figure 37.3 Bone marrow aspirate of myeloma showing plasma cells with large eccentric nuclei and basophilic cytoplasm. (See also colour plates between pages 154 and 155.)

Table 37.2 Durie and Salmon staging system.

Cell mass category: Requirements:		High (Stage III) One of A, B, C, D	Low (Stage I) All of A, B, C, D	Intermediate (Stage II)
Haemoglobin (pretransfusion) (g/dL%)	A	<85	>10	
Serum calcium (mg%)	B	>12	Normal	Neither
M-component	C	IgG > 7 g/dL% IgA > 5 g/dL% BJ > 12 g/day	<5 <3 <4	I or III
Bone lesion on skeletal survey	D	Advanced lytic disease	None/solitary lesion	

Table 37.3 MRC staging system.

		Poor prognosis (Stage III) A, C or B, C	Good prognosis (Stage I) All of A, B, C, D	Intermediate (Stage II) Not in I or III
Blood urea concentration (mM/L)	A	>10	= 8	Not in I or III
Haemoglobin (g/dL)	B	= 7.5	>10.0	Not in I or III
Performance status	C	Restricted activity	Minimal symptoms Or asymptomatic	Not in I or III

Table 37.4 Southwest Oncology Group myeloma response criteria.

A. Responsive patients who satisfy all the following criteria are considered to have achieved definite objective improvement.

1. A sustained decrease in the synthesis index of serum monoclonal protein to 25% or less of the pre-treatment value, and to less than 25 g/L on at least two measurements separated by 4 weeks. For IgA and Ig_3M proteins the synthetic index is the same as the serum concentration. For IgG proteins of subclasses 1, 2, and 4 of the synthetic index must be estimated using a nomogram.

2. A sustained decrease in 24-hour urine globulin to 10% or less of the pre-treatment value, and to less than 0.2 g/24 h on at least two occasions separated by 4 weeks.

3. In all responsive patients the size and number of lytic skull lesions must not increase, and the serum calcium must remain normal. Correction of anaemia (haematocrit > 27 vol%) and hypoalbuminaemia (> 3.0 g/dL) is required if they are considered to be secondary to myeloma. With equivocal data (e.g. non-secretors, or L-chain producers for whom the pre-treatment urine collection was lost), the following support the conclusion that an objective response has occurred.

4. Recalcification of lytic skull lesions.

5. Significant increments in depressed normal immunoglobulins (e.g. increments >200 ml/L IgM, >400 mg/L IgA, and >4000 mg/L IgG).

B. Improved patients show a decline in the serum M-protein synthesis rate to less than 50%, but not less than 25% of the pre-treatment value.

C. Unresponsive patients fail to satisfy the criteria for responsive or improved patients.

1990s and is effective in relapse. Its role as primary treatment is not clear. High-dose chemotherapy with melphalan was developed at the Royal Marsden Hospital in the 1980s and, combined with autologous marrow rescue, leads to high response rate—but unfortunately to a high relapse rate, too. When treatment was combined with total body irradiation, encouraging results were found. Results from a randomized trial carried out in France, however, suggest that there is no survival benefit to this approach compared with more simple therapies.

Maintenance therapy with alpha-Interferon has been investigated with a trend to improving remission duration. The assessment of response to myeloma is subject to a number of different analyses. One of the least complex is that of the Southwest Oncology Group, which is described in Table 37.4.

Future treatments of myeloma

Because myeloma is a clonal disease, there is hope that molecular therapies may be effective. Agents targetting vascular endothelial growth-factor receptors such as thalidomide have been investigated for myeloma but were not found to be particularly effective. Tumour cell/dendritic cell fusions have been examined as a vaccination strategy for multiple myeloma and were found to have myeloma specific cytotoxicity. Antisense oligonucleotides have been shown to have some efficacy in patients with recurrent myeloma. Nuclear factor-kappaB is a collective description of a group of transcription factors for a number of genes that include angiogenesis modulators, cell-adhesion molecules and antiapoptotic factors. There is evidence that NF-kappaB is constitutively active in myeloma. A new agent such as bortezomib, which modulates the activity of NF-kappaB, has recently been approved for the treatment of patients with advanced myeloma. This agent appears to function as a proteasome inhibitor.

Chapter 38

Skin cancer

Cinema has wide-ranging influence on fashion trends and one of the most striking examples was the mid-20th-century trend toward sun-tanning. The fashion of the Victorian era was sun-avoidance; the upper classes stayed pale in part to distinguish themselves from lower-class workers who had to toil in the sun. Yet by the 1950s, the beach culture of Southern California spread world-wide via the movies. The ill effects of chronic exposure to ultraviolet radiation on skin-ageing are well-demonstrated by Clint Eastwood. The carcinogenic effects of sunlight led to the removal of a basal cell carcinoma from the former actor, US President Ronald Reagan, whilst his eldest daughter Maureen Reagan died of melanoma.

The following two chapters discuss both non-melanoma skin tumours and melanomas.

Chapter 39

Non-melanoma skin tumours

Epidemiology and pathogenesis

Non-melanoma skin cancers comprise more than one-third of all cancers in the UK and have been described as a world-wide epidemic. The term includes two major types: basal cell carcinoma (BCC) and squamous cell carcinoma (SCC). Other less common non-melanoma skin cancers include Kaposi's sarcoma, cutaneous lymphoma, and Merkel cell carcinoma. Despite their frequency, these tumours account for only 2% of cancer deaths.

Basal cell carcinoma (BCC) is four times more common than squamous cell carcinomas (SCC). Sun damage is the major cause of both cancers, especially ultraviolet B (UVB) spectrum (290–320 nm wavelength). The UV radiation produces DNA mutations, particularly thymidine dimers in the p53 tumour suppressor gene. The incidence of skin cancer rises with latitudes approaching the equator. Light-exposed areas of the body are the most frequent sites for tumours, and occupations with high sun exposure like farming have an increased incidence of BCC and SCC. Ozone absorbs UVB, and progressive destruction of the ozone layer by fluorinated hydrocarbons may lead to increased rates. Melanin absorbs UV, and its lower levels in melanocytes of white people accounts for the higher incidence of skin cancers in white people. The benefits of melanin in areas of high UV exposure are offset against the reduced production of vitamin D3 which requires UV light, so in regions of low sunlight, black people are prone to rickets. This delicately balanced system of biological geodiversity has been abused to justify some of the most inhumane behaviour. Genetic predispositions to skin cancers include xeroderma pigmentosum, Gorlin's basal cell naevus syndrome and familial melanoma syndromes. Patients with Xeroderma pigmentosa are unable to repair the UV-induced DNA damage and develop both BCC and SCC under the age of 10 years old. Gorlin's basal cell naevus syndrome patients develop BCC in their teens and brain tumours; it is caused by a mutation of a patched gene involved in the Hedgehog pathway signal transduction. The gene name 'Hedgehog' was originally coined because mutations lead to spikes on Drosophila fruit flies. Humans have three homologues of the gene named after the two common varieties of hedgehogs, 'Indian' and 'Desert'. The third human gene was named 'Sonic' after Sega's game character. Familial melanoma is caused by inherited mutations of the CDKN2 (p16) gene (chromosome 9p21) and of CDK4 (chromosome 12q13), both implicated in insensitivity to cell-cycle checkpoints. Chemical carcinogens, including arsenic, are associated with SCC. Sir Percival Pott's description in 1775 of scrotal cancers in chimney-sweeps is thought to be due to industrial exposure to coal tar. Radiation is associated with an increased incidence of SCC, BCC and Bowen's disease (SCC *in situ*). Allogeneic organ transplant recipients are at greatly increased risk of SCC, with as many as 80% having SCC within 20 years of the graft. This may be related to the finding of genotypes five and eight of human papilloma virus in some skin SCC.

Clinical presentation

BCC begins in the basal cell layer of the epidermis, usually develops on chronically sun-exposed areas of the skin, rarely metastasizes, and is usually slow-growing. If left untreated, however, BCC may spread locally to the bone or other tissues beneath the skin. BCC starts as painless translucent pearly nodules with telangiectasia on sun-exposed skin. As they enlarge, they ulcerate and bleed and develop a rolled shiny edge sometimes referred to as a 'rodent ulcer'. They may progress slowly over many months to years, but less than 0.1% metastasize to regional lymph nodes. They occur mostly on the face, especially nose, nasolabial fold, inner canthus, usually in elderly people and are more common in men than in women.

SCC arises from more superficial layers of the epidermis and tends to be more aggressive. SCC can invade tissues beneath the skin and 1–2% spread to the lymph nodes. These cancers typically appear on sun-exposed areas of the body, such as the face, ears, neck, lips, and backs of the hands. Marjolin ulcers are SCCs arising in long-standing, benign ulcers, such as venous ulcers, or scars, such as old burns. SCCs are irregular, red hyperkeratotic tumours which ulcerate and crust. Unlike BCCs, SCCs grow more rapidly over months rather than years and occasionally bleed. Precursors to SCC include actinic keratosis and SCC *in situ* which is also called Bowen's disease. SCC *in situ* is a full-thickness malignant transformation of the epidermis that, by definition, has not invaded the dermis.

Merkel cell carcinoma is a highly malignant tumour in the basal layer of the epidermis most commonly in elderly, white patients. It consists of rapidly growing, painless and shiny purple nodules which may occur anywhere on the body. These tumours are thought to arise from neuroendocrine cells and are positive for neuron-specific enolase staining. They resemble small-cell lung cancer in their clinical course. Distant metastases are common, and treatment is with combination chemotherapy, although relapses are frequent and the prognosis is poor. Other rarer non-melanoma skin cancers include Kaposi's sarcoma, which usually starts within the dermis but can also develop in internal organs. This cancer, once extremely rare, has become more common due to its association with HIV/AIDS. It is caused by infection with an oncogenic Herpesvirus: HHV8 (human herpesvirus 8). Primary cutaneous lymphoma or mycosis fungoides, is a low-grade lymphoma that primarily affects the skin. Generally, it has a slow course and often remains confined to the skin, but progression of the tumour to a more aggressive, life-threatening stage is more likely the longer it has been present. Adnexal tumours, which start in the hair follicles or sweat glands, are extremely rare and usually benign (Figures 39.1 and 39.2).

Treatment

The goal of treatment for BCC and SCC is to eradicate local disease and achieve the best cosmetic appearance. For BCC, a complete skin examination is indicated because of the increased risk of actinic keratosis or cancers located at other skin sites in persons presenting with a suspicious lesion. For SCC, regional lymph nodes should also be examined. The main options include: surgery, which offers a single brief procedure and histological confirmation of completeness of excision; curettage, which is suitable for small, nodular lesions of less than 1 cm and yields good cosmesis; and cryotherapy, which can be used for lesions of less than 2 cm but may leave an area of depigmentation, and radiotherapy. Mohs micrographic surgery is a specialized form of excisional surgery that provides 100% microscopically controlled histologic margins. The technique involves tumour excision, mapping of the removed tissue and immediate microscopic assessment of the surgical specimen. If occult tumour extension is detected microscopically, the process is repeated until a tumour-free margin is attained. Mohs surgery is curative for 99% of primary BCCs and for 97% of primary SCCs, the highest documented cure rates. Radiotherapy has the advantages of no pain, no

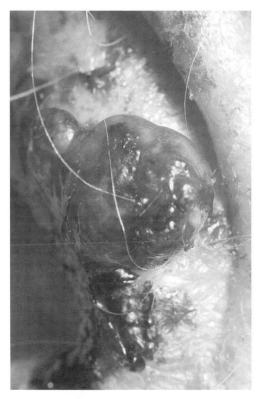

Figure 39.1 A large, raised, bleeding skin lesion on the pinna, a common site for squamous cell cancers of the skin. These tumours are related to UV exposure and may be preceded by actinic or solar keratoses. (See also colour plates between pages 154 and 155.)

hospitalization and no keloids or contracture; it preserves uninvolved tissue and produces smaller defects. It does, however, require multiple visits and results in depigmentation, and loss of hair follicles and sweat glands at the treated site. The decision between surgery and radiotherapy is based on size and site, histology, age of patient, recurrence rates and anticipated cosmetic results. Topical 5-fluorouracil chemotherapy may be used for actinic keratosis and small superficial noninvasive tumours. Side-effects include progressive inflammation, erythema, erosions and contact dermatitis. Systemic chemotherapy is reserved for treating locally advanced and metastatic disease. The most widely used regimens include cisplatin in combination with 5-fluorouracil or doxorubicin.

Prevention remains the most important aspect of the management of skin cancers and requires campaigns to increase public awareness. Children should not get sunburnt, and white-skinned people should limit their total cumulative sun

Table 39.1 A prognosis of five-year survival for patients with non-melanoma skin tumours.

Tumour	5-year survival
BCC	95–100%
SCC	92–99%

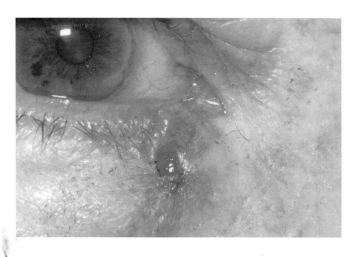

Figure 39.2 A pearly edged, ulcerated lesion characteristic of a basal cell cancer of the skin. (See also colour plates between pages 154 and 155.)

exposure. The public should be encouraged to look out for new skin lesions, and those that are not obviously benign should be seen and removed in their entirety for pathological examination within four weeks.

Prognosis

The prognosis of five-year survival for patients with non-melanoma skin tumours is given in Table 39.1.

Chapter 40

Melanoma

Epidemiology and pathogenesis

Melanoma is a tumour of melanocytes: the pigmented cells of the skin. The incidence of melanoma has increased by a factor of 3.5 between 1971 and 1997. In England and Wales, there are currently nearly 5000 people affected by this condition. The primary cause is thought to be an increase in exposure to sunlight. Risk factors for the development of melanoma, however, include being Caucasian and having dysplastic naevi or familial melanoma. It is encouraging to note that recently, there has been a stabilization of the increase in melanoma incidence. One hopes that with all the publicity, the risks of exposure to sun are at last entering into the public consciousness.

Less than 10% of all melanoma cases constitute families with an inherited predisposition to melanoma. Mutations in two genes, CDKN2A and CDK4, have been shown to confer increased risk of melanoma, but these mutations only constitute about one-fifth of all familial cases. In other families, there is linkage around the 1p22 chromosomal region. Loss of the transcription factor AP-2 is also thought to have some tumour suppressor-like role in melanoma progression.

Presentation

Patients with malignant melanoma generally present with a history of a growing mole, which may bleed or itch. Because of the public awareness of melanoma, generally there is quite rapid self-referral to GPs with these symptoms. Specialist referral to plastic surgery or dermatology is also quick, and many hospitals now offer walk-in skin-lesion clinics. In clinic, the specialist will on initial examination seek to confirm the diagnosis. If there is no evidence for metastases, he will make arrangements to excise the primary lesion. This excision requires specialist surgery with wide excision of the surrounding normal tissue. The reasons for this are firstly, concerns about the incidence of local recurrence following inadequate resection and, secondly, the need for good cosmesis. Although wide excision is practised, there is no randomized trial that supports this practice (Figures 40.1–40.4 and Table 40.1).

Staging and grading

There are four main clinical descriptions of melanoma and these are superficial spreading, nodular, lentigo maligna and acral lentiginous subtypes.

Following excision and confirmation of the diagnosis histologically, staging investigations which should include CT scanning should be performed. As a result of surgery and staging procedures, the clinical stage can be defined as follows:
Stage 1a Localized melanoma less than 0.75 mm thick

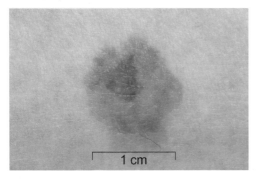

Figure 40.1 Atypical or dysplastic naevi are large naevi (moles) with irregular boarders and varied pigmentation. Atypical naevi are the precursors of melanomas. (See also colour plates between pages 154 and 155.)

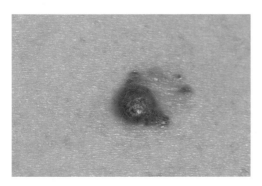

Figure 40.2 A pigmented nodular lesion with an irregular edge and adjacent satellite lesions. This was a nodular melanoma. (See also colour plates between pages 154 and 155.)

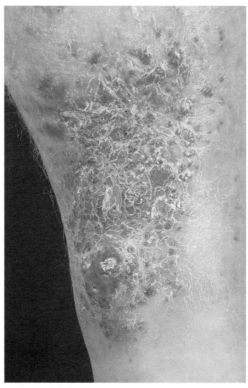

Figure 40.3 Irregular nodular pigmented lesion on the skin at the site of a previously excised malignant melanoma. This represents local recurrence of the melanoma. (See also colour plates between pages 154 and 155.)

Stage 1b Localized melanoma 0.76–1.5 mm thick

Stage 2a Localized melanoma 1.6–4 mm thick

Stage 2b Localized melanoma greater than 4 mm thick

Stage 3 Limited nodal metastases involving only one regional lymph-node group

Stage 4 Advanced regional metastases or distant metastases

There are additional widely practised staging systems, which are not included in this book. For prognostic purposes, however, pathological stag-ing is significant and includes Breslow thickness and Clark's levels. These are as follows:

Clark's level I   Melanoma confined to epidermis

Clark's level II   Penetration   into   papillary dermis

Clark's level III Extension to reticular dermis

Clark's level IV Extension   into   deep   reticular dermis

Clark's level V Invasion of subcutaneous fat

Breslow's staging system measures the vertical thickness of the primary tumour as 'Breslow's thickness', as less then 0.75 mm, 0.76–1.5 mm, 1.51–3.99 mm and greater than 4 mm.

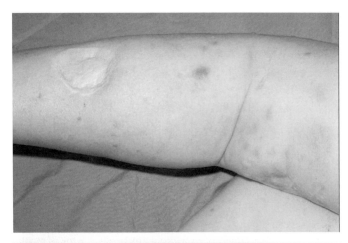

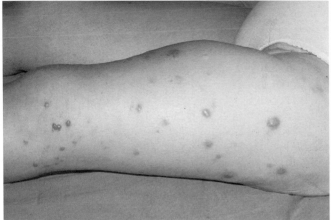

Figure 40.4 Multiple nodular skin metastases arising from a melanoma of the left calf that had been widely excised two years earlier requiring a skin graft. (See also colour plates between pages 154 and 155.)

Table 40.1 Clinicopathological features of four common forms of melanoma.

Type	Location	Age (median)	Gender & race	Edge	Colour	Frequency
Superficial spreading	All body surfaces, especially legs	56 years	White females	Palpable, irregular	Brown, black, grey or pink; central or halo depigmentation	50%
Nodular	All body surfaces	49 years	White males	Palpable	Uniform bluish black	30%
Lentigo maligna	Sun-exposed, especially head and neck	70 years	White females	Flat, irregular	Shades of brown or black, hypopigmentation	15%
Acral lentigenous	Palms, soles & mucous membranes	61 years	Black males	Palpable, irregular nodule	Black, irregularly coloured	5%

Treatment

Adjuvant therapy

There have been many studies of the use of adjuvant immunotherapy in melanoma. Adjuvant immunotherapy using the interferons has led to some conflicting findings. Some studies have been positive and others not. Cancer vaccines have been developed, enhancing anti-tumour immune responses and in some recent studies prolonged survival has been reported. Treatment with adjuvant chemotherapy has largely been without any benefit at all and have produced remarkable levels of toxicities without any effect.

Management of local skin metastases and nodal disease

The treatment of this pattern of relapse is primarily surgical. Localized recurrence is excised and nodal metastases are managed by radical lymph node dissection. There are advocates of regional infusional programmes using cytotoxic chemotherapy, but the value of this is contentious. Radiotherapy may be used where localized disease is inoperable or as an adjuvant to surgery, reducing the bulk of disease prior to definitive surgery.

Treatment of metastatic melanoma

The outlook for patients with metastatic melanoma is poor. Patients generally have disease in multiple sites, and the median survival is approximately four to six months. Treatment depends upon the patient, on his or her fitness and on the disease site. Patients with multiple disease sites are treated with chemotherapy or biological therapies or a combination of the two. The most effective chemotherapeutic drugs are dacarbazine, the nitrosoureas and vindesine. The response rate to these compounds is in the range of 5–10%. Prolonged survival is very rare, and the consensus view is that there is no advantage to the combination of single agents. New chemotherapy agents are being developed for melanoma, and there is interest in the role of Temozolomide.

It is clear that biological therapies are effective in melanoma. Within this group, the interferons lead to response rates of 10%. The median duration of a partial response is approximately four months, and of a complete response seven months. More recently, adoptive immunotherapy using interleukin 2 and LAK (lymphokine activated killer) cells has been evaluated in melanoma. The high response rates initially reported have not been confirmed, and the true response rates are in the order of 10% with a median duration of three months. Very rarely, spontaneous regression of metastatic disease occurs.

Prognosis

The most important prognostic factor is clinical stage as is reported in a group of 4000 patients treated in America and Australia. Approximately 90% of Stage 1 patients, 60% of Stage 2 patients and 30% of Stage 3 patients survive for ten years. The survival of Stage 4 patients depends upon the metastatic site. Median survival for patients with metastases in the skin is seven months, in the lung is one year, in the brain is five months, in the liver is two months and in bone is six months. The depth of tumour invasion is the most important prognostic factor for localized melanoma. This can be described according to the Clark's stage and Breslow's thickness. Ten-year survival for a lesion less than 0.75 mm thick or for a Clark's level I-melanoma is 90%, for a lesion 0.75–1.5 mm thick or Clark's level II is 80%, for a lesion 1.6–2.49 mm thick or Clark's level III is 60%, for a lesion 2.5–3.99 mm thick or Clark's level IV is 50% and for a lesion greater than 4 mm or Clark's level V is approximately 30%.

Other important survival factors have been described from multifactorial analyses. They include the type of initial surgical management, pathological stage, ulceration, the presence of satellite nodules, a peripheral anatomical location and, to a much lesser extent, patient's sex, age and tumour diameter.

The American Joint Committee on Cancer, in a study involving 17 600 patients, has provided recent information on survival. This ranges from 90% survival at five years for early-stage disease to, as might be expected, the usual miserable outlook of only 5% survival at five years for metastatic disease.

New therapies

Angiogenesis inhibitors such as Thalidomide are currently under evaluation and responses have been reported. Anti-tumour vaccination programmes have also been developed, based on the initial observation by Morton and others.

Chapter 41

Paediatric solid tumours

Epidemiology and pathogenesis

Cancer is a leading cause of death in children in England and Wales, second only to accidental injury. It is responsible for around 10% of deaths in childhood. Cancer in children is nonetheless relatively rare, affecting one in 600 children, and includes a different spectrum of cancers than adults. The solid tumours encountered in childhood are often embryonal in origin, and many are associated with an inherited predisposition. There are few areas of medicine that can rival the advances made in paediatric oncology in the second half of the twentieth century. Seven in ten children with cancer are now cured, compared with fewer than three in ten in 1962–1966. It is estimated that in 2000, 55 000 young adults in Britain aged 16–40 years were survivors of childhood cancer.

Many paediatric tumours are associated with recognized familial predispositions which are due to inherited mutations of tumour suppressor genes and therefore are inherited as autosomal, dominant traits. Examples are hereditary retinoblastoma (mutations of the RB gene on chromosome 13q14) and familial Wilms' tumours (mutations of the WT1 gene on chromosome 11p13). In contrast, environmental oncogenic factors have been less readily identified for paediatric solid tumours; one example, however, is the excess of papillary thyroid cancers in children following the nuclear explosion at Chernobyl (see Section 1 Chapter 2).

After leukaemias, which account for 22% of childhood malignancies or 440 cases per year in the UK, CNS tumours are the most common (20% or 330 cases), accounting for 2.5 in 100 000 persons under 18 years old, followed by lymphoma (NHL: 8%, Hodgkin's: 6%), neuroblastoma (8%), Wilms' tumour (6%) and bone tumours (6%).

Clinical presentation and management of CNS tumours

Tumours in the CNS occur throughout childhood; the age distribution of paediatric CNS tumours is 15% between birth and two years old, 30% from two- to five-years old, 30% from five- to ten-years old and 25% from 11- to 18-years old. In contrast to adult brain tumours, most (60%) are infratentorial and 75% are midline, involving the cerebellum, midbrain, pons and medulla. The most common tumours, accounting for 45%, are astrocytomas of varying grades. They include optic nerve gliomas, which are usually well-differentiated tumours. A further 20% are medulloblastomas, a small round-cell tumour of childhood, of neuroectodermal origin. Medulloblastomas usually arise in the posterior fossa and may seed metastases in the neuraxis by dropping them down the subarachoid space into the spinal canal. Craniopharyngiomas make up 5–10% of CNS tumours of childhood and cause raised intracranial pressure, visual defects and pituitary

Complications of therapy

Although many of the delayed effects of chemotherapy and radiotherapy in children are similar to those in adults, the effects on developing organs also produce unique late side-effects particularly on the skeleton, brain and endocrine systems. These delayed effects of multimodality therapy on the developing child are substantial and the late sequelae cause considerable morbidity in this group of patients where the long-term survival rates are high. Radiotherapy retards bone and cartilage growth, causes intellectual impairment, gonadal toxicity, hypothalamic and thyroid dysfunction, as well as pneumonitis, nephrotoxicity and hepatotoxicity. Late consequences of chemotherapy include infertility, anthracycline related cardiotoxicity, bleomycin related pulmonary fibrosis, platinum related nephrotoxicity and neurotoxicity. Up to 5% of children cured of this cancer will develop a second malignancy as a consequence of an inheriteted cancer predisposition or the late sequelae of cancer treatment. Second malignancies occur most frequently following combined chemotherapy and radiotherapy.

Chapter 42

Bone cancers and sarcomas

Epidemiology and pathogenesis

Bone tumours are amongst the oldest cancers discovered in humans according to paleopathological evidence. A bronze-age woman with bone metastases in her skull has been dated to 1600–1900 BC, whilst Saxon bones from Standlake in Oxfordshire demonstrate features of osteosarcoma in a young adult warrior. St Peregrine, born in 1260 at Forlì, Italy, is the patron saint of cancer sufferers (the feast day is on 4 May). He was due for an amputation for a sarcoma of the leg, but the cancer was cured on the night prior to surgery, following a vision of Christ. He lived a further 20 years and was canonized in 1726. The presumed origins of primary bone tumours are shown in Table 42.1.

Sarcomas are tumours of the connective tissue which supports the body and include bone muscle, tendon, fat and synovial tissue. These tumours represent less than 1% of all malignancies. They have an incidence of approximately 1–2 per 100 000 per annum. There are no known associated aetiological factors, although sarcomas rarely occur as second malignancies in areas of the body that have been previously irradiated. The most common bone tumours are osteosarcoma and Ewing's sarcoma.

Ewing's sarcoma occurs in childhood and in early adult life. Molecular biology studies have shown the presence of a specific chromosomal translocation between chromosome 22 and 11. This translocation is present in a group of small round blue cell tumours which include peripheral neuroectodermal tumours (PNETs), classic Ewing's and extraosseous Ewing's sarcoma, and these are now grouped together for treatment purposes.

Osteosarcoma occurs in two groups of patients, firstly in adolescence or early adult life and secondly in old age, where osteosarcoma complicates Paget's disease. P53 mutations are commonly seen in osteosarcoma, as are mutations in the retinoblastoma gene.

Presentation

Most soft-tissue sarcomas occur in the limbs, and patients present to their GPs with localized swelling. Patients with Ewing's tumours and sarcomas generally present with pain, and the diagnosis generally comes as a result of the classical X-ray appearances of these tumours. Fractures are common and nerve palsies may be seen where there is a cranial presentation. Patients may also present with metastases. Because of the rarity of these tumours and the requirement for a multidisciplinary specialist approach, patients with a suspected diagnosis of sarcoma should be referred on to specialist centres, where results have been shown to be vastly superior to those achieved by peripheral clinics. These tumours are usually diagnosed after a significant delay. (Tables 42.2–42.4 and Figures 42.1–42.4.)

Investigations and management

In a patient where a diagnosis of soft tissue sarcoma is suspected, an initial biopsy should be carried out by the surgeon who is to perform definitive surgery. Fine-needle aspiration cytology, core-needle biopsy and incisional biopsies are all techniques that are considered by the surgeon and, for those patients with rare abdominal or thoracic soft-tissue sarcomas, CT guided biopsies may be required. After the pathological diagnosis has been established, definitive surgery can be planned. This requires a multidisciplinary approach which takes place in the context of MR staging of the local tumour and CT definition of metastatic sites. The surgical approach requires the removal of the muscle compartment to include the fascia. This limits the risk of local relapse.

In those patients with Ewing's sarcomas and osteosarcomas, initial staging will include CT assessment of the chest, abdomen and pelvis, and MR of the primary tumour site. The initial management option for Ewing's sarcoma includes the consideration of either primary surgery or radiotherapy to control the local lesion. If the lesion is small and it is possible to have substantial resection margins, surgery is the best option with immediate endoprosthetic

Table 42.1 Origins of primary bone tumours.

Origin	Benign	Malignant
Cartilage	Enchondroma	Chondrosarcoma
	Osteochondroma	
	Chondroblastoma	
Bone	Osteoid osteoma	Osteosarcoma
	Osteoblastoma	
Unknown origin	Giant cell tumour	Ewing's sarcoma
		Malignant fibrous histiocytoma

Table 42.2 Features of cartilage derived bone tumours.

	Enchondroma	Osteochondroma (exostosis)	Chondroblastoma	Chondrosarcoma
Age	10–50 years	10–20 years	5–20 years	30–60 years
Site	Hands, wrist	Knee, shoulder, pelvis	Knee, shoulder, ribs	Knee, shoulder, pelvis
	Diaphysis	Metaphysis	Epiphysis prior to fusion	Metaphysis or diaphysis
X-Ray	Well-defined lucency, thin sclerotic rim, calcification	Eccentric protrusion from bone, calcification	Well defined lucency, thin sclerotic rim, calcification	Expansile lucency, sclerotic margin, cortical destruction, soft tissue mass
Notes	Ollier's disease = multiple enchondromata	1% transform to chondrosarcoma		

Table 42.3 Features of osteoid derived bone tumours.

	Osteoid osteoma	Osteoblastoma	Osteosarcoma
Age	10–30 years	10–20 years	10–25 years & >60 years
Site	Knee	Vertebra	Knee, shoulder, pelvis
	Diaphysis	Metaphysis	Metaphysis
X-Ray	<1 cm central lucency, surrounding bone sclerosis, periosteal reaction	Well defined lucency, sclerotic rim, cortex preserved calcification	Lytic/sclerotic expansile lesion, wide transition zone, cortical destruction, soft tissue mass, periosteal reaction, calcification

Table 42.4 Features bone tumours of uncertain origins.

	Giant cell tumour	Ewing's sarcoma	Malignant fibrous histiocytoma
Age	20–40 years	5–15 years	10–20 years & >60 years
Site	Long bones, knee	Knee, shoulder, pelvis	Knee, pelvis, shoulder
	Epiphysis & metaphysis post closure	Diaphysis, less often metaphysis	Metaphysis
X-ray	Lucency with ill-defined endosteal margin, cortical destruction, soft-tissue mass, eccentric expansion	Ill-defined medullary destruction, small areas of new bone formation, periosteal reaction, soft-tissue expansion, bone/lung-metastases	Cortical destruction, periosteal reaction, soft-tissue mass

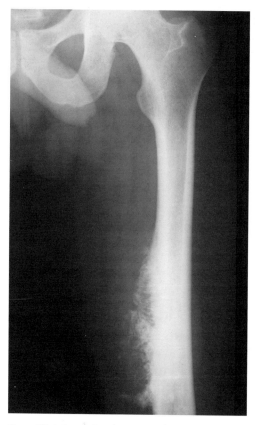

Figure 42.1 Femur chondrosarcoma showing expansile lesion with sclerotic margin, cortical destruction and punctuate internal calcification and associated soft tissue mass. These tumours are most common in middle age and occur around the knee, shoulder or pelvis.

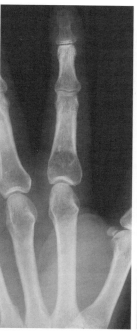
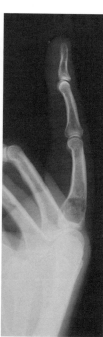

Figure 42.2 Enchondroma ring finger proximal phalynx showing well defined lucency and thin sclerotic rim with preserved cortex. These cartilage-derived tumours occur in 10–50 year olds most frequently in the diaphyses of the hand or wrist. Multiple enchondromata occur in Ollier's disease, a non-hereditary condition that is associated with an increased risk of chondrosarcoma.

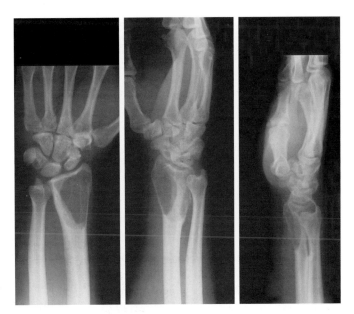

Figure 42.3 Giant cell tumour of the distal radius showing expansion and lucency with cortical destruction giving a multiloculated appearance. These tumours occur most commonly in 20–40 year olds in long bones at the epiphyses and metaphyses after closure.

replacement. For the majority of patients, however, radiotherapy remains the most important treatment modality for the control of local disease.

Osteosarcomas are rare and for this reason also best managed in specialist centres. This is particularly important for teenage patients with sarcomas. For these patients, chemotherapy, radiation, surgery and counselling all have a significant role in management. Patients with osteosarcomas are generally managed well because of the excellent results achieved using multidisciplinary specialist approaches. In osteosarcoma bone scanning as well as CT and MR scanning are essential in the initial work up of a patient. Biopsy of the tumour is required with the open approach preferred. Surgical advances have meant that bone tumours are managed so much better than they were, with the aim of limb-sparing prosthetic surgery.

Pathology

The most helpful classification of soft-tissue tumours is into tumours of fibrous tissue, fibrohistio-cytic tumours, adipose tissue tumours including liposarcomas, tumours of muscle, tumours of blood vessels, tumours of lymph vessels, tumours of synovium, tumours of mesothelium, tumours of peripheral nerves, tumours of autonomic ganglia, tumours of paraganglionic structures, tumours of cartilage and bone forming tissue, tumours of pleuripotential mesochyme, tumours of uncertain histogenesis and unclassified soft tissue tumours. This latter tumour group is extremely diverse, with at least 50 different subtypes.

These groups may in turn be divided into benign and malignant conditions. Benign tumours do not generally metastasize, and microscopic examination shows a low mitotic rate. Malignant tumours have a high mitotic rate and do tend to metastasize. Approximately one-third of tumours are low-grade and two-thirds are high-grade. Osteosarcomas are described as being of low, intermediate and high grade.

Treatment of soft tissue sarcomas

Clinical features of soft tissue sarcomas are listed in Table 42.5

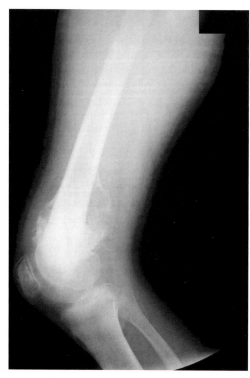

Figure 42.4 Osteosarcoma Codman triangle. Osteosarcoma of distal femur showing expansile soft tissue mass with internal calcification and cortical destruction. There is a marked periosteal reaction with lifting of the periosteum that is described as Codman's triangle which is almost always due to an aggressive malignant bone tumour extending into adjacent soft tissues.

Treatment of the primary tumour

There is considerable discussion as the appropriate management of a soft tissue sarcoma. Low-grade tumours which by definition should not spread, should be treated by surgical excision alone. Local control should result in 85–100% recovery in these patients. The situation is different for those patients with high-grade tumours, and there is debate as to whether surgery alone, surgery combined with radiation, or surgery, radiation and chemotherapy in combination is the correct approach.

Surgery

There is little argument that surgery is necessary, and the operation of first choice should be one that allows a reasonably wide margin of normal tissue to be excised with the tumour. If a good procedure is carried out, such as muscle compartmental excision, the local failure rate is 7–18%. If less radical procedures such as excision biopsy are performed, then the local failure rate is approximately 50%. More radical procedures such as amputation have a lower local recurrence rate—which is approximately 5%. Over the last decade, there has been a trend toward radical compartmental excision with limb-sparing procedures.

Adjuvant chemotherapy and radiation

After definitive surgery has been performed, the need for radiation and chemotherapy is assessed. Radiation is not given for low-grade tumours. In high-grade tumours, radiotherapy to the tumour bed has an advantage in terms of reduced local recurrence rates in extremity lesions where effective dosages can be given without risking vital structures. Local radiation has no effect upon the progression of distant metastases. Because patients with high-grade sarcomas are at great risk from the progression of their cancer to a metastatic state, adjuvant chemotherapy has been investigated in a number of trials. The original studies which were, however, non-randomized, showed an advantage to combination chemotherapy. This result has not held up, and the consensus view now is that adjuvant chemotherapy has no advantage in terms of five-year survival. This remains very much a subject for debate, however, and in many centres adjuvant chemotherapy is still administered.

Treatment of metastatic sarcoma

The treatment of metastatic soft tissue sarcomas requires the use of chemotherapy. The most effective single-agent treatments lead to responses in 15–35% of patients. Attempts are made to capitalize on this by the use of combination chemotherapy programmes. A slight increase in response

Table 42.5 Clinical features of soft-tissue sarcomas.

Tumour	Age (y)	Commonest sites	Primary therapy	5-year survival
Fibrosarcoma	20–50	Thigh, arm, head & neck	Wide excision & adjuvant radiation	90% (well diff) 50% (poorly diff)
Liposarcoma	40–60	Thigh, head & neck (rarely arise from lipoma)	Wide excision & adjuvant radiation	66% (myxoid) 10% (pleomorphic)
Embryonal rhabdomyosarcoma	0–10	Head & neck, genitourinary (botyroid)	Neoadjuvant chemoradiation & surgery	40%
Alveolar rhabdomyosarcoma	10–20	Thigh	Neoadjuvant chemoradiation & surgery	60%
Pleomorphic rhabdomyosarcoma	40–70	Thigh, upper arm	Wide excision & adjuvant radiation	10%
Synovial sarcoma	20–40	Leg	Wide excision & adjuvant radiation	40%
Angiosarcoma	50–70	Skin, superficial soft tissues	Wide excision & adjuvant radiation	15%
Leiomyosarcoma	45–65	Retroperitoneal, uterine	Wide excision & adjuvant radiation	40%

rates has been found by some groups of clinicians. This supposed advantage is however much debated. Many cancer doctors would advocate the administration of single-agent chemotherapy to their patients simply because combination therapies maximize toxicities and do not provide a significant advantage.

Treatment of Ewing's sarcomas

For patients with Ewing's tumours the last 20 or 30 years have seen a significant evolution of treatment protocols. One type of management generally consists of treatment with induction chemotherapy, followed by local treatment to the primary site with either surgery or radiotherapy or both. This will be followed by further consolidation chemotherapy.

Treatment of osteosarcomas

Similarly in sarcomas, primary chemotherapy to debulk the tumour is followed by surgery. Both chemotherapy and surgery are complex and highly specialized, requiring immense technical skill and input from many areas of medical and paramedical expertise. Patients with metastatic osteosarcoma can be cured, and once more surgery is enormously important. Surgical excision of pulmonary mestastases is considered and may be curative in a limited number of patients.

New therapies

Although there have been some developments in chemotherapy, it is not thought that chemotherapy will be the future for patients with sarcomas. Oncologists and their patients have been most encouraged by the development of Imatinib (Glevec), which is an agent that inhibits the function of BCR-ABL oncogene and of the KIT and PDGF tyrosine kinases. This agent is active in chronic myeloid leukaemia and is described in the Leukaemia section of this book. It also has activity in gastrointestinal stromal sarcomas, which are rare sarcomas of bowel. Patients who have gross metastatic disease have been seen to respond to this agent without any significant toxicity. This is clearly a wonderful development and may have a role in the management of bone tumours.

Chapter 43

Unknown primary cancer

Epidemiology and pathogenesis

For most patients who present with metastatic disease, routine examination and investigation will quickly disclose the underlying primary tumour. Occasionally, the primary tumour may be more obscure, and a number of clinical, histopathological and serological clues may help to establish the site. For 1–5% of patients, however, the primary site remains undisclosed because it is too small to be detected or has regressed. The usual histological diagnosis in these patients with an unknown primary site is adenocarcinoma or poorly differentiated carcinoma. The benefits of establishing the primary site include diagnosing treatable disease (Table 43.1), avoiding over-treating unresponsive disease and hence iatrogenic morbidity in resistant disease, preventing complications that relate to occult primary disease, such as bowel obstruction, and, finally, clarifying the prognosis. The methods commonly used to aid in the hunt for a primary site are described below.

Clinical sites of metastatic spread

Different tumours follow different patterns of metastatic spread. This may be related to chemokine and chemokine receptor expression by tumours and stromal cells (see Section 1).

Brain and meningeal metastases

Up to 30% of solid tumours develop parenchymal brain metastases. Carcinomatous meningitis is less common. Carcinomatous meningitis presents with multiple widely separated cranial and spinal root neuropathies. The diagnosis may be confirmed by finding malignant cells in the CSF. Treatment usually involves a combination of intrathecal chemotherapy and craniospinal radiotherapy. Carcinomatous meningitis most frequently occurs with leukaemias and lymphomas and occasionally with breast cancer. Parenchymal brain secondaries that may occur with any solid tumour are usually treated with whole-brain radiotherapy, although surgery may be considered for patients with solitary brain metastases and limited systemic disease (Figure 15.2).

Bone metastases

Bone metastases are a major source of morbidity in patients with cancer and often have a prolonged course. Bone metastases cause pain, reduced mobility, pathological fractures, hypercalcaemia, myelosuppression and nerve compression syndromes. Tumours that commonly metastasize to bone are lung, breast, prostate, renal, thyroid and sarcomas. Metastases usually occur in the axial skeleton, femur or humerus. If they are found elsewhere, then renal cancer and melanoma should be considered as possible primary tumour sites. Most bone metastases are lucent, lytic lesions; occasionally dense, sclerotic deposits are seen in prostate, breast, carcinoid tumours and Hodgkin's disease. The diagnosis of bone metastases is rarely complicated. The differential diagnosis is outlined in Table 43.2. See also Figures 1.4, 16.1, 16.2 and 31.2.

Lung metastases

The lungs are the second most common site for metastases via haematogenous spread. Tumours that commonly metastasize to lung include lung, breast, renal, thyroid, sarcoma and germ-cell tu-

mours. Surgical resection of pulmonary metastases is occasionally undertaken where the primary site is controlled and the lungs are the sole site of metastasis. See also Figures 2.7 and 17.1c.

Liver metastases

Of all patients with liver metastases, 60% have a colorectal primary tumour, 25% have melanoma, 15% lung cancer and 5% breast cancer. Hepatic resection for patients with up to three metastases from colorectal cancer results in five-year survivals of 30% and is the best treatment available for selected patients.

Malignant effusions

Eighty percent of malignant pleural effusions are due to lung and breast cancer, lymphoma and leukaemia. Malignant pericardial effusion is rarer than pleural effusions; breast and lung cancer account for 75%. Metastases to the heart and pericardium are 40 times more common than primary tumours at these sites, but only 15% will develop tamponade. Malignant ascites is a common complication of ovarian, pancreatic, colorectal and gastric cancers and lymphoma. Measures

Table 43.1 Treatable unknown primary diagnoses.

Chemosensitive tumours	Non-Hodgkin's lymphoma
	Germ-cell tumours
	Neuroendocrine tumours (including small-cell lung cancer)
	Ovarian cancer
Hormone-sensitive tumours	Breast cancer
	Prostate cancer
	Endometrial cancer
	Thyroid cancer

Table 43.2 Differential diagnosis of bone metastases.

Diagnosis	Pain	Site	Age	X-Ray	Bone scan, CT/MRI	Biochemistry
Metastases	Common	Axial skeleton	Any	Discrete lesions, path fracture loss of vertebral pedicles	Soft tissue extension on MRI/CT	Raised ALP, & Ca
Degenerative disease	Common	Limbs	Old	Symmetrical	Symmetrical uptake on bone scan	Normal
Osteoporosis	Painless (unless path fracture)	Vertebrae	Old (women)	Osteopenia	Normal bone scan/MRI	Normal
Paget's disease	Painless	Skull often	Old	Expanded sclerotic bones	Diffusely hot bone scan	Raised ALP & urinary hydroxyproline
Traumatic fracture	Always	Ribs	Any	Fracture	Intense linear uptake on bone scan	Normal

for long-term control of malignant effusions include sclerosis with talc, bleomycin or tetracycline for pleural effusions, drainage by pericardial window for pericardial effusions and peritoneovenous shunts for malignant ascites (Figure 46.6).

Clinical unknown primary syndromes

Five highly treatable subsets of unknown primary site have been identified which have more favourable outcomes and require distinct management:

1. Women with isolated axillary lymphadenopathy (adenocarcinoma or undifferentiated carcinoma) usually have an occult breast primary and should be managed as Stage II breast cancer. They have a similar prognosis (five-year survival is 70%).

2. Women with peritoneal carcinomatosis (often papillary carcinoma with elevated serum CA-125) should be managed as Stage III ovarian cancer.

3. Men with extragonadal germ cell syndrome or atypical teratoma present with features reminiscent of gonadal germ-cell tumours. They occur predominantly in young men with pulmonary or lymph-node metastases. Germ-cell tumour markers (alpha fetoprotein and human chorionic gonadotrophin) may be detected in the serum and in tissue by immunocytochemistry. Cytogenetic analysis for isochromosome 12p (see Figure 1.3) is positive in 90% of cases. Empirical chemotherapy with cisplatin-based combinations yield response rates of over 50% and up to 30% long-term survival.

4. Patients with neuroendocrine carcinoma of an unknown primary site overlap with extrapulmonary small-cell carcinoma, anaplastic islet cell carcinoma, Merkel cell tumours and paragangliomas. Immunocytochemical staining for chromogranin, neurone specific enolase, synaptophysin and epithelial antigens (cytokeratins & epithelial membrane antigen) are usually positive. Patients often present with bone metastases and diffuse liver involvement. These tumours are frequently responsive to platinum-based combination chemotherapy.

5. Patients with high cervical lymphadenopathy containing squamous cell carcinoma may have occult head and neck tumours of the nasopharynx, oropharynx or hypopharynx. Radical neck dissection followed by extended field radiotherapy that includes these possible primary sites may yield five-year survival rates of 30%. Adenocarcinoma in high cervical nodes and lower cervical adenopathy containing either histology, however, have a much worse prognosis and should not be treated in this aggressive fashion.

Unfortunately, the majority of unknown primary tumours do not fit into any of these subsets, and the response rates to chemotherapy are below 20%. These responses are usually of brief duration, with no impact on overall survival. The median survival is under 12 months. The exception to this rule is in the group of patients who are under 45 years old. In this group, treatment with BEP or a taxane combination is worthwhile.

Histopathologic characterization

The histopathologic characterization of unknown primaries to establish their origin includes a number of techniques: light microscopy, immunocytochemical staining, immunophenotyping, electron microscopy, cytogenetics and molecular analysis. These are described in detail in Section 1.

Serological characterization

Tumour markers are proteins produced by cancers that are detectable in the blood of patients. Ideally, serum tumour markers should be quick and cheap to measure, have high sensitivity (of more than 50%) and specificity (over 95%) and yield a high predictive value of positive (PPV) and negative (NPV) results. Under these circumstances, tumour markers may be used for population screening, diagnosis, as prognostic factors, for monitoring treatment, diagnosing remission and detecting relapse and for imaging metastases. A large number of serum tumour markers are available, and each may be valuable for any of screening, diagnosis, prognostication and monitoring treatment (Table 43.3).

Table 43.3 The most common serum tumour markers and their uses.

Name	Natural occurrence	Tumours	Comments	Screening	Diagnosis	Prognosis	Follow-up
Carcino-embryonic antigen (CEA)	Glycoprotein found in intestinal mucosa during embryonic and fetal life	Colorectal cancer (esp. liver mets) gastric, breast & lung cancer	Elevated in smokers cirrhosis, chronic hepatitis UC, Crohn's, pneumonia & TB (usu <10 ng/m)	N	Y	Y	Y
Alpha fetoprotein (AFP)	Glycoprotein found in yolk sac & fetal liver	Germ cell tumours (GCT) (80% nonseminomatous GCT), Hepatocellular cancer (50%), Neural tube defects, Down's pregnancies	Role in screening in pregnancy not cancer Only prognostic for GCT not HCC. Transient increase in liver diseases	N	Y	Y	Y
Prostate specific antigen (PSA)	Glycoprotein member of human kallikrein gene family. PSA is a serine protease that liquefies semen in excretory ducts of prostate	Prostate cancer (95%), also benign prostatic hypertrophy and prostatitis (usually <10 ng/ml)	Tissue-specific but not tumour specific although level >10 ng/ml is 90% specific for cancer	*see Section 3	Y	N	Y
Cancer antigen 125 (CA-125)	Differentiation antigen of coelomic epithelium (Muller's duct)	Ovarian epithelial cancer (75%), also gastrointestinal lung- and breast-cancers	Raised in cirrhosis chronic pancreatitis autoimmune diseases and any cause of ascites	* see Section 3	Y	N	Y
Human chorionic gondadotropin (HCG)	Glycoprotein hormone, 14KD? subunit & 24KD? subunit from placental syncytiotrophoblasts	Choriocarcinoma (100%), Hydatidiform moles (97%), Nonseminomatous GCT (50–80%), Seminoma (15%)	Screening post-hydatidiform mole for trophoblastic tumours, also used to follow pregnancies & diagnose ectopic pregnancies	Y	Y	Y	Y
Calcitonin	32 amino acid peptide from C-cells of thyroid	Medullary cell carcinoma of thyroid	Screening test in MEN 2	Y	Y	Y	Y
β-2-microglobulin	Part of HLA common fragment present on surface of lymphocytes macrophages and some epithelial cells	Non-Hodgkin's lymphoma, myeloma	Elevated in autoimmune disease, renal glomerular disease	N	N	Y	Y
Thyroglobulin	Matrix protein for thyroid hormone synthesis in normal thyroid follicles	Papillary & follicular thyroid cancer		N	Y	N	Y
Placental alkaline phosphatase (PLAP)	Isoenzyme of alkaline phosphatase	Seminoma & ovarian dysgerminoma (50%)		N	Y	N	Y

Approach to investigation of metastatic disease to establish primary site

There is a worrying tendency to over-investigate patients with unknown primary cancer while at the same time ignoring their palliative care needs. So often the greater the eminence and number of consultants whose advice is sought, the larger the number of esoteric investigations ordered, and the less well the patient and their family are informed. Investigations should be restricted to those that will alter clinical management. It is estimated that in the abscence of a localizing sympton, extensive radiological investigation lead to the identification of a primary site in less than 5% of all patients. The prognosis is generally poor, with a median survival of 3–4 months. Less than 25% of patients survive to one year, and less than 10% are alive after five years. The site of the primary is usually on the same side of the diaphragm as the metastases, and 75% of tumours are infra-diaphragmatic; of the 25% that arise above the diaphragm, nearly all arise from the lung. Where identified, the most common primary sites, in order of frequency, are: lung, pancreas, liver, colorectal, stomach, kidney, prostate, ovary, breast, lymphoid and testis. A good performance status is the most important predictor of survival, while extensive weight loss and older age are adverse prognostic factors. With the exception of the five clinical syndromes listed above, treatment other than symptom palliation is rarely appropriate.

Burnet began to champion the view that a major function of the immune system is to eliminate malignant cells. This was based upon evidence that animals can be immunized against syngeneic transplantable tumours. This theory of immune surveillance led to the identification of tumour antigens and of immunotherapy strategies to treat tumours.

Tumours in allograft recipients

The risk of cancer following an organ transplant varies with both the organ that has been transplanted and the type of cancer. The greatest risks numerically are with heart and heart–lung transplants, which often require a more aggressive regime of immunosuppression to prevent graft rejection. In addition to PTLD that is caused by the Epstein–Barr virus, the risk of Kaposi's sarcoma (caused by KSHV), cervical cancer (caused by HPV) and non-melanoma skin cancers are most dramatically increased. In the case of PTLD and post-transplantation Kaposi's sarcoma, reducing the immunosuppression may cause regression of the tumours—but this of course increases the risk of graft rejection.

Tumours in HIV patients

Studies by the WHO estimated that by December 2004, over 20 million people would have died of AIDS and 42 million people would be living with the virus. The number of people newly infected with human immunodeficiency virus (HIV) worldwide is approximately six million per year. Along with opportunistic infections, tumours are a major feature of HIV infection. The most frequent tumours in this population are Kaposi's sarcoma, non-Hodgkin's lymphoma and cervical cancer and these three are AIDS-defining illnesses. The management of cancer in the immunodeficient host requires careful attention to the balance between anti-tumour effects and the toxicity associated. Combination antiretroviral treatment has both dramatically reduced the incidence of opportunistic infections and prolonged the survival of people with HIV infection. In addition, this highly active antiretroviral therapy (HAART) has reduced the incidence of AIDS-defining malignancies and improved their prognosis. Only one million of the estimated 42 million people infected with HIV worldwide, however, are receiving HAART, as the majority of affected people live in developing countries. In addition, even in the established market economies with access to medical treatment, many individuals remain undiagnosed and consequently do not receive HAART.

Tumours in primary immunodeficiency

The cancers that occur with primary immunodeficiency syndromes are rare, and as a consequence treatment protocols and outcome data is scarce. Most patients succumb to infections, and these continue to pose a major threat to life during treatment of associated tumours.

Management of immunodeficiency-associated malignancies

The incidence of congenital immunodeficiency-associated tumours is sufficiently low for there to be little consensus upon their clinical management. In contrast, the incidence of both PTLD and KS has risen dramatically in recent years with the spread of the HIV pandemic and the marked increase in

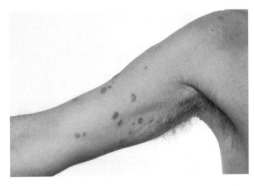

Figure 44.1 Multiple pigmented Kaposi sarcoma skin lesion in a man with HIV infection. Following antiretroviral therapy alone there was a marked regression of these lesions.

transplant surgery. The management of PTLD relies upon enhanced immunity against EBV by reducing the immunosuppression and infusing cytotoxic T lymphocytes against EBV. In addition, antiviral agents, low-dose chemotherapy and anti-CD20 monoclonal antibodies may be useful. The introduction of HAART has reduced the incidence of HIV-associated KS in established market economies where this treatment is available. More-over, early-stage KS may be successfully treated with HAART alone, leading to regression of KS. Visceral KS is usually treated with systemic liposo-mal anthracycline chemotherapy with concomi-tant HAART. Other tumours that arise in immunodeficient individuals are generally treated along conventional lines, with extra attention to the risk of infectious complications of therapy (Figure 44.1).

Part 3

The practice of oncology

Chapter 45

Paraneoplastic complications of cancer

Paraneoplastic complications of malignancy are remote effects of cancer that arise without local spread. Most of these paraneoplastic syndromes arise due to secretion by tumours of hormones, cytokines and growth factors. Paraneoplastic syndromes also arise when normal cells secrete products in response to the presence of tumour cells. For example, antibodies produced in this fashion are responsible for many paraneoplastic neurological syndromes including cerebellar degeneration, Lambert–Eaton myasthenic syndrome and paraneoplastic retinopathy.

Paraneoplastic endocrine complications

Cushing's syndrome

Cushing's syndrome is a clinical disorder resulting from the prolonged exposure to excess glucocorticoids and should not be confused with Cushing's disease, which refers exclusively to those cases that arise due to an ACTH-secreting pituitary adenoma (Table 45.1). Clinically overt Cushing's syndrome caused by ectopic secretion of adrenocorticotrophic hormone (ACTH) by non-endocrine-derived tumours is rare. In approximately 20% of cases of Cushing's syndrome the cause is ectopic ACTH secretion by a tumour which is frequently occult at presentation. For this reason, the differential diagnosis between pituitary

adenoma and ectopic ACTH is important clinically, but biochemical overlap often makes this difficult. More than half of the cases of ectopic ACTH syndrome are due to small-cell lung cancer, with carcinoid tumours and neural crest tumours (phaeochromocytoma, neuroblastoma, medullary cell carcinoma of the thyroid) accounting for a further 15%. The typical presentation is of a middle-aged, male smoker with features of severe hypercortisolism and hypokalaemic metabolic alkalosis. Patients have muscle weakness or atrophy, oedema, hypertension, mental changes, glucose intolerance and weight loss. When ectopic ACTH production arises from a more benign tumour such as bronchial carcinoid or thymoma, the other classical features of Cushing's syndrome may be present including truncal obesity, moon facies and cutaneous striae.

The diagnosis of Cushing's syndrome may be confirmed by elevated urinary free cortisol, loss of diurnal variation of plasma cortisol and failure of cortisol suppression in the low-dose dexamethasone (2 mg) test. After establishing the diagnosis, an elevated plasma ACTH level supports the diagnosis of pituitary adenoma or ectopic ACTH syndrome. Failure of cortisol to suppress following high-dose dexamethasone (2 mg four times daily for two days, or 8 mg overnight) and very high levels of ACTH (>200 pg/mL) suggest an ectopic source of ACTH. In difficult cases, a corticotrophin-releasing hormone stimulation test, selective

Table 45.1 Aetiology of Cushing's syndrome.

Type	Example
ACTH-dependent	Pituitary adenoma (Cushing's disease)
	Ectopic ACTH secretion
	Ectopic CRH secretion (very rare)
ACTH-independent	Exogenous glucocorticoid administration
	Adrenal adenoma
	Adrenal carcinoma
	Nodular adrenal hyperplasia

venous catheterization of inferior petrosal sinus with ACTH estimations, and somatostatin analogue scintigaphy and ^{99}technetium methoxy-isobutylisonitrile (MIBI) imaging may be necessary to determine the source of ACTH.

The mainstay of palliative therapy for Cushing's syndrome due to ectopic ACTH production is inhibition of steroid synthesis, although inhibition of ACTH release and blocking glucocorticoid receptors have also been attempted. Several steroid synthesis inhibitors are available, and success in these circumstances has been reported for the use of aminoglutethamide, metyrapone, mitotane, ketoconazole and octreotide. On rare occasions, laparoscopic bilateral adrenalectomy or adrenal artery embolization may be necessary to control symptoms.

Syndrome of inappropriate antidiuresis

Hyponatraemia is a common finding in association with advanced malignancy. Many factors may contribute, including cardiac and hepatic failure, hyperglycaemia and diuretics. The detection of concentrated urine in conjunction with hypo-osmolar plasma, however, suggests abnormal renal free water excretion and the presence of the syndrome of inappropriate antidiuresis (SIAD). This acronym is better than the previous term 'SIADH' (for 'syndrome of inappropriate ADH'), since there is no ADH secretion in approximately 15% of cases. In malignancy-related SIAD, tumours secrete ectopic arginine vasopressin or vasopressin-like

peptides. SIAD is most frequently associated with small-cell lung cancer or carcinoid tumours but has also been described in pancreatic, oesophageal, prostatic and haematological malignancies. Nonetheless, many factors may contribute to SIAD (Table 45.2).

Significant symptoms of hyponatraemia appear at plasma sodium levels of below 125 mmol/L with confusion progressing to stupor, coma and seizures as levels fall. Nausea, vomiting and focal neurological deficits may also occur. The clinical features depend on both the levels of plasma sodium and the rate of decline; with gradual falls in sodium, the brain cells are able to compensate against cerebral oedema by secreting potassium and other intracellular solutes. Asymptomatic hyponatraemia therefore suggests chronic SIAD rather than acute SIAD. The division into chronic and acute SIAD is of therapeutic importance as their management differs. The diagnosis of SIAD requires the demonstration of plasma hyponatraemia and hypo-osmolality in the presence of concentrated urine and normal extracellular fluid volume (Table 45.3).

The management of SIAD depends upon the rate of onset of hyponatraemia and the presence of neurological complications. Acute SIAD with an onset over two to three days, and falls in serum sodium levels in excess of 0.5 mmol/L/day are associated with neurological sequelae and require prompt correction by intravenous hypertonic saline. In contrast, the mainstay of therapy for chronic asymptomatic SIAD is fluid restriction and inhibition of tubular reabsorption of water, with drugs including the tetracycline antibiotic demeclocycline that causes nephrogenic diabetes insipidus.

Non-islet cell tumour hypoglycaemia

Tumour-related hypoglycaemia is a frequent complication of beta islet cell tumours of the pancreas which secrete insulin, but it occurs uncommonly with non-islet cell tumours. Most non-islet cell tumours produce hypoglycaemia by increased glucose use or by secreting insulin-like growth factors, formerly named 'somatomedins'. Non-islet cell tumours associated with hypoglycaemia

Table 45.2 Causes of syndrome of inappropriate diuresis (SIAD).

Source of ADH		Examples
Ectopic AHD production	Malignancy	Small cell lung cancer
Inappropriate pituitary	Malignancy	Lung cancer
secretion of ADH		Lymphoma
	Inflammatory	Pneumonia
	lung disease	Lung abscess
	Neurological	Meningitis
	disease	Head injury
		Subdural haematoma
		Surgery
	Drugs	Antidepressants (tricyclics, SSRIs)
		Carbamazepine
		Chlorpropamide
		Phenothiazines
		Vincristine
		Cyclophosphamide
		Ecstasy*
	Post-operative	
	Others	Hypothyroidism
		Porphyria
		Addison's disease

*Excessive water consumption may contribute to the development of hyponatraemia with ecstasy

Table 45.3 Diagnosis of syndrome of inappropriate diuresis (SIAD).

Essential criteria to establish this diagnosis are:
Plasma hypo-osmolality (plasma osmolality
  <275 mosm/kg H_2O and plasma sodium
  <135 mmol/L)
Concentrated urine (plasma osmolality >100 mosm/kg
  H_2O)
Normal plasma/extracellular fluid volume
High urinary sodium (urine sodium >20 mEq/L) on a
  normal salt and water intake
Exclude (i) hypothyroidism, (ii) hypoadrenalism (iii)
  diuretics

Supportive criteria for this diagnosis are:
Abnormal water load test (unable to excrete >90% of a
  20 mL/kg water load in 4 h, and/or failure to dilute
  urine to osmolality <100 mosmol/kg H_2O)
Elevated plasma arginine vasopressin levels

are usually large retroperitoneal or intrathoracic sarcomas. Unlike other endocrine complications of malignancy, hypoglycaemia is very rarely associated with lung cancer. The clinical manifestations are due to cerebral hypoglycaemia and secondary secretion of catecholamines. They include agitation, stupor, coma and seizures which may follow exercise or fasting. Tumour-related hypoglycaemia should be differentiated from other causes of hypoglycaemia including drugs such as sulphonylureas, hypoadrenalism, hypopituitarism and liver failure. In advanced malignancy the most common cause of hypoglycaemia is continued oral hypoglycaemic medication in long-standing diabetics.

Enteropancreatic hormone syndromes

Enteropancreatic hormone production is relatively uncommon in malignant disease. A variety of clinical syndromes occurs in association with hormone secretion by endocrine tumours of the

Table 45.4 Clinical manifestations of secretory endocrine tumours.

Tumour	Major feature	Minor feature	Palliative treatments
Insulinoma	Neuroglycopenia (confusion, fits)	Permanent neurological deficits	Frequent feeding Glucose Glucagon Diazoxide Octreotide
Gastrinoma (Zollinger-Elison syndrome)	Peptic ulceration	Diarrhoea Weight loss Malabsorption Dumping	Gastrectomy Proton pump inhibitors H2 receptor antagonists Octreotide
VIPoma (Werner-Morrison syndrome)	Watery diarrhoea Hypokalaemia Achlorhydria	Hypercalcaemia Hyperglycaemia Hypomagnesaemia	Octreotide Glucocorticoids
Glucagonoma	Migratory necrolyic erythema Mild diabetes mellitus Muscle wasting Anaemia	Diarrhoea Thromboembolis Stomatitis Hypoaminoacidaemia Encephalitis	Octreotide Oral hypoglycaemics
Somatostatinoma	Diabetes mellitus Cholelithiasis Steatorrhoea Malabsorption	Anaemia Diarrhoea Weight loss Hypoglycaemia	

Abbreviations: VIP, vasoactive intestinal polypeptide. H2, histamine type 2

pancreas and, less frequently, by tumours arising in other organs (Table 45.4). The majority of pancreatic islet cell tumours are malignant, with the exception of most insulinomas, and metastases are frequently present at diagnosis. For many patients, the distressing clinical manifestations arising from excessive secretion of gastrointestinal peptides require palliation, and this may be difficult to achieve. These tumours often secrete more than one polypeptide hormone and may switch their hormone production during follow-up.

Carcinoid syndrome

Carcinoid tumours arise from enterochromaffin cells principally in the gastro-intestinal tract, pancreas and lungs and, occasionally, in the thymus and gonads. One in ten patients with carcinoid tumours develops the carcinoid syndrome after contracting hepatic metastases. This avoids the first pass metabolism of 5HT and kinins in the liver so that the systemic symptoms occur. The acute symptoms are: vasomotor flushing, typically of upper body that lasts up to 30 mins, fever, pruritic wheals, diarrhoea, asthma/wheezing, borborygmi and abdominal pain. Chronic complications include tricuspid regurgitation, arthropathy, pulmonary stenosis, mesenteric fibrosis, cirrhosis, pellagra, due to secondary deficiency of trytophan and telangiectasia. The diagnostic investigation is 24-hour urinary collection for 5-hydroxyindoleacetic acid (5-HIAA), a metabolite of 5HT. Somatostatin analogues are considered by most physicians to be the first line treatment of choice for patients with carcinoid syndrome and, indeed, with most enteropancreatic hormone syndromes. Palliation of the clinical manifestations of carcinoid syndrome includes symptomatic therapy of diarrhoea with codeine phosphate, loperamide or diphenoxylate, β_2 adrenergic agonists for wheezing, and avoiding precipitating factors to reduce flushing such as alcohol and some foods.

Phaeochromocytoma

Phaeochromocytomas arise from the chromaffin cells of the sympathetic nervous system most frequently in the adrenal medulla but occasionally from sympathetic ganglia. Phaeochromocytomas commonly secrete norepinephrine and epinephrine and, in some cases, significant quantities of dopamine. Phaeochromocytomas are associated with a number of familially inherited cancer syndromes including MEN2a, MEN2b, von Hipple Lindau syndrome and neurofibromatosis. The catecholamines cause intermittent, episodic, or sustained hypertension. Further clinical manifestations including anxiety, tremor, palpitations, sweating, flushing, headaches, gastrointestinal disturbances and polyuria. These symptoms are all attributable to excessive adrenergic stimulation.

Twenty-four-hour urinary collection for urinary free catecholamines (epinephrine, norepinephrine and dopamine) is now the most widely employed diagnostic test, although some centres also measure catecholamine metabolites such as metanephrines and vanilylmandelic acid (VMA). The tumour may be localized by radiolabeled MIBG scintigarphy.

Initial treatment should be with α-blockade to control hypertension followed by β-blockade to control tachycardia. This combination will control symptoms in most patients with malignant phaeochromocytoma. If palliation is not achieved, high-dose ^{131}I-MIBG may be used as therapy for phaeochromocytoma and neuroblastoma, to reduce catecholamine synthesis.

Gynaecomastia

Gynaecomastia results from elevation of the oestrogen to androgen ratio, which may be either a consequence of decreased androgen production or activity or of increased oestrogen formation usually by peripheral aromatization of circulating androgens to oestrogens. In men with advanced cancer, gynaecomastia is most often a consequence of drug therapy: either chemotherapy (alkylating agents, vinca alkaloids, nitrosoureas), antiemetics (metoclopramide and phenothiazines), antiandrogens (cyproterone acetate, flutamide, bicalutamide). Occasionally, other tumour secretion of oestrogens or gonadotrophins may be responsible. Tumours may either secrete oestrogens (Leydig cell testicular tumours and feminizing adrenocortical tumours), or secrete androgens which are peripherally converted to oestrogens (Sertoli cell testicular tumours and hepatoma).

Paraneoplastic neurological conditions

In contrast to the metabolic and endocrine paraneoplastic conditions where products secreted by the tumours are responsible, most neurological paraneoplastic syndromes are immune-mediated. Moreover, with neurological paraneoplastic syndromes, the tumour may be asymptomatic or occult. It is thought that antibodies reacting to antigens on the surface of cancer cells cross-react with neural antigens and are the basis of these syndromes. The antibodies may be directed at ion channels; for example, the presynaptic P-type voltage-gated calcium channel in the case of Lambert Eaton myasthenic syndrome and the nictonic acetyl choline receptor in myasthenia gravis. Alternatively, antibodies may bind intracellular proteins such as Hu, a neuronal nuclear RNA-binding protein and Yo, a cytoplasmic protein in Purkinje cells of the cerebellum. The most common paraneoplastic neurological manifestations are described in association with small-cell lung cancer (Table 45.5).

Paraneoplastic dermatological conditions

A number of paraneoplastic dermatological manifestations have been described; several are listed in

Box 45.1: Oncological mnemonics

Hypercalcaemia causes

GRIM FED

Granulomas (TB, sarcoid)
Renal failure
Immobility
Malignancy
Familial (familial hypocalciuric hypercalcaemia)
Endocrine **PATH** (phaeochromocytoma, Addison's, Thyrotixicosis, Hyperparathyroidism)
Drugs (thiazides, lithium, vitamins A&D, milk alkali syndrome)

Causes of SIADH

Surgery
Intracranial (Infection, head injury, CVA)
Alveolar (pus, cancer)
Drugs ABCD (**A**nalgesics: opiates, NSAIDS, **B**arbiturates, **C**yclophosphamide,/ **C**arbamazepine / **C**hlorpromazine, **D**iuretic: thiazides)
Hormonal (hypothyroid, Addison's)

Cushinoid features

Cataracts
Ulcers
Striae
Hypertension, hisuitism
Infections
Necrosis (avascular necrosis of femoral head)
Glycouria, glycaemia
Osteoporosis, obesity
Immunosuppression
Diabetes

Phaeochromocytoma Rule of 10s

This mnemonic applies to *adults* with phaeochromocytomas
10% are extra-adrenal
10% are bilateral or multiple
10% are malignant
10% are familial

Phaeochromocytoma symptoms ('5 Hs')

Headache
Hypertension
Hypotension (postural)
Heartbeat (palpitations)
Hyperhidrosis (sweating)

Gynaecomastia

Genetic (Kleinfelters)
Youth (puberty)*
Neonate*
Anifungals (ketoconazole)
Estrogen
Cirrhosis / Cimetidine
Old age*
Marijuana
Alcoholism
Spirolonactone / Stilboestrol
Tumours (testicular & adrenal)
Isoniazid
Alkylating agents

Causes of Clubbing

Cyanotic congenital heart disease
Lung disease (Abscess, Bronchiectasis, Cystic Fibrosis, Empyema, Fibrosing alveolitis)
Ulcerative colitis / Crohn's dišease
Biliary cirrhosis
Birth defect (hereditary pachydermoperiostosis)
Infective endocarditis
Neoplasia (NSCLC, Mesothelioma, GI lymphoma)
Goitre (Thyrotoxicosis)

MEN

MEN I: 3Ps
Pituitary adenoma
Pancreatic islet cell tumours
Parathyroid
MEN II: 2Cs
Catecholamines (phaeochromocytoma)
Medullary **C**ell carcinoma of thyroid
Plus:
MEN IIa
Parathyroid tumours
MEN IIb (also known as MEN III)
Mucocutaneous neuromas

* physiological causes

Table 45.5 Paraneoplastic neurological manifestations.

Condition		Antibodies	% paraneoplastic	Underlying malignancy
Encephalomyelitis	Fluctuating confusion, anxiety, depression, impaired short term memory	anti-Hu, anti-CV2	10%	SCLC, thymoma
Subacute cerebellar degeneration	Ataxia, nystagmus, dysarthria	anti-Yo, anti-Hu, anti-VGCC, anti-Tr	50%	SCLC, ovary, Hodgkin's
Opsoclonus-myoclonus syndrome	Opsoclonus (irregular, rapid, horizontal and vertical eye movements) and myoclonus (brief, shock-like muscle spasms), intention tremor, unsteady gait	anti-Hu, anti-Ri	20–50%	Neuroblastoma, breast
Retinopathy	Night blindness, ring scotomas, photosensitivity.	anti-recoverin		SCLC, melanoma
Sensory neuropathy	Rapid progressive loss of all sensory modalities especially proprioception	anti-Hu	10–20%	SCLC
Lambert Eaton Syndrome	Proximal muscle weakness sparing eyes, power increases with repetition	anti-VGCC	60%	SCLC
Myasthenia gravis	Muscle fatigability, ptosis, ophthalmoplegia	anti-AChR	5%	Thymoma
Polymyositis	Propximal muscle weakness, rash	anti-Jo-1	10%	NSCLC, SCLC, lymphoma
Dermatomyositis	Erythematous rash, arthralgia	anti-Jo-1	20%	NSCLC, SCLC, lymphoma

Abbreviations: SCLC = small-cell lung cancer, NSCLC = non-small-cell lung cancer

Table 45.6. Amongst the most common paraneoplastic dermatological manifestation is 'clubbing', a clinical sign beloved of physicians which was first described by Hippocrates over 2400 years ago. Clubbing is characterized by softening of the nail bed and periungual erythema with loss of the normal 15° angle at the hyponychium. As this advances, bulging of the distal phalynx and curvature of the nail lead to a drum stick end appearance. Clubbing may be associated with hypertrophic osteoarthropathy, with new subperiosteal cancellous bone formation at the distal ends of long bones—particularly the radius and ulna or tibia and fibula (Figures 45.1 and 45.2).

Cachexia

Cachexia, or severe protein calorie malnutrition, is one of the most debilitating and life-threatening aspects of cancer. The mechanism of cachexia may be a combination of tumour- and host-secreted products including inflammatory cytokines such as cachectin, disruption of neuropeptide Y-regulation and aberrant melanocortin signalling. Severe weight loss shortens survival and decreases quality of life substantially; indeed, for many malignancies, weight loss of more than 10% of body weight is an independent adverse prognostic factor. The two major options for pharmacological therapy

Table 45.6 Paraneoplastic dermatological conditions.

Name	Description	Malignancy
Acanthosis nigricans	Grey–brown symmetrical velvety plaques on neck, axillae, flexor areas	Adenocarcinoma predominantly gastric
Acquired ichthyosis	Generalised dry, cracking skin, hyperkeratotic palms & soles	Hodgkin's disease, lymphomas, myeloma
Acrokeratosis paraneoplastica (Bazex syndrome)	Symmetrical psoriasiform hyperkeratosis with scales and pruritis on toes, ears & nose, nail dystrophy	Squamous carcinoma of oesophagus, head & neck, lungs
Bullous pemphigoid	Large tense blisters, antibodies to desmoplakin	Lymphomas & others
Cushing's syndrome	Broad purple striae, plethora, telangiectasia, mild hirsuitism	Small-cell lung-cancer, thyroid, testis, ovary, adrenal tumours pancreatic islet cell tumours, pituitary tumours
Dermatitis herpetiformis	Pleomorphic symmetrical subepidermal bullae	Lymphoma & others
Dermatomyositis	Erythema or telangiectasia of knuckles and periorbital regions	Miscellaneous tumours
Erythema annulare centrifugum	Slowly migrating annular red lesions	Prostate, myeloma & others
Erythema gyratum repens	Progressive scaling erythema with pruritis	Lung, breast, uterus, gastrointestinal
Exfoliative dermatitis	Progressive erythema followed by scaling	Cutaneous T-cell lymphoma, Hodgkin's disease & other lymphomas
Flushing	Episodic reddening of face and neck	Carcinoid syndrome, medullary cell carcinoma of thyroid
Generalised melanosis	Diffuse grey brown skin pigmentation	Melanoma, ACTH producing tumours
Hirsuitism	Increased hair in male distribution	Adrenal tumours, ovarian tumours
Hypertrichosis languginosa	Rapid development of fine long silky hair	Lung, colon, bladder, uterus & gallbladder tumours
Muir-Torre syndrome	Sebaceous gland neoplasm	Colon cancer, lymphoma
Necrolytic migratory erythema	Circinate area of blistering and erythema on face, abdomen and limbs	Islet cell tumour of pancreas (Glucagonoma)
Pachydermoperiostosis	Thickening of skin folds, lips, ears, macroglossia, clubbing, excessive sweating	Lung-cancer
Paget's disease of nipple	Red keratotic patch over areola, nipple or accessory breast tissue	Breast cancer
Pemphigus vulgaris	Bullae of skin and oral blisters	Lymphomas, breast cancer
Pruritis	Generalised itching	Lymphoma, leukaemia, myeloma, CNS tumours, abdominal tumours
Sign of Leser Trelat	Sudden onset of large number of seborrhoeic keratoses	Adenocarcinoma of stomach, lymphoma, breast cancer
Sweet's syndrome	Painful raised red plaques, fever, neutrophilia	Leukaemias
Systemic nodular panniculitis (Weber–Christian disease)	Recurrent crops of tender violaceous subcutaneous nodules, may be accompanied by abdominal pain and fat necrosis in bone marrow and lungs	Adenocarcinoma of pancreas
Tripe palms	Hyperpigmented velvety thickened palms with exaggerated ridges	Gastric and lung cancer

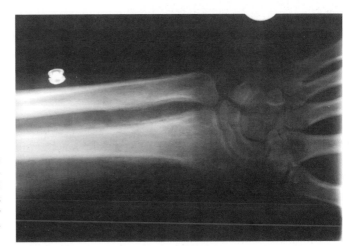

Figure 45.1 Forearm radiograph showing periosteal reaction in metaphysis and diaphysis of radius and ulnar and periarticular osteoporosis due to hypertrophic osteoarthropathy secondary to non-small cell lung cancer (squamous cell).

that aim to enhance appetite are progestagens, such as megestrol acetate, and corticosteroids. Neither these drugs, nor enteral or parenteral nutrition, however, have proved universally beneficial. Both approaches are furthermore associated with appreciable toxicity. As the molecular aetiology of cancer cachexia is unveiled, novel therapeutic strategies are emerging.

Figure 45.2 Finger-nail clubbing is characterized by increased longitudinal curving of the nail, loss of the angle between the nail and its bed and bogginess of the nail fold. (See also colour plates between pages 154 and 155.)

Chapter 46

Oncological emergencies

Hypercalcaemia

One in ten cancer patients develop hypercalcaemia. Malignancy accounts for about half of the cases of hypercalcaemia amongst hospital inpatients. Hypercalcaemia occurs most frequently with myeloma, breast, lung and renal cancers, and 20% of cases occur in the absence of bone metastases. Most patients with hypercalcaemia of malignancy have disseminated disease and 80% die within one year. Thus, hypercalcaemia is usually a complication of advanced disease and its treatment should be directed at palliation as it may produce a number of distressing symptoms (Table 46.1). The treatment of hypercalcaemia of malignancy frequently ameliorates these symptoms, and for this reason the diagnosis should always be sought and treatment instituted for the cause.

In recent years, there have been significant advances in our understanding of the biochemical processes that cause hypercalcaemia in malignancy, such that the factors involved in local osteolysis and in the evolution of humoral hypercalcaemia have now been delineated. A number of different cytokines have been implicated in the development of hypercalcaemia as a result of local osteolysis. These osteoclast-activating factors, which are released locally by metastatic tumour and stimulate osteoclastic resorption of bone, include prostaglandin E_2, tumour necrosis factors α (cachectin) and β (lymphotoxin), epidermal

growth factor and transforming growth factor β. It is probable that interleukin 1, epidermal growth factor and the tumour necrosis factors are the most important of these aetiological agents, as they enhance the release of macrophage colony stimulating factor by osteoblasts. Since osteoclasts are derived from a haematopoietic stem-cell progenitor, this release of macrophage colony stimulating factor may be fundamental to oestoclastic bone resorption.

Humoral hypercalcaemia was first described in 1941 by Albright, but it was not until the late 1980s that the humoral factor causing hypercalcaemia was characterized. In the 1970s, hypercalcaemia was thought to result from the ectopic production of parathyroid hormone. This hypothesis, however, remained unproven because the use of parathyroid hormone antisera failed to demonstrate excessive secretion of parathyroid hormone in patients with humoral hypercalcaemia. In addition, low serum concentrations of 1,25 vitamin D3 and of urinary cyclic AMP levels failed to reflect excess parathyroid hormone activity, and no parathyroid hormone mRNA was found in the tumours of patients with humoral hypercalcaemia.

In the late 1980s, polyadenylated RNA from a renal carcinoma from a patient with this syndrome was used to construct a cDNA library. This was screened with a codon preference oligonucleotide, synthesized on the basis of a partial *N*-terminal amino acid sequence from a human tumour-

Table 46.1 Clinical features of hypercalcaemia of malignancy.

General	Gastrointestinal	Neurological	Cardiological
Dehydration	Anorexia	Fatigue	Bradycardia
Polydipsia	Weight loss	Lethargy	Atrial arrhythmias
Polyuria	Nausea	Confusion	Ventricular arrhythmias
Pruritis	Vomiting	Myopathy	Prolonged P–R interval
	Constipation	Hyporeflexia	Reduced Q–T interval
	Ileus	Seizures	Wide T waves
		Psychosis	
		Coma	

derived peptide, and a 2.0 kilobase cDNA was identified. The cDNA encodes a 177 amino acid prohormone which consists of a 36 amino acid leader sequence that is cleaved to produce a 141 amino acid, mature-peptide, parathyroid hormone-related peptide (PTHrP). The first 13 amino acids of the mature peptide have a sequence homology with parathyroid hormone, and the N-terminal sequence is thought to be the parathyroid hormone receptor binding region. Parathyroid hormone-related peptide was found to be expressed in most normal human tissue where its role is as yet undetermined. The gene for parathyroid hormone-related peptide has been mapped to the short arm of chromosome 12, whilst the parathyroid hormone gene maps to the short arm of chromosome 11. The gene for parathyroid hormone-related peptide is complex and contains a six exon, 12 kilobase, single-copy sequence, encoding up to five mRNA species. Exons 2, 3 and 4 are similar to the parathyroid hormone gene.

A radioimmunoassay for parathyroid hormone-related peptide was used to screen patients with hypercalcaemia associated malignancy. The results contrasted with patients who were normocalcaemic and had malignant disease, patients with primary hyperparathyroidism and normal controls. Parathyroid hormone-related peptide was elevated in 19 of 39 patients (49%) with malignant hypercalcaemia, 12 of 74 of normocalcaemic patients (16%) with malignancy, four of 20 patients (20%) with hyperparathyroidism, but in none of 22 normal controls.

The clinical manifestations of hypercalcaemia are varied (Table 46.1) and many symptoms may

be wrongly attributed to the underlying malignancy. A diagnosis of hypercalcaemia can only be made by biochemical investigation, and so all symptomatic patients with malignancy should have their corrected serum calcium measured if treatment is likely to be appropriate:

$$\text{Corrected calcium} = \text{measured calcium} + [(40\text{-serum albumin (g/L)}) \times 0.02]$$

The mainstay of therapy is rehydration with large volumes of intravenous fluids followed by the administration of calcium lowering agents, most commonly bisphosphonates. Low calcium diets are unpalatable, exacerbate malnutrition and have no place in palliative therapy. Drugs promoting hypercalcaemia such as thiazide diuretics, vitamins A and D should be withdrawn. The cornerstone of the re-establishment of normo calcaemia is treatment with a bisphosphonate. Bisphosphonates have multiple functions in hypercalcaemia. They reduce serum calcium levels by directly affecting the osteoclast and stabilize hydroxyapatite crystals. There are two classes of effect of bisphosphonates. One group of bisphosphonates, which includes Clodronate and Etidronate, acts through their incorporation into non-hydrolysable analogues of ATP that accumulate in osteoclasts and induce apoptosis. Alternately, agents such as Pamidronate and Zoledronate inhibit an enzyme called FPP synthase, which functions in the mevalonate pathway. This leads to the inhibition of protein prenylation. The bisphosphonates of choice for malignant hypercalcaemia are currently Pamidronate and Zoledronate. Approximately 80% of patients respond to hydration and bisphosphonate treatment by normalization of serum calcium levels. Calcium levels start to normalize within the first 24 hours of treatment with bisphosphonates and reach normal levels usually within three days. It is a dogma that treatment with bisphosphonates has to be repeated, usually on a three- to four-weekly cycle. Some accumulating information, however, suggests that a single treatment may be sufficient to reset calcium homeostasis. Bisphosphonates have analgesic activity in patients with metastatic bone pain and reduce skeletal morbidity in patients with breast cancer and myeloma. In 20% of patients with hypercalcaemia, bisphosphonates do not work. Alternative treatments include the use of a somatostatin analogue such as Octreotide, which acts to reduce the serum levels of PTHrP. Other, more old-fashioned treatments include Calcitonin and Mithramycin.

Superior vena cava obstruction

Superior vena cava obstruction (SVCO) restricts the venous return from the upper body, which results in oedema of the arms and face, distension of the neck and arm veins, headaches and a dusky blue skin discoloration over the upper chest, arms and face. SVCO is caused by a mediastinal mass that compresses the vessel with or without intraluminal thrombus. Collateral circulation via the azygous vein may provide some drainage, and over a period of several weeks, collaterals may form over the chest wall. In this case the flow of blood in these collateral veins will be from above downwards into the inferior vena cava circulation. This may be demonstrated clinically as an aid to confirm the diagnosis.

The presenting symptoms of SVCO include dyspnoea, swelling of the face and arms, headaches, a choking sensation, cough and chest pain. The most important clinical sign is loss of venous pulsations in the distended neck veins. This is usually accompanied by facial oedema, plethora and cyanosis, and tachypnoea. The severity of the symptoms is determined by the rate of obstruction and the development of a compensatory collateral circulation. The symptoms may deteriorate when lying flat or bending, which further compromises

Table 46.2 Non-malignant causes of superior vena cava obstruction (SVCO).

Non-malignant causes of SVCO
Mediastinal fibrosis
Idiopathic
Histoplasmosis
Actinomycosis
Tuberculosis
Vena Cava thrombosis
Idiopathic
Behcet's syndrome
Polycythemia vera
Paroxysmal nocturnal haemoglobinuria
Long-term venous catheters, shunts or pacemakers
Benign mediastinal tumours
Aortic aneurysm
Dermoid tumour
Retrosternal goitre
Sarcoidosis
Cystic hygroma

the obstructed venous return. In nine out of ten cases, the cause of SVCO is a malignancy: most often lung cancer and disproportionately more often small-cell lung cancer, lymphoma or metastatic breast or germ-cell cancer. Rare non-malignant causes are listed in Table 46.2 (Figure 46.2).

The management of SVCO depends upon the cause and severity, along with the patient's prognosis, and includes relieving symptoms as well as treating the underlying cause. SVCO with airway compromise is an oncological emergency and delays occurring during the period when histological findings are confirmed, may adversely affect the outcome. In such circumstances, patients are treated empirically with steroids and radiotherapy. When it is safe to do so, it is important to establish the diagnosis, as this will determine the optimum treatment. A delay of no more than 1–2 days to obtain a histological diagnosis is usually appropriate. Diagnostic procedures should include plain chest X-ray, sputum cytology, bronchoscopy, thoracoscopy or mediastinoscopy, CT scans or MRI and ultrasonography and/or venography. A palpable lymph node may be amenable to biopsy, thereby providing a diagnosis.

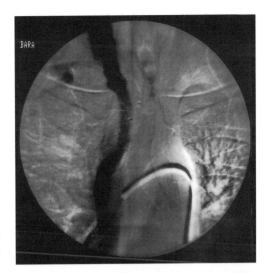

Figure 46.1 Angiogram showing superior vena cava compression at the level of the carina due to small cell lung cancer.

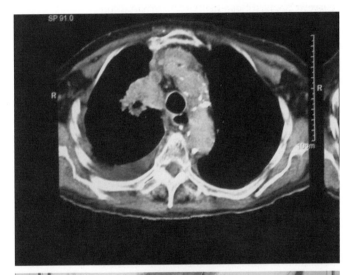

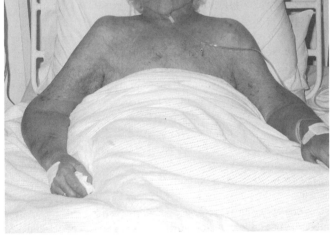

Figure 46.2 An 80-year-old woman presented with shortness of breath, headaches and swollen arms. The CT scan shows a large right hilar mass that was small cell lung cancer compressing the superior vena cava and collateral circulation. The clinical image also shows dilated veins on the anterior chest wall due to collateral circulation. The flow of blood in these veins will be from above as the blood is bypassing the obstructed superior vena cava to return via the patent inferior vena cava. (See also colour plates between pages 154 and 155.)

Patients may respond to being sat upright with oxygen therapy, and intravenous corticosteroids should be administered. In the majority of cases, radiotherapy is the most appropriate treatment modality and relieves symptoms in up to 90% of patients within a fortnight. Where a diagnosis of lymphoma, small-cell lung cancer or germ-cell tumour has been obtained chemotherapy may be the optimal initial treatment.

For patients with recurrent SVCO, or in those where other therapeutic modalities are unsuitable, insertion of expandable wire stents under radiological guidance can be effective. Studies report instantaneous symptomatic relief with an excellent response rate. A surgical bypass of the obstruction is usually reserved for patients with benign disorders. For central venous access catheter-associated SVCO and thrombosis, remove the line and commence anticoagulation. The administration of low-dose warfarin has been reported to reduce the incidence of thrombosis associated with central venous access catheters.

Spinal cord compression

Spinal cord compression is a relatively common complication of disseminated cancer and affects 5% of patients with cancer. Spinal cord compression occurs with many tumour types but is particularly frequent in myeloma and prostate cancer. Up to 30% of these patients will survive for one year. It is essential to spare these patients paraplegia by making the diagnosis swiftly and instituting treatment quickly. In general, the residual neurological deficit reflects the extent of deficit at the start of treatment, so early treatment leaves less damage. Neoplastic cord compression is nearly always due to extra-medullary, extradural metastases usually from breast, lung, prostate, lymphoma or renal cancers. Compression usually occurs by posterior expansion of vertebral metastases or extension of paraspinal metastases through the intervertebral foramina. These result in demyelination, arterial compromise, venous occlusion and vasogenic oedema of the spinal cord, all contributing to myelopathy. Seventy percent occur in the thoracic spine, 20% lumbar spine and 10% cervical spine.

The earliest symptom of cord compression is vertebral pain, especially on coughing and lying flat. Subsequent signs include sensory changes one or two dermatomes below the level of compression. A complaint of back pain with focal weakness and bladder or bowel dysfunction with a sensory level requires urgent investigation in a patient with cancer. This will progress to motor weakness distal to the block and finally sphincter disturbance. If spinal cord compression is missed, or left untreated, patients can develop severe neurological deficits and double incontinence.

Spinal cord compression should be treated as a medical emergency. High-dose intravenous corticosteroids should be initiated on clinical suspicion alone, to prevent further evolution of neurological deficit. Subsequently, plain X-rays of the spine to look for vertebral collapse should be performed, as well as MRI of the spinal axis to define the presence and levels of spinal cord compression. If appropriate, a neurosurgical opinion should be obtained regarding the potential value of surgical decompression, especially if there is vertebral instability or if the level of the compression has been previously irradiated. Otherwise, the definitive treatment is urgent local radiotherapy. It is important to provide adequate analgesia. Pre-treatment ambulatory function is the main determinant of post-treatment gait function, thus prompt diagnosis and treatment is the key to gait and continence preservation (Figures 46.3–46.5).

Malignant pleural effusions

Although not strictly an emergency, approximately 40% of all pleural effusions are due to malignancy (see Table 46.3), and it frequently indicates advanced and incurable disease. The pleural space is normally filled with 10–40 mL of hypoproteinaceous plasma that originates from the capillary bed of the parietal pleura and is drained through the parietal pleura lymphatics. A pleural effusion is often the first manifestation of malignancy. Lung and breast cancer account for almost two thirds of malignant cases. Malignant pleural effusions may be asymptomatic or cause progressive dyspnoea, cough and chest pain which may be pleuritic in

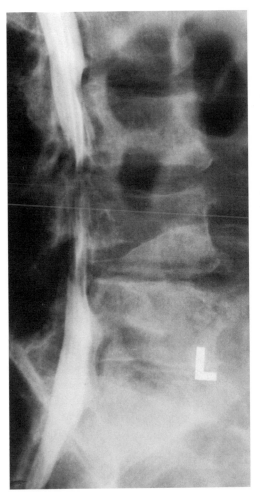

Figure 46.3 Myelogram demonstrating spinal cord compression.

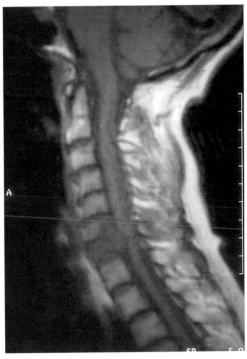

Figure 46.4 MRI scan demonstrating metastasis in cervical C7 vertebral body with soft tissue extension posteriorly to cause compression of the cervical spinal cord.

nature. Malignant pleural effusions are usually exudates. This may be confirmed by a fluid LDH exceeding 200 U/mL, a fluid-to-serum LDH ratio of more than 0.6, a fluid to serum–protein ratio greater than 0.5 and a fluid-to-serum glucose ratio of <0.5. The fluid may be blood-stained and is typically hyper-cellular containing lymphocytes, monocytes and reactive mesothelial cells; exfoliated tumour cells may be present also.

The management of malignant effusions should be tailored to the patient's symptoms, as only half of the patients will be alive at three months and over 90% of effusions will recur within 30 days of thoracocentesis. Reaccumulation of pleural effusions may be delayed by chemical pleurodesis normally using talc or tetracycline or video assisted thoracic surgery (VATS) with pleurectomy and/or talc insufflation. Pleuroperitoneal shunts or chronic indwelling catheters may be considered for patients who fail pleurodesis, but this is rarely appropriate. Pericardial effusions are relatively common but uncommonly cause tamponade emergency, with florid signs and a dramatic response to treatment (Figure 46.6).

Ascites

The most frequent malignancies causing ascites are primary tumours of the ovaries, pancreas, stomach and colon, breast and lungs. The distressing symptoms of ascites include abdominal distension or pain, dyspnoea due to diaphragmatic splinting,

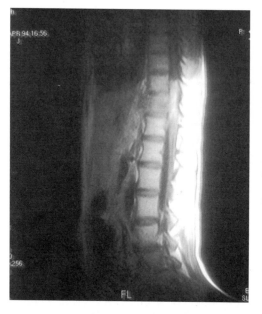

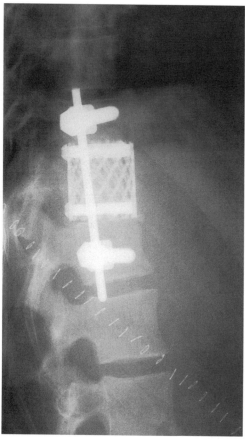

Figure 46.5 Magnetic resonance image demonstrating cord compression at T11 due to vertebral metastasis with soft tissue extension. Plain radiograph image following surgical decompression and stabilisation of metastasis.

oedema of the legs, perineum and lower trunk and a 'squashed stomach syndrome' leading to anorexia. If these symptoms are distressing, paracentesis is indicated. It offers rapid symptom relief but poor long-term control. While anti-cancer therapy may reduce the subsequent reaccumulation of ascites, if this is not an option or is unsuccessful, diuretics may be helpful. A peritoneovenous shunt may be surgically placed under general anaesthetic if the ascites cannot be controlled. Shunts are more commonly inserted under imaging control, but both these procedures are carried out rarely.

Tumour lysis syndrome

The acute destruction of a large number of cells is associated with metabolic sequelae, and is termed 'tumour lysis syndrome'. Cell destruction results in the release of different chemicals into the circulation, some of which may cause profound complications. Electrolyte release may cause transient hypercalcaemia, hyperphosphataemia and hyperkalaemia. The release of calcium and phosphate into the blood stream rarely causes any significant consequences. The calcium and phosphate may, however, co-precipitate and cause some impairment of renal function. Hyperkalaemia can be much a more significant problem and may mani-

Table 46.3 Causes of pleural effusion.

Transudate		Cardiac failure	
		Nephrotic syndrome	
		Cirrhosis	
		Protein losing enteropathy	
		Constrictive pericarditis	
		Hypothyroidism	
		Peritoneal dialysis	
		Meig's syndrome	Pleural effusion associated with ovarian fibroma
Exudate	Tumour	Primary: lung-cancer, mesothelioma	
		Secondary: Breast-, ovary cancer, lymphoma	
	Infection	Pneumonia	
		Tuberculosis	
		Subphrenic abscess	
	Infarction	Pulmonary embolus	
	Connective tissue disease	Rheumatoid arthritis SLE	
	Others	Pancreatitis	Usually left sided pleural effusion
		Dressler's syndrome	Inflammatory pericarditis and pleurisy following MI or heart surgery
		Yellow nail syndrome	Combination of discoloured hypoplastic nails, recurring pleural effusions and lymphedema. Aetiology unknown.
		Asbestos exposure	

fest as minor ECG abnormalities. Even more significant, however, are the cardiac arrhythmias, which may include ventricular tachycardia or ventricular fibrillation, and which may lead to the demise of the patient. Nucleic acid breakdown leads to hyperuricaemia and this, unless treated appropriately, can be complicated by renal failure due to the precipitation of uric acid crystals in the renal tubular system. Naturally, it is best to prevent these occurrences: we do not like our patients dying, least of all of the complications of the treatment that we have administered.

There are certain malignancies whose treatment is associated with a higher-than-usual risk of tumour lysis syndrome. These include acute promyelocytic leukaemia and high-grade lymphomas. Patients with acute promyelocytic leukaemia can develop tumour lysis syndrome, with minor trauma to the patient or infection.

In this leukaemia, there is release of procoagulants from blast cells with the risk of a devastating coagulopathy. Patients with high grade lymphomas may also be at risk from circumstances where one would not normally expect there to be a problem. For example, if these patients are started on steroids, they may develop tumour lysis because steroids have cytotoxic qualities in lymphoma. In these malignancies the risk of tumour lysis syndrome is pre-empted by intelligence! Patients are started two days prior to chemotherapy or radiation therapy with Allopurinol. The day before treatment intravenous hydration is started, and these efforts generally prevent the development of the tumour lysis syndrome. Many clinicians advise alkalinization of the urine. In practice it is, however, very difficult to achieve an alkaline urine, and there are dangers inherent in the use of significant amounts of sodium bicarbonate. A pro-

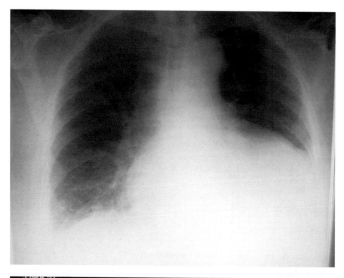

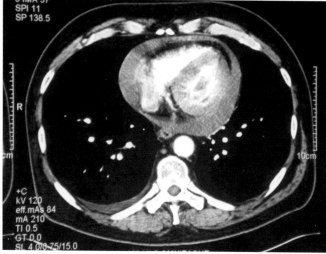

Figure 46.6 Chest X-ray showing globular enlarged heart shadow and CT scan confirming a malignant pericardial effusion due to metastatic non-small cell lung cancer. These effusions may present as a medical emergency with cardiac tamponade. The clinical symptoms include dyspnoea and cough and the signs are hypotension, tachycardia, pulsus paradoxus (fall of systolic blood pressure of >10 mm Hg on inspiration), quiet muffled heart sounds and a raised JVP with Kussmaul's sign (paradoxical rise in JVP on inspiration). The ECG may show pulsus alternans (alternating QRS voltages). The emergency treatment is by pericardiocentesis and subsequent surgical formation of a pericardial window to prevent recurrence may be necessary.

portion of patients will go on to develop tumour lysis syndrome despite these measures. For this reason, patients who are treated require careful monitoring with two-hourly measurement of serum potassium levels for the first 8–12 hours of treatment. Many clinicians will also advise ECG monitoring, but it is our experience that these monitors are generally not observed to best effect. A new drug has become recently available for the treatment of this condition. Recombinant urate oxidase converts uric acid, which is insoluble, into allantoin, which is. Clinical trials have shown that urate oxidase controls hyperuricaemia faster and more reliably than Allopurinol, and its use is indicated in children and haematological malignancy.

Myelosuppression

Neutropenia

We explain to our patients that chemotherapy puts them at risk of developing of bone-marrow suppression, because cancer treatments kill 'good' as well as 'bad' cells. In this case, the 'good' cells are the haematological progenitor cells and patients are at risk from death if the effects of treatment upon the bone marrow are not recognized. Neutropenic sepsis is very common in cancer treatment and, if undiagnosed, leads to a mortality rate approaching 20–30%. Patients with neutropenic sepsis develop fevers and rigors with associated oral ulceration and candidiasis. It is standard practice for patients with neutropenic sepsis (which is defined by septic symptoms in the presence of a white count that is lower than 1.0×10^9/L) to be admitted to hospital. The patient is resuscitated with intravenous fluids and blood cultures taken. In the absence of any obvious focus of infection, such as the urinary tract, the advantage of culturing from sites other than blood is virtually zero. Cultures from other sites merely act to swamp the microbiology lab with unnecessary requests for culture work without any positive advantage. Just 20% of blood cultures from patients with neutropenic sepsis are positive for bacterial organisms. The cause for infection is generally not clear.

Antibiotic policies vary from hospital to hospital, but there is good evidence that treatment with single-agent Ceftazidime is as effective as treatment with combination antibiotic regimens. In the UK, patients are generally admitted, though it is interesting to note that this conservative management policy is not strictly necessary. In one randomized study, treatment with oral Ciprofloxacin in the community was compared to inpatient treatment with intravenous Ceftazidime. The results were absolutely identical in terms of control of fever and patient outcome.

Over the last decade, marrow growth factors have become available and GCSF, which stimulates the marrow to produce granulocytes, has entered wide use. There is no evidence that prophylactic use of GCSF prevents neutropenic sepsis or septic deaths in any way. The evidence for its use in established infection is poor. The consensus view is that GCSF is of value only in patients with established neutropenic sepsis, who have a non-recovering marrow, and in whom, additionally, an infective agent has been identified. GCSF is of enormous value in transplantation programs,

where the mean period of time to engraftment has been reduced from 28 to 18 days by the use of these agent as previously discussed.

Anaemia

Anaemia is a very common complication of cancer and its treatment. It is estimated that up to 30% of all cancer patients will require a transfusion. In general, anaemia is cumulative and builds up over several cycles of chemotherapy. Recombinant Erythropoietin is considered to be a valuable alternative to blood transfusion. The response of patients to Erythropoietin is wide-ranging: between 20% and 60%. Haemoglobin levels increase after about six weeks of treatment with recombinant Erythropoietin. The cost of this agent used to be considered prohibitive. The cost of blood, however, is widely predicted to increase significantly because of the increased costs of testing blood for infective agents such as CJD. The pharmaceutical industry markets Erythropoietin for its effect upon the asthenia related to cancer treatment: claims are made for a far greater improvement in cancer fatigue than haemoglobin level.

Thrombocytopenia

Thrombocytopenia is not as significant a problem in the treatment of solid tumours as it is in the treatment of haematological malignancies. There is a significant risk of spontaneous major haemorrhage, as the platelet count declines below $10–20 \times 10^9$/L. Most oncologists advocate prophylactic platelet transfusions at this level or in the presence of bleeding. There are a number of regulatory molecules that stimulate early haematopoietic progenitors. These include IL-1, IL-6 and IL-11. IL-1 and IL-6 have poor efficacy and significant toxicity, but IL-11 has been licensed for the prevention of chemotherapy-induced thrombocytopenia. The pharmaceutical industry continues to develop agents for the treatment of thrombocytopenia, and the focus recently has been on analogues of Thrombopoietin which appear to have more efficacy and less toxicity than the interleukins.

Cancer-related thromboses

Patients with cancer have an increased tendency to thrombosis, a problem that was first documented by Trousseau, who sadly went on to develop venous thromboses himself and died from cancer. Patients with cancer have an increased risk of developing thromboses for two major reasons. The first may be a pressure effect: the primary tumour mass or secondary nodal masses impinge upon vasculature, producing venous stasis and thrombosis. The second reason for the increased risk is the release of pro-coagulants from the tumour. A number of tissue pro-coagulants have been described, ranging from protein S and protein C to the current view that activated factor X is released by tumours which sparks off the clotting cascade.

The incidence of venous thrombosis and thromboembolism in cancer patients is variably reported. One study looked at a group of patients presenting with DVTs. Screening of these patients showed that almost 30% had a cancer that was most commonly a pelvic malignancy. As always in medicine, there is initial positive reporting, and later studies showed the true incidence of previously undetected cancer in patients presenting with venous thrombosis to be in the order of 5%. Once cancer has been diagnosed, clinically significant thromboembolic events are remarkably common and described in about 10% of all patients. Subclinical thrombosis occurs in at least 50% of patients. The incidence increases significantly when long lines are inserted in cancer patients for the purposes of chemotherapy or supportive care. In this group of patients the incidence of thromboembolism increases to 20%. For this reason, prophylaxis with low-dose Warfarin is recommended, and this decreases the risk of subsequent thrombosis to between two and five percent. Because of the high risk of thrombosis in cancer patients, it has been suggested that anticoagulation should be prophylactically prescribed. Logically, the best way of preventing thromboembolism would be with a heparin-like compound rather than with a coumarin. At the moment, the evidence is that the low molecular weight Heparins are probably more effective than Warfarin in the prophylaxis of thromboembolism.

Chapter 47

End-of-life care

Amongst the most important elements to onco-logical care is recognizing shifting goals as the cancer progresses. The balance of benefit and side-effects of any intervention should be carefully weighed against each other. Whilst neurosurgical resection of solitary metastases from melanoma may be appropriate in some circumstances, vene-puncture for measuring the serum electrolytes in a dying patient rarely is justifiable. These decisions should involve the patient wherever possible and require skilful communication. Throughout the cancer journey, patients often enquire about their life expectancy. There is a temptation for clinicians to pluck some figure out of the air. An intelligent doctor will recognize the pitfalls of prognostication when applied to an individual and will appreciate that the median survival, the statistic most relevant in this circumstance, is the time when half the pa-tients will still be alive. Stephen J Gould explains this from a patient's perspective in the essay 'The median is not the message', published in the collec-tion 'Bully for Brontosaurus'. During the patient's journey with cancer, a number of emotions are ex-perienced. These may follow a stepwise succession originally described by the Swiss psychologist Elisa-beth Kubler Ross. In her 1969 book 'On death and dying', she records the stages as denial, anger, bar-gaining, grieving and finally acceptance.

As the cancer progresses and the patient deterio-rates, it is important that reviews are frequent and that problems are anticipated. This close follow-up is often best undertaken in the community by community palliative care services rather than bringing patients up to hospital for regular ap-pointments. This approach requires however ex-cellent communication between all the health professionals involved. This may be facilitated by patient-held records similar to those used in shared care obstetrics. The anticipation of symptoms in-cluding pain and diminishing mobility should be addressed in advance so that analgesia is quickly available to patients.

Pain control

Nerve endings, or nociceptors exist in all tissues which are stimulated by noxious agents including chemical, mechanical and thermal stimuli, giving rise to pain (Table 47.1). These stimuli are relayed by Aα, Aδ (fast transmitting fibres) and C (slow transmission of sensation) sensory nerve fibres to the dorsal horns of the spinal cord, and dif-ferent qualities of pain may use different sensory fibres.

Analgesic drugs form the mainstay of treating cancer pain and should be chosen based on the severity of the pain rather than the stage of the cancer. Drugs should be administered regularly to prevent pain, using a stepwise escalation from non-opioid, to weak opioid and strong opioid anal-gesia (Figure 47.1). Adjuvant drugs may be added at any stage of the analgesic ladder as they may have

Table 47.1 Definitions of Pain.

Term	Definition
Allodynia	Pain due to a stimulus that does not normally cause pain
Analgesia	Absence of pain in response to stimulation which would normally be painful
Dysesthesia	An unpleasant abnormal sensation, either spontaneous or evoked
Hyperalgesia	Heightened response to a normally painful stimulus
Hyperpathia	An abnormally painful reaction to a stimulus, especially a repetitive stimulus, as well as an increased threshold
Hypoalgesia	Diminished pain in response to a normally painful stimulus
Neuralgia	Pain in the distribution of a nerve or nerves
Neuropathic pain	Pain initiated or caused by a primary lesion or dysfunction in the peripheral nervous system
Nociception	The nervous system activity resulting from potential or actual tissue-damaging stimuli
Paraesthesia	An abnormal sensation, whether spontaneous or evoked

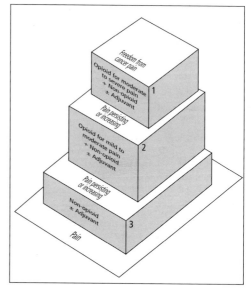

Figure 47.1 The World Health Organisation (WHO)'s three step ladder to use of analgesic drugs.

Table 47.2 Side-effects of opiates.

Side-effect	Comments
Constipation	This affects almost all patients and all patients require prophylaxis with a stimulant laxative (e.g. senna, bisacodyl) and a softener (e.g. docusate sodium) or as a combined preparation (e.g. codanthramer, codanthrusate)
Drowsiness	Generally remits after a few days
Nausea	Affects one-third of opioid-naïve patients but usually resolves within 1 week. Consider prophylaxis for 1 week
Hallucinations	An uncommon side-effect that often features images in the peripheral vision
Nightmares	Vivid and unpleasant but rare
Myoclonic jerks	Occur usually with excess doses and may be mistaken for fits
Respiratory depression	Not a problem in patients with pain

additional analgesic effect in some painful conditions. Examples of adjuvant analgesics are corticosteroids, non-steroidal anti-inflammatory drugs, tricyclic antidepressants, anticonvulsants, and some antiarrythmic drugs. Morphine is the most commonly used strong opioid analgesic and whenever possible should be given by mouth. The dose of morphine needs to be tailored to each patient and must be repeated at regular intervals so that the pain does not return between doses. There is no upper dose limit for morphine. A number of myths have however arisen around opioid prescribing that may deter prescribers as well as patients. Firstly, opioid tolerance is rarely seen in patients with cancer pain, and neither psychological dependence nor addiction is a problem in this patient group. The toxicity of opioid may also prove to be an obstacle for some patients (Table 47.2). Sedation is common at the start of opioid therapy but resolves in most patients within a few days. Similarly, nausea and vomiting may prove troublesome at the start of regular opioid dosing but usually dissipate within a few days and may be controlled with anti-emetics. Constipation develops in almost all patients on opioids, and this toxicity persists and necessitates routine prophylactic laxatives for almost everyone receiving opioids. A careful explanation of these issues will result in the acceptance of opioid analgesia by almost all patients.

Care of the dying patient

The continuing attention to the needs and comfort of a dying patient is as important as the care given to any other patient. Part of that care includes reducing the distress of relatives. Many issues may be raised by relatives that pose ethical dilemmas, and these may make you question the therapy that has been or should be given. Amongst the most frequent scenarios is the role of intravenous hydration, evaluating the balance between painful cannulation and restriction of mobility versus an uncomfortable dry mouth and thirst. To address these questions you should consider whether death from cancer is now inevitable, whether interventions would relieve symptoms and whether treatment would cause harm. Careful explanation to the relatives is essential; in this circumstance, for example, they need to be reassured that the patient is not dying because of dehydration but rather because of progression of the cancer.

Symptom control in the dying patient often requires a different route of administration, as swallowing may be difficult and agitation and restlessness are often prominent features as death approaches. A number of factors may contribute to terminal agitation, including physical causes such as pain, sore mouth, full bladder or rectum, along with emotional factors, including fear of dying and the distress of relatives. The physical causes should be addressed appropriately and unnecessary medications should be stopped. Often the best method of delivering analgesia, antiemetics and sedation is via a subcutaneous syringe driver. Similarly, oral secretions accumulating in a patient who is too weak to cough may be distressing to patient and family alike. Drug treatment for terminal secretions includes hyoscine hydrobromide—and glycopyrronium bromide, which is less sedating. It is important to recall that not all patients wish to be sedated, and this should be discussed with them and their families.

The last hours and days

For many patients with cancer, the last hours and days are heralded by a deterioration to semiconsciousness. At this time, patients are usually unable to take oral medication and prescriptions need to be reconsidered. Many medicines may be stopped altogether. Alternative routes of administration including subcutaneous, rectal and transdermal routes may be employed for other necessary medications including analgesia. Although patients may no longer be receiving medicines by mouth, oral hygiene remains an important part of overall care. It is particularly important to avoid unnecessary unpleasant interventions at this time and to adopt a practical, problem-oriented approach to symptom control.

Bereavement

Bereavement care and support includes recognizing the physical and emotional need of families and carers and continues after the patient's death. A number of features have been identified as associated with the risk of severe bereavement reactions (Table 47.3). The recognition of these risks prior to death can allow planning of care for those

Table 47.3 Risk factors for bereavement.

Patient	Young
Cancer	Short illness, disfiguring
Death	Sudden, traumatic (e.g. haemorrhage)
Relationship to patient	Dependent or hostile
Main carer	Young, other dependents, physical or mental illness, unsupported

Box 47.1: The Tibetan Book of the Dead

A fundamental tenet of Buddhism is that death is not something that awaits us in some distant future, but something we bring into the world with us and that is present throughout our lives. Moreover, rather than a finality, death offers a unique opportunity for spiritual growth with the ultimate opportunity for transformation into an immortal state of benefit to others. Among Tibet's many and varied religious traditions are esoteric teachings that address compassionate death, including the Tibetan Book of the Dead. These popular texts are manuals of practical instructions for the dying; for those who are immediately facing death; for those who have died, who are wandering in the intermediate state between lives; and for the living, who are left behind to continue without their loved ones.

Before death, friends and relatives are encouraged to bid farewell without excess drama so that neither regret nor longing is experienced by the dying, as their state of mind at death must be positive. This may be facilitated by a spiritual master (lama) whispering guiding instructions from the Tibetan Book of the Dead into the dying person's ear.

Tibetan Buddhism recognises that spiritual growth may be derived from acknowledging death and proposes detailed meditation strategies that relate to the acceptance of death in order to comprehend the nature of human existence. Four human life-cycle stages are recognised: birth, the period between birth and death, death and the interval between death and rebirth (the bardo). This post-mortem bardo lasts seven weeks and is followed by rebirth into a worldly state that is influenced by past actions or 'karma'. The cycle of rebirth (samsara) may be broken by enlightenment, culminating in the final liberation of buddhahood.

Box 47.2: Jewish Mourners' Kaddish Prayer

Glorified and sanctified be God's great name throughout the world which He has created according to His will. May He establish His kingdom in your lifetime and during your days, and within the life of the entire House of Israel, speedily and soon; and say, Amen.

May His great name be blessed forever and to all eternity.

Blessed and praised, glorified and exalted, extolled and honoured, adored and lauded be the name of the Holy One, blessed be He, beyond all the blessings and hymns, praises and consolations that are ever spoken in the world; and say, Amen.

May there be abundant peace from heaven, and life, for us and for all Israel; and say, Amen.

He who creates peace in His celestial heights, may He create peace for us and for all Israel; and say, Amen.

With a strong belief in an afterlife, mourning practices in Judaism are extensive but are not an expression of fear of death. Instead, they aim to show respect for the dead and to comfort the living. As an expression of respect, following death, the body is never left alone and on hearing of the death, friends and relatives tear a portion of their clothes. Burial is prompt, within two days, and is followed by seven days of mourning (shiva). Mourners sit on low stools or the floor instead of chairs, do not wear leather shoes, do not shave or cut their hair, do not wear cosmetics, do not work, and do not do things for comfort or pleasure, such as bathe, have sex or put on fresh clothing. Mourners wear the clothes that they tore at the time of learning of the death, and mirrors in the house are covered. The Jewish Kaddish prayer is recited for the first eleven months following a death by identified mourners and on each anniversary of the death (Yahrzeit). Remarkably, there is no reference to death in the prayer. Instead, it focuses on the greatness of God and on a call for peace.

left behind after the death. Good health professionals are not immune to bereavement, and our need for support should not be ignored.

The culture of death and dying

Just as different cultures have developed distinct explanations for the origins of life ranging from 'big bangs' and evolution to creationist genesis, similar cultural variations affect attitudes to death. Christians, Jews and Sufis believe in resurrection whilst Hindi, Buddhists and Sikhs believe in reincarnation. These cultural discrepancies must be recognized and respected particularly where patients and carers views differ (Boxes 47.1 and 47.2).

Index

Page numbers in *italics* refer to figures and those in **bold** to tables or boxes; please note that figures, tables and boxes are only indicated when they are separated from their text references. Index entries are filed in letter-by-letter alphabetical order.

PMB chemotherapy 132
polymyositis **225**
polyploidy **9**
polyvinyl chloride (PVC) 93
positron emission tomography (PET) 84
post-menopausal bleeding 133
post-transplantation lymphoproliferative disease (PTLD) 211, 215–16
predictive value **61**
prevalence 3, **61**
proctitis, radiation 113
progesterone 133
progestogens 227
prognosis 10, **11**
progression, tumour 28–9
prolactinoma 153
promotion, tumour 28–9
prophylactic surgery 37, **38**
prostate cancer 105, 114–20
  endocrine therapy 57–8, *59*
  epidemiology 114–15
  presentation and diagnosis 115, *116*, *117*
  prognosis 119
  screening 119
  staging and grading 115
  treatment 115–18, 119–20
prostatectomy, radical 117
prostate-specific antigen (PSA) 115, **209**
protein calorie malnutrition 225–7
pruritus **226**
psychiatric dysfunction 56–7
psychological aspects of cancer 65–8
psychological distress 65–6
psychological interventions 65–6
psychological risk factors 65
psychosocial problems 66
PTC gene 110
PTEN/MMAC1 gene 106
pulmonary toxicity, chemotherapy 53, *54*

quackery 69–70

radiation 23–8
  brain tumour risk 82
  dose 37–8
  ionizing 23–4, 26–8
  non-ionizing 23–4
  recall phenomenon 53
radioactive isotopes
  nuclear imaging **10**
  therapeutic 38, 40, **41**
radiology 10
radiotherapy 37–42
  bladder cancer 112–13
  breast cancer 78
  cervical cancer 132
  children 57, 199
  CNS tumours 84, 85
  colorectal cancer 103

endometrial cancer 134
external beam 38–9
fields *39*, 40
head and neck cancer 142
Hodgkin's disease 172
kidney cancer 108
lung cancer 159
lymphoma 178
prostate cancer 117
sensitivity and resistance 42
skin cancer 187
soft-tissue sarcoma 204
testis cancer 123, 124
thyroid cancer 147
toxicity 40–2, 85, 199
radon 26
randomization **62**
rankl 179
Ras genes 156, 164
RB gene 23, 156, 196
RECIST criteria 61
reconstructive surgery 37
rectal cancer
  adjuvant treatment 103
  surgery 102
  see also colorectal cancer
Reed Sternberg cells 170, *171*
relatives
  bereavement care 241–2
  dying patients 241
renal cell carcinoma 106, 107, 108–9
respiratory depression, opioid-induced **240**
RET gene 144, 146
retinoblastoma **24**, 196
  hereditary 194, 196
  Knudson's two-hit hypothesis 23, *25*
retinoblastoma gene *see* RB gene
retinoblastoma protein (Rb) 17
retinoic acid 164
retinoids 141, 142
retinopathy, paraneoplastic **225**
rhabdomyosarcoma 197–8, 205
rhenium-188 **41**
rituximab 60, 173, 178
RNA viruses, oncogenic **31**, 33
rodent ulcer 186
Rosenberg, Barnett 43
Rous, Peyton 23, 29
Rous sarcoma virus (RSV) 23
Royal Free Hospital 12
Royal Marsden Hospital 12–14

salivary gland tumours 140, 142, 143
samarium-133 **41**
sample size **62**
sarcomas 6, 200
  epidemiology 200
  paediatric 196–9
Saunders, Dame Cecily 64
Scarff–Bloom–Richardson grading system 7

Schistosoma haematobium **31**, 34
schistosomiasis 29, 34
schwannomas 83
scrotal cancer 185
second cancers
  after childhood cancer 199
  chemotherapy-induced 55–6
  Hodgkin's disease 55, 56, 173
sedation, terminal 241
selective estrogen receptor modulators (SERMs) 133
seminoma 121, 123, 124, 125
senescence 19
sensitivity, diagnostic test **61**
sensory neuropathy, paraneoplastic **225**
sepsis, neutropenic 50–1, 168, 236–7
serotonin (5HT) 150, **152**, 222
severe combined immunodeficiency (SCID) syndromes **213**
sexual dysfunction 102–3, 112
shark cartilage **71**
sick role 3
signal transduction 15, *16*
Sipple's syndrome **144**
Sister Mary Joseph nodule *137*
skin cancer 184, 185–8
  aetiology, pathophysiology and pathology 185–6
  clinical presentation 186
  prognosis **187**, 188
  treatment 186–8
  ultraviolet radiation and 25, 184, 185
  see also melanoma
small-cell lung cancer (SCLC) 156, 158
  paraneoplastic syndromes 157, 160, **225**
  treatment 159–60
small-cell tumours, testis 123
smoking 30
  head and neck cancer and 140, 141
  lung cancer and 30, 155, 156
social aspects of cancer 65–8
sociological perspective 3, **4**
sociology 72
soft-tissue sarcomas
  clinical features **205**
  paediatric 197–8
  presentation 200
  treatment 204–5
somatostatin analogues 222–3, 230
  see also octreotide
somatostatinoma **98**, 222
specificity, diagnostic test **61**
spinal axis tumours 83, 84
spinal cord compression 232, *233*, *234*
spindle poisons 44
squalamine **71**